Lecture Notes in Computer Science 9083

Commenced Publication in 1973
Founding and Former Series Editors:
Gerhard Goos, Juris Hartmanis, and Jan van Leeuwen

Editorial Board

David Hutchison
Lancaster University, Lancaster, UK
Takeo Kanade
Carnegie Mellon University, Pittsburgh, PA, USA
Josef Kittler
University of Surrey, Guildford, UK
Jon M. Kleinberg
Cornell University, Ithaca, NY, USA
Friedemann Mattern
ETH Zürich, Zürich, Switzerland
John C. Mitchell
Stanford University, Stanford, CA, USA
Moni Naor
Weizmann Institute of Science, Rehovot, Israel
C. Pandu Rangan
Indian Institute of Technology, Madras, India
Bernhard Steffen
TU Dortmund University, Dortmund, Germany
Demetri Terzopoulos
University of California, Los Angeles, CA, USA
Doug Tygar
University of California, Berkeley, CA, USA
Gerhard Weikum
Max Planck Institute for Informatics, Saarbrücken, Germany

T0212774

More information about this series at http://www.springer.com/series/7408

Paloma Díaz · Volkmar Pipek
Carmelo Ardito · Carlos Jensen
Ignacio Aedo · Alexander Boden (Eds.)

End-User Development

5th International Symposium, IS-EUD 2015
Madrid, Spain, May 26–29, 2015
Proceedings

 Springer

Editors
Paloma Díaz
Universidad Carlos III de Madrid
Leganés
Spain

Volkmar Pipek
Universität Siegen
Siegen
Germany

Carmelo Ardito
Università degli Studi di Bari Aldo Moro
Bari
Italy

Carlos Jensen
Oregon State University
Corvallis, Oregon
USA

Ignacio Aedo
Universidad Carlos III de Madrid
Leganés
Spain

Alexander Boden
Fraunhofer Institute for Applied Information
   Technology
St. Augustin
Germany

ISSN 0302-9743
Lecture Notes in Computer Science
ISBN 978-3-319-18424-1
DOI 10.1007/978-3-319-18425-8

ISSN 1611-3349   (electronic)

ISBN 978-3-319-18425-8   (eBook)

Library of Congress Control Number: 2015937373

LNCS Sublibrary: SL2 – Programming and Software Engineering

Springer Cham Heidelberg New York Dordrecht London

ⓒ Springer International Publishing Switzerland 2015
This work is subject to copyright. All rights are reserved by the Publisher, whether the whole or part of the
material is concerned, specifically the rights of translation, reprinting, reuse of illustrations, recitation, broadcasting, reproduction on microfilms or in any other physical way, and transmission or information storage
and retrieval, electronic adaptation, computer software, or by similar or dissimilar methodology now known
or hereafter developed.
The use of general descriptive names, registered names, trademarks, service marks, etc. in this publication
does not imply, even in the absence of a specific statement, that such names are exempt from the relevant
protective laws and regulations and therefore free for general use.
The publisher, the authors and the editors are safe to assume that the advice and information in this book
are believed to be true and accurate at the date of publication. Neither the publisher nor the authors or the
editors give a warranty, express or implied, with respect to the material contained herein or for any errors or
omissions that may have been made.

Printed on acid-free paper

Springer International Publishing AG Switzerland is part of Springer Science+Business Media
(www.springer.com)

Preface

In its fifth edition the International Symposium of End-User Development came to Madrid, hosted by the Interactive Systems Research group (DEI Lab) of Universidad Carlos III de Madrid and MediaLab-Prado. The collaboration between these two public entities brought this academic conference to a unique venue; a public citizen lab, always open to new ways of doing research, production, and diffusion. Its location in a lively cultural area surrounded by coworking spaces, and, specially, its reputation as an active center in the promotion of new models of technology production and the reflection on their impact in our lives and societies made MediaLab-Prado the perfect place to start closing the gap between the academic community and end users. This is one of the main goals pursued in this edition by IS-EUD, which will try to engage citizens by making more accessible the innovations in end-user development.

My world, my device, my program.

In an increasingly connected world, we use information and communication technologies in more and more of our work practices and everyday routines. End users face the challenge of adapting and combining these technologies through different kinds of artifacts for various and differing purposes, engaging in creative, often collaborative, activities to make technologies and infrastructures fit their practice. End-user development has established itself as a research discipline that connects the ergonomics of programming with the users' needs and abilities to shape the technological infrastructures we live in. The research does not aim to make everybody a "traditional" programmer, but to allow everybody to be in control of the technologies they live and work with in a way that is natural or intuitive to them, in their context and for their practices. This includes improving the concepts and interfaces for programming and configuration as well as supporting end users in their activities to share, delegate, and collaborate.

Following the path started in the 2013 edition in Copenhagen, the link with participatory design was also a topic explored in Madrid. Ubiquitous computing and the Internet of Things gained also relevance in the symposium, and we aimed at connecting to relevant societal movements like the Makerspaces and FabLabs. These emerging areas of research and development aim to change the way we interact with the world around us, and how we empower ordinary people to create and change the future. Therefore, at the core of their vision and challenge they require us to to empower end users to adapt technologies to their own needs. Therefore, discussing the contribution of EUD methods and tools becomes more timely than ever.

The full papers chairs Carmelo Ardito and Carlos Jensen, in close collaboration with the short papers chairs, Ignacio Aedo and Alexander Boden, were in charge of designing a varied and exciting program including different types of contributions and covering a broad spectrum of research related to EUD and participatory design. Thanks to the hard work of our Program Committee, the rigorous review process resulted on 10 full papers and 12 short papers accepted. An industrial paper by Airbus Spain will illustrate how the avionics industry is joining the EUD movement to provide personalization capabilities to their end users.

Our two keynote speakers will also open their talks to the public to engage nonacademics in the EUD community. David Cuartielles, cofounder of the Arduino platform and director of the Prototyping Laboratory at K3 at Malmö University's School of Arts and Communication, is one of the leading researchers in open source platforms and interaction design. Professor Dr. Albrecht Schmidt from the University of Stuttgart is a well-known researcher in the area of Human–Computer Interaction who is now involved in several projects related to the application of physical and augmented computing to different contexts. Both will enrich the symposium with their extensive expertise and inspiring points of view.

Connecting researchers and end users.

Pursuing the goal of engaging end users in the symposium, the 5th IS-EUD introduces a new category of participation again open to the public: the Playground. This special track, organized by Andrea Bellucci, Lily Diaz, and Monica Maceli, is devoted to establishing spaces for end users to interact with EUD technologies. We hope that this interaction between researchers and end users will be a first step to look for innovative ways to link the EUD research community with its stakeholders, the society.

The Workshops Chairs, Daniela Fogli and Yvonne Dittrich, managed to attract the third edition of the workshop on Cultures of Participation in the Digital Age that this year will deal with the theme "Coping with information, participation, and collaboration overload." Organized by a group of international researches with strong ties to the EUD community, including Barbara Rita Barricelli, Gerhard Fischer, Anders Mørch, and Antonio Piccinno, CoPDA 2015 offers an excellent chance to further explore the socio-technical dimension of advances in social and participatory technologies. The workshop along with the Doctoral Consortium, organized by Clarisse de Souza, Panos Markopoulos, and Simone Stumpf, took place in the Leganés Campus of Universidad Carlos III de Madrid where the Technical School was located.

The Conference General Chairs had the good fortune to count on the generous and rigorous work of a group of varied and brilliant chairs, including those in charge of the publicity (Teresa Onorati and Patrick Shih), the local arrangements (Telmo Zarraonandía and Sergio Santiago), the organization in MediaLab-Prado (Marcos García, Clara Lapetra, and Patricia Domínguez), and the volunteers. They hope and expect that you all enjoy IS-EUD 2015 as much as they enjoyed being part of its preparation.

Thanks to all for making this possible and please do not forget to enjoy also the beautiful and unique city of Madrid!

March 2015

Paloma Díaz
Volkmar Pipek
Carmelo Ardito
Carlos Jensen
Ignacio Aedo
Alexander Boden

Organization

General Chairs

Paloma Díaz   Universidad Carlos III de Madrid, Spain
Volkmar Pipek   University of Siegen, Germany

Program Chairs

Full Papers

Carmelo Ardito   University of Bari, Italy
Carlos Jensen   Oregon State University, USA

Short Papers

Ignacio Aedo   Universidad Carlos III de Madrid, Spain
Alexander Boden   Fraunhofer Institute for Applied Information
         Technology FIT, Germany

EUD-Playground Chairs

Andrea Bellucci   Universidad Carlos III de Madrid, Spain
Lily Diaz   Aalto University, Finland
Monica Maceli   Pratt Institute, School of Information and
         Library Science, USA

Industrial Liason Chairs

Marcos García   MediaLab-Prado, Spain
Alex Jaimes Larrate   Yahoo Labs, USA/Spain/India
Boris de Ruyter   Philips Research Europe, The Netherlands

Workshops Chairs

Daniela Fogli   University of Brescia, Italy
Yvonne Dittrich   IT University of Copenhagen, Denmark

Doctoral Consortium Chairs

Clarisse de Souza   Pontifícia Universidade Católica do Rio de Janeiro,
                                   Brazil
Panos Markopoulos   Eindhoven University of Technology,
                                   The Netherlands
Simone Stumpf   City University London, UK

Publicity Chairs

Patrick Shih   Pennsylvania State University, USA
Teresa Onorati   Universidad Carlos III de Madrid, Spain

Local Arrangement Chair

Telmo Zarraonandia   Universidad Carlos III de Madrid, Spain

Steering Committee

Margaret Burnett   Oregon State University, USA
Maria Francesca Costabile University of Bari, Italy
Boris de Ruyter   Philips Research Europe, The Netherlands
Yvonne Dittrich   IT University of Copenhagen, Denmark
Gerhard Fischer   University of Colorado Boulder, USA
Anders Mørch   University of Oslo, Norway
Antonio Piccinno   University of Bari, Italy
Volkmar Pipek   University of Siegen, Germany
Mary Beth Rosson   Pennsylvania State University, USA
David Redmiles   University of California, Irvine, USA
Gunnar Stevens   University of Siegen, Germany
Volker Wulf   University of Siegen, Germany

Program Committee

Ignacio Aedo   Universidad Carlos III de Madrid, Spain
Carmelo Ardito   University of Bari, Italy
Barbara Rita Barricelli   Università degli Studi di Milano, Italy
Andrea Bellucci   Universidad Carlos III de Madrid, Spain
Alexander Boden   Fraunhofer Institute for Applied Information
                                   Technology FIT, Germany
Margaret Burnett   Oregon State University, USA
Federico Cabitza   University of Milano-Bicocca, Italy

Maria Francesca Costabile	University of Bari, Italy
Boris de Ruyter	Philips Research Europe, The Netherlands
Clarisse de Souza	Pontifícia Universidade Católica do Rio de Janeiro, Brazil
Lily Diaz	Aalto University, Finland
Yvonne Dittrich	IT University of Copenhagen, Denmark
Paloma Díaz	Universidad Carlos III de Madrid, Spain
Gerhard Fischer	University of Colorado Boulder, USA
Daniela Fogli	University of Brescia, Italy
Thomas Herrmann	Ruhr-University of Bochum, Germany
Carlos Jensen	Oregon State University, USA
Benjamin Koehne	University of California, Irvine, USA
Thomas D. LaToza	University of California, Irvine, USA
Catherine Letondal	ENAC/LII, France
Monica Maceli	Pratt Institute, School of Information and Library Science, USA
Alessio Malizia	Brunel University London, UK
Panos Markopoulos	Eindhoven University of Technology, The Netherlands
Nikolay Mehandjiev	University of Manchester, UK
Anders Mørch	University of Oslo, Norway
Fabio Paternò	CNR-ISTI, Italy
Antonio Piccinno	University of Bari, Italy
Volkmar Pipek	University of Siegen, Germany
David Redmiles	University of California, Irvine, USA
Anita Sarma	University of Nebraska–Lincoln, USA
Carla Simone	University of Milano-Bicocca, Italy
Gunnar Stevens	University of Siegen, Germany
Simone Stumpf	City University London, UK
Tom Yeh	University of Colorado Boulder, USA

Additional Reviewers

Buono, Paolo	Nolte, Alexander
Daskalopoulou, Athanasia	Oleson, Alannah
Desolda, Giuseppe	Onorati, Teresa
Hill, Charles	Reyero Aldama, Gonzalo
Horvath, Amber	Romano, Marco
Kuttal, Sandeep	Turchi, Tommaso
Loser, Kai-Uwe	Valtolina, Stefano

Keynote Speeches

Programming Ubiquitous Computing Environments

Albrecht Schmidt

University of Stuttgart
Pfaffenwaldring 5a, 70569 Stuttgart, Germany
albrecht.schmidt@vis.uni-stuttgart.de

Abstract. Computing becomes a part of our everyday environment. Interaction in the "real world" is more and more determined by ubiquitous computing systems that are tailored to fit a specific environment. These systems can only be created with strong domain knowledge. End users may be the right group to develop or at least tailor such systems. We show two examples of how domain expert can program systems: one looks at how to transfer programming by demonstration to ubicomp scenarios and the other on how to use examples as recipes for a new development. In the outlook we extrapolate from current practices of sharing videos to a future where multimodal and sensor-rich examples can be continuously recorded and may become the basis for new approaches for a truly user-centered development of cyber-physical systems.

Opensource Hardware and Education

David Cuartielles

Medea - Malmö University's School of Arts and Communication,
Ö Varvsg. 11 A, Malmö University, 205 06 Malmö
david.cuartielles@mah.se

Abstract. Arduino is a free, opensource hardware platform that can be reprogrammed with a piece of opensource software. Software that reprograms hardware allows people to transform the way they understand and interact with the world because electronics are omnipresent in our everyday activities. Elevators run with microcontrollers, in an average car there are seventy microcontrollers and even a microwave oven has microcontrollers. The goal of Arduino is to empower people other than engineers to understand interaction paradigms such as physical, tangible and ubiquitous computing and to create their own interactive artifacts with digital electronics. Eventually, it democratizes learning by practical experimentation so that learners discover how to be independent, how to use things by themselves, how to exploit those things to build interactive systems by themselves and how to be critically demanding about technology.

In this talk, I will introduce the feature that makes a free hardware platform such as Arduino a powerful learning tool that foster creativity and I will talk about a vision for the computing education for the 21st century: accessible and pleasant approaches to teach kids how to reprogram the surrounding environment. To this end, I will share experiences and insights gathered from project-based learning experiments with Arduino in secondary schools.

Contents

Short Papers

Doctoral Consortium

Workshops

EUD-Playground

Keynote Speech

Programming Ubiquitous Computing Environments

Albrecht Schmidt[✉]

University of Stuttgart, Pfaffenwaldring 5a, 70569 Stuttgart, Germany
`albrecht.schmidt@vis.uni-stuttgart.de`

Abstract. Computing becomes a part of our everyday environment. Interaction in the "real world" is more and more determined by ubiquitous computing systems that are tailored to fit a specific environment. These systems can only be created with strong domain knowledge. End users may be the right group to develop or at least tailor such systems. We show two examples of how domain expert can program systems: one looks at how to transfer programming by demonstration to ubicomp scenarios and the other on how to use examples as recipes for a new development. In the outlook we extrapolate from current practices of sharing videos to a future where multimodal and sensor-rich examples can be continuously recorded and may become the basis for new approaches for a truly user-centered development of cyber-physical systems.

1   Introduction

Over the last 20 years ubiquitous computing has become reality. Phones, household appliances, TVs, cars, and even buildings have essentially become computers. Interacting with computing technologies has become an integral part of our life [1]. Embedded computers and the software and services running on them more and more shape how we perceive the world and how we interact with each other. In many cases computers even determine what we can do or what we can't do. The opportunities to create interactive experiences are manifold [2]. As many traditional electro-mechanical systems include now processing, communication, sensing, and actuation, designing such cyber-physical systems in a user-centered development process offers new opportunities and creates new challenges [3].

2   Challenges in Programming Ubiquitous Computing Systems

By creating ubiquitous computing technologies – software and hardware - we inevitably change the way people live. There are great opportunities to build new interactive tools and integrate them into our environment, but developing these systems, raises again many design and engineering challenges solved in graphical systems. How to ensure that systems are consistent and the users can guess the outcome of their actions? How can we build systems that allow easy reversal of action and that prevent users from making errors? How can we provide appropriate feedback, where on one side we expect that computing becomes invisible but on the other side we want users

© Springer International Publishing Switzerland 2015
P. Díaz et al. (Eds.): IS-EUD 2015, LNCS 9083, pp. 3–6, 2015.
DOI: 10.1007/978-3-319-18425-8_1

to be in control? These are just some of the questions we have to ask when moving to interactive systems that are part of our everyday environments.

Looking at successful ubiquitous computing environments and more specifically at smart spaces it becomes apparent, that they are developed to fit a certain context, they are targeted at specific users, and they are designed to support specific activities and tasks. Developing such systems includes the selection and deployment of hardware and the development of software. Most of the systems are unique and domain knowledge is essential to create useful systems.

3   End User Development as a Solution

Analyzing this it becomes clear (1) end users and domain experts are required in the development process, and (2) as systems are unique, programming by professionals will for most cases not be a viable option (at least not economically).

We expect that by lowering the effort required to develop and program ubiquitous computing environments, the proliferation of such technologies into homes and businesses can be facilitated. In our view, systems should be designed in a way that they have a generic functionality that can be customized and programmed by end-users and domain experts to suit their needs and to provide useful functionality.

3.1   I Can Show You - Programming by Demonstration in the Real World

When transferring skills between people "showing how to do it" and observing the person who has just learned how to do it is the most common way. In vocational training this is essential to acquire practical skills. For many people it is much easier to show how it is done than to verbalize it (or even to describe it in a formal language). Hence programming by demonstration is very common in robotics [4] as well as in the desktop world (e.g. creating Excel Macros).

In ubiquitous computing programming by demonstration is not as straightforward as it appears. What part of the action is relevant? Assuming an environment with many sensors, it is not clear which parts of the input are incidental and which parts belong to the demonstration. Just imagine the following scenario: you want to show the smart home, when to switch of the heating. You walk out of the house, lock the front door, open the garage, drive the car out, and close the garage again. This gives a clear set of events that can lead to a rule to switch the heating off when you leave. However there are pitfalls. Does this only apply to the time of day and the weekday when you demonstrated it? Is it relevant that it is dark outside (which is also sensed by the environment)? What happens if another person is at home?

In the project MotionEAP[1] we have explored this approach of programming by demonstration in an industrial context, where it is feasible to attach clear semantics to actions. Using a system that tracks the movement of users, their grapping of tools and objects, and the assembly steps performed, we only record actions that are relevant to

---

[1] http://www.motioneap.de/

the process. Using a projector and monitoring the actions by a new person we can replay the actions and adapt them to a new user's performance. See figure 1 for a photo of the system.

Fig. 1. The figure shows the MotionEAP system that allows semantically rich programming by demonstration. The system observes actions and can replay recorded sequences adapted to a new environment and users with varying performance. Left: test scenario in the lab; right: application in an industrial production process (photos curtesy to Markus Funk).

3.2 I Want it Like this, but Different – Programming Using Examples

It is often hard to describe what one wants. In many areas in real life we use things that are similar to what we want as reference, and only described the differences. I would like such a burger but with salad instead fries, or my car looks like this one, but it is blue not red. By using an example as a reference the number of things that need to be specified are typically smaller and it appears much easier for the person listening to imagine what is described. In professional programming we see a similar approach. Very rarely we start to write software from scratch. Often we take examples of pieces of code, of functions, or even whole projects that do something similar to what we want to implement. By modification and extension of examples it seems much quicker to create something that is close to what we want. It also helps to follow an agile process as based on the example one may already have a working version.

We have explored this approach for designing and implementing interactive cultural heritage applications in the context of the European project meSch[2] [5]. By creating recipes for systems, which describe instances of interactive elements and installations, information is collected for easy reuse. A recipe contains all information about hardware and software required, as well as the configuration details and the specifically developed program. Similar to cooking, a novice with some skill can just replicate the recipe in their context, whereas an expert can take the recipe as an inspiration and starting point to create their own interpretation of the system described.

---

[2] http://mesch-project.eu/

4   Towards Environments that Learn from Us

Already now it is amazing how many examples of how to do things are available on YouTube. Changing a tire, playing the guitar, cooing paella, and repairing a broken phones screen are well described with hundreds of videos. Here people make a deliberated effort to record and share. To us this is just a starting point. Extrapolating this to future interactive cyber-physical environments where capturing is continuous and multimodal one foresees that examples for everything humans do will become available [6]. If such recordings are not just videos, but include sensor information, we can imagine to have semantically rich recipes for everything mankind does.

Fig. 2. These examples from YouTube give a glimpse of the many examples individuals willing to share. Once recording becomes continuous and semantically rich through sensors, one can imagine creating editable and executable examples of people's actions.

References

1. Schmidt, A.: Ubiquitous computing: Are we there yet? Computer **43**(2), 95–97 (2010)
2. Schmidt, A., Pfleging, B., Alt, F., Shirazi, A.S., Fitzpatrick, G.: Interacting with 21st-century computers. IEEE Pervasive Computing **1**, 22–31 (2011)
3. Broy, M., Schmidt, A.: Challenges in Engineering Cyber-Physical Systems. Computer **47**(2), 70–72 (2014)
4. Billard, A., Calinon, S., Dillmann, R., Schaal, S.: Robot programming by demonstration. In: Springer handbook of robotics, pp. 1371–1394. Springer Berlin Heidelberg (2008)
5. Petrelli, D., Ciolfi, L., van Dijk, D., Hornecker, E., Not, E., Schmidt, A.: Integrating material and digital: a new way for cultural heritage. Interactions **20**(4), 58–63 (2013)
6. Billinghurst, M., Davies, N., Langheinrich, M., Schmidt, A.: Augmenting Human Memory-Capture and Recall in the Era of Lifelogging (Dagstuhl Seminar 14362). Dagstuhl Reports **4**, 151–173

Long Papers

Designing for End-User Development
in the Internet of Things

Barbara Rita Barricelli and Stefano Valtolina[(⊠)]

Department of Computer Science, Università degli Studi di Milano, Milano, Italy
{barricelli,valtolin}@di.unimi.it

Abstract. With the widespread of Internet of Things' devices, sensors, and applications the quantity of collected data grows enormously and the need of extracting, merging, analyzing, visualizing, and sharing it paves the way for new research challenges. This ongoing revolution of how personal devices are used and how they are becoming more and more wearable has important influences on the most well established definitions of end user and end-user development. The paper presents an analysis of the most diffused applications that allow end users to aggregate quantified-self data, originated by several sensors and devices, and to use it in personalized ways. From the outcomes of the analysis, we present a classification model for Internet of Things and new EUD paradigm and language that extends the ones existing in the current state of the art Internet of Things.

Keywords: Internet of Things · End-User Development · Quantified self · Life-logging · Pervasive computing · Mobile devices · Unwitting developers · End users

1   Introduction

The Internet of Things (IoT) concept was coined in 1999/2000 by Kevin Ashton and his team at MIT's Auto-ID Center [1] and rapidly spread around the world thanks to the evolution of sensor technology and its use that is becoming more and more mobile and pervasive [2]. To connect uniquely identified everyday objects in a network allows to send and receive data and at the same time to influence the behavior of the objects in two ways: automatic, on the basis of the collected data, and semi-automatic/manual, according to users' needs and/or preferences. Today, IoT is successfully adopted in several application domains and it is estimated that in 2015 the number of objects connected will be around 12 billion, while in 2020 it will be 50 billion [3][4].

Recent studies [5][6] show that the coming of IoT changed the way people use the Internet, and mobile and sensor-based devices. This tendency is more relevant in domains that present pervasive characteristics where the integration of data could help in improving quality of life and in offering an even richer and satisfying experience of use of everyday objects. This type of integration is what characterizes the so-called *lifelogging*: keeping track of the collected data through all the everyday or occasional

© Springer International Publishing Switzerland 2015
P. Díaz et al. (Eds.): IS-EUD 2015, LNCS 9083, pp. 9–24, 2015.
DOI: 10.1007/978-3-319-18425-8_2

activities that may influence people's quality of life. Lifelogging, initially conceived in the 70s as a 24/7 broadcasting of self-videos, has become today a wide spreading phenomenon, called quantified-self movement, that allows people to keep track of their habits, health conditions, physiological data, and behavior, and to monitor conditions and quality of the environments in which they work and live. Today, a continuously increasing number of lifelogging devices are on the market and become more and more affordable to the masses.

In our research, we mainly study applications of lifelogging in three domains: health, wellness, and domotics. In the health domain, people can collect data gathered through several devices for monitoring, among all, blood pressure, heart beat rate, glucose level, and coagulation factor. Lifelogging in the wellness domain allows to keep track for example of weight, sport/fitness activity, calories intake, and sleep quality. As to domotics, IoT helps in having better awareness about energy consumption, use of entertainment or work appliances, and even care of gardens/plants. Some of the most advanced IoT devices offer solutions based on artificial intelligence and expert systems for avoiding to prompt users too often and risking to bother them with too many questions. The idea to make objects and environments able to take decisions on behalf of the users aims at not disturbing and overwhelming people in their everyday lives. Although these automatic suggestions avoid to bother users by helping them in managing objects more easily, we believe that the user control over connected objects is a crucial element for IoT success. In fact, newly created Web, mobile, wearable, and pervasive applications are today designed in a more user-centered manner and particular attention is made in taking care of the user experience.

More than 20 years ago, Cypher [7] defined the end user as a "user of an application program", someone who is not a computer programmer and who "uses a computer as part of daily life or daily work, but is not interested in computers per se". In the IoT era, this concept evolves because now machines are becoming part of the social tissue and their use is common in almost every cultural context: with the growing diffusion of mobile devices, like smartphones and tablets, pervasive computing is spreading [8]. IoT allows the end users to manage physical devices, interactive systems, and quantified-self data by deciding how to create new usage scenarios and this empowers them more than ever, making them evolve, as explained later in the paper, to become end-user developers [9].

In Section 2, we describe how digital devices have become not only tools to satisfy the need of getting jobs done but also the key for taking care of social relationships (real or virtual) and to manage several aspects of personal life (e.g. financial, wellness, entertainment). Under this perspective, we describe IoT as an ecosystem of objects and services that aim at supporting the end users in extracting, merging, analyzing, visualizing, and sharing data enabling them to unwittingly transforming the data into information, information into knowledge, and knowledge into wisdom. This scenario leads towards an innovative point of view on technology and mobility, focusing diversity and agency as central aspects of a socially responsible approach to mobile computing [10]. According to this consideration, we then discuss the most consolidated definitions of end user and End-User Development (EUD) with respect to the IoT domain. Even though the EUD definitions given in scientific literature remain valid, we claim how the perspective has deeply changed. EUD in IoT is now focused on how users interact with an ecosystem of elements and how they are able to affect the way data is collected and aggregated. According to this new perspective, in Section 3 we present the current state of the art of EUD in IoT and in particular we present applications that enable the users to arrange data coming from IoT devices/sensors and to aggregate it via Social Media, Mobile and Web apps. Finally, in Section 4 we present the definition of a new EUD paradigm and language in IoT domain. Specifically, we propose a sensor-based rule language able to support the end user in aggregating and combining data originated by several sensors/devices and in creating personalized use of the quantified self-data. This language aims at enabling end user for unwittingly developing personalized IoT environments according to specific temporal, spatial, and fuzzy conditions that may affect the elements in the IoT environment.

2   End-User Development in the Internet of Things Era

The "old computing" as claimed by Shneiderman [11] is focused on what computers can do for the user, while the "new computing" regards people activity and what people can do by using computers. Users of digital devices and interactive systems are increasingly evolving from passive consumers of data and computer tools into active producers of information and software [12][13]. The potentials offered by network and connectibility of the objects does not only enrich the person's personal sphere but also offers the possibility of sharing data with other people who can be family members, friends, colleagues, or others. Data sharing contributes to the creation of a large quantity of data especially in the long term, calling for the integration of recommendation, intelligent, and distributed systems in order to help in their aggregation and exploitation. In this scenario, the end users finds themselves at the center of a complex ecosystem that they need to manage in efficient, effective, satisfactory, and aware manner. EUD represents the ideal approach for empowering the end users and make them becoming unwitting developers in their own IoT environment [14][15][16].

2.1   The IoT Ecosystem

In designing for the IoT, the attention is not focused on the development of a unique interactive system but of an ecosystem of elements (hardware and software) that exchange data through the Internet and act and react in a semi-automatic or automatic way according to events, and/or users' preferences, rules, or decisions. At the center of this ecosystem stands the end user, the one who generates (or contributes to) the data, manages the IoT elements in the ecosystem, and unwittingly develops in the IoT environment defining the interactions among the elements and the elements' behavior. The elements of the ecosystem (depicted in Figure 1) can be categorized into five groups:

Sensors. The IoT sensors are typically built-in components in electronic devices aimed at collecting data of various nature. Examples of sensors are those present in devices for weather stations, activity tracking armbands, or Wi-Fi body scales. IoT devices can be portable – meant to follow the end user everywhere (e.g. activity trackers) – or unmovable – designed for being placed in a specific place and not moved around (e.g. weather stations). Sensors and their devices can autonomously send the data they collect or wait for the end user to collect the data when they need to. They typically come with applications for enable the end user to access them (both settings and data) but can also present an embedded stand-alone interface.

Fig. 1. The IoT ecosystems. The end user plays the central role deciding what elements to connect, how to interact with them, and how they should interact with each other. (Icons made by Freepik from www.flaticon.com are licensed by CC BY 3.0).

Applications. Through them, the end user is able to access the IoT devices. They typically are of two types: bundled with specific devices or compatible with several devices. Applications are usually designed to be mobile-compliant giving the end user the chance of interacting with the devices on remote setting.

Social Media. Those applications built on Web 2.0 principles and technology that allow the end user to share content on the Internet. The relationship with IoT is that most of its devices and applications are equipped with social features that allow the end user to share the collected data with virtual communities (friends, family, or colleagues in real life or people they just know on the Web).

Recommendation Systems (RS). In the context of IoT, recommendation services aim at suggesting proper aggregation, integration and distribution strategies of data coming from sensors or other informative resources and at tailoring them according to the context of use, the users profile, and goals. However, the use of automatic suggestions might be not appreciated by the end user that may feel frustrated in using the RS features, whenever the recommendations appear to be inappropriate. To deal with this problem, some RSs offer solutions able at exploiting end user's social relationships for improving the service quality.

Other IoT users. Those people who belong to the virtual communities mentioned before. They typically share with the end user some particular interests, life choices, or other aspects. Is the end user who chooses the people to be connected with on the basis of personal searches or suggestions made by the applications (thanks to RSs).

The quantity of different types of IoT devices that are today on the market is continuously growing and their variety leads to a higher and higher level of complexity in the IoT ecosystem. To support the integration of new IoT devices and related applications into the ecosystem and understand how to better empower the end user in becoming unwitting developer of their own IoT environment, we propose a 3-dimensional model of classification (Figure 2) that is based on three peculiar aspects in IoT: space, time, and social dimension.

Space. This dimension goes from "settled" to "mobile". Elements in the "settled" area of the 3D model are typically constrained to a fixed position (e.g., home, office) and are not supposed to be used on the move. Examples of such category are devices for ambient surveillance, weather stations, energy consumption monitoring, water leak sensors. On the other hand, "mobile" elements are designed to be used in different places while accompanying the user during their movements. An example of this category of elements are wearable devices that are used to track activity, calories burning, and physiological data (e.g., fitness armbands, smartwatches).

Time. Along this axis, an element can be categorized as asynchronous or synchronous. Asynchronous elements are typically those that collect data only when the user decides to, while synchronous elements collect and analyze data on the fly when they are generated without the need of having users directly involved. Especially earlier IoT devices were not equipped with Bluetooth/Wi-Fi connectivity and a mechanical action by the users was required to connect the device with a smartphone, a tablet or a desktop PC in order to collect the data generated by the device's use. Today, most of the IoT devices are designed to be standalone and directly connected to the Internet so that the users' intervention can be very limited.

Social Dimension. An element may be designed for individual use, if it is supposed to be used by a user only, or for collective use, if the element's data are meant to be accessed by many users and not only by the element's owner. Choosing between sharing and keeping private the data collected via IoT devices can be driven by personal motivations or by default characteristics of the devices themselves; sometimes in fact, IoT devices are meant to be used individually only and the sharing of data can be achieved only using third-party applications.

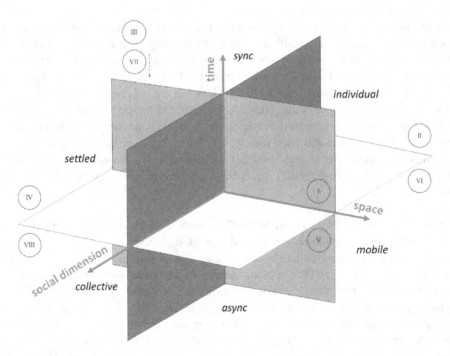

Fig. 2. The 3D model for classifying IoT devices according to space, time and social dimension

Table 1. The octants resulting from the 3D space depicted in Figure 2

Octant	Social dimension	Space	Time	Signs
I	Collective	Mobile	Synchronous	+ + +
II	Individual	Mobile	Synchronous	- + +
III	Individual	Settled	Synchronous	- - +
IV	Collective	Settled	Synchronous	+ - +
V	Collective	Mobile	Asynchronous	+ + -
VI	Individual	Mobile	Asynchronous	- + -
VII	Individual	Settled	Asynchronous	- - -
VIII	Collective	Settled	Asynchronous	+ - -

Such representation allows to identify the position of the elements in terms of octants of the 3D space. Table 1 presents all the octants in the model. The most social,
connected, flexible, and mobile elements are those located in octant 1 (+ + +), while
the elements that present less degree of flexibility and personalization and do not
follow the users in their social and real life are those octant VII (- - -). Given the flexibility of some IoT devices, it is important to keep into account that the position of the
elements in the 3D space model of classification may change in time because their
state can dynamically change according to users' behavior and preferences. It can be
used both as a tool for analyze an existing IoT ecosystem and to explore and better
understand its potentials, or as a classification to inform IoT ecosystems design that

applies EUD techniques. In particular, the classification can be of help for identifying the peculiarities of the context of use of the IoT ecosystem that is under design. According to the values of the three dimensions – space, time, and social – the designer is able to decide what EUD features are to be provided to the user, what EUD activities, and to what extent EUD can be applied without overwhelming the user. The values of space, time, and social dimensions may also influence the interaction style design that has to be adopted in a specific context of use with specific devices (e.g. mobile or desktop, touchscreen or not).

Beyond the practical uses that one can do of this model, in this paper it is used to highlight that the high complexity of IoT ecosystems may inevitably cause a shift in the traditional and more or less consolidated definitions of *end user* and *EUD*, as explained in what follows.

2.2   EUD and IoT: Evolution of Definitions and Principles

The definition of end user has experienced deeply changes in the last decade. However, there are some seminal works in the consolidated EUD scientific literature that still hold and are those that see the end user as someone interested in using digital devices just for the sake of it and not with the idea of becoming expert in the technology itself (e.g. [13], [17]). Also the definition of EUD given in [9] still sounds valid to describe the phenomenon: "a set of methods, techniques, and tools that allow users of software systems, who are acting as non-professional software developers, at some point to create, modify or extend a software artefact". In this scenario, end users are increasingly evolving from passive consumers of data and computer tools into active producers of information and software [18][12]. From an organizational point of view, end users are not necessarily experts in computer science, but in the domains they work in. In [19], Åsand and Mørch consider end users those persons who are skilled with computers, while Nardi and Miller [20] gave a classification of end user according to their computing skill level. At some point, it is possible to recognize some similarities between the two classifications: Åsand and Mørch describe regular users as those workers who are not developers and not interested in tailoring but want to use computers to perform they daily work; Nardi and Miller define the non-programmer users as workers who could also some have programming skills. On the contrary, Ye and Fischer [21] did not focus on users' classifications but on how the distinction between users and developers is going to disappear with the time's passing. There are however, some other definitions that do not reflect anymore the current scenario of IoT and this can be linked to a shift in the definition of time, space, and social dimension that are the dimensions of the 3D model of classification that we presented in Section 2.1. Nardi's definition given in [22] states that the end user is "the person who does not want to turn a task into a programming problem, who would rather follow a lengthy but well-known set of procedures to get the job done". If we consider that today the majority of digital devices are general purpose, the term job is too vague and too work-related to be used when speaking of modern technology. With the large diffusion of portable and mobile digital, pervasive systems are becoming the most diffused computing paradigm in which infrastructure and services are seamlessly available anywhere, anytime, and in any format [8]. Dourish, Anderson, & Nafus proposed in [10] an innovative point of view on technology and mobility, focusing diversity and agency as central aspects of a socially responsible approach to mobile computing. This work also connects current research in HCI, ubiquitous computing and human and social geography suggesting new perspective for design that should help in reflecting the current idea of *space*. This broadening of the space dimension in the use of digital devices leads to a revision of all those definitions of end users that consider the context of use as fundamental. Brancheau and Brown [23] confined the end users to a space that is somewhere "outside the information system department". Confining the end users at the end of design and development processes and putting distance, as suggested by Cypher [7], between them, designers, and developers is an approach that does not reflect the current society and its real expectations. Another problem with this definition is that the notion of time in today's life and the way in which we manage it have deeply changed: digital devices continuously become faster and faster allowing their users to obtain feedbacks and results very quickly. Moreover, with the computational performance, also our speed in performing actions and take decisions has increased and our expectations in terms of time saving have become very high. This has led us to reconsider the concept of *time* and to change the way in which we deal with its flow [24]. Every process becomes more and more faster and any time spent waiting for a response from a machine is seen as an unbearable waist. So, forcing the user to perform a "lengthy" set of procedures does not appear to be the right design choice. Moreover, when dealing with sensors and temporal data, there is the need to make a distinction between valid time and transaction time. The first refers to the instant in which an event actually occurs, while the second is linked to the instant in which the event has been registered in the system. Another aspect that changed in the last decade is the concept we have of the *social dimension* in which we live: the digital devices have become not only tools to satisfy the need of getting jobs done but also the key for taking care of social relationships (real or virtual).

3   EUD Activities in IoT

As widely reported in literature, EUD can be enabled by offering the end users tools that allow them to develop without having specific programming skills and knowledge about programming languages. In this Section, we first resume the most consolidated literature on EUD activities, and then we critically review the current practice of EUD by presenting and discussing the most used applications for IoT that implements EUD activities.

3.1   Literature Review

EUD covers a large area of interests, i.e. customization of applications by parameters setting, control of a complex device like a home-based heating system, script of interactive Web sites [25]. EUD allows users to configure, adapt, and evolve their software by themselves [26] and such tailoring activities, together with personalization, extension, and customization are defined in literature in different ways, sometimes referring the same concepts and sometimes referring different ones [27]. Trigg et al. [28] define a system as adaptable if it "enables user-customizable behavior". They also state that a system can be adaptable in four different ways: i) flexible systems provide generic objects and behaviors that can be interpreted and used in different ways from different users to carry out different tasks; ii) parameterized systems offer many alternative behaviors among whom the users can choose; iii) integratable systems can be interfaced to and integrated with other facilities being part of the environment or connected to remote facilities; iv) tailorable systems allow users to modify the system by building accelerators, specializing behavior, or adding functionalities. In [27], Mørch defines the tailoring activity as a way to bridge the gap between the objects that compose the interface (simple widgets such as menu items, icons, buttons or composite widgets such as menus, dialog boxes) and the underlying implementation code that defines the functionality (written in a general-purpose programming language). Furthermore, he presents three levels of end-user tailoring: by customization, by integration, and by extension. With customization users can modify the appearance of presentation objects (the ones that compose the interface) or can edit their attribute values by choosing among a set of predefined configurations. Integration allows users to add existing functionalities to an existing application. Extension permits to add new functionalities to an existing application. A further definition of tailoring is given by [29]: if the modifications that are being made on a system are on the subject matter of the tool then there is a use activity, otherwise if the modifications are made on the tool itself that can be called activity tailoring. A further classification of EUD activities has been introduced in [30]. The authors list five characteristics in the functional design of tailorable technologies by adapting what Baldwin and Clark presented in [31]: 1) splitting by reducing a single module to smaller components; 2) substituting by replacing components or parts of them; 3) augmenting by adding new modules; 4) excluding by deleting modules; 5) porting by adding a component made for another technology. In [32] another classification of users' activities is presented: the different activities are classified in two distinct classes that includes respectively those activities that allow users to choose among different behaviors by setting some parameters and those activities that imply some programming for software artifact creation or modification. Furthermore, the authors provide examples of activities belonging to the two different classes, Class 1 and Class 2. Class 1 groups together activities that support the user in setting parameters in order to choose among various behaviors available in the application. Two examples of activities that belong to this class are parameterization and annotation. Class 2 is constituted by those activities that allow the user to create or modify a software artifact, by programming in any programming paradigm. To meet the users' need of not becoming developers, programming by demonstration, programming by examples, visual programming, and macro generation are used. Examples of activities that belong to this class are modeling from the data, programming by demonstration, formula languages, incremental programming. All these classifications still apply to EUD for IoT but an important observation has to be made: in IoT, the target of EUD activities is not (only) the interface and the behavior of an interactive system, but is the whole IoT ecosystem with its elements. Therefore, we need to distinguish between those activities that can be made at three different levels: hardware, software, and data. EUD activities on hardware are those made on the devices via their bundled applications. They typically are configuration, personalization, and customization by setting parameters and choosing among existing behaviors. The activities on software targets the applications that allow to control more than one sensor/device (even of different brands) and include tailoring by integration of existing and/or new functionalities, macros, visual programming, and programming by examples. The EUD activities that can be made on data can be resumed in aggregation, filtering, and porting. In what follows, we will use the classifications presented so far for discussing the state of the art of applications that can manage data originated by more than one sensor/device and shared on Social Media, and that enable the end user to unwittingly develop their own IoT environment.

3.2   The Current State of the Art

We analyzed the most diffused applications for IoT that exploit EUD principles and we identified two main types that differ in terms of activities and interaction style. A first type of applications allow users to define sets of desired behaviors in response to specific events. This is made mainly through rules definition-wizards that rely on the states of sensors/devices. Rules can be typically chosen among existing presents or can tweaked through customization. These EUD activities can be clearly seen as belonging to Class 1 and put in place a task automation layer across all sensors/devices in the IoT environment. Such strategy is adopted by those applications that use automated rules-based engines like Atooma (http://www.atooma.com/) and IFTTT (https://ifttt.com) – by using the programming statement *IF this DO that,* and by Wewiredweb (https://wewiredweb.com/) with the statement *WHEN trigger THEN action.* With a more advanced use of these applications, the end user can exploit EUD activities that belong to Class 2 and make use of RSs (as part of the IoT ecosystem). These activities are supported by the RSs that by reading end user's pattern of use for a device can suggest compelling examples of statements that the end user can adapt to their needs. A second type of applications stems from the outstanding work done with Yahoo's Pipes (https://pipes.yahoo.com/pipes/) and can be classified to Class 2 as they typically use formula languages and/or visual programming. Applications like Bipio (https://bip.io/) and DERI pipes (http://pipes.deri.org/) offer engine and graphical environment for data transformation and mashup. They are based on the idea of providing a visual pipeline generator for letting the end user creating aggregation, filtering, and porting of data originated by sources. An advanced use of such visual paradigm is offered by WebHooks (https://developer.github.com/webhooks/) that allows the end users to even write their personal API for enabling connections with new sources of data.

Both presented typologies of EUD strategies, adoptable in the context of the IoT applications, offer a solution able to gather information from across the net and trigger specific actions when certain things happen. The first type of applications offers a very simple and easy to learn solution based on the definition of ad hoc rules that can notify the end users when something happens – e.g. when their favorite sites are updated, when they check-in in some places or their friends do, or warn them when specific weather conditions are going to take place. However, the adoption of the IF-THIS-DO-THAT/WHEN-TRIGGER-THEN-ACTION patterns are not enough to deal with more sophisticated rules based on time, space, and fuzzy conditions. On the other hand, the second type of applications offers a too complex solution for supporting the end user in expressing their preferences. Pretending that the end users are able to deal with APIs of several sensors/devices put at risk the success of the EUD approach. Another problem with the current state of the art regards the fact that in the most diffused applications the social dimension is commonly taken care of, while time and space dimensions are almost never considered. To face these problems, in the next Section we propose an extension of the IF-THIS-THEN-THAT paradigm by presenting a sensor-based rule language able to support the end user in defining rules in a more articulated way but keeping the complexity at an acceptable and accessible level. This idea is to keep the simplicity of the IF-THIS-THEN-THAT paradigm pairing it with the use of formula languages. Moreover, time and space dimension will be exploited and fuzzy conditions are adopted for expressing more loose rules in the statements.

4   A New EUD Paradigm and Language for IoT

In the most common programming languages, a control structure is a block of instructions that on the basis of specific variables and parameters chooses a direction (flow control) to follow. The flow control determines how a computer will respond when certain given conditions are in place and specific parameters are set. In the same way, in IoT domain, the end user needs to state that if a condition (e.g. the weather station says that it is going to rain in the next 12 hours) and an action (e.g. tweet this news on the end user's Twitter personal account using hashtags #weather #rain). As described before, this solution is adopted in many applications for supporting end users in creating rules for their IoT environment. The IF-THIS-THEN-THAT paradigm seems work well when end users need to be warned or notified on a specific event, but uses a very simple language that has a quite low expressive power. We propose to extend this paradigm by giving end users the possibility of setting triggers that do not depend just on one event but also on other conditions. Such conditions rely on a language with higher expressive power that draws from database management rule languages. Moreover, the paradigm allows end users to design triggers that depend also on time and space and not only on social media content, like most of the applications in the current state of the art. The introduction of time dimension allows end users to set triggers that can be fired at some specific time, delayed in case of certain conditions are verified, and may be repeated until some event happens. The space dimension gives end users the chance of linking triggers to the place/area where they currently are, where they will possibly be in the future, where they are moving into, or where some events are taking place. In literature [33][34] there is a nearly unanimous agreement on an extension of "classical" trigger languages by including time dimension.

The proposal in this field can be summarized as follows: (1) Rules should be triggered by the occurrence of time events, (2) Enabling periodically repeated triggering of the same reaction, where the period is specified by an expression returning a time duration. (3) Delaying reaction execution to some later point in time relative to the triggering event of a rule. In [35] the authors propose a set of functionalities to be implemented with triggers written in SQL:1999 standard that cover three types of temporal categories – absolute, periodic, and relative event specifications – and allow to base delay or periodic repetition on valid time or transaction time events, respectively. According to this proposal of functionalities, we can provide users with a new set of rules composition-strategies able to go beyond the simple use of an IF-THIS-THEN-THAT statement. Up to now, rules can be triggered by call events only, and reactions are always executed one time. We identified four types of rule:

1. Space Events: rules that need to be triggered if the data stream refer to a specific geographical place/area. An example: IN *"homeplace"* IF *"my sleep-controller detects that I did not sleep at least 7 hours in the last 3 nights"* THEN *"the alarm clock on my smartphone should ring at 11 PM for suggesting me to go to bed earlier"*.
2. Time Events: Rules triggered on certain absolute time events are the most common feature of time-triggers. An example: AT *"summer time"* IF *"my sleep-controller detects that I did not sleep well the night before"* THEN *"my activity tracker device should suggest me to take a walk before going to bed"*.
3. Delayed Reaction Execution: Reaction execution can be delayed by combining a call event with a temporal offset. This offset is a time-valued attribute of the related environment, thus generating "relative events". For instance, to check three months after my last blood test if I need another test, a possible rule could be: AT *"The date of my last blood test + 3 months"* IF *"the person scale says that I lost more than 10 kilograms"* THEN *"my smart watch should show a message suggesting to book a medical exam"*.
4. Repeated Reaction Execution: Repeating execution of a particular action regularly after a fixed period of time has passed. In this case the keyword EVERY could be combined with an expression of type PERIOD, e.g. EVERY MONTH, or EVERY 3 HOURS, or with even more sophisticated specifications, such as EVERY MONDAY, EVERY 2nd MONDAY IN A MONTH, or EVERYDAY EXCEPT SATURDAY.

The EUD paradigm we propose in this paper aims supporting the end user in composing such space/time-based rules for extending the well-established but not powerful IF-THIS-THEN-THAT paradigm. Our Sensor-based Rule Language follows syntax, semantics, and grammar of a Policy Rule Language proposed in [36], and is based on the ECA (Event, Condition, Action) paradigm [34]. Our language allows to specify rules stating policies for triggering actions (one or a set). The general format of a rule is the following (square brackets denote optional components):

```
RuleName: "MY RULE"
ON Sensor[s]
  [WHENEVER "Condition"]
Action: "Some Actions"
  [VALIDITY: Validity_Place-Interval]
```

A rule consists of several components. The `RuleName` component represents the rule identifier. Users can retrieve rules by means of such identifier for visualizing, sharing, dropping, or modifying them. `Sensor[s]` represents the sensor or set of sensors upon which data the rule is triggered. Each sensor exposes a set of parameters which can be used for expressing the conditions. `Condition` is an optional conditional expression. `Action` is an expression that states what happens when the condition is verified. `Validity_Place-Interval` is a special spatial and/or temporal condition also expressed by means of the condition language we developed, representing the space and time period during which the rule is enabled. For example, if the interval [EVERYDAY EXCEPT SATURDAY] is specified we know that a rule is enabled every day of the week but not on Saturday. But if `Validity_Place-Interval` is not specified, we know that the rule is always enabled. By means of `Validity_Place-Interval` it is possible to state that certain rules are not always enabled; rather, they are enabled only if an event happens in a specific place or during specific temporal intervals. Such a feature is not provided by conventional apps for IoT.

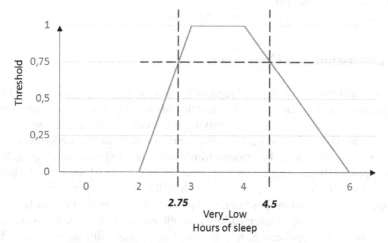

Fig. 3. Example to illustrate hours of sleep distribution

Another extension of the IF-THIS-THEN-THAT paradigm is to provide end users with a more flexible way for expressing the condition statement by incorporating fuzziness into the condition on which the events need to be triggered. This extension focuses on the linguistic values of the fuzzy condition [37], in which the fuzziness concerning the linguistic concepts are interpreted in an application context. A linguistic variable is represented by a quintuple of <v,T,X,g,m> where v is name of the linguistic variable, T is set of linguistic terms applicable to variable v, X is the universal set of values, g is the grammar for generating the linguistic term, m is the semantic rule that assigns to each term tεT, a fuzzy set on X. To illustrate our approach, we us as example an IoT environment that has a sleep monitor among its elements. Let represent a linguistic variable with a graphical distribution based on four parameters as depicted in Figure 3. Very_Low for hours of sleep is represented using trapezoidal function as Very_Low (2 hours, 3 hours, 4 hours, and 6 hours). Current IoT applications use simple statements such as "Hours of sleep <= 3 hours" to indicate when the value is very low. Using our language, users can use the statement "Quantity = $Very_Low": a set of values are related to "$Very_Low" in this comparison, rather than one single value. Fulfillment threshold is allowed to specify the condition with a degree value in the range of [0, 1]. For example, in Figure 3, we used 0.75 as the threshold to indicate that the value of hours of sleep is very low with the degree of 0.75. As a result, a value in the range [2.75, 4.5] indicates that "the number of hours of sleep is very high with a threshold of 0.75". By using our Rule Language the user can express a fuzzy condition is this way:

```
RuleName: "Quality of sleep Monitor"
ON sleep-controller AND Thermometer
   WHENEVER "the number of hours of sleep is $Very_Low"
AND "the temperature is not $Very_High"
Action: "The activity tracking device suggests me to take
a walk before going to sleep"
   VALIDITY: IN "Milan" and AT "August"
```

5   Discussion and Conclusion

The main contribution of this paper regards the analysis of the current state of EUD in the light of the development of IoT research and practice. The comprehensive overview that we provided, helps in underlying the nature of the challenges that arise today. The analysis of existing IoT ecosystem, as well as the under-design ones, according to elements and dimensions (time, space, social) may be of great help in assessing potentials and issues that may arise. From a study of the most diffused applications for IoT that provide the user with EUD tools, we identified and discuss some open problems and propose in this paper a new EUD paradigm and language to solve them. The language presented in the previous section is currently under implementation in an IoT application that is aimed at dealing with an ecosystem in the wellness domain. It consists in the design and development of an interactive visual system aimed at implementing the paradigm and language proposed and at testing its validity.

References

1. Ashton, K.: That 'Internet of Things' Thing. RFID Journal, June (2009). http://www.rfidjournal.com/articles/view?4986 (accessed on January 9th, 2015)
2. Atzori, L., Iera, A., Morabito, G.: The internet of things: A survey. Comput. Netw. **54**(15), 2787–2805 (2010)
3. Connections Counter: The Internet of Everything in Motion. http://newsroom.cisco.com/feature-content?type=webcontent&articleId=1208342 (accessed on January 9th, 2015)
4. Evans, D.: The Internet of Things. How the Next Evolution of the Internet is Changing Everything. Cisco Internet Business Solutions Group – White Paper (2011). http://www.cisco.com/web/about/ac79/docs/innov/IoT_IBSG_0411FINAL.pdf (accessed on January 9th, 2015)
5. Meder, J.: Human Empowerment in a Semantic Web of Things: Concept of a semantic platform for connected devices. Master Thesis at Uppsala University, Department of Information Technology (2014)
6. Munjin, D.: User Empowerment in the Internet of Things. Ph.D dissertation at University of Geneve, Department of Economy and Management (2013)
7. Cypher, A.: Watch What I Do: Programming by Demonstration. The MIT Press (1993)
8. Barricelli, B.R., Marcante, A., Mussio, P., Parasiliti Provenza, L., Padula, M., Scala, P.L.: Designing pervasive and multimodal interactive systems: an approach built on the field. In: Ubiquitous and Pervasive Computing: Concepts, Methodologies, Tools, and Applications, pp. 212–233. IGI Global (2010)
9. Lieberman, H., Paternò, F., Klann, M., Wulf, V.: End-User Development: An Emerging Paradigm. In: Lieberman, H., Paternò, F., Wulf, V. (eds.) End-User Development, pp. 1–8. Springer (2006)
10. Dourish, P., Anderson, K., Nafus, D.: Cultural mobilities: diversity and agency in urban computing. In: Baranauskas, C., Abascal, J., Barbosa, S.D.J. (eds.) INTERACT 2007. LNCS, vol. 4663, pp. 100–113. Springer, Heidelberg (2007)
11. Shneiderman, B.: Leonardo's Laptop: Human Needs and the New Computing Technologies. MIT Press (2002)
12. Fischer, G.: Beyond 'Couch Potatoes': From Consumers to Designers and Active Contributors (2002). http://firstmonday.org/issues/issue7_12/fischer/ (accessed on January 9th, 2015)
13. Costabile, M.F., Fogli, D., Mussio, P., Piccinno, A.: Visual Interactive Systems for End-User Development: a Model-based Design Methodology. IEEE TSMCA **37**(6), 1029–1046 (2007)
14. Costabile, M.F., Mussio, P., Parasiliti Provenza, L., Piccinno, A.: End users as unwitting software developers. In: Proc. of WEUSE 2008, pp. 6–10. ACM (2008)
15. Costabile, M.F., Mussio, P., Parasiliti Provenza, L., Piccinno, A.: Advanced Visual Systems Supporting Unwitting EUD. In: Proc. of AVI 2008, pp. 313–316. ACM (2008)
16. Barricelli, B.R., Marcante, A., Mussio, P., Parasiliti Provenza, L., Valtolina, S., Fresta. G.: BANCO: a Web Architecture Supporting Unwitting End-User Development. IxD&A, 5-6, pp. 23–30 (2009)
17. Petre, M., Blackwell, A.F.: Children as Unwitting End-User Programmers. Proc. of VL/HCC **2007**, 239–242 (2007)
18. Costabile, M.F., Fogli, D., Lanzilotti, R., Mussio, P., Parasiliti Provenza, L., Piccinno, A.: Advancing end-user development through meta-design. In: End User Computing Challenges Technologies: Emerging Tools and Applications, pp. 143–167. Information Science Reference (2007)

19. Åsand, H., Mørch, A.: Super Users and Local Developers: the Organization of End User Development in accounting company. JOEUC **18**(4), 1–21 (2006)
20. Nardi, B.A., Miller, J.R.: An ethnographic study of distributed problem solving in spreadsheet development. In: Proc. of CSCW 1990, pp. 197–208). ACM Press (1990)
21. Ye, Y., Fischer, G.: Designing for Participation in Socio-Technical Software Systems. In: Proc. of UAHCI, pp. 312–321. Springer (2007)
22. Nardi, B.: A Small Matter of Programming. MIT Press (1993)
23. Brancheau, J.C., Brown, C.V.: The Management of end-user computing: status and direction. ACM Computing Surveys **25**(5), 437–482 (1993)
24. Lee, H., Liebenau, J.: Time and the Internet at the Turn of the Millennium. Time & Society **9**, 43–56 (2000)
25. Sutcliffe, A., Mehandjiev, N.: Introduction of Special Issue on End User Development. CACM **47**(9), 31–32 (2004)
26. Pipek, V., Rosson, M.B., de Ruyter, B., Wulf, V.: Introduction. In: Proc. of IS-EUD 2009, pp. V–VI. Springer (2009)
27. Mørch, A.: Three levels of end-user tailoring: customization, integration, and extension. In: Computers and Design in Context, pp. 51–76. MIT Press (1997)
28. Trigg, R.H., Moran, T.P., Halasz, F.G.: Adaptibility and Tailorability in NoteCards. In: Proc. of INTERACT 1987, pp. 723–728. Elsevier Science Publishers (1987)
29. Henderson, A., Kyng, M.: There's no place like home: continuing design in use. In: Design at Work: Cooperative Design of Computer Systems, pp. 219–240. Lawrence Erlbaum Associates (1991)
30. Germonprez, M., Hovorka, D., Collopy, F.: A Theory of Tailorable Technology Design. Journal of the Association for Information Systems **8**(6), 315–367 (2007)
31. Baldwin, C.Y., Clark, K.B.: Design Rules: The Power of Modularity. MIT Press (2000)
32. Costabile, M. F., Fogli, D., Mussio, P., Piccinno, A.: End-user development: the software shaping workshop approach. In: End-User Development, pp. 183–205. Springer (2006)
33. Ceri, S., Cochrane, R., Widom, J.: Practical applications of triggers and constraints: success and lingering issues. In: Proc. of VLDB 2000, pp. 254–262 (2000)
34. Widom, J., Ceri, S.: Active Database Systems. Morgan Kaufmann Publisher (1996)
35. Behrend, A., Dorau, C., Manthey, R., Grundspenkis, J., Morzy, T., Vossen, G. (eds.): SQL Triggers Reacting on Time Events: An Extension Proposal Advances in Databases and Information Systems. Springer (2009)
36. Bertino, E., Cochinwala, M., Mesiti, M.: UCS-Router: a policy engine for enforcing message routing rules in a universal communication system. In: Proc. of Mobile Data Management 2002, pp. 8–16 (2002)
37. Jin, Y., Bhavsar, T.: Incorporating fuzziness into timer-triggers for temporal event handling. In: Proc. of IRI 2008, pp. 325–329 (2008)

Natural Notation for the Domestic Internet of Things

Charith Perera[1,2](✉), Saeed Aghaee[3], and Alan Blackwell[3]

[1] Research School of Computer Science (RSCS), The Australian National University,
Canberra, ACT, Australia
`charith.perera@ieee.org`
[2] Faculty of Maths, Computing and Technology, The Open University,
Milton Keynes, UK
[3] Computer Laboratory, University of Cambridge, Cambridge, UK
{`saeed.aghaee,alan.blackwell`}`@cl.cam.ac.uk`

Abstract. This study explores the use of natural language to give instructions that might be interpreted by Internet of Things (IoT) devices in a domestic 'smart home' environment. We start from the proposition that reminders can be considered as a type of end-user programming, in which the executed actions might be performed either by an automated agent or by the author of the reminder. We conducted an experiment in which people wrote sticky notes specifying future actions in their home. In different conditions, these notes were addressed to themselves, to others, or to a computer agent. We analyse the linguistic features and strategies that are used to achieve these tasks, including the use of graphical resources as an informal visual language. The findings provide a basis for design guidance related to end-user development for the Internet of Things.

Keywords: Internet of things · Smart home · End-User programming · User study

1 Introduction

In this paper, we investigate how people might program the 'smart home' domestic technologies enabled by the Internet of Things (IoT). However, rather than start by creating another new end-user programming (EUP) language, we study how people give instructions in the home as an existing natural task. Using the familiar sticky note as an experimental device, we conducted an experiment in which we asked people to write sticky notes requesting that things should be done in their homes. We wanted to compare routine requests to other people, in comparison to communication with a programmable smart home. As a control condition, we compared both of these to the use of sticky notes as a reminder to oneself.

© Springer International Publishing Switzerland 2015
P. Díaz et al. (Eds.): IS-EUD 2015, LNCS 9083, pp. 25–41, 2015.
DOI: 10.1007/978-3-319-18425-8_3

2 Background

A major category of applications for IoT devices are 'smart home' scenarios, in which domestic tasks are automated by defining policies or scripts. These scenarios appear attractive to technical enthusiasts, but actual home automation currently faces a key obstacle, in the ability to control communication between devices. Although there are many categories of automated domestic appliance (e.g. floor-cleaning robots, bread-makers, video recorders), their automated behaviours are carried out by a single device. In such cases, the functional capabilities of the device are determined by the manufacturer, with the user only needing to customize it to suit the configuration of their own house or daily schedule.

In contrast, the most challenging instances of EUP for IoT devices are those that involve information exchange – between devices and users (e.g. reminders), between devices and services (e.g. automated orders for home supplies), or between devices themselves. Many domestic information exchange tasks are activities that could in principle be carried out directly by the user, reading information from one device or context and applying it to another. For example, when you notice that the laundry powder box is nearly empty, you remember (perhaps) to buy powder next time you are shopping. However, all these little tasks consume the limited resource of human attention. One way of defining domestic EUP is that it allows people to optimize their allocation of attention, choosing between immediate direct manipulation and reminders or automation of future behaviour [1,2].

There are numerous popular examples of end-user programming services for the Web that demonstrate this strategy. For example, IFTTT[1] allows users to specify future behaviour as an if-this-then-that policy. A typical IFTTT 'recipe' might be triggered (if) every time a photo is taken on your iPhone (this), and then automatically upload it to your Twitter feed (that). IFTTT is a simple and practical EUP system [3] that automates future actions. In this paper, we explore a familiar category of home behaviour in order to gain insight to the opportunities for creating IFTTT-style automation services for the home. We focus on tasks that involve attention investment – where paying attention to something in advance, in order to define a policy, will save attention in future. The everyday term for this kind of information exchange is a reminder – creating a mechanism that transfers information at a time in the future. Similar rule-based systems include Tasker[2], Atooma[3], and Locale[4].

In terms of EUP research, there is a well-established strategy for using everyday descriptions of an automated task as a way of gaining insight into programming system design. In the method employed in Myers' Natural Programming project [4], typical studies recruit samples of representative users who are asked

---

[1] http://ifttt.com
[2] http://tasker.dinglisch.net
[3] https://play.google.com/store/apps/details?id=com.atooma
[4] http://www.twofortyfouram.com

to describe specific types of program behaviour in their own words. The key to design of valid natural programming studies is to ensure that the experimental tasks correspond to the intended application domain, and that the programming 'environment' in which the natural language description is collected properly represents the cognitive demands of the programming situation. For example, natural programming studies do not usually proceed by asking participants to give a verbal description to the experimenter, because human conversation relies on substantial elements of common ground and interpretive ambiguity that are not available in programming languages.

Our goal in this study was therefore to define an experimental paradigm that could be used to study investment of attention in the definition of domestic information exchange policies, in a manner that offered external validity with regard to the context of everyday home management. We chose to focus on the sticky note (a generic term for the product category introduced by Post-It^{TM}). One of the major uses of the sticky note in domestic contexts is indeed to implement reminders. People often write sticky notes as reminders to themselves, and place notes in a context where they expect future information exchange to be valuable – on the front door, on their keys, on their wallet and so on. In shared houses, people also write sticky notes and place them in contexts where they wish to remind other people of particular policies or requests for action. Our study generalizes beyond these familiar cases, to use the sticky note as an experimental proxy for a domestic EUP language, where the reader of the note is not yourself or another resident of your house, but an automation service that will take responsibility for future information exchange.

3   Related Work

There is a long tradition of exploring the potential design space of 'smart home' technologies through study of natural behaviours in the home (e.g. [5]), and investigating the ways in which families respond to the opportunity to program and configure existing digital technologies [6]. Sticky notes are often included in the kit of materials for cultural probe studies (e.g. Graham et al. [7]), and the sticky note metaphor has been literally rendered in home technology probes (e.g. Hutchinson et al. [8]). The refrigerator door, as a location where sticky notes and other papers are placed, is a regular focus of smart home technology, both as a versatile augmented display surface for research attention [9] and more literally in commercial products such as the Samsung WiFi-enabled fridge[5]. One can imagine that sticky notes themselves might be used as an EUP technology in future (e.g. Tarkan et al. [10]), and there are many previous systems that have augmented sticky notes in ways that might achieve this (e.g. as reviewed by Mistry et al. [11]).

Our goal in this research is to understand better the ways that people express themselves when making requests or reminders in the smart home context. This can help to design more natural EUP systems, as in the work of Myers et al.

---

[5] http://www.samsung.com/us/topic/apps-on-your-fridge

It can also be applied as a basis for Natural Language Interfaces (NLI). Many companies are currently deploying NLI for simple query and status applications, especially in mobile apps such as Google Now[6] and Siri[7]. For instance, Google Now has recently published an advertisement[8] that tackles a similar use case for smart homes. The Microsoft Cortana[9] NLI has recently been exploited in INSTEAON[10], a mobile app that aims at creating a natural language interface for IoT.

Nevertheless, when considered as a programming interface, NLIs have numerous disadvantages. The ambiguity and lack of precision in natural language remains a challenge [12], with more detailed instructions often less efficient than a concise formal notation [13]. Analysis according to Cognitive Dimensions of Notations [14] identifies that speech-based interaction (1) poses constraints on the order of doing things (premature commitment), (2) conceals information in encapsulations (poor visibility), (3) doesn't allow changes to made decisions (high viscosity), and (4) obscures links between entities (hidden dependencies). The sticky note offers an opportunity to study natural language interaction in a written context which is routinely augmented with visual cues.

4   Structure of the Study

We designed six different use case scenarios for presentation to participants in the study (see Table 1). Each scenario depicts a familiar problem likely to be faced in the home, requiring future action either by yourself (recording a reminder), by someone you live with (delivering a request) or potentially by an intelligent agent of some kind (defining a program or script). Participants were asked to write a sticky note to 'solve' the problem mentioned in each scenario, in a manner that would implicitly result in the generation of a speech act such as reminder, request, or program.

We presented each scenario on an A4 sheet, using a minimum number of words in order to encourage participants to choose their own phrasing for the resulting speech act. Instead of verbal description, the problem context was illustrated as far as possible using images from which the nature of the problem could be inferred. An example is shown in Figure 1. Our goal was to provide sufficient information to draw attention to the nature of the problem, without including any direct phrasing that might be incorporated in the participant responses. As with other studies in natural programming, we wanted participants to think about how they would approach the problem, using their own words and presentation mechanisms to write the sticky notes without being influenced by our descriptions and instructions.

---

[6] http://www.google.com/landing/now/

[7] https://www.apple.com/ios/siri/

[8] https://twitter.com/googleuk/status/525194969238478848

[9] http://www.windowsphone.com/en-us/features-8-1

[10] http://www.insteon.com/

Problem:
Toilet paper roll is used up. You don't
want to see this happen again.

How would you write a sticky note that will remind **YOU** to take necessary actions to solve this problem in the future in natural language ?

Fig. 1. Sample use case scenario sheet

Each A4 sheet included a printed rendering of a sticky note. We pasted a real sticky note on top of this printed sticky note before handing the survey sheets to each participant. Use of a real sticky note increased the naturalness of the experiment, allowing participants to imagine that these notes might be placed in their own home (several participants made unsolicited comments indicating that they did indeed imagine particular locations in which the note might be placed). Attaching a sticky note to the instruction sheet was also convenient for data collation and analysis, in that we could remove the sticky notes and arrange all six on a single page for each participant.

The six scenarios covered a range of home activities, designed to take place in different contexts within a typical house, covering different frequencies and durations of activity, and representing different degrees of complexity and cost. These are summarized in Table 1.

In each scenario, we asked the participants to write a sticky note to solve the illustrated problem. We created three variants as follows, each addressed to a different person who will carry them out (the 'addressee'):

How would you write a sticky note that will

- (version 1) remind you
- (version 2) remind someone you are living with
- (version 3) be interpreted by a machine (an intelligent robot or something that can read sticky notes)

to take necessary actions to solve this problem in the future in natural language?

Table 1. The problems described in each scenario

Context	Problem
Laundry	Washing Machine filter is clogged. This happens roughly every 3 months
Kitchen	You have prepared food for your kids and about to leave your house. You won't come back until late. Leftover food can be spoiled if it is not placed in the fridge.
Bathroom	Toilet paper roll is used up. You don't want to see this happen again.
Garage	It is summer!!!.. Your parents have asked to bring your weed eater when you visit them next time. Every summer they need your weed eater to cut their lawn.
Living Room	Some relatives come to visit every few months... Your house is usually a mess
Garbage Bins	You always forget to put garbage bags into outside bins located in front of your house so the council will pick them up on Mondays

We created six sets of experimental materials, each using the same scenarios, but with different combinations of instructions, balanced across participants. Our main within-subjects research question relates to the effect of addressee, so the three different addressee conditions were placed to minimize order effects. Issues with participant recruitment and withdrawal led to slight variations (15.9% in sets 1, 5 and 6, 14.3% in set 2, 20.6% in set 3, and 17.5% in set 4).

In addition to completing sticky notes for the six scenarios, participants completed a short questionnaire: gender, age group, profession, education, number of hours spend using computational devices, and previous programming experience. A final debriefing question asked for any further comments on the experiment.

5   Summary of Data Collected

We recruited 63 participants in Canberra, Australia. All had good working knowledge of English, either native or fluent speakers. No direct compensation was provided for participating in the study. 38 were male (60%) and 25 female (40%). Figure 2 shows the age distribution. All participants were met either in their office or at home. Most completed the tasks and demographic questionnaire in 5-10 minutes, although a small number (n=4) took 15-20 minutes.

In response to the final debriefing question, two participants requested further information about our research. Two noted that they did not know how the machines would work. One noted that she was not a native English speaker. One questioned the practicality of using sticky notes for these scenarios. Several participants also used the sticky notes themselves to provide additional explanation to the researchers. This included information on where they might place the sticky note, for example adding *In front of the door* to a sticky note *"Place the food in the fridge"* (in response to the kitchen scenario). A few participants

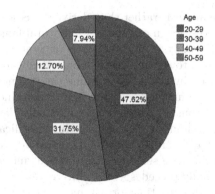

Fig. 2. Age distribution of participants

wrote an alternative method that they would prefer to writing sticky notes, for example *I would probably put an alert in my calendar* (in the garage scenario).

Based on the questionnaire responses, we constructed a measure of prior technical experience. Where a participant stated that they were familiar with multiple programming languages, they were considered to be technically experienced. In cases where the participant reported some experience of a programming language used in school, they were only placed in the technically experienced category if they were in a technical profession, or had a degree in a technical field. Although this is a relatively coarse criterion, it was less intrusive and faster to administer than more elaborate programming aptitude tests. It is possible that some participants were mis-classified as a result, but since the classification was done without reference to responses, we treat this as an unbiased source of experimental variation. Demographic data showed that the technical experience construct was correlated with gender (8 females and 26 males).

6 Analysis Method

6.1 Linguistic Analysis

Linguistic analysis involves studying the grammatical structures and meaning of a language sample. In the context of the smart home, our goal was to develop an understanding of how the communication of information between people and smart devices is linguistically framed. Linguistic framing offers insights into the mental model of users as well as their communicative practices. These, in turn, provide valuable guidelines for designing "natural" programming languages that conform to those mental models and practices [4].

Our analysis corpus consisted of 374 sentences extracted from the sticky notes. It was not possible to use automated tools due to the ambiguity caused by frequently missing punctuation in the notes. Note that although this corpus is relatively small compared to those used in automated text analysis, our goal was to make a descriptive analysis rather than derive statistical training data of the kind that would be necessary in creating a full natural language interpreter.

We proceeded with the analysis at three levels of Syntactic, Semantic, and Pragmatic, which correspond to the analysis of, respectively, form, meaning, and context of the language used by the users to frame the reminders.

At the syntactic level, we first assessed the frequency of noun phrases compared to sentences in the corpus. Furthermore, we manually classified all the sentences according to their grammatical structure. Our classification of sentences involves the grammatical differences between Declarative, Interrogative, and Imperative sentences. Declarative sentences state a fact and syntactically consist of a subject that normally precedes a verb. Interrogative sentences are constructed in the form of yes-no questions or wh-questions (i.e., questions framed using an interrogative word such as "who", "which", "where", and "how"). Imperative sentences give a command or make a request and have an understood but not always stated "you" as the subject.

We applied the standard semantic analysis method of n-gram modelling to estimate the probability of a given sequence of words. An n-gram is simply a sequence of n words that appear in the corpus in the same order immediately one after another. Using the SRI Language Modelling Toolkit [15], we built a list of most recurrent uni-grams (1-grams) and bigrams (2-grams).

We refined the n-gram list by removing common n-grams that had no direct reference to the task (e.g. "in the") as well as the phrases that were directly prompted by the scenario description presented in the experiment (e.g. "washing machine", "weed eater" and "fridge"). We then grouped the n-grams according to semantic similarity, using the ConceptNet word association API [16]. ConceptNet uses a rich commonsense knowledge base to provide an accurate measure of similarity between two concepts.

Extracting context-dependent meaning from a language sample is, however, beyond semantic analysis and is dealt with at the pragmatic level. Speech acts are used to express a certain attitude and are a central point of pragmatics. Hence, we considered the five classes of speech acts proposed by Searle [17], and classified the sentences into one of five speech act classes as follows:

Representatives: The speaker asserts his or her belief of something that can be evaluated to be true or false (e.g., a doctor's diagnosis about the presence of a disease).

Directives: The speaker expects the listener to take a certain action as a response such as by asking a question or making a request.

Commissives: The speaker commits to a future action, for instance, by making promises or threats.

Expressives: The speaker expresses his or her attitude and psychological state (e.g., thanking or apologizing) to the listener.

Declaratives: The speaker changes the status or condition of the reality, for example, by pronouncing a marriage.

6.2   Visual Language Coding

The visual/typographic elements of participants' responses were coded using the graphical language approach introduced by Bertin [18], extended by Engelhardt [19], and applied to user interfaces by Blackwell [20]. This analyses the 'graphic resources' that have been employed in a hierarchy of marks, symbols, regions and surfaces. Each of these supports a range of semantic correspondences that allow different types of design application. In our experiment, we can consider the participants writing sticky notes as implicit designers, inventing their own graphical languages in response to the task. The visual language analysis started with overall ink distribution, including multiple regions separated by whitespace (if any) and bounded regions formed by visual gestalt properties of alignment or regular containment.

The great majority of the marks made by participants were English alphabet letter forms, in most cases either uniformly uppercase, or uniformly lowercase (with appropriate grammatical capitalisation). Some distinctive capitalisation was observed – this is discussed below. A relatively small number of participants made no further use of visual language devices – they wrote conventionally from left to right, starting at the top of the sticky note, and starting a new line when necessary.

Punctuation marks were coded separately, as were other conventional symbolic forms such as emoticons and logos. A small number of respondents included pictorial elements, although these included meta-communication with respect to the task frame, such as a drawing of the door on which the sticky note should be placed. Other functional graphical devices included connecting lines, dividing lines between regions, and a small number of conventional typographic or diagrammatic forms such as tables and flowcharts with arrows and decision diamonds.

Visual language coding was performed by annotating colour scanned copies of all participant responses, marking every occurrence of the features discussed. This was done in two passes – first open coding, in which all types of visual feature in the sample were identified, and then exhaustive coding of each occurrence of that type. Some qualitatively distinctive but infrequent features were noted for discussion. Frequently occurring features were tabulated and transcribed into our statistical data set for each case in which they had been observed.

7   Findings

7.1   Linguistic Structure

In this section we make a linguistic analysis of the sticky notes. We consider features at several syntactic, semantic, and pragmatic levels: number of words (syntactic), sentence types (syntactic), request types (semantic and pragmatic), causality (semantic and pragmatic), and speech acts (pragmatic).

Number of Words. The sticky notes we used in the experiments were small in size, thus restricting the reminder messages to a limited number of words. On average, the number of words per reminder message was 9. Looking for differences between the participants, we found that the addressee of the sticky note has a statistically significant impact on the number of words, whereas technical experience (and gender) has no significant effect. The average number of words in a note addressed to yourself was 7.83, which was significantly less than those addressed to someone else (10.86) or to an intelligent machine (10.33) (ANOVA $F = (6.47, 2), p < 0.01$).

Sentence Types. Out of 374 sentences, we classified 271, 94, and 9 as imperative, declarative, and interrogative, respectively. Gender and technical experience do not impact the sentence type. However, we found a significant difference in the effect of addressee. Sticky notes addressed to an intelligent machine and the participants themselves have, respectively, the least (81) and the most number (100) of imperative sentences (Chi-Square test $p < 0.05$).

Request Types. Table 2 lists the most common n-grams. Based on the ConceptNet API, we put 'remind', 'remember', and 'don't forget' in one category (similarity score> 0.9), of 'reminder' requests. While technical experience and addressee had no effect, gender was a significant factor: significantly more male participants (228 cases out of 374) used one of these (formal) "request" phrases (Chi-Square test $p < 0.05$).

We noted that the phrases 'remember' and 'don't forget' exhibit a double negation. We found that significantly fewer cases incorporate one of these phrases when the addressee is an intelligent machine, as compared to a human (someone else or the participants themselves).

Table 2. The most important n-grams (unigrams and bigrams)

N-gram	N	Occurrences
put	1	69
clean	1	63
please	1	52
if	1	50
house	1	26
when	1	24

N-gram	N	Occurrences
remember	1	20
remind	1	19
remind me	2	14
remember to	2	13
dont't forget	2	12

Causality. Another set of related recurrent n-grams are 'if' and 'when'. These words have been used to indicate and express a cause or condition in a sentence. The results show that technical experience and having a machine as an addressee positively affects the use of these causal words in a sticky note (respectively 202/374 and 125/374 cases). Fewer of these cases were self-addressed (123/374 cases). There is a subtle grammatical difference between 'if' and 'when': 'if' is used when the outcome is not certain, while 'when' is used when it is certain. Overall, the frequency of 'if' is more than double that of 'when'. We noted that in scenarios 1, 2, and 6, where the outcome depends on a condition that may hold, the number of 'when' cases is considerably lower than that of 'if' cases. In other scenarios (3, 4, and 5) the two phrases are almost equally utilized.

Speech Acts. As anticipated by the nature of the scenarios, the dominant speech act was of directive class (296/374 cases). Moreover, the addressee had a significant impact in this matter. The sentences are more likely (108/374 cases) to convey a directive speech act when addressed to an intelligent machine (Chi-Square test $p < 0.05$). We found no commissive (promise or threat) and only one instance of expressive (expressing emotions) speech acts with a machine specified as the addressee. Also, we found no expressive speech act that was self-addressed.

7.2   Graphical Resources

The following discussion analyses the visual features observed according to their frequency across all cases, where each case represents a single sticky note. 255 out of 378 cases (67%) included one or more of the visual features discussed above. Only 2 participants used no visual features in any note, writing in 'plain' text.

Visual Regions. 45 cases divided the note into two distinct regions, always separated vertically. In 14 of these, a distinct region at the top functioned as a title, announcing the purpose of the note. In 19 cases, regions within the 'body' area were separated either by a horizontal line, or an area of blank space, with a few distinguishing one region from another by different handwriting styles in each. A further 12 cases used the conventions of written correspondence, with a salutation and farewell at the top and bottom of the note. Two participants used more elaborate decoration – highlighter pen overlay and 'bang' circle.

Text arrangement within a region was most often conventionally left- and top-justified – a natural arrangement for handwriting as it requires little advance planning. There were 11 cases in which the text block was aligned with a slant: of the left edge, of the text base lines, or both. A further 11 cases showed consistent centre-alignment of the individual text lines. This is surprising, given that it is difficult to achieve (the length of each line must be known before starting it), and does not have a clear semantic purpose.

Vertical left-alignment was used to indicate items in a list – in 5 cases prefaced by a dash, in 4 with sequential numbers, in 3 with round bullets, and in 2 cases purely implicit with no marker. Nested left indentation, as in programming language source code, was used in 5 cases.

Symbols. As noted, alphabetic letters were usually lower case with conventional capitalisation. There were also 9 cases of idiosyncratic capitalisation, usually of selected nouns. Rather than title case convention, these seemed to apply to words marking key semantic concepts in the message (e.g. "Date"), so may be related to computer idioms. Individual words were sometimes capitalised for emphasis (9 cases), or had an underscore added (7 cases).

After alphabetic letters, the most common symbol was use of an exclamation mark (26 cases). Parentheses were used to separate supplementary information in 2 cases, and long dashes to indicate pauses in 3 cases, a link in one case, and item markers as already mentioned. Algebraic symbols were used in 8 cases, often in ways that reflected typical programming language practice.

Smiley emoticons were used 6 times, in the conventional form with a circle around two eyes and mouth. There were 4 cases of other icons, using visual analogy to traffic signs, from a single participant. Finally, there were 7 cases in which a terminator symbol was added to close the message – either an underline or flourish.

Visual Semantics. Overall, it is apparent that responses included many visual features beyond those that can be captured in a text transcription, or that correspond to semantic content of speech interaction. We saw no sign of 'private' visual language. As a result, many of these could conceivably be used as design resources in multi-modal interaction systems, employing visual language devices that form a common vocabulary of written speech acts.

However, it is possible that some of these features form a specialised visual vocabulary that would not be appropriate if imposed on end-users (or alternatively, a precise notation that might have to be taught to end-users in order for them to use a visual command language competently). We therefore carried out a statistical analysis of the distribution of all these features, with particular attention to whether the 'speaker' (the participant who wrote the sticky note) or the 'listener' (the addressee of the note) suggested that a technically specialised visual vocabulary was being used.

Visual Pragmatics. Do people adjust the visual language grammar they use when they are writing a sticky note addressed to an intelligent machine, rather than another person? As with other EUP research, we might expect that people with programming experience are more likely to have experience of specific conventions of language use derived from programming.

We have three hypotheses:

H1) that there is an identifiable subset (or 'dialect', perhaps) of visual language features that are more often used when addressing machines rather than people

H2) that there is a complementary set of visual language features that are more often used when addressing people rather than machines

H3) that people with prior experience of programming are more likely to use an identifiable subset of visual language features when addressing machines

(null hypotheses are that there is no difference in frequency of features resulting from addressee of the sticky note or technical experience of the writer)

During coding, we observed several visual features that appeared characteristic of program source code layout rather than other handwriting or print conventions: use of nested indentation, use of ordered lists of steps, and use of algebraic symbols. We counted all cases in which any of these three conventions had been used, finding 52 cases. Of these, 32 were addressed to an intelligent machine, with only 10 addressed to someone else and 10 self-addressed (Chi-Square $p < 0.001$). The people writing these were more likely to have technical experience – 43 out of 52 cases (Chi-Square $p < 0.001$). Nested indent was particularly likely to be used by those with technical experience (26/27 cases, $p < 0.001$), and to be addressed to a machine (20/27 cases, $p < 0.001$). Ordered lists were also more likely to be addressed to a machine (11/16 cases, $p < 0.05$), although sample size is too small to state that there is a difference based on technical experience. Algebraic symbols were more likely to be used by those with technical experience (20/26 case, $p < 0.05$), but we cannot say whether these were more likely to be addressed to a machine. Algebra was unlikely to be used in the living room scenario (1/26 cases), which involved no numeric values. Lists were most frequently used in the living room and laundry scenarios (12/16 cases).

We observed several visual features that appeared characteristic of informal correspondence: use of salutations, emoticons, exclamation marks and visual emphasis. We found 102 cases, of which only 19 were addressed to a machine (Chi-Square test $p < 0.001$). People with technical background were less likely to use these human-like visual conventions (46/102, $p < 0.05$), in particular when addressing machines, although we did observe some cases (7 of 19, n.s.). The largest number of these features appeared in notes written to someone else (50/102 cases, $p < 0.001$), especially the use of salutations (18/20, $p < 0.001$). Emoticons were not used at all when addressing machines, and most likely to be used when addressing someone else (6/8, $p < 0.05$). Exclamation marks were relatively unlikely to be used when addressing machines (12/65, $p < 0.05$), although these cases were evenly split between technical and non-technical writers. Writers with technical experience were relatively unlikely to use visual emphasis (6/33, $p < 0.001$) with only one of these cases addressed to a machine.

We also observed trends in the overall visual structure of the notes created by people with technical and non-technical backgrounds. Those with technical background were less likely overall to divide the note into separate regions (23 out of 72 cases, Chi-Square test $p < 0.001$) and less likely overall to place a context or mode title at the top of the note (15 out of 45 cases, $p < 0.01$). These may be general habits derived from use of sticky notes in technical work, because we saw no evidence that these overall visual structures were more or less common according to either the addressee, or the task scenario.

Overall, we find that there are differences in visual language features that are used by people with technical and non-technical backgrounds when writing sticky notes (rejecting the null hypothesis for H3), and that there exist particular sets of visual language features likely to be used when addressing machines (H1) and people (H2).

8   Implications for Design

While general natural-language programming remains a challenging future ambition for EUD, our focus on the specific application domain of IoT and on the sticky note as a constrained multimodal information device suggests new opportunities for EUD.

We have shown that the graphical resources of the sticky note complement natural language understanding, by allowing the use of visual language cues that establish the context for instruction, drawing on a number of commonplace graphical conventions. This represents an opportunity for simple multimodal interfaces to support EUP in this domain, which has remained untapped. Despite the fact that systems such as IFTTT, Atooma, and Locale, incorporate a visual iconic language (e.g., rules and actions are visualized as icons), they do not support a multimodal interface capable of receiving both natural and visual language inputs in a complementary manner.

We have also identified a number of ways in which people make allowance for interpretation when addressing others (either machine or person) rather than themselves. This helps us to understand the cognitive effort involved in 'reminder' tasks, which inherently involve cognitive effort to anticipate future state. For example, the distinction between 'remember' and 'don't forget' (the case of double negation) requires implicit theory of mind judgements [21]. Our results show that, while such anthropomorphic considerations are always implicit in reminders, and sometimes involve expressive speech acts with emotional elements, communications intended for interpretation by a machine are far less likely to include such elements. The majority of existing smart home systems are used for automation solutions and thus naturally mediate communication between humans and machines at the user interface. Nonetheless, some interesting use cases have emerged beyond machine automation and have been implemented to enhance human-to-human communication such as in Remind'em app[11]. Hence, this subtle difference in the attitude of end-users towards the communication target should be taken into account while designing the user experience for smart home systems.

As might be expected, people with technical experience bring this to bear in speech acts directed toward a machine. This results in more detailed specification, with syntactic and semantic forms that resemble programming language constructs. It is interesting to note that this resemblance covers both textual and graphical modes – a consideration that should be taken into account when designing 'natural' interfaces. On one hand, it is a safe strategy to design an EUP system in compliance with the non-programmer mentality [22] (e.g., high simplicity and low expressive power), and on the other, offering a high level of expressive power can also be beneficial for non-programmers as well. Given a

---

[11] *Note 1.* http://www.remindem.in/

high level of expressive power, programmers will be able to write high quality scripts that can be reused by many end-users. Moreover, a study by Lucci et al [23] shows that expressive power is also a factor for non-programmers in deciding which smart home automation service to use.

Finally, our combined visual/textual analysis demonstrates the devices used to accommodate semantic modes such as 'if' and 'when', as a component of the conventional reminding and instruction speech acts accomplished with sticky notes. While a trigger such as 'relatives paying a visit' is accommodated in emerging event-based mashup paradigms (e.g. IFTTT), the attention investment required for modal reasoning about temporal contexts such as 'when' may involve more sophisticated combinations of natural language and other notational devices. Existing rule-based systems (e.g., IFTTT, Tasker, Atooma, and Locale) seem to disregard these subtle differences between these semantic modes as well as their effects on the design of the overall user experience.

9 Conclusion

In this paper, we have reported an experiment that explored the ways in which people express themselves, when specifying domestic tasks of the kind that will require exchange of information between IoT appliances and services. We used the familiar sticky-note, which has often been a focus of research for understanding everyday information technologies. The sticky note offers good external validity for experimentation in this area, as a mundane information technology that supports the same kinds of reminder function identified in the attention investment model of EUP. We have carried out a rigorous linguistic analysis of this naturalistic data set, considering syntactic, semantic and pragmatic aspects from both textual and visual language perspectives.

The results draw attention to numerous design opportunities emphasising the multimodal resources that are relevant in this context. These considerations extend the potential for design solutions in an area that has recently placed more emphasis on speech interaction as the primary target for natural language interfaces. By considering this kind of everyday communication from the perspective of end-user programming, we can see a variety of ways in which speech interaction with the IoT might be extended, as already demonstrated in the familiar but surprisingly rich domain of the sticky note.

Acknowledgments. This work is supported by a Swiss National Science Foundation Early Postdoc Mobility fellowship (#P2TIP2_152264), and is also partially funded by International Alliance of Research Universities (IARU)Travel Grant and The ANU Vice Chancellor Travel Grant.

References

1. Blackwell, A.F., Rode, J.A., Toye, E.F.: How do we program the home? gender, attention investment, and the psychology of programming at home. International Journal of Human-Computer Studies **67**, 324–341 (2009)
2. Dey, A.K., Sohn, T., Streng, S., Kodama, J.: icap: interactive prototyping of context-aware applications. In: Fishkin, K.P., Schiele, B., Nixon, P., Quigley, A. (eds.) PERVASIVE 2006. LNCS, vol. 3968, pp. 254–271. Springer, Heidelberg (2006)
3. Ur, B., McManus, E., Pak Yong Ho, M., Littman, M.L.: Practical trigger-action programming in the smart home. In: Proceedings of the 32nd Annual ACM Conference on Human Factors in Computing Systems, pp. 803–812 (2014)
4. Myers, B.A., Pane, J.F., Ko, A.: Natural programming languages and environments. Communications of the ACM **47**, 47–52 (2004)
5. Tolmie, P., Pycock, J., Diggins, T., MacLean, A., Karsenty, A.: Unremarkable computing. In: Proceedings of the SIGCHI Conference on Human Factors in Computing Systems, pp. 399–406 (2002)
6. Rode, J.A., Toye, E.F., Blackwell, A.F.: The fuzzy felt ethnographyunderstanding the programming patterns of domestic appliances. Personal and Ubiquitous Computing **8**, 161–176 (2004)
7. Graham, C., Rouncefield, M., Gibbs, M., Vetere, F., Cheverst, K.: How probes work. In: Proceedings of the 19th Australasian Conference on Computer-Human Interaction: Entertaining User Interfaces, pp. 29–37 (2007)
8. Hutchinson, H., Mackay, W., Westerlund, B., Bederson, B.B., Druin, A., Plaisant, C., Beaudouin-Lafon, M., Conversy, S., Evans, H., Hansen, H., et al.: Technology probes: inspiring design for and with families. In: Proceedings of the SIGCHI Conference on Human Factors in Computing Systems, pp. 17–24 (2003)
9. Taylor, A.S., Swan, L., Eardley, R., Sellen, A., Hodges, S., Wood, K.: Augmenting refrigerator magnets: why less is sometimes more. In: Proceedings of the 4th Nordic Conference on Human-Computer Interaction: Changing Roles, pp. 115–124 (2006)
10. Tarkan, S., Sazawal, V., Druin, A., Golub, E., Bonsignore, E.M., Walsh, G., Atrash, Z.: Toque: designing a cooking-based programming language for and with children. In: Proceedings of the SIGCHI Conference on Human Factors in Computing Systems, pp. 2417–2426 (2010)
11. Mistry, P., Maes, P.: Augmenting sticky notes as an i/o interface. In: Universal Access in Human-Computer Interaction. Intelligent and Ubiquitous Interaction Environments. Springer, pp. 547–556 (2009)
12. Petrick, S.R.: On natural language based computer systems. IBM Journal of Research and Development **20**, 314–325 (1976)
13. Dijkstra, E.W.: On the foolishness of "natural language programming". In: Bauer, F.L., Broy, M., Dijkstra, E.W., Gerhart, S.L., Gries, D., Griffiths, M., Guttag, J.V., Horning, J.J., Owicki, S.S., Pair, C., Partsch, H., Pepper, P., Wirsing, M., Wössner, H. (eds.) Program Construction, vol. 69, pp. 51–53. Springer, Heidelberg (1979)
14. Blackwell, A., Green, T.: Notational systems-the cognitive dimensions of notations framework. In: Carroll, J.M. (ed.) HCI Models, Theories and Frameworks: Toward a Multidisciplinary Science, pp. 103–134. Morgan Kaufmann, San Francisco (2003)
15. Stolcke, A.: Srilm - an extensible language modeling toolkit, pp. 901–904 (2002)
16. Speer, R., Havasi, C.: Representing general relational knowledge in conceptnet 5. In: LREC, pp. 3679–3686 (2012)

17. Searle, J.R.: A classification of illocutionary acts. Language in society **5**, 1–23 (1976)
18. Bertin, J.: Semiology of graphics: diagrams, networks, maps (1983)
19. Engelhardt, Y.: The language of graphics: A framework for the analysis of syntax and meaning in maps, charts and diagrams. Unpublished Ph.D. thesis, Institute for Logic, Language and Computation, University of Amsterdam, The Netherlands (2002)
20. Blackwell, A.: Visual representation. Soegaard, M., Dam, R.F. (eds.) The Encyclopedia of Human-Computer Interaction, 2nd Ed. Aarhus, Denmark: The Interaction Design Foundation (2013). https://www.interaction-design.org/encyclopedia/visual_representation.html
21. Jespersen, O.: The philosophy of grammar. University of Chicago Press (1992)
22. Aghaee, S., Nowak, M., Pautasso, C.: Reusable decision space for mashup tool design. In: Proceedings of the 4th ACM SIGCHI Symposium on Engineering Interactive Computing Systems, pp. 211–220 (2012)
23. Lucci, G., Paternò, F.: Understanding end-user development of context-dependent applications in smartphones. In: Sauer, S., Bogdan, C., Forbrig, P., Bernhaupt, R., Winckler, M. (eds.) HCSE 2014. LNCS, vol. 8742, pp. 182–198. Springer, Heidelberg (2014)

Engineering the Creative Co-design of Augmented Digital Experiences with Cultural Heritage

Paloma Díaz[1(✉)], Ignacio Aedo[1], and Merel van der Vaart[2]

[1] Laboratorio DEI, Computer Science Department,
Universidad Carlos III de Madrid, Madrid, Spain
{mpaloma.diaz,ignacio.aedo}@uc3m.es
[2] Amsterdam School for Heritage and Memory Studies,
Universiteit van Amsterdam, Amsterdam, The Netherlands
M.J.vanderVaart@uva.nl

Abstract. Ubiquitous and tangible computing is opening a new panorama for interactive applications in different domains including cultural heritage. To ideate augmented experiences that provide more enjoyable, intrinsically motivating and memorable user experiences, design thinking methods that fuel the imagination and creativity of designers are required. This design can also take profit from software engineering approaches aimed at putting rationality concepts in practice. In this paper we advocate that such complex interactive (eco)systems require a mixed approach where the benefits of both disciplines are taken into account. It is not a question of design thinking versus software engineering, but a challenge to face the process both as people-values-centered and as quality-centered. This was the motivation of the CoDICE (COdesigning DIgital Cultural Encounters) software tool that supports situated, collocated and distributed tasks and adds persistence and traceability to the co-design outcomes so that the design rationale behind the products can be made explicit.

Keywords: Co-design · Software engineering · Design thinking · Digital cultural heritage

1 Introduction

The current status of tangible and augmented computing is opening a new panorama for highly creative and interactive applications in different domains. Tangible computing provides a physical representation of digital information so that users can interact with it in a richer way as they have been doing for centuries with tangible objects [1]. Physicality has been shown as a powerful mechanism to enable tangible thinking, that is, the ability to think by means of corporal actions and the physical manipulation of objects. In turn, augmented computing focuses on augmenting the real world with digital capabilities usually relying upon wereables and mobile devices [2]. In the particular domain of cultural heritage, the benefits of tangible and augmented spaces can be exploited to support richer experiences that create more meaningful links with visitor's previous experiences, knowledge and motivations [3]. In this way, the visit to cultural spaces becomes an encounter, an experience that engages the visitor in a

© Springer International Publishing Switzerland 2015
P. Díaz et al. (Eds.): IS-EUD 2015, LNCS 9083, pp. 42–57, 2015.
DOI: 10.1007/978-3-319-18425-8_4

intrinsically rewarding activity by stimulating sensory, intellectual and emotional opportunities to interact with culture [4] in a way that might help visitors to develop long term motives to enjoy cultural heritage [3].

Designing this kind of augmented and tangible technologies that interwine human practices and expectations, interaction spaces and complex digital artifacts is rather difficult and multifaceted and cannot be satisfied just with end user programming tools as there is a need to reflect upon a complex and wicked problem. Co-design approaches where the end users voices are heard from the beginning of the ideation process by integrating them into multidisciplinary teams [5] make it possible to address design as such a creativity-driven activity. The goal is to go beyond function-al requirements and end user empowering tools to focus on user motivations, expecta-tions and experiences when interacting with digital objects and systems. This design paradigm requires setting up design spaces where heterogeneous teams can collabo-rate effectively. For this to be possible methods have to provide means to enable non-experts to express and discuss their ideas with software developers and designers. To enable non experts to describe their problems and ideas in a natural and expressive way they use techniques that make it possible to explain, make tangible things or act and play [6,7]. Moreover, creativity methods are generative, that is, they guide the members of the team to explore the problem and co-create solutions through a cyclic and evolving process. On the other side, sofware engineering (SE henceforth) me-thods have been used for more than four decades to put rationality concepts into prac-tice [8]. Their mathematical models and visual languages [9] impose serious barriers in the discussion of design options with end users but they also provide some advan-tages in long term and distributed projects. Thus, SE methods force designers to apply a systematic, disciplined, repeatable and measurable processes that guarantee the quality of the final product. They also provide additional advantages including com-plete analysis and design documentation, traceability of requirements and designs, and unambiguity of the specifications that will contribute to ease software evolution and maintenance [10].

In this paper, we posit that in order to develop complex interactive systems both approaches, design thinking [11] and SE, should complement each other in a holistic process that benefits from both disciplines and makes it possible to integrate end users not only in creation activities but also in more reflective practices that involve ideat-ing digital futures. This is the main purpose of CoDICE (COdesigning DIgital Cultur-al Encounters) a software platform developed within the meSch project [12]. One of the goals of this project is to envision smart objects that will enhance the experience with cultural heritage for which a number of co-design workshops and activities in-volving cultural heritage professionals (CHP), end users, designers, software engi-neers and developers are held. CoDICE assists such heterogeneous teams in co-design tasks through three design spaces: situated design, ideation and convergent design. In the context of the tool, end users are non-technically skilled people, including CHPs, who want to take part in a collaborative process to ideate new ways to engage visitors in their museums and institutions using smart objects.

The remaining of the paper starts with a review of some related works about the integration of design thinking and SE, after which the tool is presented using five design principles that guided its iterative development. Section 4 includes the description of a use case about the co-design of a specific prototype that illustrates the main benefits of the tool and, finally, some conclusions are drawn in Section 5.

2   Related Works

Klein and Hirschheim describe software development as a design activity that should be regarded not only in terms of efficacy and efficiency, but also as a social action that *"deals with behavioral issues concerned with changing conditions and forms of social behavior brought about by the design outcomes"* [8]. This conception is aligned with design thinking approaches that also consider designers as behavior shapers [13], so we will assume this conception of software development in order to understand how SE and design thinking can be balanced in a holistic approach.

The definition of software development as a social action roots on Max Weber's theory that categorizes actions according to the forces that drive them [14]. As illustrated in Figure 1, such forces can be rational or non-rational. Rational forces are related with objective criteria (formal rationality) and principles (substantive rationality) such as efficacy, cost, reliability or the need to apply a specific method to reach the goals. Examples of rational forces that chiefly drive SE approaches might be to use a specific technology to optimize an industrial process decreasing the time spent or to deploy a mobile version of a magazine to increase the number of potential readers. On the other side, non-rational actions are chiefly fired by subjective, personal and sociocultural based criteria like emotions, aesthetics or resonance. Examples of this kind of forces, that are usually the fulcrum of design thinking practices, might be to redesign a product to make it more personally meaningful for end users or to deploy technology that respects the cultural practices of a community.

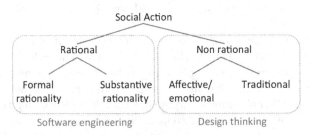

Fig. 1. Focus of SE and design thinking in the forces that drive social action

Our point is that both approaches should be complementary when developing interactive systems that in most cases deal with wicked problems. Wicked problems cannot be solved easily because their requirements change, are not clear, difficult to identify or even contradictory [15]. In such a context, SE fails to provide on its own a solution using analytical processes and metrics that do not take into account the non rational forces that make a product successful and enjoyable, or what Christopher Alexander called the *"quality without a name"* [16]. Similarly, design thinking tends to minimize the benefits of being systematic and rational in terms of quality assurance, maintainability and repeatability, issues that are particularly relevant in multidisciplinary and distributed teams. A holistic approach, combining the benefits each of them brings to the table, might help to balance rational and non-rational forces.

A first step to integrating SE and design thinking can be found in the attempts to establish usability engineering as a discipline, by combining the system-driven approach of SE with the user-driven approach of user-centered design [17]. SE methods also started their own journey to meet user-driven development by including usability as a quality criterion, usability patterns and heuristics as a design aid and by applying usability evaluation and iterative design [18]. However, as pinpointed in [6], in SE the participation of the user was considered only to identify problems with the user interface. For interactive systems design, however, this is just the tip of the iceberg. What would be required is participation with stakeholders, including end users, during all the design phase: to frame ideas, discuss options, and design and test solutions. However, the analytic methods of SE are too complex as facilitate end user participation as they might feel more comfortable with less formal techniques.

An interesting approach to merge both disciplines is reported in [9] where authors transform the constructs of a SE method into tangible pieces that can be used in combinations with other physical elements such as post-its. In this way, they provide a flexible working space where mixed groups of software engineers, designers and end users can discuss ideas in an expressive way but also including structured concepts from SE. Other works are focused on improving design thinking by making use of technology to support the design process. For example, in [19] a distributed user interface to work with affinity diagrams using different devices is presented. A similar approach but combining physical and digital objects is described in [20].

3   Balancing Design Thinking and Software Engineering in CoDICE

The work described in this paper goes a step further in the integration of SE and design thinking by mixing practices of both domains in a smooth way, that is, without imposing methods that could compromise the quality nor the novelty of the final product. In our experience, trying to adopt SE methods in the early stages of the ideation process might compromise the capacity to devise highly innovative ideas as nontechnical users do not always feel comfortable with the analytical and rigid abstractions managed in SE. In any case, it is not a matter of SE *versus* design thinking but a question of SE *and* design thinking, being able to apply process models where discipline and creativity, rationality and emotions, quality-centered and people-centered can coexist. With this idea in mind, the approach proposed here applies a SE perspective to document in a persistent and meaningful way the design thinking outcomes and, conversely, it broadens the scope of SE engineering approaches by recognizing the value of the ideation phase, that is previous to the elicitation of requirements and implies being able to understand wicked problems and imagine how to solve them without imposing constraints from the very beginning. The ultimate goal of CoDICE is to respect the flexibility and expressivity of creativity methods and to be able to rationalize the process to understand why decisions were taken.

3.1   The Scenario: Co-designing Smart Objects in the meSch Project

We faced the challenge of balancing SE and design thinking practices within the context of co-designing digital enhanced encounters with cultural heritage in the meSch project [12]. The meSch project aims to integrate technology in cultural heritage sites whilst keeping the physicality of the real pieces as the core of the interaction process. Thus the project relies upon the use of tangible interfaces that will enhance the experience with the physical object or environment but will not divert attention to other elements, like mobiles and tablets or screens. In this paper we will refer to these augmented experiences as digital encounters with cultural heritage. The use of the word encounter instead of visit tries to highlight the role these augmented experiences should play in providing richer, more active and meaningful connections between visitors and cultural heritage by establishing long term motives as defined in [3]. The project assumes a co-design approach and, therefore, a multidisciplinary consortium where three European museums participate (Allard Pierson Museum, Museo della Guerra and Museon) holds co-design workshops to ideate and co-create smart objects. The workshops ran during the first year of the project were a valuable source of information to envision the design spaces and entities required in CoDICE and they also provided the perfect context to iteratively design the tool by getting feedback from a team including managers, researchers, designers, CHPs and software developers.

3.2   Design Principles and Spaces

CoDICE is a software tool aimed at helping heterogeneous teams in the co-design of digital encounters with cultural heritage. It supports some of the tasks of multidisciplinary teams, made up of designers, developers, CHPs and end users, who work together to envision the scenarios of use and the prototypes that will make it possible to generate enriched encounters with cultural heritage. CoDICE does not empower end users to create digital encounters with cultural heritage since this is a wicked problem that requires a deep understanding of how an encounter and a smart object can improve the user experience that should be ideally faced in multidisciplinary tools. Thus, the tool provides a platform to share different ideas and outcomes to help each participant, including end users, to reflect upon such digital encounters.

As discussed in the previous section, the vision of CoDICE is to be able to bridge the gap between two apparently disjoint approaches: design thinking and SE. The outcomes of hands-on creativity workshops can be used to feed ideation processes, and since these outcomes are digitized and organized in a meaningful way they can help to specify concepts, features or the design rationale behind the ideas explored by the co-design teams. Being able to access all this information during software design does not only provide useful feedback to inform the rest of the development but also makes it possible to keep the emotions and feelings that inspired the ideas throughout the whole process. Understanding why implementing a specific prototype was relevant requires more than technical and quality details; it requires understanding the process that led to take the decision to move from an idea to a design and from a design to a working prototype. The tool is being implemented following an iterative process based on formative evaluations with the members of the consortium as well as with other external users. These formative evaluations help to understand the kind of support that software tools could provide in co-design activities without compromising efficacy or creativity. After the observations done in the co-design workshops held during the first year of the project and taking into account the literature [5, 8, 9, 10, 21, 23, 24, 25], we identified five design principles that help us to describe the main features and functionalities of the tool. These principles do not pretend to be comprehensive; they just put the focus on well-known features of the design process.

Principle 1. Design is Divergent and Convergent
This is a basic principle of design thinking that recognizes the value of the ideation phase to frame the problem properly and to stimulate creativity during the divergent phase, as well as the need to narrow the branch of potential designs and make choices according to some (rational or non-rational) criteria during convergent design [21].

In the context of CoDICE, the move from divergent to convergent is materialized as the bridge between design thinking and SE practices. The main assumption is that both approaches should be complementary, respecting the benefits each of them brings to the table: discipline and creativity, rationality and emotions, quality-centered and people-centered. Whilst guaranteeing the flexibility and expressiveness of design thinking methods to co-ideate smart objects, it is also necessary to produce clear specifications that could guide the implementation and provide the necessary design rationale that justifies the decisions taken. Consequently, CoDICE will organize the design space considering both approaches, making it possible the transition from divergent to convergent design and the generation of specifications that could inform the implementation process. In particular, three spaces are considered (see Figure 2): situated resources gathering, divergent design and convergent design.

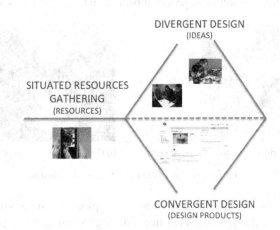

DIVERGENT DESIGN
(IDEAS)

SITUATED RESOURCES
GATHERING
(RESOURCES)

CONVERGENT DESIGN
(DESIGN PRODUCTS)

Fig. 2. Design spaces in CoDICE

The *Situated resources gathering* is the space where co-designers can collect useful or inspirational material while visiting the physical environment where the digital artifact is going to be deployed and used. *Divergent design* is the space aimed at generating ideas that may or may not turn into design products. This space makes it possible to keep track of all the ideas that emerged during the co-design workshops, assuming two of the classical tenets of Osborn's brainstorming [22]: generate lots of ideas and defer judgment. Ideas that didn't succeed at a specific moment in the project, probably due to some constraints, might be worth to revisit later so keeping track of them could be useful. This phase is previous to the elicitation of requirements in SE and it is included to provide some software support to the ideation process required in any complex domain where the problem has to be explored before thinking on solutions. Finally, the *Convergent design* is the space where co-designers turn ideas into design products that will be implemented. Taking as a seed the ideas generated in the previous phase, some design entities are generated to specify what has to be implemented and why.

Principle 2. Design Happens in Different Spaces and at Different Paces
As stated by Sanders and Westerlund [23], co-design happens in different spaces: the experienced physical space, the workspace and the future situation of use. The possibility of doing part of the co-design in the physical space where the product is supposed to be deployed or in the context recreated by the product might help to better understand the scenarios of use and the needs or expectations of the participants. However other activities, like specifying or exploring concepts further can be done in other spaces. CoDICE deals with different design spaces by implementing a real time system with a Distributed User Interface (DUI) where a variety of devices are used in different design spaces to perform the tasks in the best way. Thus, team members will be able to use mobile devices to collect items when studying the physical space using an Android application called CoDICE-mobile (see Figure 3.a) and to work with tablets, laptops, interactive tables or other devices to work individually or collaboratively in ideas generation and solutions proposal using CoDICE desktop (see Figure 3.b).

a) Taking photos, videos and notes in onsite visits   b) Collocated discussion of ideas and designs

Fig. 3. CoDICE distributed vision of codesign

Co-design is also social, the more ideas you explore the more possibilities to get a better final product [24]. However, when working in teams, participants have different rhythms of working. Some might require more time to understand the problem or to further elaborate their initial thoughts. To meet this requirement, CoDICE supports both synchronous and asynchronous collaboration.

Principle 3. Richness of Expression Encourages All Kinds of Participants to Externalize their Ideas.

Though CoDICE is a software tool, it has to allow different ways of expression not necessarily mediated by software. In some occasions, people are more expressive using non-digital media, like plasticine, pens and paper or their own bodies [9]. This is particularly true during the ideation phase, when participants are exploring and framing the problem and need richer ways to express their own ideas. Being constrained by the functionalities and affordances of software tools in this phase might be quite frustrating have a negative impact on creativity.

Opposite to works like [19, 20], the approach of CoDICE is not to create tangible environments to digitize techniques like brainstorming, storytelling or prototyping, but to be able to collect and organize the outcomes of these techniques. This approach was adopted after the first iteration in the prototype design when the meSch partners evaluated a software application to work with Affinity Diagrams and both CHPs and designers stated they preferred to use physical objects during the ideation phases instead of being forced to use a software tool.

Therefore, CoDICE does not impose any specific co-design technique with a view to encouraging team creativity. Depending on the available resources, the abilities of the team members or the goal pursued, different techniques can be used. What is important it to keep track of what was done and why, and to be able to revisit the process to look for the design rationale or to rescue ideas that were previously discarded. Concepts have to be also held in a useful and purposeful way that can support further steps in a co-development process. By useful we mean that co-designers can use it to document their design process; by purposeful we mean that co-designers understand the meaning of each activity they perform with the tool and how this activity contributes to the whole design process.

Principle 4. All the Outcomes of the Design Process Should be Held in a Persistent and Meaningful Way

This principle implies providing persistent storage of design outcomes, whether they are software design entities like user requirements or less structured ideas gathered through pictures, textual descriptions or stories. In this way, the design rationale behind the final products can be built by revisiting the material created during the co-design workshops. As discussed by Carroll and Rosson in [25], design rationale makes it possible to understand a product in depth, not only its properties or functionalities but also the reasons and principles that inspired its development as well as its impact on human behavior. Having a meaningful storage of outcomes also makes the purpose of each design activity explicit, something that in many occasions is not obvious for non-professional designers such as CHPs or end users.

CoDICE will make it possible to store all kind of design outcomes, including those that did not become design concepts in further steps of development. Figure 4 depicts the data model including the concepts and relationships considered in CoDICE. Next paragraphs describe the semantics of each component.

Ideas Space. Ideas are the outcomes of the divergent design phase. Analyzing the domain problem, the following kinds of ideas are supported:

- *Object* is the concept used to reflect upon the features of the physical elements in the environment, such as collections or sub-collections of a museum or a unique object. It can also be used to model the physical object that will be converted into a smart object. This concept is based on the Artifact analysis method [26] and has been included to push co-designers to analyze in-depth the physical objects, their features, interaction affordances and constraints, and the emotions and feelings they inspire, as a potential and preliminary way to envision digital futures for them.
- *Encounter* is the concept used to collect information on potential augmented experiences with cultural heritage objects or sites. They are defined in an informal way usually through pictures, comics or videos, since they are just ideas on how to augment the interaction.
- *Augmented concepts* are the digital artifacts or smart objects that could be implemented to support the augmented *encounters* with the physical *objects*. Again the description is quite informal for the same reasons.

Persona. Persona is a well-known technique to identify user profiles [27] that is used in CoDICE as the gluing concept linking the two spaces. They represent the fictional users of an augmented object and the ones for which encounters are devised. This concept might help to focus on a goal-oriented-design as they are described in terms of goals, skills and expectations.

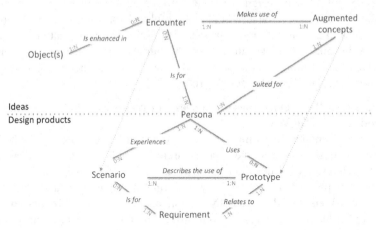

Fig. 4. Linking CoDICE entities

Design products. In this space, some of the ideas generated during the divergent design turn into design products that will be further implemented. In particular the following options are considered:

- *Scenarios* are the evolution of encounters. To be able to move an encounter to the design space it has to be linked to at least one *persona* and one *augmented concept*. If the encounter is not useful for any persona nor uses any kind of new artifact, then it doesn't make sense to develop it further; it requires further exploration in the ideation space. Scenarios provide more detailed information including the kinds of experiences covered for which Falk's Visitor Identity Model is used [28]. This is the unique element in CoDICE exclusively related to the cultural heritage domain, since it classifies the kind of user experiences of the visitors of museums.

- *Prototypes* are the specification of the smart objects that will be implemented and they are transformations of *augmented concepts*. Similarly to Scenarios, *augmented concepts* can only be transformed into prototypes if they are useful for at least one *persona* and can be used in at least one *encounter*.
- *Requirements* are the software requirements that have to be fulfilled in the implementation. Five kinds of requirements are considered: functional, usability, user, data and technical. Requirements can be related to other requirements and can be subject to dependencies with other requirements.

Other elements included in the tool to facilitate its use are the Resources that are the pieces of content (image, video, files, etc.) that can be reused throughout the design process and Workshops, which is a way to group ideas and designs.

Principle 5.   The Process has to be Traceable to Understand the Design Rationale Behind the Design Outcomes
This is a basic feature of any software specification and consists of providing links among related entities, to be able to look at the specification from different perspectives and to understand what decisions were taken [10]. Which entities have to be linked and why, depend on the design domain, since the paths created by the links should help designers to understand the product and check its quality from a holistic point of view. The design challenge here is to identify meaningful paths for the heterogeneous members of the development team, ranging from end users to CHPs or software developers. Traceability might also help to bring some of the emotions generated during creative design thinking into the whole development process.

CoDICE provides a number of links among entities in the same or different space (see Figure 4). Relationships are shown in the interface and can be used to validate the transformation of Ideas into Design Concepts. Thus, as described before, an *Augmented concept* cannot be moved to a prototype if there isn't any Encounter that makes use of such a concept. Transforming ideas into design products is a process guided by a wizard that first does a validation to check the concepts the idea is linked to and then encourages designers to fill a SWOT (strengths, weaknesses, opportunities and threats) matrix to justify their decision.

4   Architecture and Implementation

CoDICE is implemented as a real time distributed and multi-device system. To support design principle 2 ("Design happens in different spaces and at different paces") there are two user interface clients: CoDICE-mobile, that supports situated ideas gathering, and CoDICE-desktop used for divergent and convergent design. CoDICE-mobile is implemented as an Android application and it makes it possible taking notes, pictures and videos that are made available in CoDICE-desktop. In turn, CoDICE desktop is a Rich Internet Application implemented with Microsoft SilverLight technology and, therefore, it can be used with any Internet browser. To support concurrent edition the ASP.NET SignalR library is used, so all the updates are automatically saved in the database. The tool can be used in different devices so that different working modes (collocated and non collocated, individual and group based) are allowed. Figure 5 shows the Gallery of Augmented Concepts (ideas about potential prototypes) in CoDICE-desktop as an example of the user interface. The figure shows the collection of augmented concepts developed till now in the project. Some of these concepts evolved to prototypes (for example The Loupe or the Companion Novel) while others were discarded for several reasons (such as the Memento Mori). From the gallery, components can be accessed, deleted or created. The interface of specific components is shown in the next section (Figures 6 and 7).

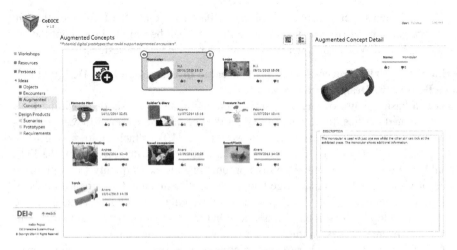

Fig. 5. CoDICE-desktop interface

5   Use Case: The Design of the Loupe

In this section we describe a real use case of the tool to illustrate how it can support co-designers in their ideation and design tasks. Since the tool was being implemented at the same time co-design workshops were taking place, this use case is a reverse engineering example that helps us to make explicit the reasons that might make a prototype of a smart object a potential tool to support a digital encounter with cultural heritage by showing the rationale behind its design. The different subsections go deeper into the process that was followed to end up implementing the Loupe as a meSch prototype and how they are documented in CoDICE.

5.1   Early Personas and Encounters

During the first project meeting of the project in February 2013 a co-design workshop took place in Sheffield. This workshop focused on familiarizing all team members with some design thinking principles, including the development of personas and what are called encounters and augmented concepts in CoDICE. Many of the outcomes of this first workshop were not created for a specific museum, but were designed to suit various museum needs, based on the diverse backgrounds and experience of the three partner museums that were present at the event.

One of the *Personas* that was created at this workshop was Emma, a 71 year old retired craft teacher with a broad interest in culture. This persona represents a considerable part of the visitor demographic of the Allard Pierson Museum (APM). One of the *Encounters* that was particularly relevant for this museum, that was developed during this first co-design workshop, was that of layered content (see Figure 6). Many museums, including APM, contain objects for which many layers of information are available. Consequently, a single object can be used to tell many different stories and can be linked to other objects in various ways. One of the challenges of the curatorial team faces is to choose which layers of content will be shared with the public, and which stories will be told. However, research on the behavior of museum visitors has shown time and again that many of them perform browsing behavior [29, 30], looking for content that most closely matches their personal interest at that specific point in time. To facilitate this behavior, some museums have started to explore ways in which multiple layers or stories can be offered to their audiences, to provide them with more choice. Some of the personas and encounters that were developed during this first co-design meeting were later recorded using CoDICE-desktop so they can be revised and reused further. The information held for the *Encounter* includes a description, the emotions that it could raise in visitors, the physical *Objects* it might be used for and the *Personas* that could benefit from it. In the figure, the Augmented Concepts that finally can implement this scenario are also shown (the Loupe and the Monocular). Comments and all kinds of resources can be also attached to the Encounter so additional information can be linked to understand its relevance and evolution. All this information was not generated in the first workshop; the concept evolved through a period of time after more reflection was done and practical cases were developed.

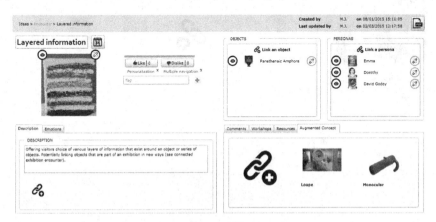

Fig. 6. The Layered information encounter

5.2   Museum Specific Development

In the spring of 2013, the Waag Society, another meSch partner, facilitated a co-design workshop at the APM. Here, the encounter of offering layered narratives was revisited and combined with a specific concern of the museum. As the APM highly values visitor interaction with original artifacts, it was concerned that screens might have a negative effect on visitors' engagement with objects. During this workshop, the *augmented concept* of the Monocular was developed as a way to offer layered narratives. The idea behind this device was that additional content was brought to visitors in front of only one eye, giving them the opportunity to look at the real object with the other eye. By turning the monocular, or pressing specific buttons, visitors could alternate between the various layers of content. After discussing the potential use of this device by various *personas*, several restrictions came to light. Firstly, many visitors enjoy the museum as a social space. The functionality of the Monocular meant that only one visitor could see the presented content at any given moment, which might restrict social interaction. Secondly, visitors such as Emma, who are elderly and suffer from poor eyesight, not be able to use this device.

Moving on from this concept, the Loupe was presented to the project partners in August 2013. This device, a small screen embedded in a case in the shape of a magnifying glass, offered content in response to how the device was handled, again focusing on adding new layers of content to the existing museum offer. Through its physical qualities (its loupe shape) this augmented concept maintained the association with close-looking at objects, but used a screen that could be shared amongst visitors. As a consequence, in CoDICE the 'layered narratives' encounter had two augmented concepts linked to it, one of which (the Monocular) had not been implemented due to usability issues.

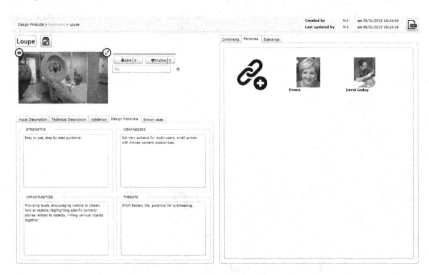

Fig. 7. The Loupe prototype specification. Apart from other information, prototypes include a SWOT matrix that includes the different issues that were considered to implement the concept

5.3   Cross-Pollination and Sharing

Like the APM, other museums within the consortium were part of co-design processes in which they explored the augmented concepts and encounters that would match their specific museum needs. At the Museon, way-finding had been identified as an important challenge, which could label an *Encounter* in CoDICE. The physical features of the Loupe, initially designed to offer visitors layered content, seemed to hold potential for way-finding in this second museum context. In CoDICE, this resulted in two different *Encounters* being linked to one *Augmented concept* an information that can increase the perception of the need to move on implementing it as a prototype. Unlike the APM, the Museon catered to an audience of young people, predominantly of primary school age. The range of personas linked to the concept therefore expanded. After tests with the loupe as a way-finding tool in the Museon, it became apparent that their younger audience became so engrossed in the act of way-finding, that they had very little eye for the objects on display. On this basis, the Museon decided to not explore the potential of the Loupe as way-finding tool any further. However, information about this development was added to CoDICE since for other kind of audiences this functionality can still be considered increasing the number of scenarios where the Loupe as a smart object enhancing the user experience makes sense.

5.4   Consolidation and Further Development

In its short lifespan, the augmented concept of the Loupe had been explored by various parties and linked to different encounters and personas. It was rejected by the Museon, but this didn't mean the concept was forgotten about. For although the Loupe proved unsuitable as a tool for way-finding (encounter) for younger audiences (persona). This augmented concept was still linked to another persona and encounter, namely that of providing layered content to an older audience. An initial informal usability test of this concept was carried out at the APM in the summer of 2014. This test proved successful and in the autumn of 2014 a curator of the museum created new content for the Loupe, based on what was learned from the usability test. Again all this information was added to the tool and even pdf reports can be created, so the process can be tracked. A larger device evaluation took place in early 2015. Having proven its use, the Loupe has now been upgraded from an augmented concept to a design product in the tool. CoDICE might facilitate further development of the tool.

6   Conclusions

This paper describes an approach to integrate the systematic flow and rationale forces of SE with the non-rationale forces and generative ideation methods of design thinking in order to support a holistic process to design augmented computing ecosystems. The proposal is based on five design principles (design is divergent and convergent; design happens in different spaces and at different paces; richness of expression encourages all kinds of participants to externalize their ideas; all the outcomes of the design process should be held in a persistent and meaningful way; the process has to be traceable to understand the design rationale behind the design outcomes) that have led the implementation of a real-time concurrent system using a DUI that makes it possible to support teamwork in collocated and distributed sessions.

From the meSch project experiences and the formative evaluations performed, we learnt that in long term, multidisciplinary and distributed projects involving the creation of complex interactive systems, forcing creative teams to be systematic pays off. Being able to revisit the preliminary ideas you had or to visualize their evolution provides a better understanding on the final outcomes and on the reasons that motivated your decisions. In a domain application like cultural heritage where many different issues have to be considered to ideate digital futures, including user motives and motivations, visitors and curators expectations, features of the collection and the physical environment, economical and technical constraints and so on, being forced to reflect further on the digital encounters and the personas that might benefit from them might help to take more rationale decisions about the integration of technologies. Moreover, sharing ideas among different groups helps to reuse concepts and explore them further in other contexts, as happened with The Loupe in APM and Museon. We also realized that SE techniques might be hard for non-technical people but design thinking techniques also might create confusion when the purpose and utility of each activity performed isn't clear. The ability to link the outcomes of such activities into a comprehensive space like the one provided by CoDICE might help to have a clear idea of the whole picture and understand the development process and the forces that drove it.

Acknowledgments. meSch is funded by EC FP7 'ICT for access to cultural resources' (ICT Call 9: FP7-ICT-2011-9) under the Grant Agreement 600851.

References

1. Ishii, H., Ullmer, B.: Tangible bits: towards seamless interfaces between people, bits and atoms. In: Proc. of CHI 1997, March 22–27, 1997
2. Heim, M.: Virtual realism. Oxford University Press (1998)
3. Dindler, C., Iversen, O.S.: Motivation in the museum - mediating between everyday engagement and cultural heritage. In: The Nordes Conference, Oslo, August 2009
4. Csikszentmihalyi, M., Hermanson, K.: Intrinsic motivation in museums: why does one want to learn? In: Falk, J.H., Dierking, L.D. (eds.) Public institutions for personal learning: Establishing a research agenda, pp. 66–77. American Association of Museums, Washington D.C. (1995)
5. Sanders, E.B.N.: ``Scaffolds for building everyday creativity'', design for effective communications: creating contexts for clarity and meaning. In: Frascara, J. (ed.) Allworth Press, New York, New York (2006)
6. Elizabeth, B.N., Sanders, E.B., Binder, T.: A framework for organizing the tools and techniques of participatory design. In: Proceedings of the 11th Biennial Participatory Design Conference (PDC 2010). ACM, New York, NY, USA, pp. 195–198 (2010)
7. Martin, B., Hanington, B: Universal Methods of Design: 100 Ways to Research Complex Problems, Develop Innovative Ideas (2012)

8. Klein, H.K., Hirschheim, R.: Rationality concepts in information system development methodologies. Accounting, Management and Information Technologies, **1**(2), 157–187 (1991). http://dx.doi.org/10.1016/0959-8022(91)90017-9

9. Luebbe, A., Edelman, J., Steinert, M., Leifer, L., Weske, M.: Design thinking implemented in software engineering tools. 8th Design Thinking Research Symposium (DTRS8), University of Technology, Sydney, Australia, September 2010

10. Pressman, R.S.: Sofware Engineering a Practitioner's approach. 7th ed. MC Graw Hill (2010)

11. Zimmerman, J., Forlizzi, J., Evenson, S.: Research Through Design as a Method for Interaction Design Research in HCI (2007). Human-Computer Interaction Institute. Paper 41

12. Petrelli, D., Ciolfi, L., van Dijk, D., Hornecker, E., Not, E., Schmidt, A.: Integrating material and digital: a new way for cultural heritage. Interactions **20**(4), 58–63 (2013)

13. Kolko, J. Toughts on interaction design. Morgan Kaufmann (2010)

14. Weber, Max: The Nature of Social Action. In: Runciman, W.G. (ed.) Weber: Selections in Translation. Cambridge University Press (1991)

15. Buchanan, R.: Wicked Problems in Design Thinking. Design Issues **8**(2), 5–21 (1992)

16. Alexander, C.: The timeless way of building. Oxford University Press (1979)

17. Nielsen, J.: Usability engineering. Morgan Kaufmann (1993)

18. Seffah, A., Metzker, E.: The obstacles and myths of usability and software engineering. Commun. ACM **47**(12), 71–76 (2004)

19. Harboe, G., Doksam, G., Keller, L., Huang, E.M.: Two Thousand Points of Interaction: Augmenting paper notes for a distributed user experience. Distributed User Interfaces: Usability and Collaboration. Human–Computer Interaction Series, pp. 141–149 (2013)

20. Klemmer, S.R., Newman, M.W., Farrell, R., Bilezikjian, M., Landay, J.A.: The designers' outpost: a tangible interface for collaborative web site. In: Proceedings of the 14th annual ACM symposium on User interface software and technology (UIST 2001), pp. 1–10 ACM, New York, NY, USA (2001)

21. Rhea, D.: Bringing Clarity to the "Fuzzy Front End". In: Laurel B. (ed.) Design Research: Methods and Perspectives (2003)

22. Osborn, A.F.: Applied imagination: Principles and procedures of creative problem-solving. Scribners, New York (1953)

23. Sanders, E.B.-N., Westerlund, B.: Experiencing, exploring and experimenting in and with co-design spaces. In: Proc. Nordic Design Research Conference 2011 (2011)

24. Warr, A., O'Neill, E.: Understanding design as a social creative practice. In: Proceedings of the 5th conference on Creativity \& cognition (C\&C 2005), pp. 118–127. ACM, New York, NY, USA (2005)

25. Carroll, J.M., Rosson, M.B.: Design rationale as theory. HCI models, theories and frameworks: Toward a multidisciplinary science, pp. 431–461 (2003)

26. Díaz, L.: Developing design education and knowledge for heritage. In: Proceedings of the 7th Conference of the Turkish Design History Society, 5T A New Affair: Design History and Digital Design Museums, Yazar University, Izmir, Turkey, 17–18 May, 2012. (In press.)

27. Cooper, A.: The inmates are running the asylum. Macmillan (1999)

28. Falk, J.: Identity and the museum visitor experience. Left Coast Press (2009)

29. Falk. J.: The Museum Experience. Whalesback Books (1992)

30. Klein, H.J.: Tracking Visitor Circulation in Museum Settings. Environment and Behavior **25**(6), 782–800 (1993)

A Review of Research Methods in End User Development

Daniel Tetteroo[(✉)] and Panos Markopoulos

Eindhoven University of Technology,
Eindhoven, The Netherlands
{d.tetteroo,p.markopoulos}@tue.nl

Abstract. This article gives a structured overview of the field of End User Development, and its related fields of End User Programming, End User Software Engineering and meta-design. We have analyzed 93 papers from these fields that have been published between 2004 and 2013 in major and relevant journals and conference proceedings. The article discusses the methods, purpose and impact of the research that was analyzed, and points towards trends within the research community, as well as research gaps that need to be addressed.

Keywords: End-user development · End-user programming · End-user software engineering · Meta-design · Survey

1 Introduction

End user development (EUD) and the related fields of end user programming (EUP), end user software engineering (EUSE) and meta-design concern the modification and creation of software artefacts by end-users. These fields have been studied for well over three decades now [13], and span a wide variety of domains and end-users [11]. They have matured to an extent that they have warranted a dedicated bi-annual symposium (IS-EUD) since 2007.

A recent survey by Ko et al. has provided a much needed overview of the topics that have been, and are still being studied within EUSE, and provides an outlook into what remain areas to be explored further in the future [11]. Such a survey could be complemented with an analysis of the research methods that have been used, and the impact particular types of research have had. Knowledge about a field's preference for particular research methods and purposes is imperative for its further development, since it can expose potential research gaps and trends that need to be addressed. In other HCI related fields, such as Mobile HCI [10] and Children's HCI [8], surveys on the research methods used in those fields have indeed helped identify such gaps and propose directions for future research.

Accordingly this paper presents a structured literature survey of the research methods that have been used in the fields of EUD, EUP, EUSE and meta-design in the last decade, i.e., between 2004 and 2013. The remainder of this paper discusses the results of this survey, as well as the implications of our findings for future research.

© Springer International Publishing Switzerland 2015
P. Díaz et al. (Eds.): IS-EUD 2015, LNCS 9083, pp. 58–75, 2015.
DOI: 10.1007/978-3-319-18425-8_5

2   Research Methods and Purposes

There are several different ways to classify research methods and purposes, but we chose to adopt the classification scheme that was developed by Kjeldskov and Graham [10] for the field of MobileHCI and later used by Jensen and Skov in their review of research methods in children's technology design [8]. This classification scheme is based on the work of Wynekoop and Conger [17] and although it's accuracy has been critiqued (amongst others by [10] themselves), in our opinion it is currently the best classification scheme covering HCI research methods. The scheme by Kjeldskov and Graham classifies HCI research over two dimensions: research method and research purpose. It distinguishes eight research methods, and five research purposes for the field of HCI. Below we discuss shortly the categories from the two classification dimensions, as defined by Kjeldskov and Graham [10]. Readers are encouraged to consult [10] and [17] for a more elaborate discussion of the methods and purpose definitions.

Table 1. Summary of research methods, their strengths, weaknesses, and use (adapted from Kjeldskov and Graham [10])

	Method	Strengths	Weaknesses	Use
Natural setting	**Case studies**	Natural setting Rich data	Time demanding Limited generalizability	Description, explanations, developing hypothesis
	Field studies	Natural setting Replicable	Difficult data collection Unknown sample bias	Studying current practice Evaluating new practices
	Action research	Firsthand experience Applying theory to practice	Ethics, bias, time Unknown generalizability	Generate hypothesis/theory Testing theories/hypothesis
Artificial setting	**Laboratory experiments**	Control of variables Replicable	Limited realism Unknown generalizability	Controlled experiments Theory/product testing
Environment independent setting	**Survey research**	Easy, low cost Can reduce sample bias	Context insensitive No variable manipulation	Collecting descriptive data from large samples
	Applied research	The goal is a product which may be evaluated	May need further design to make product general	Product development, testing hypothesis/concepts
	Basic research	No restrictions on solutions Solve new problems	Costly, time demanding May produce no solution	Theory building
	Normative writings	Insight into firsthand experience	Opinions may influence outcome	Descriptions of practice, building frameworks

2.1   Research Methods

Case Studies. Case studies are intensive empirical studies of small numbers of entities, such as organizations, groups and individuals [17]. They have been defined by Yin as *"empirical enquiries that investigate a contemporary phenomenon within its real-life context, especially when the boundaries between phenomenon and context* *are not clearly evident"* [18]. Usually, the data collected is qualitative. Case study results are usually hard to generalize, given their origin in a specific case. However, they can provide rich insights into specific cases and are particularly suitable for hypothesis generation and explaining complex phenomena.

Field Studies. Field studies are studies taking place in the real world. They range from (usually qualitative) ethnographic studies to (usually quantitative) field experiments. They offer increased ecological validity over artificial settings, but offer limited or no control, and can be laborious and complicated to conduct.

Action Research. Action research combines both action and research within the same process and aims at generating knowledge by improving practice, and improving practice by the application of knowledge [2]. Typically, this implies researchers participating in the intervention or activity studied, simultaneously evaluating the results. The advantages are firsthand experience, and the possibility to apply theory to practice directly. Disadvantages are the limited generalizability and the laborious efforts required for conducting action research.

Lab Experiments. All research that takes place in an artificial environment setting is qualified as lab experiment in the scheme of [10]. Typically, researchers use lab experiments to perform context independent studies of specific phenomena. Lab experiments range from true experiments with manipulation of independent variables, to loosely structured usability evaluations that summarize impressions and anecdotes afterwards. Lab experiments have the advantage that they are usually easier and cheaper to conduct compared to field studies, but might lack ecological validity.

Survey Research. Research that systematically samples a population through questionnaires or interviews. Responses are collected directly and are independent of context. This research is typically applied for collecting large amounts of data and is relatively cheap to perform. On the other hand, survey research might incur a respondent bias, and is typically cross sectional, providing a snapshot image of a phenomenon, thus unable to capture how processes evolve over time.

Applied Research. Environment independent research method based on intuition, experience, deduction and induction, used to analyze a specific research problem [17]. Typically, the desired outcome or goal is known, but the methods and techniques for achieving this goal are unknown. The advantages of applied research are that it is goal-directed, and that it typically leads to a product. On the downside, solutions might be not generalizable, or may not materialize at all.

Basic Research. Basic research is about developing theories and frameworks in situations where the problems are well known, but the methods and solutions are unknown. Such research is often time consuming and may fail to produce any result, but has the advantage of allowing for a high level of creativity in the search for solutions.

Normative Writings. This category includes all writings that do not describe actual research, such as concept development or 'truth' writings [17]. Examples are descriptions of future research directions, 'oeuvre'-writings that reflect on a longer period of research on a particular topic, and papers that present an opinion or intuitively correct ideas and concepts.

2.2   Research Purpose

In addition to the research method, the classification scheme also distinguishes between five different research purposes:

Understanding. Research aimed at understanding the particulars of a phenomenon studied.

Engineering. Research aimed at the original development of a tool or technology.

Re-engineering. Research aimed at the engineering of modifications or extensions to an existing tool or technology.

Evaluating. Research aimed at the assessment, validation and assurance of tools, technology, models and frameworks.

Describing. Research aimed at describing the ideal properties of a system or situation.

3   Classification of Research Methods in End User Development

In this section we present a classification of selected research papers from the fields of EUD, EUP, EUSE, and meta-design.

A total of 93 conference and journal papers were classified using the before mentioned scheme. These publications are all full research papers on EUD, as well as the related fields of EUP, EUSE and meta-design that have been published in the following major, relevant conferences and journals between 2004 and 2013 which are the mainstream venues for publishing related research:

- Conference on Computer-Human Interaction (CHI), ACM
- Conference on Advanced Visual Interfaces (AVI), ACM
- Conference on User Interface Software and Technology (UIST), ACM
- International Symposium on End-User Development (IS-EUD), EUSSET
- Visual Languages and Human Centered Computing (VL/HCC), IEEE
- Journal of Visual Languages and Computing, ACM
- International Journal on Human Computer Studies, Elsevier
- Interacting with Computers, Oxford University Press
- Transactions on Computer Human Interaction (TOCHI), ACM

Although there is a significant body of relevant and high-quality short papers that have been presented at e.g., CHI and IS-EUD, we chose not to include these papers for two reasons: the resulting set of articles would be too large for this survey to be feasible, and given that short papers are often preliminary reports of studies that are later published as full papers, including short papers would introduce a bias caused by 'double-counting' the research methods used in these studies.

To ensure sufficient validity, all papers were independently coded by both authors. The inter-rater reliability scores for research method (0.88) and research purpose (0.82) were found to be sufficiently reliable. Articles with conflicting classifications were reread, discussed, and reclassified in order to achieve consensus.

Table 2. Classification of research on end-user development. The numbers refer to indexes in the appendix 'reviewed end-user development research papers bibliography'.

	Case studies	Field studies	Actio research	Lab experiment	Survey research	Applied research	Basic research	Normative writings
Under-stand		3, 50		7, 8, 9, 15, 23, 35, 36, 48, 67, 68, 71, 72, 85	69	74		
Engineer						1, 4, 16, 17, 19, 21, 22, 24, 25, 27, 29, 32, 33, 34, 37, 38, 39, 40, 42, 44, 46, 49, 51, 54, 56, 59, 60, 61, 62, 65, 66, 70, 73, 76, 77, 79, 82, 83, 88, 89, 91, 93		
Re-engineer				53		2, 52, 80, 81, 84, 87		
Evaluate	30, 40	25, 27, 42, 66, 70, 84		16, 17, 21, 22, 24, 34, 37, 38, 40, 44, 51, 52, 53, 54, 55, 58, 59, 60, 61, 73, 76, 87, 88, 91, 93		1, 2, 39, 74, 75, 77		
Describe	11, 13, 31, 41, 78	5, 44, 45, 52, 61, 82		10, 12, 14, 43	90	18, 30, 75	28	6, 20, 26, 47, 57, 63, 64, 78, 86, 92

As has been the case in previous research that has used this classification scheme (e.g. [8, 10]), some papers were found to clearly fit in more than one category. Hence, the total number of classifications (135) is larger than the number of papers that were classified (93). 55 papers received a single classification, 34 papers received two classifications and 4 papers received three classifications. As such the percentages used below total to over 100%.

Table 2 shows clearly that most of the selected papers fall in the categories applied research (58 out of 93 papers, 62%) and lab experiments (43, 46%). Field studies (14, 15%), normative writings (10, 11%), case studies (7, 8%) and survey research (2, 2%) were found to be considerably less common. No action research studies were found, and only one publication describes basic research. The classification shows a strong bias towards artificial setting environments (46%) and independent setting environments (73%), and a much less significant role for natural setting environments (23%).

The purpose of most research was to engineer (42, 45%) and evaluate (39, 42%), although describing (30, 32%) and to some extent understanding (17, 18%) were frequent purposes as well. Only 7 papers (8%) concerned re-engineering.

The most frequent method-purpose combinations are engineering as applied research (42, 45%) and evaluations performed in a lab setting (25, 27%), followed by lab experiments aimed at understanding (13, 14%).

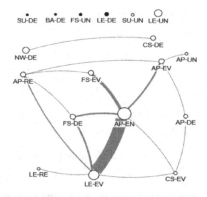

Fig. 1. Network graph showing the relationships between different classification categories. The four-letter codes denote the method (first two characters) and purpose (last two characters) of a publication. The size of the nodes corresponds with the number of papers that received a classification, while the thickness of the edges illustrates the strength of the relationship between two classification categories.

Fig. 1 shows the relationships between classifications. Clearly, many papers (22, 24%) describe the engineering of a system, or re-engineering thereof, (AP-EN, AP-RE) followed by a lab evaluation (LE-EV). The strong link between (re-)engineering and lab evaluation becomes even clearer by looking at the percentage of AP-EN and AP-RE papers that are followed by a lab evaluation: 46% of the 48 papers describing (re-)engineering follow up with a lab evaluation. Considerably fewer of such (re-)engineering attempts are followed by evaluations in a natural setting environment; 7 papers, or 15% of all (re-)engineering research is followed up by such an evaluation. Papers classified as descriptive basic research (BA-DE), descriptive survey research (SU-DE), descriptive lab experiments (LE-DE), and field studies, survey studies, and lab studies aimed at understanding (FS-UN, SU-UN, LE-UN) did not receive any additional classifications.

3.1 Development of the Field over Time

Fig. 2 shows the distribution of the publications included in this survey over time. Clearly, the numbers are higher for the years in which the IS-EUD symposia were held (2009, 2011, 2013). Overall, there is a slightly positive trend in the number of publications in this domain.

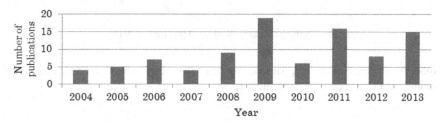

Fig. 2. Number of publications included in this survey, per year. The peaks in 2009, 2011, and 2013 are caused by the IS-EUD symposia in those years.

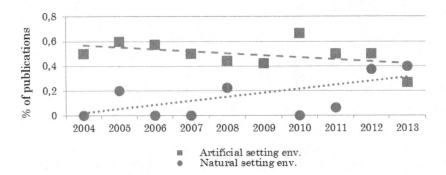

Fig. 3. Percentages of studies done in an artificial setting environment and a natural setting environment. The dashed and dotted lines are trend estimations based on a least-squares fit for artificial and natural setting environment respectively.

While the number of publications gives an indication of the overall activity in the surveyed fields, it is also interesting to analyze whether the nature of the research performed has changed over the years. Fig. 3 shows the relative number of publications on research performed in artificial and natural setting environments. Traditionally, artificial setting environment research has been dominant, but there is a trend towards a more balanced situation.

Fig. 4 shows the development of research purpose frequency over time. Research for engineering seems to become less prominent, while descriptive research is on the rise. There seem to be no clearly identifiable trends for research with other purposes, though research aimed at re-engineering remains consistently scarce.

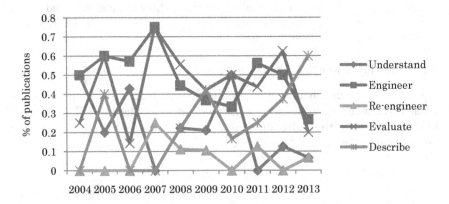

Fig. 4. Development of research purpose over time. The values indicate the percentage of publications for a given year with a specific purpose.

3.2   Research Impact

We have also analyzed the impact of the publications included in this survey by considering the number of citations per publication.

The number of citations per publication ranged from none (several publications) to 92 ([15]). There is a large spread in the number of citations between individual publications (Mdn=3.00, SD=16.32); The five most influential publications ([3, 4, 6, 15, 16]) account for almost 44% of all citations.

As is to be expected, there is a strong correlation between the year of publication and the average number of citations (rs(10) = .875, p = .001); earlier publications on average have a higher number of citations.

Table 3. Citations per classification category. The category labels (e.g., AP-EN) consist of the first two characters of the research method (e.g., APplied research), and the first two characters of the research purpose (e.g., ENgineering).

Classification category	Nr. Publ.	Nr. Citations	Avg. cit. / publ.	Median cit. / publ.
AP-DE	3	8	2.67	2.00
AP-EN	42	404	9.62	4.00
AP-EV	6	34	5.67	1.50
AP-RE	6	45	7.50	5.00
AP-UN	1	1	1.00	1.00
Applied research	**59**	**492**	**8.48**	**4.00**
BA-DE	1	1	1.00	1.00
Basic research	**1**	**1**	**1.00**	**1.00**
CS-DE	5	8	1.60	2.00
CS-EV	2	13	6.50	6.50
Case studies	**7**	**21**	**3.00**	**2.00**
FS-DE	6	19	3.17	2.00
FS-EV	6	28	4.67	5.50
FS-UN	2	11	5.50	5.50
Field studies	**14**	**58**	**4.14**	**4.00**
LE-DE	4	13	3.25	3.00
LE-EV	25	287	11.48	4.00
LE-RE	1	2	2.00	2.00
LE-UN	13	146	11.23	5.00
Lab experiments	**46**	**448**	**10.42**	**5.00**
NW-DE	10	157	15.70	1.00
Normative writings	**10**	**157**	**15.70**	**1.00**
SU-UN	1	4	4.00	4.00
SU-DE	1	1	1.00	1.00
Survey research	**3**	**5**	**2.50**	**2.50**

Table 3 shows the distribution of citations amongst the different classification categories. Publications describing applied research (median 4.00 citations per publication), field studies (4.00) and lab experiments (5.00) are cited more often than publications with other research methods. The discrepancy between the average and median number of citations per publication for applied research, lab experiments, and normative writings, is caused by a number of highly cited research papers using these methods. This effect is especially strong in the case of normative writings, since two of the most cited publications ([4, 16]) have received this classification. Interestingly, evaluations performed in a natural setting environment (i.e. CS-EV:6.50 and FS-EV:5.50) are more impactful than evaluations performed in an artificial setting environment (LE-EV:4.00).

Overall, publications describing research aimed at understanding (median 5.00 citations per publication), and research aimed (re-)engineering (4.00) and evaluations (4.50) are the most influential. Descriptive writings (2.00) are somewhat less influential. The most influential journals on the surveyed fields are Interacting with Computers (median 8.00 citations per publication) and the International Journal on Human Computer Studies (6.00). The most influential conference is CHI (13.50).

Table 4. Classification categories ranked by number of publications and median citations. The shading of the cells in the last column indicates the extent to which the publication ranking of a category deviates from its citation ranking. Orange cells indicate categories that have fewer publications than expected based on their impact, green cells represent categories that have more publications than would be expected. Darker colored cells indicate higher deviations.

Classification category	Rank by # publications	Rank by median citations	Difference in ranks
AP-DE	11	10	1
AP-EN	1	6	-5
AP-EV	5	14	-9
AP-RE	5	4	1
AP-UN	14	15	-1
BA-DE	14	15	-1
CS-DE	9	10	-1
CS-EV	12	1	11
FS-DE	5	10	-5
FS-EV	5	2	3
FS-UN	12	2	10
LE-DE	10	9	1
LE-EV	2	6	-4
LE-RE	14	10	4
LE-UN	3	4	-1
NW-DE	4	15	-11
SU-UN	14	6	8
SU-DE	14	15	-1

Table 4 shows the classification categories ranked by the number of publications, and the median citations. The last column of Table 3 shows the difference between these rankings, and thereby reveals some interesting discrepancies between the amount of work that is published in certain categories, and the impact of that work. Most striking are the discrepancies for case-study evaluations, and field studies and survey research aimed at understanding. Given the impact of the work from these categories, one would expect significantly more publications. Similarly, applied research-style evaluations and descriptive normative writings are published more often than one would expect from the impact of that work.

4   Discussion

Our study reveals a number of interesting aspects about the research on EUD and its related fields of EUP, EUSE, and meta-design.

First, the number of publications on these topics is increasing. The increase indicates a growing interest of the research community in the issues that are addressed by EUP, EUD, EUSE and meta-design. However, a recent survey by Liu et al. [12] shows that the role of these fields within the CHI community has diminished. Although the internal cohesion with these fields is high, they are relatively isolated from the rest of the CHI community. Arguably, more inter-domain research would strengthen the position of EUP, EUD, EUSE and meta-design as research fields, and would increase their importance for the greater CHI community.

It is clear that the research surveyed in this article is dominated by the engineering of systems and subsequent (formative) lab evaluations of these systems. Evaluations that take these systems into the field are much less common. A similar finding was reported by Kjeldskov and Graham in their review of research methods in Mobile HCI [10]. They provide two explanations for the relative abundance of applied research and lab studies, and the lack of natural setting research, that apply to this survey as well: First, applied research and lab experiments are simply easier to conduct and manage than field studies. Furthermore, the roots of end-user development are in the field of computer science, which traditionally has had a strong bias towards engineering and evaluations in artificial environments. Although there is an overall preference for studies in an artificial setting environment, Figure 3 shows this preference is slowly fading while the number of studies in natural setting environments is increasing. This is a necessary shift that needs to continue, since only in-the-field research can ensure the ecological validity of the paradigms, frameworks, and methods developed. Furthermore, such research is able to account for the influence of contextual and organizational factors on EUD, whose importance has been stressed often, amongst others by [5]. The value of natural setting environment research has been confirmed by our survey; evaluations performed in natural setting environments are more influential than evaluations in artificial setting environments.

Another observation that can be made from our survey is the lack of action research and basic research. Although there is still a debate about using action research in HCI [7], and a similar lack of action research has been reported in other fields (e.g., [10, 17]), the lack of action research in the field of end-user development is remarkable. Action research seems particularly suitable for the evaluation of EUD systems in natural environments, since it promotes a similar strain of end-user empowerment; just as EUD removes the distinction between programmers and users of software, action research removes the distinction between researchers and participants. In action research, both researchers and end-users are committed to improve work practices *and* to generate knowledge through this process. Kjeldskov and Graham, in their review of MobileHCI research methods, attribute the lack of action research in their field to a rather limited established body of theoretical knowledge and an unwillingness to implement these technologies in real life, mainly due to high costs of the technology. Although the field of EUD might not suffer from such high costs, the number of reports on the evaluation of EUD systems in a practical context is very limited (8 papers). This might indeed point to a lack of understanding as to what enables

end-users to engage in EUD activities in actual life. It is therefore worrying that research aimed at understanding seems to be taking place mainly in artificial setting
environments. Such research will not be able to identify factors related to context and
organization that need to be understood before attempts to deploy EUD systems can
be successful, as pointed out by e.g., [9, 14]. The need for field studies aimed at generating understanding is also visualized by Table 4; although only few of such studies
have been performed, they attract great interest from the community.

The number of papers that focus on the re-engineering of existing systems is quite
small compared to the number of papers that report on engineering efforts to develop
a completely new system. Although this is to be expected for any technological field,
it is somewhat surprising for the specific case of EUD. As any software needs basic
functionality that is valuable for users before the need for tailoring and modification
arises, EUD comes naturally as a software authoring extension to existing, general
purpose software systems. Therefore one would expect to see more re-engineering in
EUD than in other fields;

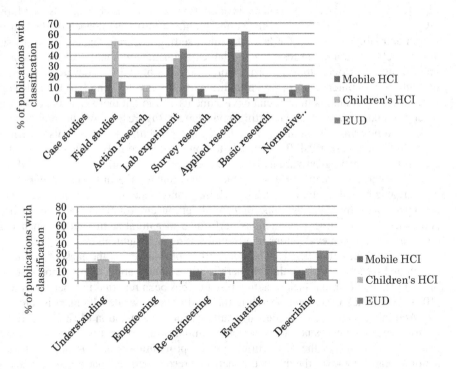

Fig. 5. Comparison of classification results of research method surveys in the fields of Mobile
HCI [10], Children's HCI [8] and EUD

Fig. 5 shows a comparison of the classification results of this study, and that of two
previous surveys in the field of MobileHCI [10] and Children's HCI [8]. The results of
our survey are remarkably similar to those of the MobileHCI survey. Both surveys
reveal a scarcity of natural setting environment research (especially compared to the
Children's HCI survey), and an abundance of applied engineering and lab evaluations.

The results from the survey of Children's HCI research methods are somewhat different, in that their review shows a relatively high preference for field study evaluations. However, a general pattern is visible over all three surveys: Case studies, action research, survey research, basic research and normative writings are not often encountered, while lab experiments and applied research are mainstream practice in all the three fields. Similarly, studies focused on understanding and re-engineering are less common than studies focused on engineering and evaluating. It is remarkable that such a pattern is recognizable despite the differences in the surveyed domains. This raises the question whether this pattern can be considered the footprint of HCI research in general. It might be that the very nature of HCI as a field favors particular types of publications, with a focus on applied engineering and subsequent lab evaluations.

There is however another explanation for the pattern that seems to occur across HCI research. All three studies have used the same classification scheme by Wynekoop and Conger [17]. The large clusters of applied engineering and lab evaluation research might contain a more nuanced picture that is currently obfuscated by the coarseness of the classification scheme. A closer look at the publications that were classified as lab study evaluations (LE-EV) reveals that the majority of these publications (16 out of 25) report on structured usability evaluations with quantitative measures. However, the same classification has been applied to true experiments with manipulation of independent variables (4) and loosely structured evaluations that summarize impressions and anecdotes afterwards (2). Moreover, these publications significantly differed in the size of the experiments (between 5 and 48 participants), participant characteristics (e.g., students and colleagues recruited as a convenience sample to actual end-users) and research context (e.g., actual lab vs. in-the-field). In our opinion, clustering these very different publications in a single category results in a skewed or at least indiscriminate picture of the research methods used. It appears that such discussions on research methodology would benefit from a classification scheme that caters for this diversity, such that more nuanced developments and trends in the research methods practice within HCI research fields can be visualized.

The number of publications per research method and purpose gives a good indication of the popularity of such research for the surveyed fields. Similarly, the number of citations per classification category gives an indication of the impact of such research. Ultimately, by combining these data sets, we are able to reveal discrepancies between what *is* published, and what *should be* published. Table 3 reveals that, although in general the number of publications within a certain category is in line with the impact of these publications, there are some exceptions. Notable are the apparent lack of case-study evaluations, and field studies and surveys aimed at understanding. There are only few publications within these categories, but the publications available are amongst the most highly valued publications in the surveyed fields. Similarly, the number of descriptive normative writings, and evaluations using an applied research methodology are far greater than one would expect based on their impact.

Although these findings are no reason for a massive trend-shift in EUD research, they should not be ignored by the research community. EUD and its related fields are still relatively isolated from other HCI research, while this survey has shown the necessity for adopting less techno-centered research approaches that are commonly found in HCI. By addressing the challenges and opportunities for future EUD research that we have outlined here, the impact of its research for the greater HCI community can increase.

5   Limitations

This survey has used the classification scheme that was proposed by Kjeldskov and Graham in their survey of methods in Mobile HCI [10] and has also been used by Jensen and Skov in their review of methods in the field of children's HCI [10]. While, in our opinion, this scheme currently is the best available scheme for classification of HCI research, it leaves (too) much room for interpretation. For example, the distinction between case studies and field studies is not at all clear – a 'problematic' example is [1]. Furthermore, while the number of papers that use lab experiments is high, this number needs to be interpreted with caution. Under the definition that Kjeldskov and Graham have used for lab experiments, this category includes all experiments that happen in an artificial setting environment. However, we think it is worth distinguishing between a true experiment with manipulation of independent variables, a usability evaluation with a structured set of tasks and quantitative measures, and a loosely structured evaluation that just summarizes impressions and anecdotes afterwards. Also, sometimes, evaluations may be conducted in a series, which means that in the same study, authors report finding bugs, fixing them, and testing improved versions of the system – in this case what is reported is not a lab experiment but the convergence to a better engineered system.

6   Conclusion

We have presented a survey on the methods and purpose of research performed in the fields of end-user development, end-user programming, end-user software engineering and meta-design between 2004 and 2013. After reviewing 93 publications, we found that activity in these fields is increasing, but also that research in these fields is strongly dominated by the engineering of systems and the subsequent evaluation of these systems in a lab setting. All the while, natural setting environment research is scarce; more of this research is needed in order to improve the ecological validity of the existing knowledge, as well as to increase the understanding on the influence of factors that cannot be considered in a lab setting, such as context and organization. Finally, an evaluation of research impact reveals opportunities for case-study evaluations, and field studies and surveys aimed at understanding.

References

1. Andersen, R., Mørch, A.I.: Mutual development: a case study in customer-initiated software product development. In: Pipek, V., Rosson, M.B., de Ruyter, B., Wulf, V. (eds.) IS-EUD 2009. LNCS, vol. 5435, pp. 31–49. Springer, Heidelberg (2009)
2. Anderson, G.L., Herr, K.: The Action Research Dissertation: A Guide for Students and Faculty. SAGE (2005)
3. Dey, A.K., et al.: A CAPpella: programming by demonstration of context-aware applications. In: Proc. CHI 2004, pp. 33–40. ACM, New York (2004)
4. Fischer, G., et al.: Beyond binary choices: Integrating individual and social creativity. International Journal of Human Computer Studies 63(4–5), 482–512 (2005)

5. Fischer, G., et al.: Meta-design: a manifesto for end-user development. Commun. ACM. **47**(9), 33–37 (2004)

6. Fujima, J., et al.: Clip, connect, clone: combining application elements to build custom interfaces for information access. In: Proc. UIST 2004, pp. 175–184. ACM, New York (2004)

7. Hayes, G.R.: The relationship of action research to human-computer interaction. ACM Trans. Comput.-Hum. Interact. **18**(3), 15:1–15:20 (2011)

8. Jensen, J.J., Skov, M.B.: A review of research methods in children's technology design. In: Proceedings of the 2005 conference on Interaction design and children, pp. 80–87. ACM (2005)

9. Kierkegaard, P., Markopoulos, P.: From top to bottom: end user development, motivation, creativity and organisational support. In: Piccinno, A. (ed.) IS-EUD 2011. LNCS, vol. 6654, pp. 307–312. Springer, Heidelberg (2011)

10. Kjeldskov, J., Graham, C.: A review of mobile HCI research methods. In: Chittaro, L. (ed.) Human-Computer Interaction with Mobile Devices and Services, pp. 317–335. Springer, Berlin Heidelberg (2003)

11. Ko, A.J., et al.: The state of the art in end-user software engineering. ACM Comput. Surv. **43**(3), 21:1–21:44 (2011)

12. Liu, Y., et al.: CHI 1994–2013: mapping two decades of intellectual progress through co-word analysis. In: Proceedings of the 32Nd Annual ACM Conference on Human Factors in Computing Systems, pp. 3553–3562. ACM, New York (2014)

13. McLean, E.R.: End Users as Application Developers. MIS Quarterly. **3**(4), 37–46 (1979)

14. Mehandjiev, N., et al.: Organizational view of end-user development. In: End User Development, pp. 371–399. Springer (2006)

15. Wong, J., Hong, J.I.: Making mashups with marmite: towards end-user programming for the web. In: Proc. CHI 2007, pp. 1435–1444. ACM, New York (2007)

16. Wulf, V., et al.: Component-based tailorability: Enabling highly flexible software applications. Int J Hum-Comput St. **66**(1), 1–22 (2008)

17. Wynekoop, J.L., Conger, S.A.: A review of computer aided software engineering research methods. In: Nissen, H.-E., et al. (eds.) Information Systems Research: Contemporary Approaches & Emergent Traditions, pp. 301–326. North-Holland, Amsterdam (1991)

18. Yin, R.K.: Case study research: Design and methods. Sage publications (1994)

Appendix A: Reviewed Research Papers on EUD, 2004-2013

1. Abraham, R., Erwig, M.: Goal-Directed Debugging of Spreadsheets. Proc. VL/HCC 2005. pp. 37–44 IEEE, Washington, DC, USA (2005).

2. Abraham, R., Erwig, M.: UCheck: A Spreadsheet Type Checker for End Users. J. Vis. Lang. Comput. 18, 1, 71–95 (2007).

3. Andersen, R., Mørch, A.I.: Mutual Development: A Case Study in Customer-Initiated Software Product Development. In: Pipek, V. et al. (eds.) End-User Development. pp. 31–49 Springer Berlin Heidelberg (2009).

4. Ardito, C. et al.: An Ontology-Based Approach to Product Customization. In: Costabile, M.F. et al. (eds.) End-User Development. pp. 92–106 Springer Berlin Heidelberg (2011).

5. Ardito, C. et al.: Enabling End Users to Create, Annotate and Share Personal Information Spaces. In: Dittrich, Y. et al. (eds.) End-User Development. pp. 40–55 Springer Berlin Heidelberg (2013).

6. Ardito, C. et al.: End Users As Co-designers of Their Own Tools and Products. J. Vis. Lang. Comput. 23, 2, 78–90 (2012).

7. Beckwith, L. et al.: Effectiveness of End-user Debugging Software Features: Are There Gender Issues? Proc. CHI '05. pp. 869–878 ACM, New York, NY, USA (2005).
8. Beckwith, L. et al.: Tinkering and Gender in End-user Programmers' Debugging. Proc. CHI '06. pp. 231–240 ACM, New York, NY, USA (2006).
9. Blackwell, A.F. et al.: How do we program the home? Gender, attention investment, and the psychology of programming at home. Int. J. Hum.-Comput. Stud. 67, 4, 324 – 341 (2009).
10. Bogart, C. et al.: Designing a Debugging Interaction Language for Cognitive Modelers: An Initial Case Study in Natural Programming Plus. Proc. CHI '12. pp. 2469–2478 ACM, New York, NY, USA (2012).
11. Bolmsten, J., Dittrich, Y.: Infrastructuring When You Don't – End-User Development and Organizational Infrastructure. In: Costabile, M.F. et al. (eds.) End-User Development. pp. 139–154 Springer Berlin Heidelberg (2011).
12. Booth, T., Stumpf, S.: End-User Experiences of Visual and Textual Programming Environments for Arduino. In: Dittrich, Y. et al. (eds.) End-User Development. pp. 25–39 Springer Berlin Heidelberg (2013).
13. Cabitza, F., Simone, C.: LWOAD: A Specification Language to Enable the End-User Develoment of Coordinative Functionalities. In: Pipek, V. et al. (eds.) End-User Development. pp. 146–165 Springer Berlin Heidelberg (2009).
14. Cao, J. et al.: A Debugging Perspective on End-User Mashup Programming. Proc. VL/HCC 2010. pp. 149–156 IEEE, Washington, DC, USA (2010).
15. Cao, J. et al.: End-user Mashup Programming: Through the Design Lens. Proc. CHI '10. pp. 1009–1018 ACM, New York, NY, USA (2010).
16. Cappiello, C. et al.: Enabling End User Development through Mashups: Requirements, Abstractions and Innovation Toolkits. In: Costabile, M.F. et al. (eds.) End-User Development. pp. 9–24 Springer Berlin Heidelberg (2011).
17. Carmien, S.P., Fischer, G.: Design, Adoption, and Assessment of a Socio-technical Environment Supporting Independence for Persons with Cognitive Disabilities. Proc. CHI '08. pp. 597–606 ACM, New York, NY, USA (2008).
18. Carroll, J.M.: Co-production Scenarios for Mobile Time Banking. In: Dittrich, Y. et al. (eds.) End-User Development. pp. 137–152 Springer Berlin Heidelberg (2013).
19. Celentano, A., Maurizio, M.: An End-User Oriented Building Pattern for Interactive Art Guides. In: Costabile, M.F. et al. (eds.) End-User Development. pp. 187–202 Springer Berlin Heidelberg (2011).
20. Costabile, M.F. et al.: Supporting End Users to Be Co-designers of Their Tools. In: Pipek, V. et al. (eds.) End-User Development. pp. 70–85 Springer Berlin Heidelberg (2009).
21. Deng, Y. et al.: Designing a Framework for End User Applications. In: Costabile, M.F. et al. (eds.) End-User Development. pp. 67–75 Springer Berlin Heidelberg (2011).
22. Dey, A.K. et al.: A CAPpella: Programming by Demonstration of Context-aware Applications. Proc. CHI '04. pp. 33–40 ACM, New York, NY, USA (2004).
23. Díaz, P. et al.: Web Design Patterns: Investigating User Goals and Browsing Strategies. In: Pipek, V. et al. (eds.) End-User Development. pp. 186–204 Springer Berlin Heidelberg (2009).
24. Dörner, C. et al.: Supporting business process experts in tailoring business processes. Interact. Comput. 23, 3, 226 – 238 (2011).
25. Eagan, J.R., Stasko, J.T.: The Buzz: Supporting User Tailorability in Awareness Applications. Proc. CHI '08. pp. 1729–1738 ACM, New York, NY, USA (2008).
26. Fischer, G. et al.: Beyond binary choices: Integrating individual and social creativity. J. Organ. End User Com. 63, 4–5, 482 – 512 (2005).
27. Fogli, D.: Cultures of Participation in Community Informatics: A Case Study. In: Dittrich, Y. et al. (eds.) End-User Development. pp. 201–216 Springer Berlin Heidelberg (2013).
28. Fogli, D.: End-User Development for E-Government Website Content Creation. In: Pipek, V. et al. (eds.) End-User Development. pp. 126–145 Springer Berlin Heidelberg (2009).

29. Fogli, D., Parasiliti Provenza, L.: A Meta-design Approach to the Development of e-Government Services. J. Vis. Lang. Comput. 23, 2, 47–62 (2012).
30. Fogli, D., Piccinno, A.: Co-evolution of End-User Developers and Systems in Multi-tiered Proxy Design Problems. In: Dittrich, Y. et al. (eds.) End-User Development. pp. 153–168 Springer Berlin Heidelberg (2013).
31. Fogli, D., Provenza, L.P.: End-User Development of e-Government Services through Meta-modeling. In: Costabile, M.F. et al. (eds.) End-User Development. pp. 107–122 Springer Berlin Heidelberg (2011).
32. Fujima, J. et al.: Clip, Connect, Clone: Combining Application Elements to Build Custom Interfaces for Information Access. Proc. UIST '04. pp. 175–184 ACM, New York, NY, USA (2004).
33. Garzotto, F., Megale, L.: CHEF: A User Centered Perspective for Cultural Heritage Enterprise Frameworks. Proc. AVI '06. pp. 293–301 ACM, New York, NY, USA (2006).
34. Ghiani, G. et al.: Creating Mashups by Direct Manipulation of Existing Web Applications. In: Costabile, M.F. et al. (eds.) End-User Development. pp. 42–52 Springer Berlin Heidelberg (2011).
35. Grigoreanu, V. et al.: End-user Debugging Strategies: A Sensemaking Perspective. ACM Trans. Comput.-Hum. Interact. 19, 1, 5:1–5:28 (2012).
36. Grigoreanu, V. et al.: Males' and Females' Script Debugging Strategies. In: Pipek, V. et al. (eds.) End-User Development. pp. 205–224 Springer Berlin Heidelberg (2009).
37. Grigoreanu, V.I. et al.: A Strategy-centric Approach to the Design of End-user Debugging Tools. Proc. CHI '10. pp. 713–722 ACM, New York, NY, USA (2010).
38. Guo, P.J. et al.: Proactive Wrangling: Mixed-initiative End-user Programming of Data Transformation Scripts. Proc. UIST '11. pp. 65–74 ACM, New York, NY, USA (2011).
39. Hale, P. et al.: User-driven Modelling: Visualisation and Systematic Interaction for End-user Programming. J. Vis. Lang. Comput. 23, 6, 354–379 (2012).
40. Van Herk, R. et al.: ESPranto SDK: An Adaptive Programming Environment for Tangible Applications. Proc. CHI '09. pp. 849–858 ACM, New York, NY, USA (2009).
41. Hess, J. et al.: Involving users in the wild—Participatory product development in and with online communities. Int. J. Hum.-Comput. Stud. 71, 5, 570 – 589 (2013).
42. Ioannidou, A. et al.: AgentCubes: Incremental 3D End-user Development. J. Vis. Lang. Comput. 20, 4, 236–251 (2009).
43. Jeong, S.Y. et al.: Improving Documentation for eSOA APIs through User Studies. In: Pipek, V. et al. (eds.) End-User Development. pp. 86–105 Springer Berlin Heidelberg (2009).
44. Kandogan, E. et al.: A1: End-user Programming for Web-based System Administration. Proc. UIST '05. pp. 211–220 ACM, New York, NY, USA (2005).
45. Kanstrup, A.M.: Designed by End Users: Meanings of Technology in the Case of Everyday Life with Diabetes. In: Dittrich, Y. et al. (eds.) End-User Development. pp. 185–200 Springer Berlin Heidelberg (2013).
46. Karger, D.R. et al.: The Web Page As a WYSIWYG End-user Customizable Database-backed Information Management Application. Proc. UIST '09. pp. 257–260 ACM, New York, NY, USA (2009).
47. Kierkegaard, P.: Beefing Up End User Development: Legal Protection and Regulatory Compliance. In: Costabile, M.F. et al. (eds.) End-User Development. pp. 203–217 Springer Berlin Heidelberg (2011).
48. Kissinger, C. et al.: Supporting End-user Debugging: What Do Users Want to Know? Proc. AVI '06. pp. 135–142 ACM, New York, NY, USA (2006).
49. Ko, A.J., Myers, B.A.: Barista: An Implementation Framework for Enabling New Tools, Interaction Techniques and Views in Code Editors. Proc. CHI '06. pp. 387–396 ACM, New York, NY, USA (2006).

50. Koehne, B. et al.: Identity Design in Virtual Worlds. In: Dittrich, Y. et al. (eds.) End-User Development. pp. 56–71 Springer Berlin Heidelberg (2013).
51. Kulesza, T. et al.: Where Are My Intelligent Assistant's Mistakes? A Systematic Testing Approach. In: Costabile, M.F. et al. (eds.) End-User Development. pp. 171–186 Springer Berlin Heidelberg (2011).
52. Kuttal, S.K. et al.: Debugging Support for End User Mashup Programming. Proc. CHI '13. pp. 1609–1618 ACM, New York, NY, USA (2013).
53. Kuttal, S.K. et al.: Versioning for Mashups – An Exploratory Study. In: Costabile, M.F. et al. (eds.) End-User Development. pp. 25–41 Springer Berlin Heidelberg (2011).
54. Little, G., Miller, R.C.: Translating Keyword Commands into Executable Code. Proc. UIST '06. pp. 135–144 ACM, New York, NY, USA (2006).
55. De Lucia, A. et al.: Generating Applications Directly on the Mobile Device: An Empirical Evaluation. Proc. AVI '12. pp. 640–647 ACM, New York, NY, USA (2012).
56. Lunzer, A., Hornbaek, K.: RecipeSheet: Creating, Combining and Controlling Information Processors. Proc. UIST '06. pp. 145–154 ACM, New York, NY, USA (2006).
57. Maceli, M., Atwood, M.E.: From Human Crafters to Human Factors to Human Actors and Back Again: Bridging the Design Time – Use Time Divide. In: Costabile, M.F. et al. (eds.) Proc. IS-EUD 2011. pp. 76–91 Springer Berlin Heidelberg (2011).
58. Maceli, M., Atwood, M.E.: "Human Crafters" Once again: Supporting Users as Designers in Continuous Co-design. In: Dittrich, Y. et al. (eds.) End-User Development. pp. 9–24 Springer Berlin Heidelberg (2013).
59. Macías, J.A., Castells, P.: Providing end-user facilities to simplify ontology-driven web application authoring. Interact. Comput. 19, 4, 563 – 585 (2007).
60. Macías, J.A., Paternò, F.: Customization of Web applications through an intelligent environment exploiting logical interface descriptions. Interact. Comput. 20, 1, 29 – 47 (2008).
61. Namoun, A. et al.: User-centered Design of a Visual Data Mapping Tool. Proc. AVI '12. pp. 473–480 ACM, New York, NY, USA (2012).
62. Neumann, C. et al.: End-user Strategy Programming. J. Vis. Lang. Comput. 20, 1, 16–29 (2009).
63. Ortiz-Chamorro, S. et al.: Hypertextual Programming for Domain-Specific End-User Development. In: Pipek, V. et al. (eds.) End-User Development. pp. 225–241 Springer Berlin Heidelberg (2009).
64. Pantazos, K. et al.: End-User Development of Information Visualization. In: Dittrich, Y. et al. (eds.) End-User Development. pp. 104–119 Springer Berlin Heidelberg (2013).
65. Prahofer, H. et al.: The Domain-Specific Language Monaco and Its Visual Interactive Programming Environment. Proc. VL/HCC 2007. pp. 104–110 IEEE Computer Society, Washington, DC, USA (2007).
66. Repenning, A., Ioannidou, A.: Agent Warp Engine: Formula Based Shape Warping for Networked Applications. Proc. AVI '08. pp. 279–286 ACM, New York, NY, USA (2008).
67. Robertson, T.J. et al.: Impact of High-intensity Negotiated-style Interruptions on End-user Debugging. J. Vis. Lang. Comput. 17, 2, 187–202 (2006).
68. Robertson, T.J. et al.: Impact of Interruption Style on End-user Debugging. Proc. CHI '04. pp. 287–294 ACM, New York, NY, USA (2004).
69. Rode, J. et al.: End-Users' Mental Models of Concepts Critical to Web Application Development. Proc. VL/HCC 2004. pp. 215–222 IEEE Computer Society, Washington, DC, USA (2004).
70. Rossen, B., Lok, B.: A crowdsourcing method to develop virtual human conversational agents. Int J Hum-Comput St. 70, 4, 301 – 319 (2012).
71. Rosson, M.B. et al.: Design Planning by End-user Web Developers. J. Vis. Lang. Comput. 19, 4, 468–484 (2008).
72. Rosson, M.B. et al.: Design Planning in End-User Web Development: Gender, Feature Exploration and Feelings of Success. Proc. VL/HCC 2010. pp. 141–148 IEEE Computer Society, Washington, DC, USA (2010).

73. Ruthruff, J.R. et al.: Interactive, Visual Fault Localization Support for End-user Programmers. J. Vis. Lang. Comput. 16, 1-2, 3–40 (2005).
74. Scaffidi, C. et al.: Fast, Accurate Creation of Data Validation Formats by End-User Developers. In: Pipek, V. et al. (eds.) End-User Development. pp. 242–261 Springer Berlin Heidelberg (2009).
75. Scaffidi, C.: Sharing, Finding and Reusing End-user Code for Reformatting and Validating Data. J. Vis. Lang. Comput. 21, 4, 230–245 (2010).
76. Scaffidi, C. et al.: Using Scenario-based Requirements to Direct Research on Web Macro Tools. J. Vis. Lang. Comput. 19, 4, 485–498 (2008).
77. Scaffidi, C. et al.: Using Traits of Web Macro Scripts to Predict Reuse. J. Vis. Lang. Comput. 21, 5, 277–291 (2010).
78. Schümmer, T., Haake, J.M.: Shaping Collaborative Work with Proto-patterns. In: Pipek, V. et al. (eds.) End-User Development. pp. 166–185 Springer Berlin Heidelberg (2009).
79. Sestoft, P., Sørensen, J.Z.: Sheet-Defined Functions: Implementation and Initial Evaluation. In: Dittrich, Y. et al. (eds.) End-User Development. pp. 88–103 Springer Berlin Heidelberg (2013).
80. Souza, C.S. de et al.: Semiotic Traces of Computational Thinking Acquisition. In: Costabile, M.F. et al. (eds.) End-User Development. pp. 155–170 Springer Berlin Heidelberg (2011).
81. De Souza, C.S., Cypher, A.: Semiotic Engineering in Practice: Redesigning the CoScripter Interface. Proc. AVI '08. pp. 165–172 ACM, New York, NY, USA (2008).
82. Spahn, M., Wulf, V.: End-User Development of Enterprise Widgets. In: Pipek, V. et al. (eds.) End-User Development. pp. 106–125 Springer Berlin Heidelberg (2009).
83. Stav, E. et al.: Using Meta-modelling for Construction of an End-User Development Framework. In: Dittrich, Y. et al. (eds.) End-User Development. pp. 72–87 Springer Berlin Heidelberg (2013).
84. Stevens, G. et al.: Appropriation Infrastructure: Supporting the Design of Usages. In: Pipek, V. et al. (eds.) End-User Development. pp. 50–69 Springer Berlin Heidelberg (2009).
85. Subrahmaniyan, N. et al.: Testing vs. Code Inspection vs. What else?: Male and Female End Users' Debugging Strategies. Proc. CHI '08. pp. 617–626 ACM, New York, NY, USA (2008).
86. Syrjänen, A.-L., Kuutti, K.: From System Development toward Work Improvement: Developmental Work Research as a Potential Partner Method for EUD. In: Costabile, M.F. et al. (eds.) End-User Development. pp. 123–138 Springer Berlin Heidelberg (2011).
87. Toomim, M. et al.: Attaching UI Enhancements to Websites with End Users. Proc. CHI '09. pp. 1859–1868 ACM, New York, NY, USA (2009).
88. Tsandilas, T. et al.: Musink: Composing Music Through Augmented Drawing. Proc. CHI '09. pp. 819–828 ACM, New York, NY, USA (2009).
89. Velasco-Elizondo, P. et al.: Resolving Data Mismatches in End-User Compositions. In: Dittrich, Y. et al. (eds.) End-User Development. pp. 120–136 Springer Berlin Heidelberg (2013).
90. Wajid, U. et al.: Alternative Representations for End User Composition of Service-Based Systems. In: Costabile, M.F. et al. (eds.) End-User Development. pp. 53–66 Springer Berlin Heidelberg (2011).
91. Wong, J., Hong, J.I.: Making Mashups with Marmite: Towards End-user Programming for the Web. Proc. CHI '07. pp. 1435–1444 ACM, New York, NY, USA (2007).
92. Wulf, V. et al.: Component-based tailorability: Enabling highly flexible software applications. Int J Hum-Comput St. 66, 1, 1 – 22 (2008).
93. Zhu, L., Herrmann, T.: Meta-design in Co-located Meetings. In: Dittrich, Y. et al. (eds.) End-User Development. pp. 169–184 Springer Berlin Heidelberg (2013).

My Program, My World: Insights from 1st-Person Reflective Programming in EUD Education

Ingrid T. Monteiro[1,2(✉)], Clarisse S. de Souza[1], and Eduardo T. Tolmasquim[1]

[1] SERG - Semiotic Engineering Research Group,
Departamento de Informática, PUC-Rio, Rio de Janeiro, RJ, Brazil
ingrid@ufc.br, clarisse@inf.puc-rio.br,
eduardot@aluno.puc-rio.br
[2] Universidade Federal do Ceará, Campus de Quixadá, Quixadá, CE, Brazil

Abstract. An important factor underlying the entire EUD enterprise is how to incorporate basic computer programming in school curricula. Rapidly increasing initiatives towards this goal have typically explored two kinds of abilities associated with learning how to program: logical problem solving and digital (multimedia) storytelling. In this paper we report on an exploratory qualitative study with a group of middle school children from a one-semester computational thinking acquisition class. We combined three technologies with which participants: (i) created a game; (ii) explored the representation of implicit and explicit meanings in their game; and (iii) created a scripted asynchronous Web-based conversation with their teacher about their game. We concluded that this combination can not only introduce new forms of 1st-person expression through software in basic education, but also and more importantly give teachers and learners a lead into program reflection, one of the most powerful concepts in programming and computing.

Keywords: Computational thinking acquisition · Programming as self-expression · Reflective computing

1 Introduction

As the number of users who engage in software configuration, digital content creation or non-expert computer programming, for personal, professional or community purposes increases, research challenges posed by *end user development* (EUD) grow in number and magnitude. EUD is about software created *by* and *for* end users, who do not have the necessary skills (or intent) to deal with the kind of generic information processing abstractions that constitute the gist of professional knowledge used by expert software developers. Therefore, there is probably not a better instance of 'software development as reality construction' [1] and interpersonal communication mode and *medium* than EUD.

In this paper we report on an exploratory qualitative study with a group of middle school children from a one-semester computational thinking acquisition class. We combined three technologies with which participants: (i) created a game; (ii) explored the representation of implicit and explicit meanings in their game; and (iii) created a

© Springer International Publishing Switzerland 2015
P. Díaz et al. (Eds.): IS-EUD 2015, LNCS 9083, pp. 76–91, 2015.
DOI: 10.1007/978-3-319-18425-8_6

scripted asynchronous Web-based conversation with their teacher about their game. Their *1st-person* experience in (i), (ii) and (iii) allowed us to detect and relate co-referential meanings expressed in different programs, as well as to see how personally meaningful aspects of programs and programming came through as self-expression communicated in new digital languages and modalities.

We found strong indications that the use of selected technologies for (i), (ii) and (iii) can not only introduce new forms of 1st-person expression through software in basic education, but also and more importantly give teachers and learners a lead into program reflection. Informally defined, reflection is a program's ability to compute upon (parts of) *itself*, that is, to take (parts of) itself as input and effectively produce self-referential output by modifying its own code or data at runtime. Reflection lies at the heart of such advanced areas in computing as artificial intelligence and distributed self-tuning systems, for example, but some versions of it are much closer to an end user's EUD activities than we might first guess. For example, programs that compute on data about data (metadata) are essential for the *Semantic Web* [2] and constitute the basic computing infrastructure of *big data* applications, which are gaining importance among scientists, investigative journalists, and other groups of end users.

Our study with middle school children has shown that participants could interpret, elaborate and communicate computer program meanings with considerable natural-ness and effectiveness, weaving a mesh of interrelated digital discourse signs, some of which reflexively referenced. Results point at interesting directions that can be further explored in EUD education, a line of argumentation that we will develop in the fol-lowing sections. In section 2 we briefly present our position regarding EUD education and in section 3 we describe our study's aims, context, procedures and findings. In section 4 we discuss our findings in view of related work, present our conclusions and comment on our plans for future work.

2   Educating End Users for Future EUD Activities

The Web 2.0 has promoted dramatic changes in the role that end users play in techno-logical development. Fischer, for example, emphasizes the shift from *consumers* to *producers* [3], while Preece and Shneiderman talk about shifting from *readers* to *leaders* [4], with a special emphasis on the social and political roles that users can now play on-line. In view of such changes, many Computer Science (CS) researchers and educators have been calling the attention of their peers and public policy makers to the importance of basic CS education since early school years, often referred to as *computational thinking acquisition*, or CTA for short (see for example [5, 6, 7]). In the last twenty years or so, a large volume of research has been devoted to under-standing, supporting and expanding early CTA. Whereas some propose to do it even without computers (cf. *CS unplugged* [8]), others have designed and developed spe-cific CTA environments such as Scratch [9], Alice [10], AgentSheets [11], Greenfoot [12] or NetLogo [13], for example.

Early CS education in middle and high school should certainly leverage one's ability to engage in EUD later on. Results can meet a widely diverse collection of purposes ranging from personal device customization to non-expert software development [14, 15], including scientific research activity [16, 17]. Because EUD is fundamentally driven by personally meaningful purposes, an investigation of self-expression and interpersonal communication of intent *in* and *by means of* programming may lead to more powerful tools for the interpretation and communication of meanings in programs by end users and novices [18, 19, 20]. The salience of personal motives in EUD can also facilitate access to certain patterns of self-expression that, we believe, can contribute to the study of program meaning communication in professional software development [20, 21, 22].

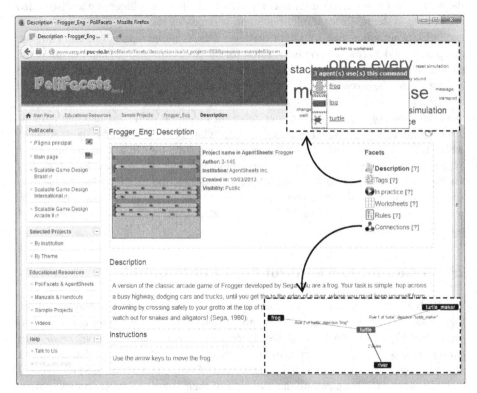

Fig. 1. An example of *PoliFacets'* tags and connection facets

In *Scalable Game Design Brasil*[1] (SGD-Br) we aim to help learners develop their ability to communicate ideas through programs [23]. Middle and high school students and teachers create games and simulations using AgentSheets [11]. They can then explore and analyze meanings, forms of expressions, as well as relations between the two, with **PoliFacets** [24], a Web-based system that we have developed specifically to support the elaboration of connections between communication intent and

---

[1] http://www.sgd-br.inf.puc-rio.br

expression in novice programming. The purpose of using *PoliFacets* is to raise the learners' awareness of program representations and structures and to help them see how these contribute to the game play experience. The system automatically analyzes AgentSheets projects that students upload to the Web. The analysis generates a set of *facets,* which are either explicit representations of program meanings that are implicit in AgentSheets visual code, or alternative representations of meanings that stand out explicitly in the visual code. One of the facets is filled out manually by the students, namely the game description and instructions for playing. In Fig. 1 we show the main page about one sample game (Frogger), which corresponds to the description facet. There are also examples of *PoliFacets'* tags and connection facets. The former represents the entire set of commands and their corresponding frequency of use in the game program. The latter represents hidden dependencies among agents' behavior. This deconstructive approach has been chosen because our primary target is to enhance young end users' ability to interpret, critique, appropriate creatively, adapt and develop software.

In the next section we report on an in-depth study carried out with a small group of volunteers from a CTA class in one of SGD-Br partner schools. The primary purpose of the study was to see how personal meanings and self-expression would emerge in the students' programming activities.

3   Study Aims, Context, Procedures and Findings

Our study is part of a long-term research on digital discourse production [25]. The goal this time was to see how personally meaningful aspects of programs and programming came through as self (*1st person*) expression communicated through *digital discourse.* For us digital discourse is the intentional expression of personally elaborated meanings in the form of a computer program whose output *delivers* such discourse and *enables* its intended effects. A digital discourse *producer* (the analog of a natural discourse *speaker*) is therefore engaged in *programming* the content and form, the temporal and spatial conditions, the means and modalities for his or her *digital speech acts* (which consist of shorter, longer or even infinite chains of digital *utterances*). The distinctive feature of the digital stance compared to the natural one is thus that the producer must specify the structure of algorithmic discourse delivery, which shifts the attention to the production *process* rather than the production *object.*

3.1   Setting, Participants and Procedures

The empirical data for this research was collected from 8th-grade students of an American school outside the United States. All the material used in the study was produced in the context of a *programming* class with a total of 18 students, 6 of which volunteered to participate in the specific extra-class activities required for this study. The teacher, anonymized as *Mr. Tobias*, was an experienced middle school educator.

The main part of Mr. Tobias's one-semester course consisted of playing with, inspecting and then reconstructing (or building new games based on) three illustrative game projects distributed with AgentSheets: *Frogger*; *Space Invaders*; and *Sokoban*. Once they began to program their own (version of existing) games, they learned to upload them to **PoliFacets** and to explore the games' facets (see section 2).

By the end of the semester, when the data collection for our study was carried out, all 18 students had learned how to create games with AgentSheets and how to explore game program facets in **PoliFacets**. All of them had also programmed *their own* (version of an existing) game, using AgentSheets visual programming language and style.

The participants of this study were 6 self-selected students from Mr. Tobias's class, coincidentally three males and three females (gender balance was not a requirement in this study). They were 13 years old on average and had different nationalities (two were Spanish, two were American, one was Israeli and the other was a citizen of the Arab Emirates). This small group of participants, which nonetheless corresponded to 1/3 of the entire class, provided us with a large volume of multiple types of interrelated data, discussed below.

The participants' tasks was to use **SideTalk**, a Web-based computer-mediated communication system that they had never seen before, and program a scripted asynchronous conversation with Mr. Tobias about one of their games documented in **PoliFacets**. The task scenario was fictional, although totally realistic. It proposed that Mr. Tobias had to go on a trip and asked the students to showcase one of their games to him using **PoliFacets** and **SideTalk**.

The showcasing was to be a scripted navigation of **PoliFacets** pages, with students' dialogs in **SideTalk**. They should tell Mr. Tobias what the selected project content was, or what it meant, or whatever the participant wanted to say about it. In Figure 2 we show a snapshot of a dialog in P3[2]'s programmed conversation with Mr. Tobias about her "Frogger" game. Grammar and spelling have not been corrected.

SideTalk is an extension to Firefox built on top of CoScripter, a macro recorded of the Web [26, 27]. When *programming* scripted asynchronous conversation to communicate with somebody else, an end user must: (1) select and record all desired navigation and interaction with existing Web pages; (2) edit (optionally) and save the recorded script; (3) enter the dialog creation mode; (4) create/edit messages, called dialogs (like the one shown in Fig. 2), which must be associated with selected script steps (not all steps need dialogs); (5) save and test the resulting conversation; and (6) iterate steps (4) and (5) if needed. When *engaging* in **SideTalk** conversations, an end user must only read and interact with the messages on the browser's side bar, which may include not only clicking on buttons, but also entering information in text areas, toggling options, selecting list items, and so on. Occasionally he or she may be instructed (by the author of the dialogs) to interact directly with the Web page on main browser area (see layout in Fig. 2) before resuming the conversation on the side bar.

---

[2] All participants but the teacher are referred to with a label Pn (P1 ... P6).

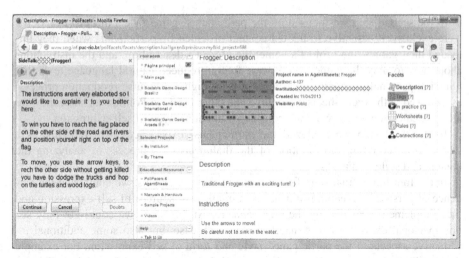

Fig. 2. An example of form and content of scripted asynchronous communication *via* *SideTalk*

There are three programming challenges in *SideTalk*. The first is to make a plan with the asynchronous communication content, form, order of message delivery, and all the other details of digital discourse structure. The second is to create, debug and prepare[3] the Web navigation and interaction script with CoScripter. The third challenge is to select the right script step with which to associate individual dialogs and compose a message for each dialog, with the aid of an HTML editor. Participants had to face these challenges and produce digital discourse with *SideTalk* showing Mr. Tobias one of their games in *PoliFacets*. The task specifically required that they talked about three facets of the selected game (see section 2), in whichever order: 'description'; 'in practice' (with the execution of the game); and a third facet of their own choice.

The study was carried out in three segments: an introduction to *SideTalk*; the planning and programming of *SideTalk* conversations in accordance with the proposed scenario; and finally answering post-activity open-ended questions in an electronic form. The introduction to *SideTalk* started with a demonstration made by one of the research team members. She then taught the participants the necessary details of script recording, dialog creation and dialog editing in *SideTalk*. The planning and programming segment was the core of the activity. Answering the questionnaire helped us collect personal information about participants such as their nationality and mother tongue, as well as their reactions to using *SideTalk* and achieving the proposed task.

We followed a qualitative analysis procedure in four steps. In the first one we inspected all six games chosen by the participants. We compared each one of them with the original game project distributed with AgentSheets (if there was one) and looked at learning support material with the aim of finding traces of *self-expression*. Our approach to self-expression was a radical one: every new (different) element introduced by a participant was taken as a manifestation of personal (subjective) content.

---

[3] Advanced users will occasionally substitute constants for variables in the script and use customized input controls (more at www.serg.inf.puc-rio.br/sidetalk).

In the second step we focused on the participants' game facets in **PoliFacets**. We were exclusively attentive to textual content provided by participants when they uploaded their games: the project's name; the project's description; and the instructions about how to play the game. These were freely produced natural language texts that hinted at personally meaningful aspects of prior digital discourse production processes achieved with AgentSheets. Of course, the other facets in PoliFacets, since they are automatically generated, were not considered in our analysis of self-expression.

In the third step we analyzed the participants' experience with **SideTalk** as a whole, from counting the duration of the dialog creation process to analyzing the content and style of dialogs.

In the fourth and final step, for each one of the participants, we contrasted the evidence of personally meaningful aspects from all three sources of self-expression and the complement provided by the questionnaire. At this stage we could not only see how personal expression was manifested in each case, but also some additional informative aspects of the participants' style and form of self-expression. For example the distribution of expressive signs across all three sources and how (if at all) such signs added new meanings to one another could be clearly seen. This showed if one participant was more comfortable or effective in one context but not in the others. For illustration, in Fig. 2 P3 explicitly says that her description in **PoliFacets** was "not very elaborated" and so she would give Mr. Tobias a better explanation in **SideTalk**.

The result of our analysis was triangulated with data collected from an interview with Mr. Tobias. He went through all the six scripted conversations, as the legitimate receiver of the messages in **SideTalk** dialogs, and talked to the interviewer about how the personality of each student came through his or her digital discourse produced with **SideTalk**. He also gave his own assessment of this technology as an additional tool in CT teaching and learning, as well as of his personal experience in having this kind of computer-mediated communication with his students.

3.2   Findings

In this paper we explore findings that are pertinent to discussing EUD education. Table 1 summarizes relevant information about our findings.

Table 1. General study information and indicators

	P1	P2	P3	P4	P5	P6
Gender	Male	Male	Female	Female	Male	Female
Script Steps	8	9	11	7	5	10
Dialogs	9	10	8	7	5	8
Visited pages	6	3	4	3	3	3
Words (averg.)	10.22	31.40	45.25	11.86	15.80	40.63
Topics	9	6	6	5	4	5

All numbers should be taken as absolute quantitative indications without any statistical connotation. The number of script steps (max = 11; min = 5) is indicative of navigation and interaction activity involved in the participants' visitation of their projects' facets in *PoliFacets*. The number of dialogs (max = 10; min = 5) is indicative of how many times the participants have addressed their teacher while showcasing their projects' facets. The number of visited pages (max = 6; min = 3), as a rule, is an indication of whether participants have kept to communicating about the established number of facets (three in the proposed task scenario) or have added more material. The average number of words per dialog is an indication of the participants' style of communication (max = 45.25 is more 'talkative'; min = 10.22 is more 'terse'). Finally, the number of topics introduced in the communication (max = 9; min = 4) indicates roughly how many aspects of the project have been mentioned.

In Table 2 we indicate how participants position themselves in a *continuum* of self-expression with 7 sequentially marked points (min = 0; max = 6). A participant's position in the *continuum* (the corresponding column) is determined by a cumulative count of instances from the following types of evidence:

- **In AgentSheets**: personally contributed agent names and depictions; changes in agent behavior, game space structure, game levels, and messages to users; or a different game altogether.
- **In *PoliFacets***: the use of 1ˢᵗ-person pronouns in game descriptions and instructions; personally contributed game title; and the quantity and quality of information filled in by the user.
- **In *SideTalk***: in addition to items summarized in Table 1, the style of communication; the use of 1ˢᵗ-person pronouns; the explicit invocation of the interlocutor in dialog messages; and the presence of emotional and attitudinal signs.

Participants' positions in Table 2 thus indicate the volume of comparable personal content in the data collected from activity with AgentSheets, *PoliFacets* and *SideTalk*. The representation should therefore be interpreted relationally and qualitatively, which explains why we are not using 'scores'. The column labeled as *Point 0*, which represents the absolute absence of self-expression signs, is empty because there were (even if minor) manifestations of "self" in digital discourse produced by all six participants. *Point 6*, however, is not an absolute scale maximum. It represents only the *champion's* position in the corresponding context (see row headers).

Table 2. General study information and indicators

	Point 0	Point 1	Point 2	Point 3	Point 4	Point 5	Point 6
AgentSheets		P3	P6	P4	P1	P2	P5
PoliFacets		P4	P3	P1	P6	P5	P2
SideTalk		P1	P4	P5	P2	P3	P6

AgentSheets is a visual programming environment and games communicate meanings mainly in visual form (win, lose and error messages being the typical exceptions). *PoliFacets* has visual and verbal signs, but most verbal signs are automatically generated by the system as explanations or annotations to the deconstruction of program representation and structures. The only *personal* content in game facets in this version of the system comes from games' names, descriptions and instructions, filled in by game authors when they upload the project to *PoliFacets*. *SideTalk*, however, is an essentially verbal environment, especially for beginners (who typically haven't learned the skills that they would need if they wished to include images, sound and video in HTML documents). Consequently, expression and communication in these three contexts require very different kinds of sign production and manipulation skills.

If we take columns corresponding to Point 1 and Point 2 to be the low end of the *continuum* and those corresponding to Point 5 and Point 6 to be the high end, it is interesting to see that while P2 and P5 stayed at the high end of self-expressive communication with AgentSheets and *PoliFacets*, they lost their position to P3 and P6 when using *SideTalk*. P3 was at the low end with AgentSheets and *PoliFacets*, but leaped to the high end when using *SideTalk*. P6 is an interesting case of progression, from low, to center, to high end, as she moved from one system to the next, shifting from visual to verbal communication. As a curiosity (since we cannot draw general conclusions in this qualitative study), all three male participants (P1, P2 and P5) consistently showed poorer self-expressiveness when using *SideTalk*. Although female participants P3 and P6 made (remarkable) progress in self-expression when using *SideTalk*, the other female, P4, did better with AgentSheets and stayed consistently nearer to the low end of the self-expression *continuum*.

In AgentSheets, P5 produced a truly *new* game, using programming elements learned in class. The game had a main character (controlled by the player) with a proper name (*Connor*) and a number of anonymous 'bad guys' (instances of an agent class named *badguy*). The behavior of agents was also loaded with personal values and choices. For example, whereas *Connor*'s weapon could fire once every 0.2 seconds, the *bad guys*' weapon was slower, shooting once every 0.34 seconds. The game could not be *won*, and the challenge was to keep *Connor* alive for longer than in previous game play sessions (there was not an automatic counter in the play, however; the player would have to keep track of time if he or she wanted to engage in a competition). As a final token of self-expression imparted by P5 in his game, the message sent to the player when *Connor* got shot by a *bad guy* was: "*If you can't take the heat, get out of the kitchen!*". Regardless of the fact that his naming and phrasing choices may have been taken from other sources (like another game or a popular expression in American culture), he made these choices by himself and expressed them in his own digital discourse.

Still in AgentSheets, P2 made significant changes in the phrasing of the winning message sent to the player in his version of *Frogger*. While the message in the originally distributed version was "I made it!" (implying that this was the *frog's* voice speaking of *its own* achievement), P2 used "*Yay I did it, thanks man*" for level 1 and "*You Beat The Game!! Thank You For Playing*" for level 2. The remarkable expressive features in P2's communication are, first, the invocation of the player as his (P2's) explicit interlocutor and, second, the emotional expression of *personal* contentment when he thanks the player for playing (with him, possibly).

One last example of effective self-expression was P1's choice to take a classmate's picture and use it as the visual depiction of the main character in his reconstructed version of *Sokoban*. The name of the agent, in accordance with the playful choice, was *'averagejoe'*, teasing his classmate once again.

In *PoliFacets* there was relatively less room for self-expression, although the change in modality (from mainly visual to verbal) was an important factor. P5 was the only participant to use personal elements extensively while naming his game. His AgentSheets project was initially named *"Programming Project game thingy"* and changed to *"La locura of the dudes"* in the final version of his project uploaded to *PoliFacets*. More expressive material, however, was collected in the game descriptions and instructions. Verbal communication there had explicit and very expressive personal elements in them, as seen in the following excerpts (no grammar and spelling corrections have been made).

"Try to defeat the green dudes. You are the yellow dude. Use W,A,S,D to move. Good luck!" P5

"Sokoban with some weird controls. Will make anyone who has played normal sokoban, freakout!" P1

"This is a Frogger adaptation made by me, everything is original, as I drew and gave directions to all of the agents. Use the arrows to move the frog and get past all of the obstacles, remember, if you cheat, you shall die. Cars and trucks shall maul you and kill you fiercely, you cant swim, remember that." P2

"Traditional Frogger with an exciting turn! Use the arrows to move! Be careful not to sink in the water. Don't get run over by the trucks/logs and turtles! ENJOY" P3

"Wall-E is having trouble cleaning up again. He has to get the crate to the red box, so it can be disposed of. Once he arrives, the box sends him to another world – with the crate. Wall-E must get the box into the new brown box so he can go back home and rest." P6

Self-expression in *SideTalk* was remarkably more elaborate than in previous cases. Although this was in part due to our study's design (since the object of communication was an AgentSheets game, as presented in *PoliFacets*), the form and content of expressive signs was sometimes surprising. Here are some examples of evidence we found.

"Good luck, you will need it. =)" P2 saying that his game is challenging (with emoticon).

"Use the instructions I shared with you at the beginning of my presentation and enjoyyyy. The second level is pretty hard so you are going to have to try your very best. GOOD LUCK" P3 saying that her game is enjoyable and especially challenging

"Hello Mr. Tobias, this is José [...] I didn't use any help, I did it all myself, and I am proud to present it." P2 expressing how proud he is of his game

"Why don't you give this game a try? [...] I've added a step counter to make the game a little more exciting. Try to keep it under 40! Trust me, that's harder than it sounds!" P6 saying that the original game was not so exciting and that she needed to improve the game somehow; also saying that the game may not look exciting to Mr. Tobias, who could "give it a try" and see that the game "is harder than it sounds"

"I guess this is bye :(I hope you enjoyed my game and the side talk presentation. Thank you, [P3's name]" P3 saying good bye to Mr. Tobias, since this was the end of the school semester and she was not sure to see him again in the next semester.

"The instructions arent very elaborted so I would like to explain it to you better here." P3

"Here is a description on what the game is about. I did not put one because I forgot." P4

"The description is the most fun to write, in my opinion, because you can be as creative as you want with it" P6

"Sometimes, I accident[al]ly pressed the new agent button instead of the new [depiction] button, so there are agents that ar[e]n´t used in the game or have any rules" P2

One of the participants, P1, unlike all others, adopted an extremely impersonal style in **SideTalk**, using the scripted communication almost exclusively to give Mr. Tobias instructions about how to interact with **PoliFacets**. In the following piece, the only personal ingredient is the use of the 1st person in "my agents". Notice that he says that "agents use commands", rather than "he" has used commands to program his agents.

"Click on "tags" if you wish to see which one of my agents used which commands." P1

In view of the evidence above our findings can be articulated around three main points. Firstly, although all participants have been able to produce *verbal* digital discourse about a piece of their own *visual* digital discourse, **self-expression in both modalities can be remarkably different** (as is the case with *natural* discourse). We also found a case of poorer self-expression in both modalities (P4's), which *per se* is not necessarily indicative of lack of digital discourse production skills (given that some people have more difficulty to express themselves in natural discourse settings).

Secondly, most participants (P2, P3, P5, P6) have been able to produce **very expressive interpersonal communication in one modality or other**. It is noteworthy that the high end communicators of visual self-expression in Table 2 were males, whereas the high end communicators of verbal self-expression were females. The point of this observation is that both **males and females have been equally competent to *program* highly expressive digital discourse**.

Finally, given the design of this study, all participants except one (P1) have taken the opportunity raised by the task scenario to **add semantic and pragmatic value to previous programming activity**. The **SideTalk** conversation was typically a commentary on the quality of their previous programming project. It was interesting to find that P2, P3 and P4 have used **SideTalk** communication to explain or compensate for certain communication flaws in previously produced digital discourse and that P6 has explicitly manifested modality preferences (*"you can be as creative as you want with it"*). P3 has also implied that she thinks she has done a good job with **SideTalk** (*"I hope you enjoyed [...] the side talk presentation"*).

The triangulation of these findings with the material collected in the interview with Mr. Tobias confirmed the validity of our analysis. In the following passage he confirms that *SideTalk* dialogs add significant ingredients to the meaning of the participants' AgentSheets games (in this case he is talking about the programmer's *confidence*).

"[P4] doesn't have, like, the same level of confidence that [P2] or [P3] have. They were very wordy. Maybe [P1], too, somehow, someway, doesn't [either], you know, cause they both [P1 and P4] used very few words".

The teacher also underlines the value of *personal* digital discourse in the context of CT teaching. He highlights the emotional connection achieved with *SideTalk* conversation and the importance of reflection enabled by digital *meta-discourse* (*SideTalk* discourse about AgentSheets and *PoliFacets* discourse).

"I liked it a lot. I think the tool is fantastic. It has this personal touch to it. I think that 'cause they were addressing me specifically, and this was between me and them, it was a great opportunity for them to kind of have a closure of the class and kind of, you know, have a way of [...] connecting with me."

"I think that would help them make better games [...]. I think it has the potential to give them awareness, which could stimulate actually computational thinking 'cause they'd think deeper about what they did and why they did it."

4   Discussion and Conclusion

We now proceed to discuss the insights that our investigation of 1st-person reflective programming activities with a small group of CT learners have brought to us regarding EUD education. We identify three lines of thought to discuss. The first one is the significance of educating end users **to view computer programming as a means of self-expression** (*1st person* digital discourse). The second is the significance of **reflective programming**, that is, building a program that takes another program as input (*SideTalk* taking *PoliFacets* as input). The third one is the significance of producing **1st-person digital discourse about other instances of 1st-person digital discourse**, which is another (semantic) dimension of *reflection*, compared to the (syntactic) structural one discussed in our second line of thought.

Although CTA initiatives have long explored and emphasized the fact that learners gain a new way to express themselves by learning how to program (see for example [28] and [29]), only a smaller proportion of research is explicitly targeted at developing and expanding the learners' communicative skills and ability to tell somebody else what they mean by way of programming (see for example [30, 31]). The larger portion is involved with the development of problem solving skills and abstract thinking. Our research is part of the smaller group and shares with [31] the notion that CT education at school should go beyond computational thinking and into computational participation [23, 24].

Our study has explored reflective programming in more than one sense. On the one hand, we have proposed that participants engage in building a program that takes another program as input. This structural reflective programming is not usually reported in research about CT education and we were encouraged by the fact that the participants in our study were not daunted by the proposed task. Quite contrarily, they took the activity naturally and – as evidence reported above shows – some have even *played* with the new programming possibilities they discovered. We must, however, underline the fact that this group had the technical assistance from the researchers, whenever they encountered a major difficulty in programming *SideTalk* in their first encounter with the technology. Even so, we believe that the conceptual challenge of planning and realizing computer-mediated communication that runs in parallel with the execution of a recorded script is by itself a significant task in reflective programming. Moreover, at the triangulation stage, the participants' teacher was also undaunted by the task and explicitly said that, in his opinion, *SideTalk* could be used productively in CT classes.

The relevance of training end users to develop structural reflective programming skills cannot be underestimated. The Web 2.0 is full of opportunities for end users to produce mashups, a kind of software that regularly takes third-party data and programs as input [32]. At a closer look reflective programming touches on another big theme in technology, the use of linked data. In a recent publication, Fletcher [33] discusses Semantic Web challenges illustrated by a pet food query. In his words, *"if our pet is a fresh water turtle (in American and Australian English), then in the UK it might be referred to as a terrapin. If our pet is a land turtle (in American English), then it might be called a tortoise in the UK and Australia. Furthermore, veterinarians and animal societies might refer to our pet as a chelonian."* (pp. 270-271) In his view, query languages should be able to handle such terminological differences by integrating data and metadata into the same query evaluation process. Although Fletcher is discussing how new technology should *work*, we must not forget about how it could, should or would *be used* by people who need the information. Clearly, the ability to express reflective queries would require more sophisticated computational thinking skills than that acquired by (re)constructing simple computer games.

This leads us into the third line of thought to discuss our study's findings, one that involves producing 1st-person digital discourse *about* previously produced 1st-person digital discourse, a *self-reflected* programming task. As we have seen, most participants explicitly explained, commented or even presented corrections to the games they had previously programmed. This added new meanings to the initial program, especially in the sense of adding more *context* information for the teacher to interpret not only the game itself, but also relevant aspects of the game programming activity (in the authors' perspective).

Recently reported research claims that preparing middle school children to use *big data* has become a requirement in education [34]. This should be taken against the backdrop of discussions about the *Pragmatic Web*, the next step ahead of the Semantic Web. For researchers like Singh [35], for example, the Semantic Web is lacking significantly in *contextual* information needed for the correct interpretation of what the available data actually *means* (for both information providers and information consumers). Building on Singh's critique, the *Pragmatic Web Manifesto* [36] clearly states that we should develop technologies that can deal with the context of data production and use. In our view, the significance of our findings in this respect is that they point in the direction of learning activities that can do important things. On the one hand, they can raise the learners' awareness of their *own* blunders in expressing their thoughts through digital discourse (which might easily be delivered in the form of *data* instead of a program). On the other, such activities can help the learners in developing digital discourse strategies to communicate (and hence collaborate) with others as part of a social construction of meaning *of* and *through* computer programs. These ultimately constitute the essence of the *Pragmatic Web*, which we can expect to be the main dwelling of end user developers in the coming years.

Our future steps in this research involve further empirical studies about 1st-person digital discourse, in reflective and non-reflective activities, using different technologies. Our mid-term aim is to propose a framework with which to explore the design and evaluation of EUD in social interaction achieved through the programming of digital discourse, which ultimately delivers and achieves both the programmers' and the users' digital speech acts.

Acknowledgements. The authors thank the volunteers who contributed to their research. They are also thankful to their sponsors and supporters: FAPERJ, CNPq, The AMD Foundation and AgentSheets, Inc.

References

1. Floyd, C.: Software development as reality construction. In: Floyd, C., Zullighoven, H., Budde, R., Keil-Slawik, R. (eds.) Software Development and Reality Construction, pp. 86–100. Springer (1992)
2. Lassila, O.: Web metadata: a matter of semantics Internet Computing. IEEE **2**, 30–37 (1998)
3. Fischer, G.: End User Development and Meta-Design: Foundations for Cultures of Participation. J. Organ. End User Comput., IGI Global **22**, 52–82 (2010)
4. Preece, J., Shneiderman, B.: The Reader-to-Leader Framework: Motivating Technology-Mediated Social Participation. AIS Transactions on Human-Computer Interaction **1**, 13–32 (2009)
5. Wing, J.M.: Computational Thinking. Commun. ACM **49**, 33–35 (2006)
6. Lu, J.J., Fletcher, G.H.: Thinking About Computational Thinking. ACM SIGCSE Bull. **41**, 260–264 (2009)
7. National Research Council Committee for the Workshops on Computational Thinking. Report of a Workshop on the Pedagogical Aspects of Computational Thinking. The National Academies Press (2011)
8. Bell, T., Witten, I., Fellows, M.: Computer Science Unplugged. Publication date 1998. http://www.csunplugged.org (last visited in December 2014)
9. Resnick, M., Maloney, J., Monroy-Hernández, A., Rusk, N., Eastmond, E., Brennan, K., Millner, A., Rosenbaum, E., Silver, J., Silverman, B., Kafai, Y.: Scratch: programming for all. Communications of the ACM. **52**(11), 60–67 (2009)

10. Kelleher, C., Pausch, R.: Using storytelling to motivate programming. Communications of the ACM. **50**(7), 58–64 (2007)
11. Repenning, A., Ioannidou, A.: Agent-Based End-User Development. Communications of the ACM. **47**(9), 43–46 (2004)
12. Kölling, M.: The Greenfoot Programming Environment. ACM Trans. Comput. Educ. **10**, 14:1–14:21 (2010)
13. Wilensky, U.: NetLogo. Center for Connected Learning and Computer-Based Modeling, Northwestern University, Evanston (1999). http://ccl.northwestern.edu/netlogo
14. Lieberman, H., Paternò, F., Wulf, V. (eds.): End User Development. Springer (2006)
15. Ko, A.J., Abraham, R., Beckwith, L., Blackwell, A., Burnett, M., Erwig, M., Scaffidi, C., Lawrance, J., Lieberman, H., Myers, B., Rosson, M.B., Rothermel, G., Shaw, M., Wiedenbeck, S.: The State of the Art in End-user Software Engineering. ACM Comput. Surv. **43**, 21:1–21:44 (2011)
16. Segal, J.: Some problems of professional end user developers. In: Proceedings of the IEEE Symposium on Visual Languages and Human-Centric Computing, pp. 111–118. IEEE Computer Society (2007)
17. Cohen, A., Haberman, B.: Computer Science: A Language of Technology. ACM SIGCSE Bull. **39**, 65–69 (2007)
18. Phelps, R., Ellis, A., Hase, S.: The role of metacognitive and reflective learning processes in developing capable computer users. School of Education Papers, pp. 481–490 (2001)
19. Cao, J., Riche, Y., Wiedenbeck, S., Burnett, M., Grigoreanu, V.: End-user mashup programming: through the design lens. In: Proceedings of the SIGCHI Conference on Human Factors in Computing Systems, pp. 1009–1018. ACM (2010)
20. Hillenbrand, E., Palmer, J.D.: Writing Software to Be Understood: An Exercise in Ginger Using Literate Programming. J. Comput. Sci. Coll., Consortium for Computing Sciences in Colleges **26**, 106–112 (2010)
21. Gaspar, A., Langevin, S.: Restoring "coding with intention" in introductory programming courses. In: Proceedings of the 8th ACM SIGITE Conference on Information Technology Education, pp. 91–98. ACM (2007)
22. Raskin, J.: Comments Are More Important Than Code. ACM Queue **3**, 64–65 (2005)
23. de Souza, C.S., Salgado, L.C., Leitão, C.F., Serra, M.M.: Cultural appropriation of computational thinking acquisition research: seeding fields of diversity. In: Proceedings of the 2014 Conference on Innovation & Technology in Computer Science Education, pp. 117–122. ACM (2014)
24. Mota, M.P., Faria, L.S., de Souza, C.S.: Documentation comes to life in computational thinking acquisition with agentsheets. In: Proceedings of the 11th Brazilian Symposium on Human Factors in Computing Systems, Brazilian Computer Society, pp. 151–160 (2012)
25. de Souza, C.S., Leitão, C.F.: Semiotic engineering methods for scientific research in HCI. Morgan & Claypool, San Francisco (2009)
26. Monteiro, I.T., de Souza, C.S., Leitão, C.F.: Metacommunication and Semiotic Engineering: Insights from a Study with Mediated HCI. In: Marcus, A. (ed.) DUXU 2013, Part I. LNCS, vol. 8012, pp. 115–124. Springer, Heidelberg (2013)
27. Leshed, G., Haber, E.M., Matthews, T., Lau, T.: CoScripter: automating & sharing how to knowledge in the enterprise. In: Proceedings of the SIGCHI Conference on Human Factors in Computing Systems (CHI 2008), pp. 1719–1728. ACM, New York (2008)
28. Kelleher, C., Pausch, R.: Using Storytelling to Motivate Programming. Commun. ACM **50**, 58–64 (2007)

29. Resnick, M., Maloney, J., Monroy-Hernández, A., Rusk, N., Eastmond, E., Brennan, K., Millner, A., Rosenbaum, E., Silver, J., Silverman, B., Kafai, Y.: Scratch: Programming for All. Commun. ACM **52**, 60–67 (2009)
30. Burke, Q., Kafai, Y.B.: The writers' workshop for youth programmers: digital storytelling with scratch in middle school classrooms. In: Proceedings of the 43rd ACM Technical Symposium on Computer Science Education, pp. 433-438. ACM (2012)
31. Kafai, Y.B., Burke, Q.: The social turn in K-12 programming: moving from computational thinking to computational participation. In: Proceeding of the 44th ACM Technical Symposium on Computer Science Education, pp. 603-608. ACM (2013)
32. Cypher, A., Dontcheva, M., Lau, T., Nichols, J.: No Code Required: Giving Users Tools to Transform the Web. Morgan Kaufmann Publishers Inc. (2010)
33. Fletcher, G.: On reflection in linked data management. In: 2014 IEEE 30th International Conference on Data Engineering Workshops (ICDEW) (March, 2014), pp. 269–271 (2014)
34. Buffum, P.S., Martinez-Arocho, A.G., Frankosky, M.H., Rodriguez, F.J., Wiebe, E.N., Boyer, K.E.: CS principles goes to middle school: learning how to teach "big data". In: Proceedings of the 45th ACM Technical Symposium on Computer Science Education, SIGCSE 2014, Atlanta, Georgia, USA, pp. 151–156. ACM, New York (2014)
35. Singh, M.: The Pragmatic Web. IEEE Internet Computing **6**(3), 4–5 (2002)
36. Schoop, M., Moor, A.D., Dietz, J.L.: The pragmatic web: a manifesto. Commun. ACM. **49**(5), 75–76 (2006)

End-User Development in Second Life: Meta-design, Tailoring, and Appropriation

Valentina Caruso[1], Melissa D. Hartley[2], and Anders I. Mørch[3(✉)]

[1] Swiss Federal Institute for Vocational Education and Training, Lugano, Switzerland
valentina.caruso@iuffp-svizzera.ch
[2] Department of Special Education, West Virginia University, Morgantown, USA
melissa.hartley@mail.wvu.edu
[3] Department of Education, University of Oslo, Oslo, Norway
anders.morch@iped.uio.no

Abstract. We present a case study of a distance education program for training special needs educators online, using the 3D virtual world Second Life (SL) as the main platform. The study explores two aspects of end-user development (EUD): 1) the professor's role as a designer of the learning environment, and 2) the students' use of the environment to collaboratively tailor virtual 3D objects. We used a qualitative approach to collect and analyze data, and we used the participants' spoken utterances and turn taking as our main source of data. We developed a conceptual framework for analysis using meta-design, tailoring, and appropriation as key concepts. The findings suggest that non-technical users of SL (special needs educators in our case) are able to develop and tailor advanced virtual 3D objects with access to online help resources, and the immersive nature of the 3D environment keeps the participants engaged and motivated during the collaboration and tailoring activities.

Keywords: 3D virtual world · Appropriation · Empirical analysis · End-user tailoring · EUD · Meta-design · Second life · Special education · Teacher education

1   Introduction

Using 3D virtual immersive environments, such as Second Life (SL), offers users the feeling of being together in a real setting [2]. Everyone interacts during live time, while viewing a visual representation of one another, as an avatar. This 3D virtual environment is a great arena for studying end-user development (EUD) because users are provided with tools at multiple levels of abstraction: 1) *Interaction*: specific tools for verbal and nonverbal (mediated) communication, 2) *end-user tailoring (EUT)*: artefacts and generic tools can be tailored by skilled users for their own and other users' purposes, and 3) *meta-design*: SL provides a design environment for advanced users (designers) to create interactive spaces for end-users to interact; these spaces will often include EUT-enabled artifacts and tools.

We studied an online teacher education course designed for special needs educators. The professor created the virtual campus and the students have used this campus to collaboratively create role-play scenarios as part of their online learning activities,

© Springer International Publishing Switzerland 2015
P. Díaz et al. (Eds.): IS-EUD 2015, LNCS 9083, pp. 92–108, 2015.
DOI: 10.1007/978-3-319-18425-8_7

making use of EUT-enabled tools and artifacts during the process. We studied one of the courses in this program with a focus on the role of EUD in this environment. We used a qualitative approach as part of a case study [23] for data collection and analysis and we analyzed participants' spoken utterances and turn-taking using interaction analysis [12]. We developed a conceptual framework for analysis using meta-design [5], tailoring [9, 18] and appropriation [19, 22]. Our findings suggest that non-technical users are able to tailor advanced 3D objects with access to online help (handbook and video instructions), and the immersive nature of the 3D virtual world keeps the users engaged and motivated during the collaboration and tailoring activities. The professor created the flexible learning environment using the embedded Second Life build feature.

The rest of the paper is organized as follows. We describe the related work in the intersection of virtual worlds and EUD. In Section 3, we present the basic concepts we have used to inform data classification and analysis. In Section 4, we present the design of the virtual learning environment. In Section 5, we describe the methods used to collect, classify and analyze data. In Section 6, we present and analyze our data. In Section 7 we compare our findings with the findings reported in the related work. At the end we summarize our findings and suggest directions for further work.

2   Related Work

Second Life (SL) is a multi-user virtual environment (MUVE) where individuals interact in real time as avatars with people and virtual objects in three-dimensional space [20]. MUVEs offer users new opportunities to design advanced learning environments composed of computer-based tools and virtual spaces for interaction and staging of authentic learning activities (e.g. a virtual university campus with classrooms and smaller discussion areas, see Figure 1) with resources that would be difficult to match in a traditional classroom setting.

Fig. 1. Two buildings of virtual campus in Second Life™ used in the distance education program (Left: Main Classroom; right: Small Group Building)

Previous research in MUVEs studied different aspects of interaction in these online environments, such as collaboration and design to create new content. For example, Gürsimsek (2014) carried out a multimodal social semiotic analysis for investigating how several users interpret and use SL resources to communicate, collaborate and co-produce new digital content. His findings have shown that the quality of co-design and co-creation depend on the social interactions and on a variety of resources that the virtual world can provide (e.g. 3D modeling tools, several marketplaces for reusable 3D objects, etc.). Furthermore, by re-examining the different theories of meta-design in virtual worlds, Koehne et al. [15] show that some open-ended environments have tools and virtual spaces for empowering end-users to tailor the systems toward their needs.

Wang & Wang [21] argued that the level of co-presence is an essential element that affects significantly the design processes in collaborative virtual worlds by increasing the sense of "being together." Along the same line, Jarmon [11] showed that users report increased social presence in SL, which she termed as an "embodied sense of social presence" (p. 1) and attributed it to being able to move avatars through space in real time. Moreover, Allmendinger [1] suggested that the sense of social presence in virtual worlds also might be related to non-verbal signals made by avatars. However, implementing non-verbal signals in virtual worlds is not an easy task for developers, and successful adoption varies across the virtual worlds available (e.g. a gesture command menu is available in SL inventory, invoked on a Mac by ⌘-G).

Koehne et al. [14] conducted an ethnographic study in LOTRO and Second Life and developed a socio-technical model of 'identity' to further investigate identity formation as a design process in online environments. They found that skillful activities of the online character define the users' identification with the avatar. However, this model of identity is focused on experiences gained mainly from studying the design and use of avatars, as a form of self-presentation. The model's general usefulness needs to be tested by applying the framework to other aspects of identity development as well. We focus on the relationship of end-user development and motivational aspects of learning.

Studies have reported findings that open-ended learning environments with embedded design environments could facilitate appropriation through a wider range of user activities and diverse contexts. For example, Huang et al. (2010) argued that providing highly interactive learning experiences is essential in such virtual learning environments. They also pointed out the appropriation of tools can promote creativity in problem solving and increase motivation for participation. People appropriate a technology by assigning it with personal meanings or associating personal emotions to it, which will sometimes imply making changes to the technology, other times seeing the use of it in a new way [18]. However, based on the literature we have surveyed, little research seems to have addressed the relationship of appropriation and motivation in SL.

3   Basic Concepts: Meta-design, Tailoring and Appropriation

Meta-design has been considered a new conceptual approach to system development where new forms of collaboration and design can take place. According to Fischer et al. [5] "meta-design characterizes objectives, techniques, and processes for creating new media and environments allowing 'owners of problems' (that is, end users) to act as designers. A fundamental objective of meta-design is to create socio-technical environments that empower users to engage actively in the continuous development of systems rather than being restricted to the use of existing systems" (p.1).

Previous research has reported applications of meta-design, e.g. in terms of tools and techniques for design in use, end-user tailoring, and customization. For example, Henderson & Kyng [9] provided a framework for continuous development of application systems at different levels of abstraction, and Mørch [18] suggested tools for customization, integration and extension to support the levels. Moreover, Costabile et al. [4] argue that software environments should be tailorable by domain-expert users at runtime in order to adapt the software to the specific work contexts and the preferences and habits of the users.

Meta-design, as conceived by Fischer and colleagues, is arguable a design concept for describing further development of technology by distinguishing design-time activities from use-time activities [5], whereas later extensions to it have made it a socio-technical framework by including ethnographic studies as part of use-time analysis [14, 15]. Taking this one step further, we define appropriation from a socio-cultural perspective according to Wertsch as "the process of taking something that belongs to others and make it one's own" [22, p.53]. Implied by this perspective is the idea that knowledge is constructed during appropriation, and that students play an active role in the process [3, 7]. The connection between appropriation as a form of advanced technology use and the social construction of knowledge has been studied in teacher education research. For example that appropriation occurs when learners (teachers in training) adapt the information in a way that is meaningful to them [3, 7]. Furthermore, Laffey & Espinosa [16] suggest that teachers appropriate and use a technology (hardware and software) in order to expand their repertoire of teaching strategies, but also found that the technology sometimes fall short of its expectations.

Appropriation is also a technology concept, and Pipek [19] connects appropriation with design in use and tailoring. He describes appropriation as "an ongoing design process that end users perform largely without any involvement of professional developers" [19, p. 5]. Based on two long-term empirical studies, he identified advanced user activities with collaboration tools (groupware) in two workplace settings, and proposed appropriation support to aid the activities. Pipek characterized this appropriation as "a collaborative effort of end users ... to make sense of the software in their work context" [19, p. 5]. The appropriation support combines communication, demonstration and negotiation with tailoring tools. This would help the teams to create a shared understanding of how the collaboration tools worked and thus contribute to a more informed and shared work context for the team members.

4   Designing the Learning Environment: Buildings and Activities

The second author created the learning environment from scratch, using Second Life's build feature (a design environment) based on skills she acquired through a workshop offered by Sloan Consortium (now called Online Learning Consortium), where she learned how to build a "box" and how to put content inside of a box. Below we describe two types of functionality that can be built with the SL box as basic building block: virtual buildings and learning activities and tools.

4.1   Designing Virtual Buildings

After taking the workshop, the professor-as-designer spent time playing in SL to practice making virtual buildings. She built the buildings by creating multiple boxes and linking them together, as shown in Figure 2a. There were restrictions on the size of an individual object; therefore, multiple boxes were put together to create the size of the building that was needed.

Fig. 2. a) Left: Building a box in Second Life, b) right: changing the size attributes of a box

In order for the main classroom to appear as one large lecture hall, the interior walls of the boxes were set to "phantom" and made transparent, as shown in Figure 2b. When an object is phantom in SL, one can walk through the object compared to merely being transparent. While fewer boxes could have been used, the main classroom had six boxes linked together in order to create the look and feel the designer wanted. Originally, the room was built with fewer boxes, but the interior windows looked too large and stretched in this configuration, so more boxes were added to make the buildings appear more natural. Once the walls were created, faculty built one large floor from a box so that the texture on the floor would look uniform.

After the interior walls were created, the professor changed each "texture" of the exterior of each box to give the objects the appearance of a building. It was the intent to make the buildings look similar to the architectural design of the downtown campus in real life (Figure 1). She then linked the boxes and the floor together. After the main area was created, she built a foyer by adding another box and making the interior walls of the box transparent and "phantom." The professor then built the floor for the foyer by building a box and adjusting the dimensions (Figure 2B). Several other pieces were also created and finally linked together.

In addition to the main classroom, it was necessary to build small group buildings for collaborative work. Each group building included a group table with chairs, as well as a lounge area with a sofa and chairs. The group buildings were 60 (virtual) meters apart to avoid sound interference between groups while talking. The small group buildings the professor created by combining two boxes and making the interior walls of the boxes transparent and "phantom," and the texture of the boxes was changed to account for floors and walls (including windows) without building separate boxes. After the prototype group building had been created, multiple copies were made by duplication of the original, in total five group rooms per instructor have been created.

4.2   Designing Learning Activities and Tools

The learning environment was designed to maximize collaboration and student engagement. When envisioning the main classroom, the online instructors wanted a space where students could meet as a large group (N=30-40) and engage in interactive lecture. The professor had visited other instructors' classes in SL and thought that flipping through slides in SL while students sat in a seat and watched was less engaging than students physically moving their avatar to participate. Therefore, a decision was made to design the space so that students would walk from display board to display board (Figure 3).

Fig. 3. Professor lecturing and asking questions at each display board, walking through slides

Each lesson begins with an activator, where students' prior knowledge is activated to begin the lesson. The activator typically involved a review of the previous lesson, or a question involving content to be discussed in the current lesson. The activator was one of the slides for the day's lesson. After the slides were uploaded using Keynote (Macintosh version of PowerPoint) as jpeg files into SL, the professor changed the texture of each display board to show each slide. Students participated in the activator by creating a notecard, writing their answer on the notecard, i.e. Activator_Studentname, and then sending it to their professor.

After the activator, students walk over to the display boards in the room for interactive lecture (Figure 3). The display boards showed content for the lesson, and there were individual activities throughout the lesson. After interactive lecture, students worked in groups for the remainder of the session. During this time, students worked collaboratively to solve problems. In addition to solving problems, students were asked to create a role-play scenario for their classmates to practice skills surrounding one of the topic areas taught in class (i.e. interpersonal problem solving, effective communication skills, etc.).

As part of this assignment, students had to learn how to build boxes to disseminate their materials, create notecards and put them inside the boxes, and allow their boxes to be "purchased" for $0L. These were the same kind of boxes the professor used to create the campus buildings described in the previous section, but in this case the students did not have to connect boxes. They changed the texture of their box to customize the look and feel. To add content to their box, students dragged a notecard from their box and dropped it into the "Content" section in the building editor (in Figure 4 all of these skills are demonstrated).

Fig. 4. Skills demonstrations for use of boxes in students' learning task of giving presentations

5   Methods

Collaboration and tailoring (i.e. appropriation) were investigated in two sections of a graduate-level special education teacher preparation course held at a North-American University. The course was arranged after working hours and used Second Life as the primary educational platform and all course sessions were held online. Thirty four (N=34) preservice teacher students took part in seven one-hour class sessions, divided into: interactive lectures of theoretical concepts (15 minutes), individual activities (5 minutes), small group activities in separate rooms (30 minutes), and role-play activities (10 minutes). The students were novice SL users before starting. The data we show (Excerpts 1-3 in Section 6) are extracts from a 30-minute group activity.

A qualitative research analysis was employed, combining a case study [23] and virtual ethnography [10]. According to Yin [23], a case study is the appropriate method when 'how' or 'why' questions are being investigated, and when the researchers have no influence over the participants who were interviewed, or during the observation of the online course. Data collection techniques were video-recorded observation and interviews. The first and third authors were the observers, and the first author carried out the interviews. According to virtual ethnography [10], all sessions were observed at a distance in the virtual world and video-recorded with screen capture software, using BSR, Camtasia and SnagIt (in total 15 hours of raw video data). Afterwards, some interviews were conducted with voluntary students and the professor, using chat and voice (headset), according to the interviewees' preferences.

In order to manage and classify the data material each session and interview were stored in a separate file, and transcribed in its entirety using linguistic conventions according to interaction analysis [12]. When selecting the data excerpts, we focused on a common scenario where groups of students created and customized boxes allowing them to perform the learning tasks. Within the same scenario, we organized the data thematically into four macro categories: meta-design, customization, collaboration and tailoring, and scaffolding for appropriation. Thus we categorized our data by a combination of top-down (theory based) and a bottom-up (data-driven, open coding) iterative classification process. Selected data are reproduced as excerpts numbered 1-4 in next section, which serve to illustrate and substantiate the claims we make.

6   Data and Analysis

Each subsection below is organized as follows: 1) short context description, 2) illustrative example of "raw" data (italicized) and 3) brief description of findings in common sense terms. The transcript notation used in the data presentations includes these symbols: (..) short pause, ((text)) comment by researcher, [..] excluded (not audible) speech, :: abruption of talk.

6.1   Customizing The Box Tool (Excerpt 1)

In the first excerpt, pre-service teachers are working in small groups (four or five members). We follow the group consisting of Heather, Janet, Mandy, and Stacy. After creating a scenario for the role-play activities, they need to create notecards, intended as instructions for the actors, which are then put in the boxes. When we start on the excerpt below the group is ready to make the box:

> Stacy: OK, now we need somebody to make the box.
>
> Heather: Y'all go together and do that. I kind of... can we build it in here?
>
> Stacy: I'm not sure if we can or not.
>
> Heather: I think we can build it here ((wherever they are in SL)), we just have to put it in our inventory before we leave. I have one (...) started; I'll try to get it so you can see it.
>
> Janet: Exactly.
>
> Stacy: Ok.
>
> Heather: That's a fancy box. Is it changing:: the scenery on it or are you changing that? (..)
>
> Mandy: Yeah, can you see it?
>
> Heather: Yeah, I can ((laughs)) (..) OK, tell me when you... we get something that you like.

In this instance, the group of learners attempts to collaboratively design the box, wishing to simultaneously perform the joint tasks. By creating and working on the same artifacts at the same time, the learning experiences becomes more collaborative and artifact-oriented than just communicating with peers. However, one of the students (Stacy) is unsure if this is possible ("*I'm not sure if we can or not*"). Heather has already started to do it on her own and works on a local version of the box to be shared by the others through the SL inventory. In other words, the work in the group is not exactly collaborative design (simultaneously performing joint design tasks); rather it is collaboration by seeing and talking, individual tailoring, and sharing.

6.2   Further Adjustments to The Box Tool by Collaboration and Tailoring (Excerpt 2)

The following excerpt shows the same group of preservice teachers, now trying to understand how to further modify the box to allow for information sharing of a document describing a role-play. The information to be put in boxes are referred to as note cards, and intended as instructions for the role-players.

Mandy: *How do I make the box (..) ahm:: have a price of nothing? What do I...?*

Stacy: *There should be a spot on there that says... with a... I think it's down toward the bottom where it says ahm, the price or whatever and you have to set it to zero dollars. Let me see if I can...*

Mandy: *Oh pay... about object (..) I'll have to make it for sale.*

Stacy: *Yeah.*

Mandy: *Features, ahm:: (..) I'll have to look it up. I'm trying to build. If you guys want to talk, I'll still listen (..) All right. I did have the note (..) So:: what exactly do we want to put in this box? I'm guessing do we need to put a little snippet of (..) what part of this case we're going to talk about and what skill we want them to practice on?*

Janet: *yes prolly*

Janet: *Mandy, are you still looking up how to make box zero dollars*

Mandy: *no, found it*

Mandy: *trying to put a note card inside*

Janet: *ok cause it said it was zero just making sure*

Mandy: *OK, see if you can access that notecard in there now.*

Stacy: *When I try to click... you mean when you click on it?*

Mandy: *Right.*

Heather: *I can buy the box. I'm trying to get the notecard that says Franklin, right? Mandy, did you label it Franklin?*

Mandy: *Yes, that's it.*

In the excerpt, Mandy takes the active role of modifying the box tool ("*I'm trying to build. If you guys want to talk, I'll still listen*"). The other students comment on the work, test it, and eventually they get it to work. The students struggle with understanding the notion of a box having a value of zero Linden dollars. The "business metaphor" permeates in SL, in this case that boxes must be made for sale in order to be used. This is not obvious to the students who are newcomers to SL. However, when this is understood, they figure out how to make a work around by setting the value to zero Linden dollars. Now, the note card can be accessed and they have accomplished their task.

Appropriation in this context (as well as in Excerpt 1) reveals two dimensions, one technical (building, modifying, testing) and the other verbal (explaining to each other, asking questions, confirming partial results, etc.), and both dimensions are clearly present in the data and relevant for the activity and motivation. What is actually "built" by one student is not extraordinary advanced from the point of view of computer science; i.e. setting parameters in property sheets (see Figures 2 & 4). However, when accomplished, it gives them a feeling of pride that we hear when listening to the video conversations.

6.3   Scaffolding Appropriation by Using an Online Handbook (Excerpt 3)

The users we observed were newcomers to SL, and the professor prepared multiple ways of scaffolding the learning activities. She created a "getting started handbook" [8] and several instructional videos for specific situations. The use of the handbook is shown in the following excerpt where the students create a notecard for giving instructions for the role-play.

Mandy:	In our handbook that we have did it say how to put a card in there (..) or was it on-line that the instructions were there?
Janet:	Give me a second, Mandy, I think I have the instructions but I need to walk away from the computer real fast.
Heather:	I'll see if I can help too. I remember doing it for that activity but let me go play around, see what I can find (..) Mandy, what did you put under ahm:: content permission?
Mandy:	I didn't even click on that, ahm::
Heather:	Go under content and click on permissions and see what you have selected there.
Mandy:	It has all checked ahm:: (..) Maybe I need to put share there (..) Anyone (..) ok (..) see if that works and you can buy it now.
Heather:	How did you pick it up, Mandy?
Mandy:	I have no idea. I just started cracking up laughing because I have no idea why it's on my lap ((laughs)).
Heather:	Somebody else has it. Janet, you have it on you.
Janet:	How do I get it off, it's squashing me!
Heather:	If you right click it'll say drop ((laughs)) (..) It's floating above the window (..) (..) There are two tie-dye boxes floating above the window.
Mandy:	Yeah, I see them.

The excerpt shows the necessity of giving students some examples and instructions for scaffolding their activities. When the professor incorporates an online handbook and short video instructions, she ensures that students feel more confident with the virtual environment.

When creating the box, the students need to set permission for sharing documents. They refer to the online handbook for this task, and as a result they make changes to some attribute values in the property sheet of the box. They enjoy the activity because they can *"play around"* with the various configurations and move the box in different orientations and shapes (e.g. *"it's on my lap"*, *"it's squashing me!"* and *"it's floating above the window"*). Afterward, the students insert the note card, which will be read by other students to start educational role-playing and concept application. It is worth noticing that the work to do this takes some time and is partly done individually as Janet needs to *"walk away from the computer real fast"* and Heather needs to *"play around"*. Thus appropriation reveals a "two-mode" process, involving collaboration and coordination on one hand and individual tailoring (customization) on the other.

6.4   Immersive Nature of Second Life Engages Students in Learning Activities (Excerpt 4)

This excerpt is part of the interview with the professor at the end of the course. It addresses a question raised by the interviewer regarding getting her students engaged for the educational activities and how it compares to a face-to-face class.

> *Professor:* *That's a good question. I would say, engagement (..) - wise (..) it's the same on-task behavior, from what I've seen, I've seen more on-task learning, um (..) in Second Life, so for example, when (..) um. And this is a different course, but, like, when I assigned, um, students to work to::like, collaboratively in my face to face courses. As I'm coming around, they're doing other things, and th::like, when I'm coming around in Second Life, and I'm flying around the buildings, the students are (..) actively engaged in what they're doing. They're not having side conversations, and I don't know - I don't know why that is, but they're:: they're typically, like, engaged in the content the whole time. And sometimes, they don't even know I'm there, like I'll fly around the outside of the building, and not even come in (..) And so they don't know that I'm there, but they're actually talking about the content instead of having a side conversation about something else.*

When immersed in the virtual world, students perform their tasks in a realistic manner. In addition, the students were deeply involved in the task all the time and less side tracked, which is different from the professor's face-to-face classroom experiences where students often have side-conversations.

7   Discussion

We discuss our findings by identifying recurrent patterns in our data and comparing them with the findings reported in the related work we surveyed in sections 2 & 3.

7.1   Meta-design, Tailoring, and Appropriation

The findings show that professional educators (a professor of education and a class of pre-service teachers) are able to design and appropriate advanced 3D objects through an engaging process of collaboration in the 3D virtual environment Second Life (SL), despite little knowledge of computer science. This was possible by the professor's training and an environment created according to principles of meta-design, which according to Fischer et al. [5] include that "owners of problems" act as designers. In our case the owners of problems are a professor and the preservice teachers, who act in their capacity as domain-expert users [4]. The preservice teachers (students) created notecards for preparing learning activities such as role-play scenarios, and they customized boxes for sharing the notecards with peers.

The basic building block used by the professor to create the learning environment is the "box tool", allowing both buildings and boxes for students' further tailoring to be created (see Section 4). Buildings required connecting boxes (a form of tailoring by integration) whereas modifying them required customization [18]. In spite of the generic nature of the SL box (i.e. serving multiple purposes, allowing multiple forms of collaborative activity), they were also specific enough so that in combination they gave the users a sense of being immersed in a "real" world (e.g. Excerpt 4).

The appropriation process revealed that learners were able to accomplish demanding technical tasks (as seen by preservice teachers) by collaboration and tailoring, and by suggesting multiple alternatives to resolve open-ended issues (e.g. Excerpt 3). Despite the fact that in some instances customizing the box tool gave the users some unforeseen challenges (as shown in Excerpt 2), we firmly believe that this form of appropriation was beneficial for them in terms of self-confidence in accomplishing an online learning activity in real time (this is evident in that they had a lot of fun and were able to "play around", see Excerpt 3 and Section 4).

7.2   The Relationship of Collaboration and Tailoring

Appropriation combines collaboration and tailoring [19]. In Pipek's studies collaboration included activities such as communication, demonstration and negotiation. Our data shows detailed examples of the intertwining of collaboration (talk to coordinate a group's common task) and tailoring (e.g. Excerpts 1 & 2). Asynchronous and synchronous communication tools support collaboration in distributed work (as opposed to collaboration in front of same computer). Whereas in the previous work the focus has been on asynchronous communication tools, e.g. sharing tailoring files [13], our work focuses on real-time (synchronous) communication in a virtual world. Using interaction analysis as our main method, we could study the moment-by-moment spoken utterances exchanged in the groups as they worked on their learning tasks.

Furthermore, we have focused our analysis on appropriation and its sub-processes. In related work we study and provide support for other aspects of interaction in virtual worlds as well, such as role-play and collaboration [2] and scaffolding [17]. Our data shows that tailoring is an individual activity separate from but intertwined with small group collaboration. The group members take turn in doing customization work (see Excerpts 1-3). Despite being separate sub-processes, collaboration and tailoring are integrated. Collaboration involves talking (testing a modification, asking questions, confirming status, etc.), whereas tailoring is for the most part non-verbal activity (supported by the tailor's individual reasoning and local problem solving, which we could not capture with our data collection techniques). On the other hand, if we had interviewed those participants who customized the boxes (e.g. Heather in Excerpt 1, Mandy in Excerpt 2, Janet in Excerpt 3), we could perhaps get a more detailed transcript of how this sub-process of appropriation unfolded at the level of retrospectively thinking aloud. This is one shortcoming of our work and identifies an area for further work by combining social science and cognitive science research methods.

7.3   Scaffolding Complex Tasks

Scaffolding is essential to make appropriation manageable and not hindering the learning activities. In our complete data set, we have examples of three types of scaffolding: 1) teacher intervention, not shown in this paper [17], 2) online handbook (Excerpt 2), and 3) video instructions (not shown for space reasons).

Scaffolding is the fine art of striking a balance in instruction, between the "soft liner" (under constrained; hindering completion by giving excessive space for trial and error) and the "hardliner" (over constrained; hindering completion by limiting experimentation and exploration of alternatives).

Fischer [6] distinguished three *learning levels* corresponding to the scaffolding continuum from soft liner to hardliner for social media learning environments: 1) Fix-it level (learning does not delay work, but little understanding is required), 2) reflect level (temporary interruption, fragmented understanding), and 3) tutorial level (systematic presentation of a coherent body of knowledge, substantial time committment). Our preservice teachers could relate to all of the three levels in their appropriation work. Designers of computer-based learning environments need to identify the levels of learning of relevance to the task, to design optimal scaffolds.

7.4   Engagement and Motivation

The findings from our study indicate that the SL experience and the "feeling of being together" keep the pre-service teachers engaged and motivated in all of their learning activities. When the professor in Excerpt 4 describes the sense of social presence created by avatars and the immersion created by the 3D environment, she acknowledges the prevalence of student engagement. The environment did not easily lead to distraction of the learning activity as it could happen in a real classroom. However, we do not know enough of the individual activities of the students to suggest how these off-line activities unfolded and what, if any, intermediate results that could have contributed to the collaborative work were (other than the time spent off-line and the results individual students brought back to the group). For example, did they they encounter any problems, or explored alternative strategies of tailoring.

7.5   Implications for Design

We have studied an online teacher education course arranged entirely in the virtual world of Second Life, enrolling 34 students. We hypothesize that a synchronous collaboration environment like Second Life will not be suitable for much larger groups of simultaneously interacting participants due to the complexity of managing the learning activities. On the other hand, large online courses, referred to as MOOCs, enroll up to thousands of students around the world (although a large percentage of the students may not intend or will be able to complete an online course). Further work ought to explore the integration of asynchronous discussion forums prevalent in today's MOOCs (e.g. cMOOCs) with 3D virtual worlds to enable immersive and motivating interactions. This integration could bridge the synchronous/asynchronous divide and offer a chance to introduce experiential and social learning in open and distance education through immersive simulations. For example, students could be divided into smaller communities (N<40) with time slots for joint problem solving and learning activities, and provided with tools for collaboration and tailoring.

8   Summary and Conclusions

This paper presented a case study of a distance education program for training special needs educators online, using Second Life. The study explored two aspects of EUD: 1) the professor's role as a designer of the learning environment, and 2) the students' use of the environment to collaboratively tailor virtual 3D objects.

Our findings suggest that non-technical users of SL are able to develop a flexible learning environment with basic training (the professor) and the users (pre service teachers) could tailor advanced virtual 3D objects with access to online help resources. Furthermore, we explored the role of engagement and motivation for learning, and found that the immersive nature of the 3D environment keeps the participants motivated and engaged during the collaboration and tailoring activities.

Moreover, we analyzed the moment-moment-interaction of the activity to identify sub processes of appropriation. Despite revealing a "two mode" process composed of collaboration and coordination as verbal activity (e.g. asking questions, confirming status, etc.) and tailoring as individual non-verbal activity (e.g. customizing boxes), users integrated collaboration and tailoring.

However, these findings are in part limited by the lack of sufficient interviews with students to investigate further private (off line) tailoring activities.

Our findings suggest directions for further work, including exploring the implications (for education, for computer science) of non-expert users profiting from engaging in collaboration and tailoring digital artifacts in a dynamic and immersive virtual environment. Further work should also explore the combination of collecting and analyzing data with research methods from social and cognitive sciences, and employing qualitative and quantitative methods.

Acknowledgements. The first author (Caruso) was a visiting researcher at InterMedia, University of Oslo while the research was carried out. The second author (Hartley) built the virtual campus on a private island provided by WVU's College of Education & Human Services. The third author (Mørch) received funding from Dept. of Education, University of Oslo, to explore Second Life as a platform for distance education courses.

References

1. Allmendinger, K.: Social Presence in Synchronous Virtual Learning Situations: The Role of Nonverbal Signals Displayed by Avatars. Educational Psychology **22**(1), 41–56 (2010)
2. Caruso, V., Mørch, A.I., Thomassen, I., Hartley, M., Ludlow, B.: Practicing collaboration skills through role-play activities in a 3D virtual world. In: Huang, R., Kinshuk, Chen, N.-S. (eds.) The New Development of Technology Enhanced Learning, pp. 165–184. Springer, Heidelberg (2014)
3. Cook, L.S., Smagorinsky, P., Fry, P.G., Konopak, B., Moore, C.: Problems in Developing a Constructivist Approach to Teaching: One Teacher's Transition from Teacher Preparation to Teaching. The Elementary School Journal **102**(5), 389–413 (2002)
4. Costabile, M.F., Fogli, D., Lanzilotti, R., Mussio, P., Parasiliti Provenza, L., Piccinno A.: Advancing end user development through meta-design. In: End User Computing Challenges and Technologies: Emerging Tools and Applications, pp. 143–167. IGI Global, Hershey (2008)
5. Fischer, G.: End-user development and meta-design: foundations for cultures of participation. In: Pipek, V., Rosson, M.B., de Ruyter, B., Wulf, V. (eds.) IS-EUD 2009. LNCS, vol. 5435, pp. 3–14. Springer, Heidelberg (2009)
6. Fischer, G.: A conceptual framework for computer-supported collaborative learning at work. In: Goggins, S.P., Jahnke, I., Wulf, V. (eds.) Computer-Supported Collaborative Learning at the Workplace, pp. 23–42. Springer, Heidelberg (2013)
7. Grossman, P.L., Smagorinsky, P., Valencia, S.: Appropriating Tools for Teaching English: A Theoretical Framework for Research on Learning to Teach. American Journal of Education **108**(1), 1–29 (1999)
8. Hartley, M.D., Ludlow, B.L., Duff, M.C.: Using Second Life in Teacher Preparation: Getting Started Handbook for Students, https://docs.google.com/document/d/162BjvWPxZ1p04VIoESaO_nMRZ1uaDS3MuEED0NxK3l8/edit#
9. Henderson, A., Kyng, M.: There's no place like home: continuing design in use. In: Design at Work, pp. 219–240. Laurence Erlbaum Associates, Hillsdale (1992)
10. Hine, C.: Virtual Ethnography. Sage Publications, London (2000)
11. Jarmon, L.: Pedagogy and Learning in the Virtual World of Second Life. Encyclopedia of Distance and Online Learning **3**, 1610–1619 (2008)
12. Jordan, B., Henderson, A.: Interaction Analysis: Foundation and Practice. The Journal of the Learning Sciences **4**, 39–103 (1995)
13. Kahler, H.; Supporting Collaborative Tailoring, Ph.D Thesis, Roskilde University, Denmark (2001)
14. Koehne, B., Bietz, M.J., Redmiles, D.: Identity design in virtual worlds. In: Dittrich, Y., Burnett, M., Mørch, A., Redmiles, D. (eds.) IS-EUD 2013. LNCS, vol. 7897, pp. 56–71. Springer, Heidelberg (2013)
15. Koehne, B., Redmiles, D., Fischer, G.: Extending the meta-design theory: engaging participants as active contributors in virtual worlds. In: Piccinno, A. (ed.) IS-EUD 2011. LNCS, vol. 6654, pp. 264–269. Springer, Heidelberg (2011)

16. Laffey, J.M., Espinosa, L.M.: Appropriation, mastery and resistance to technology in early childhood preservice teacher education: case studies. In: Proceedings CRPIT-2003, pp. 77–82. Australian Computer Society, Darlinghurst (2003)
17. Mørch, A.I., Hartley, M.D., Ludlow, B.L., Caruso, V., Thomassen I.: The teacher as designer: preparations for teaching in a second life distance education course. In: Proceedings ICALT-2014, pp. 691–693. IEEE Computer Society, Washington DC (2014)
18. Mørch, A.I.: Evolutionary application development: tools to make tools and boundary crossing. In: Isomäki, H., Pekkola, S. (eds.) Reframing Humans in Information Systems Development, pp. 151–171. Springer, London (2011)
19. Pipek, V.: From Tailoring to Appropriation Support: Negotiating Groupware Usage, Ph.D Thesis, University of Oulu, Finland (2005)
20. Sardone, N.B., Devlin-Scherer, R.: Teacher Candidates' Views of a Multi-User Virtual Environment. Technology, Pedagogy and Education 17(1), 41–51 (2008)
21. Wang, R., Wang, X.: Mixed reality-mediated collaborative design system: concept, prototype, and experimentation. In: Luo, Y. (ed.) CDVE 2008. LNCS, vol. 5220, pp. 117–124. Springer, Heidelberg (2008)
22. Wertsch, J.V.: Mind as Action. Oxford University Press, Oxford (1998)
23. Yin, R.K.: Case Study Research: Design and Methods. Sage Publications, London (2003)

Extreme Co-design:
Prototyping with and by the User
for Appropriation of Web-connected Tags

Andrea Bellucci[1]([✉]), Giulio Jacucci[2,3], Veera Kotkavuori[3],
Barış Serim[3,4], Imtiaj Ahmed[3], and Salu Ylirisku[4]

[1] Department of Computer Science, Universidad Carlos III de Madrid,
Madrid, Spain
abellucc@inf.uc3m.es
[2] Helsinki Institute for Information Technology HIIT,
Aalto University, Espoo, Finland
[3] HIIT, Department of Computer Science, University of Helsinki, Helsinki, Finland
{giulio.jacucci,veera.kotkavuori,imtiaj.ahmed,baris.serim}@helsinki.fi
[4] School of Arts, Design and Architecture, Aalto University, Espoo, Finland
salu.ylirisku@aalto.fi

Abstract. We describe a field prototyping project where open-ended
prototype tools for web-connected tags are weekly co-designed and programmed with and by the user. We call this approach Extreme Co-design
to denote how design is inscribed in Extreme Programming sessions
with rapid cycles of use, design and development that allow extensive
exploration and experiencing of appropriation scenarios. Such an approach is particularly suited for repurposing malleable technologies such
as RFID/NFC, which can take a variety of affordances and be applied
for many uses, in particular acknowledging trends such as composition at
end-user level of web functionality. We analyse the results of a one-month
field work highlighting how to document explored ideas, appropriation
scenarios, use try-outs, developed features and gained insights. We discuss this successful approach as a design tactic for unfinished products to
foster end-users' creativity through situated use and show how Extreme
Programming and in-situ deployment supported meaningful designer-
user interactions that resulted in the advancement of the initial design.

Keywords: Appropriation · Field study · Co-design · Extreme programming · In-situ deployment

1 Introduction

Since computation has left the desktop to become embedded into mobile devices
and tangible objects to support people in their everyday activities, the panorama
of modern IT has grown in complexity and the need to design open-ended systems that "allow the unexpected" has become more pressing. In the same way
a screwdriver could become a tool to open paint bins, interactive appliances

© Springer International Publishing Switzerland 2015
P. Díaz et al. (Eds.): IS-EUD 2015, LNCS 9083, pp. 109–124, 2015.
DOI: 10.1007/978-3-319-18425-8_8

can be reconfigured in ways that cannot be envisaged at design time, especially in the case of technologies such RFID/NFC. This makes design a never-ending reflective process that continues with the use and requires the practical involvement of the end-user to disclose technology adoption, use and appropriation, as exemplified by design-in-use practices [11], field studies on appropriations [8] and everyday design [7]. Following Suchman's perspective that an action cannot be interpreted as separated from the environment in which it has been accomplished [26], usages need to be observed and evaluated in everyday settings with field approaches rather than formal laboratory studies. Field research of everyday design practices [7] and domestic appropriations of tangible tokens to web content [17] uncover a plethora of use scenarios and ideas of appropriations that are not readily supported by simple implementations or laboratory prototypes, indicating the potential to pursue design of open-ended technologies through continuously evolving prototypes and in-situ deployment. To this end, novel agile approaches that allow the deployment of always-available exploratory prototypes in real-world settings are needed to design technologies informed by user practices and experiences and to gain practical insights from the end-user's personal experience [12].

Our intention is to discuss an approach to design *with* and *by* the user we called Extreme Co-Design, to denote how design is inscribed in Extreme Programming sessions with rapid cycles of use, design, development and in-situ deployment that allow extensive exploration and experiencing of appropriation scenarios. In this paper, we present results from a one month field study with one family in which weekly co-design sessions were organized alternating use, design and development of an open-ended tangible technology (the T4Tags open prototype) that exploits NFC to link digital web content to physical objects at home. Findings from the analysis of appropriation scenarios show how the Extreme Co-Design approach allows for a wide exploration of the design space through use try-outs that capitalize on end-users' knowledge of the domestic space, their practices and interpersonal relations. Gained insights allowed to reflect on how to derive implications to design open-ended technologies that assist end-user's creativity.

2   Background

Our work draws on the literature on domestic appropriations of tangible technologies, end-user development of tangibles and iterative co-design from use.

2.1   Re-interpreting Tags as Domestic Technologies

Tags as tokens and links to digital information have been investigated for more than two decades as material for interaction design. An often cited early example of tags to digital information is Durrell Bishop's Marble Answering Machine [22] where voicemails are represented by coloured marbles. The Marble Answering Machine is an instance of a tokens+constraint interface [27] that models tokens as discrete physical objects representing digital information, and that offers constraints suggesting how tokens can be manipulated. Other research prototypes have explored different scenarios of the tokens+constraint framework for linking digital information to physical tags. WebStickers [19] uses barcode stickers as bookmarks to web content. Souvenirs [21] allows people to connect photos to physical memorabilia that remind them of a particular holiday, trip or event. MyState [10] provides a way to augment any kind of object with tags that can be annotated through mobile phones and published to a social networking site as a status update. While such designs have been influential in research, showing possibilities that might be supported through tangible artifacts [25], the challenge of actual end-user appropriation of such solutions has been neglected. Recently, through extensive field studies, Tokens of Search [17] have revealed how domestic appropriation of tokens to web affords a variety of unanticipated possible use scenarios that are not easily supported by a single prototype. The variety of needs and appropriation possibilities can be ascribed to the specificity and diversity of use contexts that include aesthetic, social and material aspects [28]. Given the challenge of supporting these appropriation possibilities, approaches that allow end-user involvement in field could be particularly effective.

2.2 End-User Development of Tangibles

Several projects lowered the technical barriers for developing tangible interaction at the hardware composition level, by using simplified input mechanisms and providing toolkits of ready-to-use physical widgets such as sensors and actuators, like the case of Phidgets [9]. Other projects tackled the problem from the software level and provided languages and prototyping environments that ease the acquisition and management of raw data from input/output devices, such as Papier-Mâché [16]. Designing interactive tangibles demands a rich and grounded understanding of device re-combinations in the physical space and how technology becomes part of everyday practices by inspiring new appropriations [13]. For instance, by reflecting on common use scenarios of RFID technologies, Marquardt et al. [20] revisited RFID tags for the end-user and developed a do-it-yourself design strategy to build custom tags with enhanced capabilities, such as reader awareness, visibility and information control. RFID is a particularly versatile technology that can be exploited in different contexts and applications as demonstrated by OnObject [6], which provides a toolkit to rapidly program gestural-based interaction with physical objects, and the more recent TagMe [2] that allows the end-users to tag objects and easily develop intertwined interactions with mobile devices. By providing the technological substratum those projects represent a first step toward more articulated designs of flexible and open-ended technologies, as researchers argued that practical experiments are needed that allow to materialize abstract concepts and ideas through the in-situ deployment of prototypes [12].

2.3   Co-design from Use

Designing "for, with, and by users" has been researched in participatory design movements for decades [5] and given the challenges of ubiquitous technologies has found renewed interest ([14], [15], [3]). User-oriented design of tangible applications benefits from real-world deployment, since it has long been agreed that ubiquitous interaction cannot be evaluated in the vacuum of a laboratory [7] and that it is necessary to provide realistic conditions for the exploration of complex design spaces in order to enable constructive interactions between designers and users[4]. Capitalizing on informed participation, design-in-use has increasingly embraced agile development techniques to continuously iterate the development of prototypes while in use, making design practical and gaining insights of situated use of otherwise abstract ideas. Heyer et al. [12] proposed the RAID design approach that fosters longitudinal studies with an open prototype, which functionality is shaped over the time according to use. The approach is made of three iterative stages: (1) the design of an exploratory prototype from previous experience, (2) the observation and documentation of use try-outs, and (3) the analysis of gathered information to produce the next iteration of the prototype in terms of new implemented features).

There are other documented cases of in-situ deployment of a prototype for co-design, such as BubbleBoard [18], a visual answering machine deployed in five households with the goal of discovering appropriations over the time. Other researchers promoted the concept of non-finito products [24], in which exploiting incomplete technologies that can be used in different ways become a design choice and the exploration of the design space is carried out through the continuous evolution of prototypes in parallel with real usage.

3   Extreme Co-design

In this research we studied the application of the Extreme Co-Design tactic to explore the development of technologies with undefined purposes and indeterminate usages, informed by direct observations and reflections of situated uses. Our contribution is to adopt Extreme Programming (XP) and provide insights of its integration in a process for the co-design of open-ended technologies exploring appropriation scenarios. XP [1] is an unconventional development model that gives prominence to the rapid availability of usable prototypes to accelerate the exploration of the design space through rapid cycles of software release. Its core principles of promoting iterative development and being customer-centered and scenario-driven meet the critical demand of having a continuously working prototype always available. Attempts to combine XP with user-centered design are not new [23]. Nevertheless, while they showed to speed up the design process, further research is needed to understand the potential of XP with respect to end-user development practices. We describe the application of the Extreme Co-Design approach with the in-situ deployment of the T4Tags open prototype and discuss the findings of our field study alternating use, design and development.

3.1   The T4Tags Initial Prototype

T4Tags builds upon the concept of Tokens of Search [17] and provides a platform that allows the user to easily link physical objects to web content via NFC. While Tokens of Search implements limited functionality, e.g., only one single URL could be associated to a physical token and the content can be read only at a designated spot in the house, T4Tags is designed to be as open-ended and versatile as possible: (1) there are no limitations on the number of URL that can be associated to a token and (2) users can read the content of a token with their mobile phones, thus extending uses to more ubiquitous scenarios.

The main design principle was to assemble the prototype as an open toolbox that provides means for: (a) the users to be able to easily implement envisioned scenarios and (b) the designers-developers to rapidly extend the prototype to support future appropriations. The toolbox of T4Tags consists of (see Figure 1):

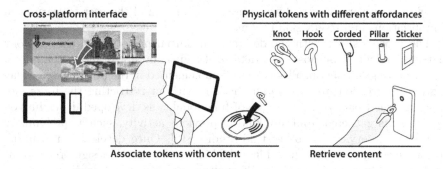

Fig. 1. The T4Tags open prototype.

- a set of 3D-printed physical tokens with different shapes, colors and affor-dances with embedded NFC tags and NFC stickers;
- a web server that stores the content of the physical tokens;
- a web interface that allows to edit the content of a token by adding or removing (drag and drop) web links. Being web-based, the application can run via a web browser from any computer or mobile device and, therefore, it is not needed to install a resident application in specific devices;
- a tray that embeds a WiFi-connected device with a NFC reader that is used, in combination with the web interface, to access the content of a token by retrieving its NFC identification number;
- an Android mobile phone that runs an application to retrieve and display the content of a token;

T4Tags implements a core set of functionality, informed by findings of previous studies [28][17]. Users can associate any number of web URLs to a token. To do so, they first put the token they want to use over the tray, making the reader to retrieve the id of the token together with the associated content. The user can then add or remove content by dragging and dropping URL addresses from a browser to the window of the web interface (see Figure 1). This functionality is implemented through websockets that connect the reader and the web interface to the server in order to maintain the synchronization of content. Users can then retrieve the content of a token either by placing it on the tray again or by using a mobile phone with an installed Android application that automatically recognizes the NFC tag and displays the list of associated URLs retrieved from the server.

3.2 Research Approach

The motto of the Extreme Co-Design approach is *"prototyping with and by the user"*. The core idea is based on the integration of Extreme Programming with co-design sessions as a tactic to quickly deploy an evolving prototype that can be readily and continuously evaluated by the user thus allowing the designer to reflect on a variety of real-world usage scenarios and the user to learn from appropriations and to envision new uses.

The process starts with the design of an initial prototype of a technology that has undefined purpose, a variety of design affordances and potentially a variety of usages. Functionality is loosely implemented in the prototype in a way it gives the freedom to explore interactions without restricting the users into pre-established patterns. A core set of functionality is developed depending on requirements gathered from any kind of previous activity, such as preliminary workshops, interviews or other field studies [12]. Once developed, the initial prototype is deployed in-situ and inscribed into a one-month design process that involves weekly co-design sessions alternating use, design and development.

While co-design sessions give a reflective account of various daily situations as articulated by participants, real-world deployment allows participants to use the prototype to support existing practices and construct novel solutions devised from their usage experience. In a domestic setting, this allows participants to generate use scenarios at different times of the day and in private spaces that are not accessible during co-design sessions. Participants are asked to record their interactions with the system in a *diary*, documenting use with pictures and videos. The *diary* would serve as a communication artifact to support the dialogue between participants and researchers that would weekly visit the deployment site to run the co-design sessions. During the weekly sessions, researchers collect impressions and feedback about participants experience with the systems as well as usage scenarios they were able to document but also non-usage of implemented features and misusing. Co-design sessions are the meeting point between users and designers, in which the latter learn from situated uses of the prototype and are able to determine the new design choices that would alter the prototype and materialize in features to be added, modified or removed. The evolution of the prototype occurs during the week after each session, in which designers consider opportune responses to the try-outs. Alternatively, the prototype could also be altered during the co-design session itself in the case designers become aware of envisioned scenarios that were no readily supported by current prototype and the issue can be quickly fixed or implemented in-situ.

In order to analyze usage try-outs, together with the *diary* from participants, a template-based *journal* is created that designers can fill in to document ideas, scenarios, use trials of scenarios without the need of new implementations and use trials of implemented features. The *journal* is intrinsically a working document and contains information regarding usage scenarios such as when they were firstly envisioned and/or enacted, authors, actors, a short description and any kind of related material such as photos, videos or excerpts from interviews. The templates are meant to keep track of usages and appropriations and offer an accessible way to organize observations regarding successfully repeated usages, abandonment after use or non-use of a feature.

4   Field Study

An in-depth study was performed in a household in Finland with the aim of exploring how the prototype would be adopted to support existing practices of the family or inspire appropriations and new social organizations. The initial T4Tags prototype was deployed in-situ and remained in the household for four weeks. During the first visit all the necessary hardware and software were provided to the family, which included: (a) the device, the NFC reader, used to link physical tokens to web content, (b) the mobile phone used to retrieve tokens content and, (c) a set of physical tokens of different shapes, colors and affordances. The web server was installed in one of the family computers.

They were then interviewed about their normal routines, family life and organization and computer use, including Internet (e.g., what they use Internet for, if children are allowed to connect to web alone, etc.). After the interview, the main functionality of the system were introduced with an example of sharing photos with friends. The family was showed how a photo could be associated to a NFC sticker and then, for instance, by attaching the sticker to a postcard it is possible to create a digitally-augmented message to send to a friend. After the example of use, a brainstorming session was undertaken, from which participants came up with many ideas and scenarios. Some of them were ready to be tried out, while others required some tweaking and programming and eventually they would have been available in the following weeks of the field trial.

Participating Family. The family studied consists of four members: father, mother and two daughters. Pseudonyms are used to protect members anonymity. The father, Kari, is a researcher. The mother, Päivi, works as a cultural producer. Kari and Päivi have two daughters Sini and Anna. Sini is 12 years old and Anna is 9 years old. The family lives in a spacious apartment house in southern Helsinki. According to Kari's words, the family provided an eclectic sample for the purposes of the study: *"[...] there's a woman who would not care less about technology. And if it works for such a person, then it will work for many others. And we have kids who are kind of normal usual girls [...] they're curious for new* *kind of things and they would be delighted to adopt something that they find helps them create some good experiences.* " All family members use their smart phones and the parents also use laptops to access the Internet. In general, Internet is used mainly for individual purposes (e.g., working, playing or shopping) and watching shows and series from Yle Areena[1] and Netflix[2], since the family does not have TV. They also have a tablet in their entrance hall that shows the weather and when the trams and buses go.

Data Collection and Analysis. The interviewing was done partly in Finnish and partly in English. A Finnish researcher interviewed the family weekly and the English speaking researcher attended the first co-design session on the premises and the other sessions via Skype. The interviews were video taped and transcribed to both Finnish and English. The family members documented their experiences with the system throughout the study with the help of photos, videos and notes (the *diary*). The transcriptions were inspected to fill in the template-based *journal* with information about usage scenarios. Next, we present the analysis of how tokens were used.

5   Results

The T4Tags prototype was able to support purposeful interactions between users and designers that resulted in the advancement of the design, such as appropriating features, proposals for new features, for transforming existing features, and implementation of transformations into existing features.

5.1   Exploration of Usage Scenarios

At the end of the field trial, we were able to document 14 distinct scenarios organized in three categories we detail below (see Table 1 at the end of the paper).

Tokens as Prompts for Content. Tokens as a means to retrieve content were mostly exploited to augment other objects in the household (Scenario 10 and 11). Participants wanted to capitalize on the physicality of existing objects and they firstly devised the idea of embedding a NFC sticker into soft toys to retrieve media content through some interaction with the augmented toy. Kari attached a sticker to a Hello Kitty toy after having added a web link to a song into the token. He also connected the smartphone to the radio speakers. He then gave the toy to Sini and, when she placed the toy sitting on top of the phone (see Figure 2, on the left), the song started to play from the speakers . The kids were really excited and wanted to share the rewarding experience with their friends as

---

[1] http://areena.yle.fi/tv

[2] https://www.netflix.com/global

Table 1. Scenarios according to categories. *The scenarios were "Only envisioned", in the case T4Tags does not provide any support for usage and no ad-hoc features were develope; "Not tried", if technical support was available but the scenario was not tested; "Tried and abandoned" if the scenario was tried but abandoned after first use, and; "Succesfully repeated usage" if the scenario was tried in different occasions all along the field study.

Category	Id and Name	Short description	Informed by	*Try-out	Developed Features
Tokens as prompts for content	7. Personal content	Everyone in the family would have one token defined by color/form for her personal use	2	Not tried	Already supported Google Drive
	5. Memento	Tokens to store things to remember informed by their affordances	7	Successfully repeated usage	Already supported Google Drive
	10. Toy	Augment toys with tokens to provide digital content	–	Successfully repeated usage	Autoplay
	11. Poster	Augment static posters with tokens to retrieve content	10	Successfully repeated usage	Autoplay
	12. Cleaning Podcast	A token that contains an audio record that motivates and instructs on cleaning	10	Not tried	Already supported
Tokens as triggers of actions	6. Password	Tokens used as passwords to log in to other applications	–	Only envisioned	–
	8. Accessory	Tokens as accessory to wear	7	Only envisioned	–
	9. Pairing	Use tokens to pair devices, for instance pair a mobile phone with a TV so that the content read with the phone would appear in the TV	–	Successfully repeated usage	Pairing service
	13. IFTTT	Use tokens to trigger IFTTT actions	6	Only envisioned	–
	14. Pottermore	Use the token as a trigger to open a game	6, 10, 11	Successfully repeated usage	Pairing service
Tokens for shared activities	1. Personal and Shared calendar	Add and share events on ones calendar by using the tokens. Tokens for a calendar that has the time tables of the whole family, but also the events from all (free time/work) calendars of each person	–	Tried and abandoned Only envisioned	Google Calendar
	2. To-do	Tokens would contain one thing to do in the household. By reading the token it should be possible to mark the task as done	–	Successfully repeated usage	Already supported
	4. Gift	Token to be given as a gift to people in or outside the family	3, 5, 7	Not tried	Google Drive
	3. Reward	Markers for childrens weekly duties to be done in order to get allowance	2, 6	Not tried	Google Drive

Fig. 2. Usage scenarios from the field study. From left to right: Scenario 10 (Toy), Scenario 11 (Poster) and Scenario 5 (Memento).

well. Kari said: *"[...] when I made it work Sini wanted immediately to show it to Anna and then Anna wanted to show it to Laura (Anna's friend) and then came Ritva and Vesa (family friends) to visit the same day and they wanted to show it to them."* The successful try-outs of the toy scenario engaged participants in thinking on other possible reconfigurations of the same idea. In fact, they later decided to augment the static content of a movie poster with a sticker that would trigger a trailer of the movie from Youtube.com (see Figure 2, in the middle).

Tokens could also work as a place where users can put things they have to remember (Scenario 5). They could contain both the description of what it needs to be done as well as instructions on how to do it. For instance, T4Tags was used by Kari to attach a list from Wunderlist[3] to a token and create a "reminder". He then put it on his pillow (see Figure 2, on the right) for remembering to help his daughter with her piano homework before going to sleep. The physicality of the token worked as a knot in a handkerchief and Kari realized that he reminded the content of the token without reading it. Other ideas of possible usages of the Memento scenario were proposed, even if not explored, such as using the token as a reminder for paying bills or as a card from hairdresser or a dentist with information of next appointments.

Tokens as Triggers of Actions. As the field study progressed, the family devised several ways of using the tokens to trigger meaningful actions, such as to log in to applications or services. Kids, for instance, could use it as a password for WiFi, Yle Areena or Netflix. Kari suggested that the token password (Scenario 6) could work only in certain hours, for instance the kids could have access to Netflix in the afternoon, but not when it is time to go to sleep, thus highlighting that the platform should support more articulated functionality of end-user tailoring that allows to program the context-aware behavior of tokens. Kari actually wondered if tokens could be programmed as IFTTT[4] applications (Scenario 13). This means that a token would become a trigger to create

---

[3] https://www.wunderlist.com/es/

[4] https://ifttt.com

powerful connections with online digital channels and, via simple rules, develop intertwined interactions between the digital and the physical world that allow to use the token, for instance, to switch on/off the lights or update the Facebook profile. This idea was envisioned during the closing co-design session and therefore there was not time for further developments or implementations.

During the last week of use Kari, Sini and Anna came up with the scenario of opening a game in the computer with a token (Scenario 14). Kari attached a token into a stick that was called *magic wand* and then used the wand to open a game called Pottermore[5] in the computer by touching the reader with it, as if he was casting a spell. Kari was surprised how positive reactions the wand application triggered: *"[...] it was emotionally quite appealing, which is visible in how Sini, who is very reluctant in showing emotionally loaded expressions, responded to the event with a 'wow!'."*

Tokens for Shared Activities. One of the most appealing ideas for the family about how to use the tokens came up very early in the first workshop. It was described as the "to-do application" (Scenario 2). All tokens would contain one thing to do in the household and by scanning a token with the phone it would be possible to mark a task as done. To make domestic chores organized and motivating, the to-do list could be associated with Wunderlist or other already existing application and the things to do could be a video, audio or a picture, not just text. The family could gather around a table at a fixed time and distribute the to-do tokens or each person could take a token once they have time and this could become a new shared routine. Päivi said that: *"the children are motivated to do household chores in an absolutely different way if the they decide the chores together and then they can choose any."*. They envisioned, and enacted during a co-design session, that the communication between family members could be done as simply as having a certain place for the tokens, for example a bowl. If the bowl is full of things to do in the morning and, when the mother comes home in the afternoon, she notices that the bowl is only half full, she immediately knows that the other members of the family have done housework that day. When talking about the family's daily routines and ways of organizing the daily life it became apparent that there is a need for new ways of coordinate shared activities as well as improving the internal communication about the schedules of each family member. A first scenario was developed that allowed participants to add and physically share events from personal calendars by using the tokens, which required the implementation of a new feature that exploited Google Calendar APIs to link events to tokens. Since they make heavy use of paper-based calendars to organize their routines (see Figure 3), the family was particularly willing to try the functionality. However, after a first try they decided to not pursue the development any further, since they realized the technology did not fit into their current practices of using calendars. They did not want to change all their calendars to Google since everyone was currently using a different kind of calendars. Päivi concluded that: *"[...] we felt we did not want to put our lives on*

---

[5] An online game inspired on Harry Potter: https://www.pottermore.com

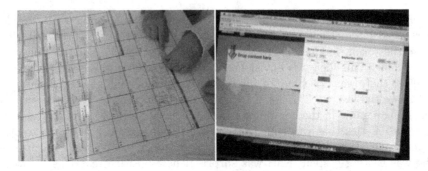

Fig. 3. Personal calendar scenario. Discussion during the co-design session (left) and the implemented Google Calendar feature (right).

Google calendars. So we did not use the calendar application." Even though the calendar application was not found useful, the example inspired new to develop during the field study. For instance, a discussion of a design for a shared calendar system started. The calendar was envisioned to contain the time tables of the whole family and also the events from all free time and work calendars of each person. This was envisaged would better support the organization of family's shared events.

These scenarios demonstrate deep knowledge of the participants about the domestic space, different activities that take place within, conventions established among family and interpersonal relationships. Tokens in some cases has been associated not only with web content but with specific items and places within house. When tokens are used as messaging devices to facilitate communication among family, this also requires a knowledge of conventions about where to leave the token so that it can be seen. Various ideas like using calendars and limiting the functionality of tokens to certain time periods (such as before bed time or after doing homework) are shaped by routines and also interpersonal relations between family members (mothers authority over children). These, in turn, called for extended functionality as described below.

5.2 T4Tags after the Extreme Co-design

Field studies on appropriations of web connected tags [18][17] reveal that discovering new routines in the circumstances of existing practices and engaging users in forming new practices around novel technologies is hampered by static prototypes that cannot be adapted or modified at use time. That was not the case with T4Tags, which supported enactment and usage try-outs of unanticipated scenarios through the rapid evolution of the original prototype in response to users' feedback through use. Various scenarios were envisioned by users that were not supported by the original prototype and required the implementation of additional features. For instance, one design response was to have calendars attached to physical objects or to share digital archives from the cloud. To this end, T4Tags was shaped to provide an interface[6] for enabling users to create

---

[6] We exploited the Google APIs: https://developers.google.com/apis-explorer

links to events from their Google Calendar accounts and files from Google Drive or their personal hard drive (in this case files were automatically uploaded to Google Drive). Another feature was implemented that exploited the ubiquity of T4Tags, especially the fact that web content could be displayed in any kind of browser-enabled device. The feature invented by Kari (Scenario 9) was called "Pairing" and consisted in creating associations between devices in a way users can choose to automatically display content on different devices at the same time. For instance, by associating a NFC sticker to a laptop, the pairing service allowed to display on the laptop the content of a token read with the mobile phone, as happened in the Scenario 14 (Pottermore).

On the other hand, designing for appropriation requires a degree of under-designing and possible removal of features along the process. Indeed, in few instances pre-configured parts became an obstacle for appropriation. For instance, when family wanted to embed solid NFC tokens into the plush toy, the plastic casing around the tokens proved to be an obstacle and Kari demanded the unadulterated NFC tag itself (this problem has been later resolved by using a sticker instead). This suggests that the design of tokens could be left unfinished and the users could design their own tags in ways that are more meaningful to them, for instance, exploiting configurability through templates of 3D-printed tokens that could be modified or designed from scratch.

6   Discussion and Conclusion

The evolution of the prototype promoted discoverability for both designers and users and accelerated the invention of new usage ideas. While at the beginning (first co-design session) participants were trying to use the technology for existing needs they already have, like organizing their daily routines with calendars, in the latest sessions the appropriation led to the creation of new practices at home, as shown in Scenario 10, 11 or 14. Moreover, our findings show how the interactions between the users and the designer-implementers through the prototype enabled local appropriations to be translated into suggestions that were relevant to the implementation of features that support meaningful user experience.

In this discussion we consider firstly how the development of new features led to the widening of the use space of tokens linked to digital information. The exploration highlights considerations for the development of serendipitous systems, where the same technology is appropriated deeply and for long but the diversity of uses are transient. We finally provide reflection on the role of Extreme Co-Design as a tactic for the development of open-ended technology and outline directions for future research.

Chain Reaction Exploration of Uses. The field work with T4Tags demonstrated that pursuing the timely development of features is an effective strategy —if compared with previous research [18][17]— that resulted in the expansion of the use space in the domestic environment. Shaping the prototype during use favored the experimentation and experiencing of complex usage scenarios and embodiments that, in turn, informed the invention of new scenarios. For instance, Google Calendar allowed the experimentation of Scenario 1 that led the family to envision new uses of a shared calendar that could better fit into their routines. Google Drive support was developed for Scenarios 7. Again, even if this specific scenario was not tried, it inspired the invention of Scenarios 5, 4 and 8. In particular, Scenario 5 (Memento) was explored throughout the entire field study and shows how the Extreme Co-Design approach enables technology to fit into the context of use. We were able to document, in fact, the use of the token as a reminder at different time of the day, by different people and in different context. The functionality implemented to support Scenario 9 enabled the usage try-out of Scenario 14 (Pottermore game), which activated the most emotional and playful user experience during real-world use.

Developing Serendipitous Technology. Our findings show that tokens were used to store media content, make information tangible, log in to applications, be kept as memories or gifted, amongst others. Having a continuously available prototype gave users the freedom to explore multiple usages of tags that were timely re-configured to support different models of use, from a vehicle for sharing information between family members, to a means to trigger specific actions in the household or to support individual practices. This exhibits a multiplicity of uses some of which with an transient others with a more habitual character. While some specific developed features can be used rarely and ephemerally the tags technology as a whole is appropriated deeply and for long. An approach such as Extreme Co-Design that exploits incompleteness as a design strategy and provides rooms for the end-user to participate could be a solution to build technologies that need serendipitous and quick means to be used.

On the Role of Extreme Co-design. If we think of the Extreme Co-Design as a method, crucial for the success is the process of translating local appropriations influential to the implementation of features into the suggested system, since the approach emphasizes on the implement-ability of ideas directly into the prototype. The following aspects demonstrated to be foundational for a successful approach:

1. The designer-developer must be able to communicate the foundations as well as the versatility of the technological agenda, for instance, that the intended system is an open-ended technological exploration with some key technological functionality.
2. The current prototype must be a sketch of how it could be tackled. The users need to able to construct relevant appropriations, and spin-off ideas, with the proposed prototype. A prototype in an unfinished form fosters the user engagement [24] allowing the system to adapt to user experience.

3. A wide degree of tailorability must be provided to empower end-users to materialize the experience of their everyday actions and needs into technical features of software development. This can be exemplified by Scenario 6 (Password) and 13 (IFTTT), in which users needed to develop more complex re-configurations of tags functionality to design their own organizing system.

We acknowledge some aspects of the research that are not explored in this paper. For instance, making the Extreme Co-Design strategy scalable to the community reveals a series of potential issues that needs further investigation, such as how to implement a sustainable process increasing the number of users while maintaining the efforts of the designer-developer. Moreover, while XP demonstrated to be successful for the thorough exploration of the use space with only one family and in a restricted time frame, it is necessary to test its applicability in case of long-term studies with a greater number of families. Scalability introduces issues to the use of XP that need to be considered, such as how to decide what feature to implement and how to communicate changes. Finally, even if our study uncovered a wide range of meaningful use scenarios, it takes time to appropriate a new technology and longitudinal studies are needed to understand the effect of novelty usage and gain insights that are more representative of the normal use of the technology.

Acknowledgments. This research has been partially funded by TIPEx Project (TIN2010-19859-C03-01), by the UC3M Postdoctoral Mobility Scholarship Programme 2014, by the Academy of Finland (286440, Evidence) and by the EU through EIT ICT Labs.

References

1. Beck, K.: Extreme programming explained: embrace change. Addison-Wesley Professional (2000)
2. Benavides, X., Amores, J., Maes, P.: Tagme: an easy-to-use toolkit for turning the personal environment into an extended communications interface. In: CHI EA 2014, pp. 2197–2202. ACM (2014)
3. Binder, T., De Michelis, G., Ehn, P., Jacucci, G., Linde, P., Wagner, I.: Design things. MIT Press (2011)
4. Botero, A., Kommonen, K.H., Marttila, S.: Expanding design space: design-in-use activities and strategies. In: Proc. DRS 2010 (2010)
5. Briefs, U., Ciborra, C.U., Schneider, L.: Systems Design For, With, and by the Users. North Holland (1983)
6. Chung, K., Shilman, M., Merrill, C., Ishii, H.: Onobject: gestural play with tagged everyday objects. In: Adj. Proc. UIST 2010, pp. 379–380. ACM (2010)
7. Desjardins, A., Wakkary, R.: Manifestations of everyday design: guiding goals and motivations. In: Proc. C&C 2013, pp. 253–262. ACM (2013)
8. Dourish, P.: The appropriation of interactive technologies: Some lessons from place-less documents. CSCW **12**(4), 465–490 (2003)
9. Greenberg, S., Fitchett, C.: Phidgets: easy development of physical interfaces through physical widgets. In: Proc. UIST 2001, pp. 209–218. ACM (2001)

10. Hardy, R., Rukzio, E., Holleis, P., Wagner, M.: Mystate: sharing social and contextual information through touch interactions with tagged objects. In: Proc. Mobile-HCI 2011, pp. 475–484. ACM (2011)
11. Henderson, A., Kyng, M.: Design at work. chap. There's No Place Like Home: Continuing Design in Use, pp. 219–240. L. Erlbaum Associates Inc. (1992)
12. Heyer, C., Brereton, M.: Design from the everyday: continuously evolving, embedded exploratory prototypes. In: Proc. DIS 2010, pp. 282–291. ACM (2010)
13. Humble, J., Crabtree, A., Hemmings, T., Åkesson, K.-P., Koleva, B., Rodden, T., Hansson, P.: "Playing with the Bits" user-configuration of ubiquitous domestic environments. In: Dey, A.K., Schmidt, A., McCarthy, J.F. (eds.) UbiComp 2003. LNCS, vol. 2864, pp. 256–263. Springer, Heidelberg (2003)
14. Iacucci, G., Kuutti, K.: Everyday life as a stage in creating and performing scenarios for wireless devices. Personal and Ubiquitous Computing 6(4), 299–306 (2002)
15. Iacucci, G., Kuutti, K., Ranta, M.: On the move with a magic thing: role playing in concept design of mobile services and devices. In: Proc. DIS 2000, pp. 193–202. ACM (2000)
16. Klemmer, S.R., Li, J., Lin, J., Landay, J.A.: Papier-mache: toolkit support for tangible input. In: Proc. CHI 2004, pp. 399–406. ACM (2004)
17. Lee, J.J., Lindley, S., Ylirisku, S., Regan, T., Nurminen, M., Jacucci, G.: Domestic appropriations of tokens to the web. In: Proc. DIS 2014, pp. 53–62. ACM, New York
18. Lindley, S.E., Banks, R., Harper, R., Jain, A., Regan, T., Sellen, A., Taylor, A.S.: Resilience in the face of innovation: Household trials with bubbleboard. Int. J. of Human-Computer Studies 67(2), 154–164 (2009)
19. Ljungstrand, P., Redström, J., Holmquist, L.E.: Webstickers: using physical tokens to access, manage and share bookmarks to the web. In: Proc. DARE 2000, pp. 23–31. ACM (2000)
20. Marquardt, N., Taylor, A.S., Villar, N., Greenberg, S.: Rethinking rfid: awareness and control for interaction with rfid systems. In: Proc. CHI 2010, pp. 2307–2316. ACM (2010)
21. Nunes, M., Greenberg, S., Neustaedter, C.: Sharing digital photographs in the home through physical mementos, souvenirs, and keepsakes. In: Proc. DIS 2008, pp. 250–260. ACM (2008)
22. Poynor, R.: The hand that rocks the cradle: Gillian crampton smith is making the royal college of art's computer related design program a multimedia powerhouse. ID-NEW YORK-DESIGN PUBLICATIONS- 42, pp. 60–65 (1995)
23. Rittenbruch, M., McEwan, G., Ward, N., Mansfield, T., Bartenstein, D.: Extreme participation-moving extreme programming towards participatory design. In: Proc. PDC 2002 (2002)
24. Seok, J.M., Woo, J.B., Lim, Y.K.: Non-finito products: a new design space of user creativity for personal user experience. In: Proc. CHI 2014, pp. 693–702. ACM (2014)
25. Shaer, O., Hornecker, E.: Tangible User Interfaces: Past, Present, and Future Directions. Found. Trends Hum.-Comput. Interact 3(1–2), 1–137 (2009)
26. Suchman, L.: Human-machine reconfigurations: Plans and situated actions. Cambridge University Press (2007)
27. Ullmer, B., Ishii, H., Jacob, R.J.: Token+constraint systems for tangible interaction with digital information. TOCHI 12(1), 81–118 (2005)
28. Ylirisku, S., Lindley, S., Jacucci, G., Banks, R., Stewart, C., Sellen, A., Harper, R., Regan, T.: Designing web-connected physical artefacts for the 'aesthetic' of the home. In: Proc. CHI 2013, pp. 909–918. ACM (2013)

Building and Using Home Automation Systems: A Field Study

Alexandre Demeure[1(✉)], Sybille Caffiau[1], Elena Elias[2], and Camille Roux[2]

[1] LIG, INRIA, Universités de Grenoble, Grenoble, France
alexandre.demeure@inria.fr, sybille.caffiau@imag.fr
[2] Floralis, Universités de Grenoble, Grenoble, France
{elena.elias,camille.roux}@multicom-ergonomie.com

Abstract. These last years, several new home automation boxes appeared on the market, the new radio-based protocols facilitating their deployment with respect to previously wired solutions. Coupled with the wider availability of connected objects, these protocols have allowed new users to set up home automation systems by themselves. In this paper, we relate an in situ observational study of these builders in order to understand why and how the smart habitats were developed and used. We led 10 semi-structured interviews in households composed of at least 2 adults and equipped for at least 1 year, and 47 home automation builders answered an online questionnaire at the end of the study. Our study confirms, specifies and exhibits additional insights about usages and means of end-user development in the context of home automation.

Keywords: End user development · Home automation · Field study

1 Introduction

Ubiquitous computing has become a fact, even if in the different way than Weiser originally envisioned [1]. Widespread deployment of networks has supported interpersonal communication and enabled people to access information such as news and encyclopedias, as well as services such as GPS-enabled navigation systems and weather forecast. This range of services is now offered almost everywhere and at anytime via smartphones, tablets or even laptops and has become part of everyday life. Ubiquitous computing also takes place at home based on gateways such as ADSL modems and set-top boxes, providing Wi-Fi local networking with high-speed connection to the Internet as well as rich multimedia services including TV, audio and video sharing. While this mostly represents how Ubiquitous Computing is currently taking place in households, a minority of them is also equipped with a home automation system.

There has been a recent trend in the past few years in the home automation domain: the emergence of radio based technologies (e.g. Z-wave[1] or enOcean[2]) that

---

[1] http://www.z-wave.com/what_is_z-wave
[2] https://www.enocean.com/

© Springer International Publishing Switzerland 2015
P. Díaz et al. (Eds.): IS-EUD 2015, LNCS 9083, pp. 125–140, 2015.
DOI: 10.1007/978-3-319-18425-8_9

enable households to be equipped with sensors and actuators in a way that is much more easy to install and cheaper than previously available through wired solutions such as KNX[3]. Typically, it now becomes possible to get equipped with a home automation system (box plus sensors and actuators) from €150. A quite complete kit can be bought for about €500, which is comparable to the cost of a PC or a tablet. The improvements of their user interfaces and the support those boxes gives using several sensors/actuators technologies tend to lower some of the barriers identified in previous works [2, 3] (cost of ownership, difficulty of preparing the infrastructure, inflexibility and poor manageability of the system) and transform the way people interact with the technology, which calls for new usability and usage studies.

While the literature on home automation systems users, uses and services is wide and varied, a quite complete and up to date review of these studies can be found in [4]. Our goal was to confirm, precise and get additional insights about why and how home automation box users do program their system.

In the rest of the paper, we first describe our protocol and households we recruited. We then discuss our findings and compare them to related works.

2   Study

This study took place in the east of France from spring to autumn 2014. We collected data from inhabitants who has been using a home automation box (such as the Zipabox, Zibase, Vera, eeDomus[4]) for at least one year in their home (at the time of the study) and can be considered as Do-it-yourselfers (as named in [2]).

By sampling participants as such, we aimed at getting an overview of current home automation real setups, the devices and services in use in such households, and their different usages. We also focused on the programs that inhabitants created to fulfill their needs via this system, in particular with regards to how they express such needs via the respective programming tools.

The study was conducted in 10 households, sampled and recruited from forums and researchers' acquaintances. It is composed of two parts: First, the technical referent (i.e. guru (G)) of the households answers an online questionnaire about the structure of the home (e.g. number of rooms), the identity of the inhabitants (age, technology habits, jobs...) and the home automation system characteristics (name of the box, when was it installed, kinds of sensors and actuators). The collected data defines participants' profiles, verifying their fitness in this study (...), as well as help prepare for the second part of the procedure.

A few days after the participant completes the online questionnaire, two members of the households (guru (G) and companion (C)) were interviewed in situ for about 80 minutes. The interviews were video-recorded and photographs were taken after the participants gave consent. During the analysis phase, the videos were textually transcribed before being analyzed and interpreted. During the first 10 minutes, both guru

---

[3] http://www.knx.org/

[4] http://zipabox.domadoo.com, http://www.zodianet.com, http://getvera.com, http://www.eedomus.com

and companion were asked to represent everything they considered as part of the automation system in their home, using A4 paper and pencils. They were then asked to detail and explain the drawings in turn, which led to a description of their view of the installation. Although incomplete, this description highlighted the most significant home automation elements for household members. The semi-structured interview that followed concerned usages of their home automation system (with guru and companion) as well as technical installation and maintainability (with guru only). All participants were French-speaking and interviews were led in French. At the end of the interview, the participants received gift vouchers of €80.

3   Participants

Our study concerned households that can manage their home automation system by themselves (i.e. Do-it-yourselfers as named in [2]). In order to better profile these households, we first posted a link to an online questionnaire on home automation French-speaking forums[5], asking for home automation systems that were in used as well as households characteristics (e.g. members, location). 47 persons (46 males and 1 female) freely answered the questionnaire. Analysis of the questionnaire allowed us to make a list of most commonly used home automation systems.

Table 1. Technical equipment of households

Household	Name	Sensors	Actuators	Programs
H1	Zibase	<5	<5	~15
H2	eeDomus	~20	~50	>150
H3	Crestron	~40	~40	~15
H4	eeDomus	~40	~20	~30
H5	Vera 3	~15	~20	~30
H6	Zibase	~15	~15	~60
H7	HomeSeer 3	~50	~50	~40
H8	Zipabox	~15	~15	~15
H9	Zibase	~15	~20	~60
H10	eeDomus	~15	~15	~30

We then recruited 10 households that were composed of at least two adults, located in or around the south-east of France and equipped with one of the home automation system from the list. Due to location, only some of them were found via the first questionnaire, while others were recruited via forums and acquaintance. In addition to the adult members, 6 households were formed of a couple with 2 children, 1 household with 1 child and 1 household with 3 children. All households were house-owners and lived in a house (composed of 3 to 9 rooms) except the inhabitants of the 8th

---

[5] http://forum.eedomus.com, http://forum.micasaverde, http://fibaro.com, http://abavala.com/forums, www.touteladomotique.com/forum, Google+ communities (S.A.R.A.H, toute la domotique, Domotique Info).

household, who live in a flat. Table 1 summarizes the technical equipment of the households (density levels of actuator, sensor and program are informal values from observation during house visits).

In each household, the guru happened to be male (data consistent with whom answered the online questionnaire). Due to their work domain or their training, 7/10 gurus were knowledgeable in computer science (cf. Table 2). No companion was found knowledgeable in computer science although 4 of them did have scientific training in biology or medical domains.

Table 2. Inhabitants

Guru	Age	Job	Knowledge of computer science	Companion's Job
G1	41-55	Security agent	-	Factory worker
G2	26-40	Technical translator	X	Child-minder
G3	26-40	Electrician	X	Teacher
G4	26-40	Infrastructure security	X	Interior designer
G5	41-55	Engineer	X	Health
G6	26-40	Computer Scientist	X	Realtor
G7	41-55	Manager	X	Engineer Biologist
G8	26-40	Technician	-	Nurse
G9	26-40	Railway technician	-	Administrative officer
G10	26-40	Computer Scientist	X	Manager

4   Analysis

In this section, we will first discuss roles and usages we found with respect to the literature. We will then present how households did choose their home automation system and present an installation overview of home automation in which every household we met can be projected. Last, we will present how these household members controlled and programmed the systems.

4.1   Roles and Usages

Roles. Despite different types of participants (see Table 2), the relationship of household members to the home automation system was quite similar: First, only one member of the household was really interested in setting up and maintaining the home automation system, the male adult (which is consistent with the online survey we led: 46/47 participants were males). The other adult member usually had a more distant relationship with the system, is not really interested what it can do and how, and do not want to spent time dealing with the technology. Actually, she considered the home automation as a hobby for her companion that they have to live with rather than a useful addition to the household. However, they are satisfied when the system works (they find it useful) and get frustrated when it does not.

At least one child lives in 8/10 interviewed households. While we did not interview them, none played an active role in future evolutions of the system, or its installation. The technology seemed to be adapted to them, so they became passive users and often a source of inspiration for gurus' scenarios programming. For example, G5 told us that he programmed the lights in the corridors to turn off automatically because his children often forget to do so.

With respect to [2], the roles identified in the households are *gurus* and *consumers*. No interviewed householder contained a resident who helped the gurus maintain the system (called *assisters* in [5]).

Table 3. Usages of home automation by interviewed households

	Intrusion detection	Monitoring	Automatic control	Heating	Reminder Notification
H1	-	Inhabitants (Camera)	-	Shutters Heaters	-
H2	-	Inhabitants (Camera) Energy consumption	Lights, portal	Heaters	Outing the trash, it's time to go at school
H3	Camera	-	Lights	Shutters	-
H4	Alarm	Inundation, smoke	Swimming pool (filtration)	Heaters	Sensors' state
H5	Alarm, presence simulation	-	Climate, shutters, lights	Shutters	-
H6	Camera	-	Lights	Heaters Shutters	Presence detection (children, guests)
H7	Camera	Energy consumption, Temperature, humidity	Lights, swimming pool (filtration)	Heaters Shutters	-
H8	Alarm	Energy consumption	Shutters	Heaters	-
H9	Camera, presence detection	-	Lights	Heaters Shutters	-
H 10	Camera, alarm	Inhabitants (Camera) Temperature Inundation	Lights, kettle	-	End of the laundry cycle

Usages. The reasons why interviewed households acquire home automation boxes are consistent with literature [3, 4, 6]: Primary motivations are related to energy saving, automatic control and security (intrusion detection). Once this first objective is satisfied by a first installation, evolutions are performed in order to improve the first objective or to take into account new ones (e.g. Activity monitoring, notification). According to the motivation "Experiencing Benefits Increases Interest in Upgrades" [3] several of the evolutions are opportunistic: Gurus create new usages because they found themselves in a situation in which they found home automation systems useful. For example, G2 and G10 used their cameras (installed for intrusion detection) to watch their children play in the living room while lying down in their bed on Sundays.

Table 3 summarizes the usages of home automation by the interviewed households. H5 and H8 wanted to achieve a state of peace of mind as identified by [2, 3, 7]. H2, H3, H6 and H7 were more focused on comfort by delegating some domestic tasks to the system. For G2, these tasks were repetitive, time-consuming and/or unrealizable when household members are not present. To achieve its goal, the home automation system must be applied in a non-intrusive manner. As a consequence, G2 tried to make the system as autonomous as possible so that it acts without needs for others inhabitants to explicitly interact with it. *"It is also what makes my wife feel the home automation less imposing or perceivable because once it is in place, the rules are almost... Finally I would say we no longer modify the implementation, as the home lives its life by itself"*.

4.2   Choice of the Home Automation System

Choosing your home automation system is a task only the guru performed. All the interviewed gurus looked for information about several boxes before buying theirs. They found information on dedicated websites or forums where existing users share their experiences. Four main criteria are cited: economic (price of the set-up box and available sensors and actuators), origin (national product or not) (H9), ease of installation and ease of maintenance. Future users often check compatibility with all connected objects already present at their homes or that they plan to add. For instance, G1 wanted the system to be able to pilot his shutters. Most of the gurus also expressed their concern about having a box able to deal with as much as protocols as possible.

Three households changed their home automation box to migrate toward a more up to date hardware or more powerful and easy to use systems (H2, H4 and H7). However, most of the evolutions concerned adding or removing devices and services. From interviews, we identified three reasons to make the home automation system evolve. First, like all technical installation, home automation system components deteriorate with time so sensors and actuators have to be replaced. Second, in order to fulfill new needs, devices and services may be added. Third, as pointed out by [3], an important motivation for guru is about managing the home automation system, experimenting new devices or services as a hobby.

Evolutions of the home automation system are planned, organized and technically installed by the guru. C2, C4 and C6 intervened in this process to modify an initial installation. For example, C2 asked her husband to switch off the vocal reminder when children are not awake. Moreover, when they plan to include new equipment, or to program a new functionality, gurus usually try to take into account their wife's needs. For example, G7 said he considers the Wife Acceptance Factor (WAF) of any equipment before buying it. That is to say that his wife has to accept the inclusion of the device, considering esthetical aspects but also that the targeted usage will be at least tolerated by her.

4.3   Installation Overview

With respect to [2], we found that the media controller was not considered as being part of the home automation system although every household was equipped with

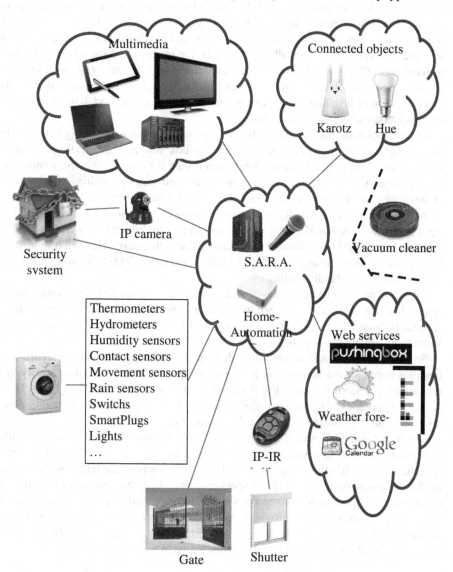

Fig. 1. Devices, services and their connections

advanced media controller. The reason may be that multimedia systems are now widespread: almost every new TV is UPnP compliant and setting up a NASS system is quite common. The other reason is that multimedia systems can work alone, there is no technical need to weave it with into the home automation system, it appears as a separate system, although communications with home automations are possible and sometimes done.

Fig. 1 illustrates the devices we observed in participant's household as well as their connections. No one had all these devices but every participant household can be projected in this schema. What participants tended to consider as home automation is the home automation box coupled with sensors and actuators, automatic gates, shutters. H2, H7, H9 and H10 installed S.A.R.A.H. (or planned to do so soon) in addition to their box. This software enables participant to use voice recognition in order to control their actuators as well as multimedia systems or connected objects. S.A.R.A.H. was installed on PC distinct to the home automation box but accessed sensors and actuators through the box.

Every participant had a multimedia system enabling video streaming between devices (often based on UPnP). Although every box was able to handle multimedia services, height households did not integrated it with the rest of the home automation. They indeed did not need such an integration, as their usage of multimedia and home automation was clearly separate. They were using their multimedia system via dedicated software such as XBMC[6]. However exceptions were found first in household equipped with S.A.R.A.H., who used it to control multimedia rendering. H7 programmed some lights to be turned on when a TV was turned on. H2 used it to help the family routine along: music was played in the bathroom at 7:00 then in the kitchen at 7:15, following the family routine.

Situation was similar for automatic vacuum cleaner: Four participants had such a device but only H2 tried to integrate it with the home automation system, without success because of API problems. His goal had been to trigger the cleaning process when family members were out.

Seven participants had a subsystem dedicated to security. G3 clearly separated it from his home automation system for security reason. He managed the security system via its dedicated software. For the other participants (H2, H4, H6, H7, H9, H10), security was achieved using sensors, shutters and IP cameras. For the later ones, both home automation system and dedicated software were used.

We found some connected objects in participants' household. The most popular was Karotz, present in seven households. It was, or had been, mainly used to notify inhabitants (e.g. "it's time to go to school" or "today wastes are taken out") or as an aesthetic camera+microphone+loud speaker device (e.g. one participant used it to check whether his child was doing homework from his workplace, eventually launching a "do your homework" notification to the child). However, due to the recent decision of the Violet Company to stop the support, some participants simply stop using it. Others turned toward Open-Karotz, an alternative open-source solution.

---

[6] http://kodi.tv/

Last, six participants (H1, H2, H4, H5, H7 and H8) has been interoperating their home automation system with google calendar. This was due to its availability everywhere online, their previous familiarity with the application, often considered better than other calendars provided by their home automation system in every aspect. Other web services were also used such as IFTTT[7], weather forecast and pushing box to send notifications.

4.4   Controlling the System

We observed that inhabitants were interacting with the system throughout 5 interfaces, namely: PC, smartphone, tablet, Karotz, S.A.R.A.H. (vocal command) and dedicated remote controllers for shutters or multimedia. According to our online questionnaire, 36/47 gurus daily interact with the system via a PC or a smartphone. Main usages were for monitoring energy consumption (25/47 use PC and 23/47 use SmartPhone), monitoring system state (39/47 use PC and 28/47 use SmartPhone) and controlling devices (31/47 use PC and 42/47 use SmartPhone). Programming scenarios was achieved almost exclusively using the household's personal computer or laptop (40/47).

Households equipped with S.A.R.A.H. use it to control multimedia (H9), lights and shutters (H2, H7). H2 also used it as a timely reminder for children to go to school. Overall inhabitants that used S.A.R.A.H. were satisfied, but they expressed concerns related to false positive detections. H9 and H7 had to uninstall the system when it was unable to recognize vocal command of the female inhabitant.

Karotz was used the most to send vocal notifications. For instance, G4 says us: *"every morning at 7h45am, if the temperature is less than 5°C then it [Karotz] says: "be careful it's cold outside""*. It has to be noticed that the producer of Karotz recently stopped its support so households had to turn toward open source solution or stopped using it completely.

Last, consistently with [3], all households told us that they considered very important to keep usual ways of interacting with the home such as light switch, remote controllers and switches for shutters and multimedia. Two reasons were cited: First, inhabitants anticipated difficulties of guests confronted to non-standard interaction technologies. Second, they felt more comfortable with the idea of having "traditional" backups as the home automation system turned to be sometime unreliable.

4.5   Scenarios / Programs

We asked participants to present their scenarios (sometime called rules) in order to get a better understanding on how they were programmed. The first finding was the diversity of strategies for naming scenarios. G8 both named scenarios with respect to the device involved (e.g. Plug2), the actions to be triggered (e.g. rain alert), the state of a device to be reached (e.g. full open) or a goal to be achieved (e.g. comfort). Seven gurus used the system's ability to group rules for factorizing conditions

---

[7] https://ifttt.com/

(e.g. sunset) or for expressing semantic proximity (e.g. all rules related to lights time-out). G10 named groups with respect to the environmental property of the targeted change (e.g. Light, Heating). For the Heating group, rules were named with respect to the schema DAYTYPE – ACTIONCONDITION, where DAYTYPE was either a week day, weekend or holiday while other groups where only named by combining related conditions and actions. DAYTYPE was actually used as a way to contextualize rules such as "turn on heating in the morning". Last, H6 used professional naming convention for his scenarios, prefixing names by '#' when scenarios were dedicated to configure devices, '@' when it concerned the system's reaction to events and '_' when scenarios had to be hidden from user interface (equivalent to the private attribute in object programming).

ECA Structure. Contents of the scenarios were either: 1) configuration instructions for a device (e.g. to set up measurement frequency for sensors), 2) scenes (i.e. a configuration of actuators) that could have been defined either by programming or by example or 3) Event Condition Action (ECA) rules. For this later, subtle differences differentiate boxes of the participants:

- ZiBase offers a simple ECA structure, it is possible to specify one event (called stimuli), to express conditions with conjunctions and disjunctions (called criterions) and a list of actions that may contain call to other rules.
- eeDomus offers a slightly different structure. Rules may contain 4 parts: 1) temporal conditions (called schedules), 2) events and conditions other than temporal (called Criterions) that can be combined with conjunctions and disjunctions 3) actions that may contain calls to other rules and 4) notifications such as mailing, texting, etc…
- HomeSeer enables users to regroup rules and to factorize conditions and actions via these groups. Rules have a WHEN THEN structure, the WHEN part containing conditions and events combined through disjunctions of conjunctions. It is also possible to trigger events in the THEN part. For some specific case, G7 wanted to use conditions intertwined. As it was not possible via Homeseer, he used Visual-Basic to program the functionality instead.
- Zipato rules are based on Skratch [8] and enable users to specify quite complex instructions flows, although G8 regretted the absence of control loop such as "do this every N seconds". Rules start with a "when" statement that specify the event which will trigger the rule. IF THEN ELSE and REPEAT structures can be used inside the rule to control instructions execution. While powerful, this can also turn complex. G8 had to use advanced instructions such as "join" (stop other executions of the same rule) and "stop" (stop this execution of the rule) in order to make one of his program work, even though he clearly stated that he did not really understand the meaning of these instructions.
- Programming with Vera is more scene-centered. Users define scenes (devices configuration) and can associate triggers and schedules to them. Conditions cannot be directly expressed inside scenes. Vera enables users to use Lua[8] language to express more complex scenarios.

---

[8] http://www.lua.org/

- Last, Creston offers an application so complicated to program (or even read) rules that we were not able to evaluate it subsequently. The rules used by H3 were complicated to set up even though he was helped by a friend whose job was to install such systems. We can only say that it seems to be based on ECA rules.

Importance of Time. We observed the importance of time in scenarios. All the participants dealt with some time-based rules, for instance to pilot heating system depending on week days, week-ends or holidays. Many participants were not plainly satisfied with the temporal representation offered by their home automation system to trigger rules. As a consequence, they managed to interface with google calendar, either by using dedicated plugins (everyone but H8) or by deploying a google script polling the box with current calendar events (H8). Reasons expressed by participants for doing so lied in their continuous personal and/or professional use of google calendar and wide-spread availability unlike the one proposed by their home automation system.

G2 programmed a quite specific morning scenario, playing music first in the bathroom, then in the kitchen 15mns later. Based on the clock, vocal notifications triggered for kids to go to school and, depending on the day, for throwing the trash. G6 used timeouts to open or close his shutters sequentially as doing it simultaneously led to blowing fuses. G7 used timeouts to turn lights off 1 minutes after any movement was detected by the related sensor. He also considered duration of state to prevent his shutters opening and closing several times at sunset (which is an hour managed by the box, as sunrise): "if the luminosity has been less than 600lux for 10 minutes, then close the shutters".

Usage of Dedicated Modules. In most boxes, it was possible to use modules (i.e. functions) to alleviate scenarios programming. For instance, G1 used in his scenarios a modules provided by Zibase to pilot his thermostat. He first tried to implement the desired behavior by himself but encountered problems due to hysteresis consideration, and therefore adopted the module as soon as it was made available, needing only to configure it for his needs. eeDomus also propose such a template mechanism called "programmation" (ie: programming). A *programmation* is a pre-specified scenario that users have to instantiate and configure for their needs.

For all home automation systems, modules appear as black boxes and are available through constructor websites or directly on the market. We observed that most of the modules were proposed by other users who were expert enough to program them using more advanced languages, such as Lua or Visual Basic. This stresses the importance of the community of users for novice households. Indeed, current or future users help each other to choose home automation box, and deal with installation or programming problems. All of our participants used forums, either as mere readers or as active participants. G5 uses to frequent forum to help other users or exchange with module developers. For instance, he talked profusely with the creator of a VMC manager module, helping to debug it, providing logs and hints. He really enjoyed this experience: *"there is often a lot of follow-up, people are having fun helping others, which is nice"*.

Importance of Interoperability. Except for Creston, all boxes offered some kind of interoperability with other services or devices, mainly through dedicated modules or the possibility to send and receive HTTP requests. G8 was probably the participant that used HTTP the most, although he was not familiar with networks beforehand. His first motivation for using HTTP was to avoid buying dedicated modules for integrating Karotz into his scenarios. He also used HTTP request inside scenarios to send SMS throughout the household set-top box, send notifications via the pushing box web-service, pilot his IP cameras or get informed about electricity rate changes (night/day). Symmetrically, with the help of a friend, he set up google scripts to get interface his calendar with the box, sending HTTP requests to his box containing current agenda events. Other participants used HTTP request to interoperate with external services, for instance G10 used the weather forecast web-service of his town with X-PATH queries to retrieve relevant data.

Another kind of interoperability was about managing shutters and gates as some of them did not offer open APIs. A workaround was to use IP to IR (infrared) devices that were taught association between IR signals and HTTP requests. From the home automation box perspective, this was integrated through the definition of virtual devices.

Variables and Virtual Devices. Seven gurus defined variables for their programs. These variables aimed at representing states (e.g. is the home occupied?), specific values (e.g. how many degrees represent *cold* or *warm* for the heating system), virtual devices (e.g. defining a tailored alarm aside from the one provided by the box by waving together Karotz, as well as a dedicated alarm system and contact sensors). Except in the case of ZiBase and Creston boxes, it was possible for gurus to specify the name of variables which helped users to make sense of them and to use them inside scenarios.

Comments. We found that although rules were most of the time expressed using pseudo natural language, the meaning was not clear enough for participant to explain them to us in return. Some participants explicitly stated that there was a lack of commentary support. The situation was even worse for ZiBase users that have to deal with variables named V1 to V32. G6 and G9 had to maintain a Microsoft Excel^{TM} stylesheet aside their box in order to remember the meaning of each variable.

Comments were also lacking when participants were debugging/tuning their scenarios. For instance, G10 spent time to find the correct detection threshold allowing his motion sensor to ignore the cat that occasionally walks around the door and didn't need the lights. He had to try multiple values for the cat to be ignored while the children weren't for instance. Threshold values were noted aside from the system as there was no commentary support available.

4.6   Testing

The most common way the gurus tested programs was by trial and error, running the program and observing the resulting behavior(s) within the house. However some problems occurred a long time after the program was set up. For instance, two of the households (H2 and H7) did mention that they had to reprogram their shutter for them not to close when night is detected while the corresponding French-window is open. Indeed, they experienced summer evenings where inhabitants stayed late in the garden and found the shutters suddenly closed (originally to keep home temperature ideal). When undesired behavior was reported (by guru or another member of the household), the guru endeavored to debug and fix it. This may mean looking in the system's traces whether messages from sensors were received (which may happen when a sensor battery is low). Traces are also used preventively when programming to check whether rules were triggered, actions performed or events received, even by gurus that do not have computer science training (e.g. G1 used traces to debug his Karotz).

Testing the completion of actions was sometimes rendered impossible. This was the case for G9 who wanted to check whether shutters were opening or closing during the day: During winter, both G9 and his wife go to work before sunrise and come back after twilight so it was not possible for them to check by themselves whether everything happened as programmed. As a consequence, G9 programmed notifications to be sent on his phone whenever shutters were opened or closed, which reassured him even after debugging was done.

In the same vein, testing scenarios sometimes implied to shorter evaluation delays. For instance G9 shorten its heating scenario evaluation frequency from every 10 minutes to every 10 seconds in order to test Hysteresis thresholds. G10 also had to modify the energy consumption measurement frequency of a smart plug alimenting his washing machine in order to be able to detect when it really stopped.

Another strategy was to set up a virtual device to simulate real one and see what happen when setting up specific values. For instance, G5 simulated temperature changes to validate his heating scenarios.

Some boxes provided a test button (eeDomus, ZiBase) associated with scenarios. It actually triggered the ACTION part of the rule, allowing the guru to validate the action. However, it turns to be insufficient as pointed out by G6 for whom it was really difficult to program the EVENT-CONDITION part of scenarios. Indeed, finding out the right sensor values or the right conditions turned out to be the real challenge. G10, for instance, spent time to tune his heating scenarios to take into account holidays, sunset and twilight, sensed lights, presence detection and so on.

A more useful functionality, proposed by a couple of boxes (eeDomus, HomeSeer) was the possibility to navigate between rules and their associated devices or services. This was used by G10 to preventively check the impact of a modification (e.g. removing a sensor) on the system. G8 also used it to turn off scenarios that impact devices in use in scenario he wants to add. For instance, he disenabled scenarios controlling lights when he wanted to test a newly bought light.

5   Discussion

Unlike what was observed in [2] and [3], only two of the households we interviewed did equip their homes with automation systems after major renovations (H7) or building a new home (H9). The gurus of these two households were not able to find skilled professional able to integrate home automation system with the heater (H9) or the electric and data networks (H7). They had to deal with the installation by themselves, which turned to be quite difficult for the heating system of H9. However, H7, H9 and other households took advantage of the fact that their automation system used radio protocol to deploy the home automation system with minor changes to the home: "only" aesthetical consideration had to be taken into account so that other household members did not reject the system outright. This tends to confirm that the evolution of home automation technologies (radio protocols) and the lower costs enable more people to equip with automation systems.

We found that the fundamental motivation of gurus to equip their household was related to their hobbies. Most of them follow the news about home automation, frequent dedicated forums, try to be up to date. The decision to get the technology was often made because of the availability of the new generation of home automation system. Lowering energy consumption, improving security (intrusion detection) or comfort are also real objectives but serve more as a justification for others. This means that most of them are happy to spend time installing and tuning their home automation system. G8 even regretted that it was sometimes too easy, talking about its tailored alarm system: "I was almost frustrated because I did it within 2 minutes and in the end I did not enjoy fiddling with the system, it was almost too simple".

Seven of the gurus we interviewed had some background in computer science, which may explain why they did not encountered extensive problems in programming. However even G1, G8 and G9 who do not have such a background, were able to program their scenarios and make them work. All programming system we considered are based on the Event-Condition-Action (ECA) paradigm, as already pointed out by [9] and [10], peoples are able to use it to express what they want. However, we found that home automation systems provide quite different ways to express ECA rules, it would be interesting to further investigate on forums the advantages and disadvantages of each as perceived by users. One limit that we identified was about grouping rules (and variables) related to a same objective into a consistent object. The roundabout way to deal with that is naming related rules with a same prefix but it does not provide a higher level of abstraction (and understanding) for gurus. We think that some effort should be put in providing ways for gurus to build higher-level abstraction from rules, variables and devices. Virtual devices may be a way to tackle that problem, activity may be another one [11].

It has to be noticed that programming is not limited to specifying ECA rules, some gurus made use of more generalist languages such as Visual Basic, Lua or even google scripts (JavaScript). Of course, only gurus with quite knowledgeable in programming made use of them. What really surprised us was how widespread the usage of HTTP APIs, provided by online services (e.g. weather forecast) or Karotz, was. G8 is the most significant case for that. Although he had no training in computer science, once he understood the principle of HTTP request, he was able to use them numerous times in his programs to communicate with Karotz, online services, his IP to IR bridge and even google script. Every system we considered did offer a way to send HTTP request, some also offer ways to specify HTTP request to be received (by specifying a virtual device as for G8). It seems to us that it is a quite simple and powerful way to make things communicate inside the home, even for non-professional programmers.

Current home automation systems lack of support for conception. This manifested through the inability for gurus to enter comments related to the threshold values they use, the meaning of their variables or the raison d'être of some rules. More generally speaking, we think that home automation systems should provide support for the conception process: expressing needs, considering options, discussion, adding tests, bug tracking etc. In some sense, this is close to Mennicken's claims [3] for the necessity of taking into account the different stages for creating a smart home. These stages would have to provide support for higher level goal or even for expressing household values [11, 12] and could lead a first step for integrating other household members who currently prefer staying aside. Indeed, gurus' companions seemed to be mere passive users of the system and this is somehow surprising when considering that they have been literally living inside the system for at least one year. This may be due to a lack of interest in that kind of technology but also on the feeling of being unable to take control of it. For instance, C2 expressed her desire to disable smartphones and TV during the dinner time, therefore using the system to enforce a family rule but she just thought that it was impossible. Other companions manifested interest when talking about high-level goal (e.g. managing stocks, keeping the home quiet when the baby was sleeping).

Last, we have to stress the importance of home automation online communities that exist around dedicated websites and forums. While gurus are currently quiet isolated geographically (only G9 physically knew someone with who to talk about home automation), these online communities are the main source of information as to give and share advices about systems, devices, installation problem, etc. It represents also a source of inspiration of possible usages and a place to discuss feedbacks. As pointed out by [4] and observed on services like IFTTT, rules created by the community can be proposed to gurus in order to inspire them. What we suggest is that not only rules should be made available in such a way but also discussions, goals, problems and solutions, etc. In other word, we suggest that it would be interesting to tackle end user development for the smart home from a social perspective and build tools accordingly.

6   Conclusion

We presented a study about current households equipped with a home automation system installed and managed by inhabitants themselves. We interviewed 10 households composed of at least 2 adult members that have lived with their system for at least one year. Our goal was to confirm, precise and get additional insights about why and how home automation box users program their system.

We observed that roles of gurus and consumers are defined before the introduction of the home automation system and they do not seem to change over time. We established the topography of devices and services and noticed that there were similarities across households. We also noticed that vocal interaction was getting popular via S.A.R.A.H.

We compared the programming languages proposed by the different systems, all are based upon ECA structures but presenting subtle differences. The interoperability between sensors, actuators, and connected objects does not seem to appear difficult to use by the gurus when taking into account their choice of box. Thanks to forums and online communities, they learn how program and capitalize on the features of their box.

Based on these observations and the conclusions of related works, we presented several research avenues for home automation system in the discussion.

Acknowledgements. This work has been supported by the European Catrene project AppsGate.

References

1. Rogers, Y.: Moving on from weiser's vision of calm computing: engaging ubicomp experiences. In: Dourish, P., Friday, A. (eds.) UbiComp 2006. LNCS, vol. 4206, pp. 404–421. Springer, Heidelberg (2006)
2. Bernheim Brush, A.J., Lee, B., Mahajan, R.: Home automation in the wild: challenges and opportunities. In: CHI 2011. Vancouver, Canada (2011)
3. Mennicken, S., Huang, E.M.: Hacking the natural habitat: an in-the-wild study of smart homes, their development, and the people who live in them. In: Kay, J., Lukowicz, P., Tokuda, H., Olivier, P., Krüger, A. (eds.) Pervasive 2012. LNCS, vol. 7319, pp. 143–160. Springer, Heidelberg (2012)
4. Mennicken, S., Vermeulen, J., Huang, E.M.: From today's augmented houses to tomorrow's smart homes: new directions for home automation research. In: UBICOMP 2014, pp. 105–115. Seattle, Washington, USA (2014)
5. Poole, E., Chetty, M., Grinter, R., Edwards, W..: More then meets the eye: transforming the user experience of home network management. In: DIS 2008, pp. 455–464 (2008)
6. Björkskog, C.: Human Computer Interaction in Smart Homes (2007)
7. Takayama, L., Pantofaru, C., Robson, D., Soto, B., Barry, M.: Making technology homey: finding sources of satisfaction and meaning in home automation. In: UbiCom 2012, Pittsburgh, PA, USA (2012)
8. Maloney, J., Resnick, M., Rusk, N., Silverman, B., Eastmond, E.: The Scratch Programming language and Environment. ACM Trans. Comput. Edication, 10 (2010)
9. García-Herranz, M., Haya, P., Alamán, X.: towards a Ubiquitous End-user Programming System for Smart Spaces. J. Univers. Comput. Sci. **16**, 1633–1649 (2010)
10. Ur, B., McManus, E., Pak Yong Ho, M., Littman, M.L.: Pratical trigger-action programming in the smart home. In: CHI 2014, pp. 803–812. Toronto, Ontario, Canada (2014)
11. Demeure, A., Caffiau, S., Coutaz, J.: Activity based end-user-development for smart homes: relevance and challenges. In: Workshop HyperCities (Intelligent Environments), Shanghai, pp. 141–152 (2014)
12. Davidoff, S., Lee, M.K., Yiu, C., Zimmerman, J., Dey, A.K.: Principles of smart home control. In: Dourish, P., Friday, A. (eds.) UbiComp 2006. LNCS, vol. 4206, pp. 19–34. Springer, Heidelberg (2006)

FRAMES – A Framework for Adaptable Mobile Event-Contingent Self-report Studies

Julian Dax, Thomas Ludwig[✉], Johanna Meurer, Volkmar Pipek, Martin Stein, and Gunnar Stevens

Institute for Information Systems, University of Siegen, Siegen, Germany
{julian.dax,thomas.ludwig,johanna.meurer,volkmar.pipek,
martin.stein,gunnar.stevens}@uni-siegen.de

Abstract. With the emergence of smart, sensor-equipped mobile devices, the gathering and processing of data concerning the everyday lifestyles of the people using these devices has become a matter of course within the field of HCI. New standards in mobile technologies provide new opportunities for empirical studies, which allow researchers to explore people's everyday lives unobtrusively. Furthermore, mobile, sensor-based approaches enhance empirical studies by automatically recognizing events of interest such as the arrival at specific locations. In this paper we describe how end-user development can be used to empower researchers without technical expertise to adjust their empirical studies to the individual dynamics of daily life. To do so, we implemented and evaluated the framework 'FRAMES' that allows researchers to flexibly specify and adopt mobile event-contingent self-report studies. The evaluation shows the potential of our framework for spontaneous customizations of the study without the need for redeployment or modification of the application.

Keywords: Self-report · End-user development · Mobile devices · Complex event processing

1 Introduction

Today smartphones and tablets are widespread throughout the population. Due to the fact that mobile devices have become constant companions for most people, their locations are implicitly determined by their owners who dynamically change locations [1]. Mobile applications use the sensors which are integrated in the devices (such as GPS, microphone, Bluetooth, accelerometer, etc.) to support their owner in a situation. With the rising popularity of mobile devices, a number of research approaches as well as technical solutions related to capturing and studying user behavior 'in the wild' have arisen [2–4]. Specifically, smartphones, as silent companions, allow researchers to gain insights into people's individual everyday lives. This in turn enables them to perform new kinds of so-called self-report studies using smartphone applications which support the recording of participants' experiences [5].

Whenever researchers are interested in certain aspects of the smartphone owners' lives, it means they often have to deal with routine behavior which is hard to capture.

© Springer International Publishing Switzerland 2015
P. Díaz et al. (Eds.): IS-EUD 2015, LNCS 9083, pp. 141–155, 2015.
DOI: 10.1007/978-3-319-18425-8_10

This can cause several recall-related problems which worsen in proportion to the time which elapses between the occurrence of the event itself and the recording of it [6, 7]. Reports that can be made either during or immediately after the occurrence of the event can help to address this challenge. In particular, "event-contingent studies" request users (automatically) to submit their reports immediately after or during the occurrence of a subject of matter (event) [8]. However, how researchers adjust such event-contingent studies based on the actual dynamics of a user's life presents a huge challenge. This paper deals with the research questions: (1) How can researchers be enabled to react dynamically to the subjects of matter in advance; and (2) how can researchers take advantage of IT-support to study individual user behavior in-situ and to react to the dynamically changing mobile context during an empirical study? In the following, we analyze related work and the specific methodological approaches to study users' behaviors 'in the wild' and possibilities that the field of end-user development (EUD) offers. Based on this literature review, we derived an approach that allows the flexible combination of smartphone sensors and event-contingent dynamical configurations. We implemented the framework "FRAMES", which is intended to support researchers in defining and adjusting their studies, and encourage 'researched' users to respond to open as well as closed questions triggered by certain events. Further, we evaluated FRAMES' usability qualitatively. In addition to discussing the results of the evaluation with regard to EUD and studying mobile contexts, we also draw conclusions on the usability and applicability of EUD in the context of event-contingent studies.

2   Capturing Everyday Experiences in Mobile Contexts

The rapid dissemination of mobile devices and their ever-increasing role in our everyday lives fosters methodological approaches which allow researchers to appropriately study mobile behavior 'in the wild' [9]. Especially within the field of HCI, new approaches arose, which enable behaviors and actions in mobile contexts to be captured by observing the use of mobile devices. These approaches also provided new options for requesting in-situ feedback in connection with observed behavior.

Mobile probes are contextual and dynamic self-documenting tools for studying people's actions in mobile contexts as well as their related intentions, motivations or attitudes [10]. (Mobile) diary studies [6] and the experience sampling method [11] are viewed as appropriate methods for capturing users' data in situ [12]. They include user-driven reporting of their own behavior in mobile contexts. In diary studies, based on researchers' specifications, users decide when and which information is worth reporting. There are forms of voice-based diaries or photo-based diaries [9] as well as combined methods designed for specific contexts [13]. All the forms have in common that the entries and contextual data (e.g. location, time) have to be reported manually [14]. Brandt et al. [15] present variations in which users in specific situations send so-called 'snippets'. These are short diary notes which allow the users to complete the entry at a later time.

These traditional paper-based diary studies are comparable to the experience sampling method, with the main difference being that experience sampling actively reminds the user to report details on his/her current situation at specific times. But both methods are too time-consuming and by completing the entries users are crowded out of the current context [16, 17]. These self-reporting methods do, however, offer the opportunity to capture the user's intention, which is another important source of information when attempting to understand participants' every day contexts.

Life-logging technology represents another approach for gathering detailed information about users' behavior. Life-logging is a concept that aims at automatic recording of user behaviors and consists of "the continuous capture of personal data: such as photos from one's field-of-view, location, audio, biometric signals and others, with the aim of supporting the later recall and reflection over one's life events and experiences" [4]. Due to the fact that nowadays a mobile device has become a highly personalized tool for individuals, it is more or less omnipresent – at hand at any time and in every place [1]. Thus mobile data logging represents a significant part of life logging. Data logging means that a device automatically collects various context and usage data, which would otherwise be very hard and time-consuming to capture, without any user interaction at all [18].

There are already approaches that combine automatic data logging with self-reporting mechanisms. Froehlich et al. [18] present a system that combines the logging of phone data with mobile experience sampling by triggering surveys at specific moments of interest. Liu et al. [19] argue that mixed methods are required to gather appropriate information about users' behavior.

Although there are currently several approaches for gathering in-situ information about a user, they all struggle with several issues: researchers failing to precisely define situations or actions of interest in advance [6], (to some extent resulting in) participants misidentifying or missing relevant events [6, 8], which can lead to belated note taking or sampling [8]. Our study aims to address these issues and examines how researchers can be supported by IT to allow flexible definitions and modifications of study interests on the one hand and assistance for participants to recognize relevant situations and events on the other hand.

3 End-User Development

To empower researchers to dynamically adjust the framework according to their particular interests of "in the wild"-studies we followed an EUD approach. EUD is defined by the ambition to develop "methods, techniques, and tools that allow users of software systems, acting as non-professional software developers, to create, modify or extend a software artifact at some point" [20]. The paradigm of EUD is based on the vision of tailorability. It asks how end users can be provided with support to incorporate and adapt software artifacts to their work practice. Hence, in this definition the efforts of EUD aim to soften the boundaries between end users and professional developers as well as within use and development.

We are, therefore, dealing with the issue of adaptability. This concept goes back to the definition of Henderson and Kyng [21] who focus on adaptable components of artifacts within a specific context of use: "The distinction then is: if the modifications are to the subject matter of tool then we think of it as use; if the modifications are to the tool itself, then it is tailoring" [21]. According to this definition, adaptability is a relative term that refers to the application context. However, the claim of adaptability necessitates differentiation within EUD-research. This is because a distinction has to be made between the research related to end-user participation *during the design-phase*, and research related to study adjustments during runtime. While the first aims to address the users' specific requirements, the latter promotes higher flexibility of the system, on which we focus.

According to Henderson and Kyng [21], tailorability should be understood as an important feature of software artifacts to enable situated development. From this stance, customization is relative to the use context and leads to a fundamentally new design methodology. Once monolithic architectures that were hard to adapt to new requirements had been overcome, much research and development was carried out to create more flexible software systems. As a result, modern software architectures provide more sophisticated opportunities for tailoring software artifacts in the use context. Particularly in the field of CSCW, several research prototypes have been built as proofs by construction following the principle of radical tailorability [22]. Prominent examples for Domain-oriented Design Environment are JANUS [23], OVAL, Prospero [24], FreEvolve [25] or CoCoWare [26]. EUD research on tailorable software architectures strongly intersects with research on software architectures for Software Product Lines. Both rely on the same idea of flexibilization. Yet, studying tailoring in isolation, EUD research has a techno-centric tendency to see flexibility as an end in itself. In particular, by reading design studies such as OVAL [22] or Prospero [24], EUD seems to be reduced to the technical challenge of increasing flexibility, following the idea that more flexibility automatically leads to more - and in this view - better EUD. Research that follows such a paradigm mainly reduces EUD to a quantitative problem of optimizing the trade-off between enhancing flexibility and dealing with increasing complexity; it thus loses the emancipatory ambition.

Thus the challenge for providing benefits by applying concepts of EUD to the design of self-report frameworks is to lower the cost of learning while keeping or broadening the scope of applicability. To do so, it becomes necessary to address the question: What kind of flexibility makes sense and is needed in the specific domain context of mobile event-contingent self-report systems? This, then, becomes the center of our research. In order to provide such an ideal EUD-environment, we have to provide the right flexibility at the right time, in the right place and in the right way. As previously mentioned, this task cannot be solved simply by increasing the tailoring options of an application; furthermore, to support the fact that various researchers have diverse interests, it becomes necessary to consider carefully which elements are required.

4   A Concept for an Adaptable Mobile Event-Contingent Self-report System

The literature review shows that several approaches for capturing mobile everyday experiences and behavior exist, but that they fall short in terms of flexibility. EUD concepts offer opportunities which allow researchers to study issues arising from participants' everyday lives 'in the wild' more easily. They also provide tools to modify the study design. In order to develop ICT support for an adaptable mobile event-contingent self-report system, we intend to show how the aforementioned implications of the EUD discourse can be applied. Based on the literature review, Table 1 shows the challenges to be faces when adjusting an event-contingent study to the dynamics of context-based field-work according to an EUD viewpoint. Based on these, we derived the design implications for the frameworks' architecture.

Table 1. Literature-based Design Challenges and resulting Technical Implications

No	Identified Issue	Design Challenge	Technical Implications
1	Current tools focus mainly on researchers with considerable technical experience.	Enable researchers without any programming skills to conduct event-contingent self-report studies.	Avoiding unnecessary application details or configurations and relying on graphical user interfaces to set up studies.
2	Current tools focus on particular studies needing a particular line of inquiry but struggle to provide an overall framework.	Enable identification and definition of varying and commonly shared attributes of studies. Differentiation between flexible and fixed subjects of matter.	Incorporate shared aspects of different studies at implementation level; all variable parts must be tailorable (e.g. locations or situations of interest).
3	Current tools struggle with flexibility and lack a systematic approach to allow modifications towards adaption on different research contexts.	Enable flexibility of the study's focus and utility and allowing researchers to filter and fuse data according to their interests which need to be addressed flexibly.	Enable flexibility of the study's focus and utility to allow researchers the ability to filter and fuse data according to their interests.
4	Tools do not deliver insights into the data during ongoing studies.	Allow researchers to monitor data collection during the study, to make adjustments.	Providing options for accessing collected data in ongoing studies.
5	Current approaches do not allow a dynamic reaction on changing study foci.	Enable researchers to be able to dynamically define events and to distinguish relevant information from noise.	Providing options for adjusting the studies during runtime to revise or readjust events.

5   Implementation of FRAMES

The overall goal of the architecture is to present researchers with a universal framework to define events of interest and start predefined surveys on the mobile device, when these events occur – especially for technical non-experienced researchers. We therefore implemented a framework for adaptable mobile event-contingent self-report studies (called FRAMES), which has been developed on the backdrop of the aforementioned technical needs, facing the challenge of providing researchers with a universal mobile self-reporting framework that is flexible enough for studies 'in the wild' and that allows changing study foci.

5.1   Complex Event Processing

The circumstances causing the occurrence of an event can be very complex. Thus, a system-automated recognition of such events needs to be highly flexible and extensible. A promising approach is the use of complex event processing approaches. "Complex event processing (CEP) is a set of techniques and tools to help us understand and control event-driven information systems" [27]. Luckham defines a complex event as one that can only happen if other events happened before.

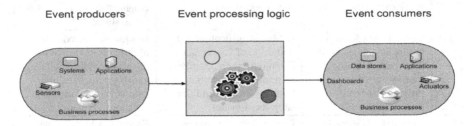

Fig. 1. Architecture of CEP-based systems (Etzion & Niblett, 2010)

In CEP systems or engines (CEPE) events are generated by three different kinds of event producers: sensors, other IT systems and the CEPE itself [27]. The CEPE can be a source for events by aggregating simpler events into more complex ones. The CEPE's event processing logic is able to recognize patterns in a stream of events and reacts to the occurrence of these patterns. These patterns are defined in an "event pattern language" (EPL) [27]. Based on these patterns, rules are defined that combine a pattern with one or more actions which should be carried out when the particular pattern occurs. The actions can be defined in EPL as well, but oftentimes it is also possible to define them in a general purpose programming language.

As events are the central entity in CEPEs, they are a natural fit for event-contingent studies. CEPEs also allow the creation, deletion and modification of rules and patterns at runtime, which renders them very adaptable to the changing needs of researchers. From a purely software engineering standpoint, the use of CEPEs leads to a separation of event detection and the rest of the system. Thus modifying the definition of rules for event detection does not require redeployment or any change to the rest of the system.

5.2   Supporting Researchers to Define Studies

As pointed out earlier, one of the main challenges in setting up event-contingent studies is the ambiguity that arises from a lack of precision when introducing the topic of interest to the participants. Researchers provide ill-defined situations or events, making it cumbersome for study participants to identify the relevant events. This may not only cause the study to produce data which is only partially useful, but also makes it difficult to compare different studies. Thus we developed a web-based editor based on EPL which allows researchers to define events using a graphical user interface (GUI). The editor (Fig. 2) ensures that researchers define those situations which are relevant to the study, rendering them unambiguously recognizable by mobile devices equipped with the appropriate sensors.

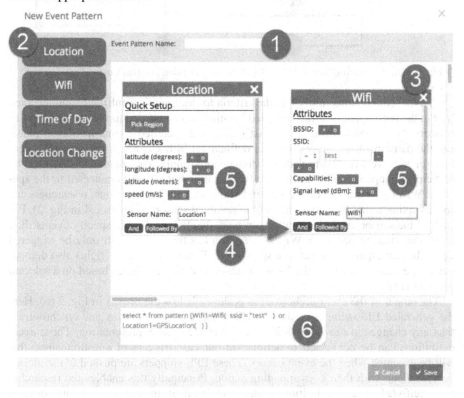

Fig. 2. Web Based Editor for Event Definition

In this example it is possible to see how the researchers can create event patterns that can be recognized by the participants' devices. Firstly, (1) researchers name the patterns they are going to create. From the available sensors list (2), they can drag and drop relevant sensor events to the canvas (3). The list of sensors can be extended easily by providing JSON-based sensor descriptions including a name for the sensor as well its list of attributes and how these can be compared to each other (e.g. greater/less than, etc.). Generally, the sensors available in the editor are a fixed set of all currently available sensors. Even though it is easy to extend the editor with new sensors (as described), its respective counterpart has to be implemented / configured on the device (e.g. if the researcher aims to use a specific device capable of collecting data from a particular sensor that is not covered by the framework currently used for sensor data collection). These sensor events can be connected (see 4 in figure 2 for non-connected events and 4 in figure 3 for connected events) through "AND", "OR" or "Followed-by" connections.

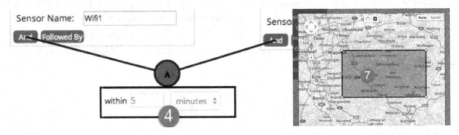

Fig. 3. Left: Connecting two events - Right: Setting location attributes using "quick setup"

"AND"-connections imply that the criteria for the event are fulfilled simultaneously, e.g. the participant is at the specified location and connected to the specified Wi-Fi network. "OR"-connections imply that one of the specified events has taken place; e.g. the participant is connected to the defined Wi-Fi but is not at the specified location (or vice versa). "Followed-By"-connections imply a sequential order, e.g. the participant happened to be at the specified location but left and connected to the specified Wi-Fi afterwards. For "AND" and "Followed-By" connections, researchers can specify a timeframe for occurrence of the involved sensor events (see 4 in Fig. 2). For each of the sensor events, attributes can be defined (5) to further specify events. E.g. using the attribute SSID for Wi-Fi events implies that events will only be triggered when the participants connect to a specific Wi-Fi network. Fig. 2 (right) also demonstrates the "quick setup" of the location sensor to define attributes based on a selected geo region (7).

The output of the event orchestration is shown below the canvas in Fig. 2 (6). Here the generated EPL-snippet is shown. The snippet and the canvas are synchronized, thus any changes to one of both is reflected in the other representation. These event definitions can be connected to actions (in our case triggers of questionnaires) that will be executed when the event occurs. These EPL-snippets are pushed to the mobile devices along with their corresponding action. Principally this enables the researcher to specifiy/adapt his definition easily and push it to the participants' devices immediately without changing any source code or adjusting settings. In the following we will describe how the mobile client is designed handle these definitions.

5.3   Mobile Event recognition

In order to detect the events defined by the researchers, we used the Esper complex event processing engine. Esper is an open source CEPE (Complex Event Processing Engine) that has been ported to Android and is only about 6MB in size. Further we used the Funf framework [28] to capture sensor data from the smartphone from more than 15 sources including e.g. location, Wi-Fi and running apps. This data is then sent to Esper. The EPL patterns, which were defined on the server, are downloaded via a REST API as soon as they become available. This API provides a JSON file containing the EPL and the ID-numbers of the actions it should trigger, which in our case are surveys initially. The Esper CEPE is designed as a background service and communicates with the rest of the application using Android's intent system: Sensor data is sent to the CEPE using these intents and when a complex event is found, another intent is sent back to the application. The application reacts to this intent via a common broadcast receiver by presenting the respective survey to the user. This architecture (as shown in Fig. 4) is easily extendable with new sensorial inputs. Yet as these sensors are hardware- and operating system-specific, both the reading of the sensor data and forwarding the data to the Esper CEPE need to be carried out manually.

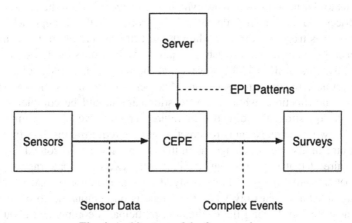

Fig. 4. Architecture of the framework

6   Evaluation

To evaluate FRAMES, we conducted two types of evaluation. The first was a technical functionality test 'in-the-wild' whereby various events were defined and tested to discover if the respective action is triggered (Fig. 5, left). The second evaluation took the form of a usability and applicability study of the web frontend (Fig. 5, right).

Fig. 5. Technical (left) and Usability Evaluation (right)

6.1   Technical Evaluation

Within the technical evaluation of FRAMES, we equipped four students with mobile devices and pre-installed our framework. After this we defined four event patterns in the backend system. The first pattern was expected to trigger when the students were on campus. At first, we did not take into account that this first defined pattern matched every time when a new location was added to the CEPE. This resulted in two students receiving prompts to complete the same survey several times during their stay at the university. The solution could be to alter the event pattern definition slightly, so that it only triggers once a day. Next we defined a more complex event: the student's phone detecting a certain Wi-Fi network is the trigger designed to switch on the screen of the phone. This was used for precise indoor location detection. It enabled us to define a questionnaire which was triggered when the student drew near to our offices and used his mobile phone. The problem with this approach was that the notification was triggered directly when the screen was turned on, i.e. at a time when users generally want to accomplish a certain task. It is possible to add a pause after the event triggers in the CEPE; however, at the time of the study, our visual editor was not yet able to support this feature. Another way to address this problem would be to show notifications whenever a questionnaire should be completed, instead of showing the questionnaire directly. In future versions, we plan to implement both options. Showing the questionnaire directly, and not requiring the user first to tap on a notification can also be advantageous in that the participant is "forced" to answer the questionnaire at that very moment. Besides these two event patterns, we further defined a pattern which triggered every day at 10a.m. and another one which triggered every day at 10 a.m. but only when the phone is on campus. Both of these patterns worked as expected. During the evaluation, participants complained about decreased battery life. This was caused by the gathering of sensor data and could already be addressed to some extent by the implementation of our own location tracking mechanism, as the one used by the funf framework was very energy consuming. However, logging sensor data will always take a certain toll on battery life.

6.2   Usability Evaluation

Our second type of evaluation focused on the interaction concept of FRAMES and its usability from an end user perspective. We were primarily concerned with identifying whether and in which ways the application would be used; what difficulties in use might be encountered; and if the designed components are adequate from an EUD point of view. The philosophy behind the evaluation process was derived from the notion of 'situated evaluation' [29] in which qualitative methods are used to draw conclusions about the real-world use of a technology involving experts. The aim here is not to measure the relationship between evaluation goals and outcomes, but to derive subjective views from the experts about how useful and relevant the technology might be in use.

We therefore conducted three workshops with experts in the field of qualitative research and additionally enlisted a group of five researchers to evaluate the usability in practice. We asked the participants to use the "thinking aloud" - protocol, which is "the single most valuable usability engineering method" according to Nielsen [30]. The "thinking aloud" method is a qualitative method, whereby participants describe their thoughts while using the software. This way, researchers can gain insights into the participants' understanding of the software. According to Nielsen [30], thinking aloud studies should be conducted with three to five participants. For this reason, we chose five participants (A-E) for our evaluation (Table 3). We aimed at a cross selection of participants ranging from privacy research or social science to crisis research. By focusing on different areas, our aim was a comprehensive overview of possible end users. All interviews were audio-recorded and transcribed for later data analysis.

Table 2. Evaluation participants

No.	Role	Research Area	Technical Experienced
A	PhD student Information Systems	Crisis Research	Yes
B	PhD student Social Science	Elderly Research	No
C	PhD student Information Systems	Mobility Research	Yes
D	Senior researcher Privacy	Privacy Research	Yes
E	PhD student Social Science	Usability Research	No

We separated the evaluation into three segments: (1) An introduction to the editor, (2) a user-study to fulfill certain tasks with the editor and (3) a less structured open feedback at the end. Within the introduction, the framework as well as its motivation was explained to the researchers. In the second phase, the participants were asked to define the following five events:

1. An event that is triggered when a participant is on campus;
2. An event that starts every morning at eight o'clock;
3. An event that is triggered when a participant is on campus at eight o'clock;
4. An event that is triggered whenever a participant changes his location;
5. An event that is triggered whenever the participant leaves campus.

In the third phase, participants were given the opportunity to make suggestions for improvement, summarize their experiences, and explore the editor on their own. The results of the evaluation can be summarized in four categories:

1. *EPL Text Field / Expert Mode:* It was especially the technically-experienced participants (C, D) who recognized the potential of the text field where users could define EPL-code (Fig. 2, no 6). One of the technically non-experienced participants (B) accidentally clicked on the text field and modified the code by mistake. The participant suggested locking this particular text field. Such functionality was asked to shift the current view to an expert mode, where technically experienced users can modify the code directly by themselves. Since most of the EPL-code is the same, participant E wanted to conceal the identical parts, just allowing the modification of changeable fields.

2. *Complex Event Definitions:* For the participants, it was often not obvious whether an event was single or complex (participant B). It was especially difficult to recognize events like location in combination with location changes as being a complex event. Further, participant A mentioned that it hadn't been conveyed that each event pattern needs its own label before it can be saved. It was not clear to any of the participants how the various event patterns could be combined. Participants B, C and D missed an option for linking two event windows. "Can one event be followed by two other events?" (Participant B). One suggestion was not to link events using lines and logical operators but instead to nest events within other events. "Why did you not simply make 'And' boxes?" (Participant D) That means a grouping of events within other events and organizing their relations with "and", "or" or "followed by".

3. *Fixed vs. Dynamic Events:* The decision to distinguish between fixed (e.g. locations) and dynamic events (changed locations) and to integrate all of them in the left sidebar without any visual separation was considered to be problematic by all participants. "We are talking about two different things... First, the fixed states and then those that have a transitional character" (participant B). Participant D suggested a working surface, where only the possible options relating to combinations of fixed and dynamic states are presented.

4. *Comments and Feedback:* Participants A and B both suggested integrating tool tips or explanations of each event as they are not always self-explanatory. They asked for a function allowing them to comment on events or event patterns so that other users could assess the pattern's intents directly. "We need a textual description of what we have modeled" (Participant E). In addition to such explanations, the participants requested options for giving feedback on event patterns.

7   Discussion and Conclusion

Being interested in certain aspects of smartphone owners' lives means that researchers generally have to deal with routine behavior that is hard to capture. New standards in mobile technologies - such as smart, sensor equipped mobile devices - offered researchers new opportunities for field-work, allowing them to explore people's everyday mobile lives. However, field-work can take place in a wide range of contexts and settings which require a variety of alternatives to gather and process empirical data. Be that as it may, researchers, who are interested in empirical qualitative studies, often have no programming skills that allow them to configure or adapt new or existing tools according their investigation interests. Challenging this issue, we analyzed related work on mobile event-based self-report studies. Based on the literature review, we identified the requirements for a universal framework including smartphone sensors and event-contingent dynamical configurations. Mobile, sensor-based approaches enhance empirical studies by automatically recognizing interesting events such as the arrival at specific locations. Methodically, we chose an EUD approach to design the framework flexibly and render it adaptable 'in the wild', particularly enabling those researchers who have no technical training. Based on these requirements, we have implemented the framework "FRAMES" which is intended to support both research-ers in defining and adjusting their studies, and users to respond to open and closed questions triggered by certain (complex) events. In particular, the framework aims to provide a flexible combination of smartphone sensors and dynamical event-contingent configurations.

We employed qualitative user studies to evaluate FRAMES according to the chal-lenges raised not only when providing users with a universal framework but also regard-ing usability issues questioning whether researchers are able to make use of the system in different settings. With regard to the first point (1) it emerged that the researchers are able to set-up the self-report studies using FRAMES related to the scenarios without any programming skills. After a short introduction it was possible for all users to define rules without modifying the client's software at implementation level. This indicates that the EUD-approach is appropriately included into the framework. Additionally, FRAMES aims to incorporate most of the sensorial capabilities of today's devices as postulated in the second point (2). Particularly in the mixed scenarios, researchers were forced to use different sensors. Furthermore, in the more open-ended discussions, users stated that they could imagine adopting the system according to their particular research contexts and interests.

Further (also addressing issue 3), even if context specific sensors are used, FRAMES can easily be extended for this purpose. Yet, as mentioned above, this needs to be extended at software level ("fixed parts"). This can be carried out unproblematically but nevertheless requires programming knowledge.

Regarding the fourth aspect (4), FRAMES is integrated into another application [31] responsible for uploading and visualizing collected data. Nevertheless, based on this visualization, it emerged that researchers were able to modify current studies as demanded in (5). This can easily be accomplished by using FRAMES as the architec-ture allows rule definitions to be pushed and exchanged during runtime.

In general, FRAMES incorporates the advantages of other prototypes, e.g. [2, 18, 19] by eliminating the necessity of participants having to recognize events and dy-namically adjusting studies to users' actual lives. This has several advantages: for example, very complex event descriptions can be expressed in EPL, which would be extremely hard to recognize manually. It also facilitates the study of many different kinds of events without confusing or overburdening the participant. Lastly, because FRAMES runs as a background service, event recognition is accomplished conti-nuously and does not need to be activated by the participant. This way, users do not need to think about the study permanently and actively remember their data entry task continuously, but are rather only reminded of it when necessary.

In this work, we have focused strongly on the researchers' point of view. Within the scope of future work, we plan to include the issue of a cooperative study design that would allow research groups to work together. Furthermore, we plan a long-term evaluation of the framework in real life research settings. This might provide more detailed insights into the usefulness of the framework and whether the EUD-approach is appropriate settled 'in the wild'. In particular, a long-term study could provide in-sights, if the formal definition of events fits with researcher's interests. Moreover, we want to explore how the editor could help researchers to a better understanding of the event patterns they are defining. One participant in our usability evaluation suggested the automatic generation of a description text for the modeled event patterns or sharing them with other users. Simulating incoming events in the editor and considering if and when the pattern is triggered could potentially be another way to help researchers develop patterns in a more interactive way. Moreover, we are investigating possibilities to port the framework to different mobile and desktop operating systems.

References

1. Fortunati, L.: The mobile phone: local and global dimensions. In: Nyíria, K. (ed.) A Sense of Place. The Global and the Local in Mobile Communication, pp. 61–70. Wien (2005)
2. Böhmer, M., Hecht, B., Johannes, S., Krüger, A., Bauer, G.: Falling asleep with angry birds, facebook and kindle – a large scale study on mobile application usage. In: Proceedings of the 13th International Conference on Human Computer Interaction with Mobile Devices and Services, pp. 47–56. ACM, Stockholm, Sweden (2011)
3. Do, T., Gatica-Perez, D.: By their apps you shall understand them: mining large-scale patterns of mobile phone usage. In: Proceedings of the 9th International Conference on Mobile and Ubiquitous Multimedia, p. 27. ACM (2010)
4. Gouveia, R., Karapanos, E.: Footprint tracker: supporting diary studies with lifelogging. In: Proceedings of the Conference on Human Factors in Computing Systems, pp. 2921–2930. ACM (2013)
5. Christensen, P., Mikkelsen, M.R., Nielsen, T.A.S., Harder, H.: Children, Mobility, and Space: Using GPS and Mobile Phone Technologies in Ethnographic Research. J. Mix. Methods Res. 5, 227–246 (2011)
6. Bolger, N., Davis, A., Rafaeli, E.: Diary methods: capturing life as it is lived. Annu. Rev. Psychol. 54, 579–616 (2003)
7. Redelmeier, D.A., Kahneman, D.: Patients' memories of painful medical treatments: Real-time and retrospective evaluations of two minimally invasive procedures. Pain 66, 3–8 (1996)
8. Wheeler, L., Reis, H.T.: Self-Recording of Everyday Life Events: Origins, Types, and Uses. J. Pers. 59, 339–354 (1991)
9. Brown, B.A.T., Sellen, A.J., O'Hara, K.P.: A diary study of information capture in working life. In: Turner, T., Szwillus, G., Czerwinski, M., Paternò, F. (eds.) Proceedings of the Conference on Human Factors in Computing Systems, pp. 438–445. ACM (2000)
10. Hulkko, S., Mattelmäki, T., Virtanen, K., Keinonen, T.: Mobile probes. In: Proceedings of the 3rd Nordic Conference on Human Computer Interaction, pp. 43–51. ACM (2004)
11. Consolvo, S., Walker, M.: Using the experience sampling method to evaluate ubicomp applications. IEEE Pervasive Comput. 2, 24–31 (2003)
12. Kahneman, D., Krueger, A.B., Schkade, D.A., Schwarz, N., Stone, A.A.: A survey method for characterizing daily life experience: the day reconstruction method. Science 306, 1776–1780 (2004)
13. Dörner, C., Heß, J., Pipek, V.: Fostering user-developer collaboration with infrastructure probes. Inf. Syst. J., 45–48 (2008)
14. Church, K., Smyth, B.: Understanding mobile information needs. In: Proceedings of the 10th International Conference on Human Computer Interaction with Mobile Devices and Services, pp. 493–494. ACM (2008)

15. Brandt, J., Weiss, N., Klemmer, S.R.: txt 4 l8r: Lowering the burden for diary studies under mobile conditions. In: ACM (ed.) Extended Abstracts on Human Factors in Computing Systems 2007, pp. 2303–2308. ACM New York (2007)
16. Möller, A., Kranz, M., Schmid, B., Roalter, L., Diewald, S.: Investigating self-reporting behavior in long-term studies. In: Proceedings of the Conference on Human Factors in Computing Systems CHI 2013, p. 2931. ACM, New York, USA (2013)
17. Robinson, M.D., Clore, G.L.: Belief and feeling: Evidence for an accessibility model of emotional self-report. Psychol. Bull. **128**, 934–960 (2002)
18. Froehlich, J., Chen, M.Y., Consolvo, S., Harrison, B., Landay, J.A.: MyExperience: a system for in situ tracing and capturing of user feedback on mobile phones. In: Design, pp. 57–70. ACM (2007)
19. Liu, N., Liu, Y., Wang, X.: Data logging plus e-diary: towards an online evaluation approach of mobile service field trial. In: Proceedings of the 12th International Conference on Human Computer Interaction with Mobile Devices and Services, pp. 287–290. ACM (2010)
20. Lieberman, H., Paternò, F., Wulf, V.: End User Development. Springer, Netherlands (2006)
21. Henderson, A., Kyng, M.: There's no place like home: continuing design in use. In: Greenbaum, J., Kyng, M., (eds.) Design at Work Cooperative Design of Computer Systems, pp. 219–240. Lawrence Erlbaum Associates (1991)
22. Malone, T.W., Lai, K.-Y., Fry, C.: Experiments with Oval: a radically tailorable tool for cooperative work (1995)
23. Fischer, G., Girgensohn, A., Nakakoji, K., Redmiles, D.: Supporting software designers with integrated domain-oriented design environments. IEEE Trans. Softw. Eng. **18**, 511–522 (1992)
24. Dourish, P.: Developing a reflective model of collaborative systems (1995)
25. Stiemerling, O., Wulf, V.: Beyond "Yes or No" - Extending Access Control in Groupware with Awareness and Negotiation. Gr. Decis. Negot. **9**, 221 (2000)
26. Kruse, H.C.J., Slagter, R.J., Ter Hofte, G.H.: Collaborative component software: The CoCoWare framework and its application (2000)
27. Luckham, D.C.: The power of events: an introduction to complex event processing in distributed enterprise systems. In: Bassiliades, N., Governatori, G., Paschke, A. (eds.) RuleML 2008. LNCS, vol. 5321, p. 3. Springer, Heidelberg (2008)
28. Indulska, J., Bettini, C., Campbell, R., Mascolo, C., Aharony, N., Pan, W., Ip, C., Khayal, I., Pentland, A.: Social fMRI: Investigating and shaping social mechanisms in the real world. Pervasive Mob. Comput. **7**, 643–659 (2011)
29. Twidale, M., Randall, D., Bentley, R.: Situated evaluation for cooperative systems. In: Proceedings of the 1994 ACM conference on Computer supported cooperative work, pp. 441–452. ACM (1994)
30. Nielsen, J.: Usability Engineering. Morgan Kaufmann (1993)
31. Ludwig, T., Scholl, S., Pipek, V.: PartS: Participatory Sensing for In Situ Capturing of People's Behavior from an End-User Perspective (2015) (in review)

Social-QAS: Tailorable Quality Assessment Service for Social Media Content

Christian Reuter[✉], Thomas Ludwig, Michael Ritzkatis, and Volkmar Pipek

Institute for Information Systems, University of Siegen, Kohlbettstr. 15, 57072, Siegen, Germany
{christian.reuter,thomas.ludwig,
michael.ritzkatis,volkmar.pipek}@uni-siegen.de

Abstract. More than 3 billion people use the Internet, many of whom also use social media services such as the social network Facebook with about 1.35 billion active users monthly or the microblogging platform Twitter numbering approximately 284 million active users monthly. This paper researches how a tailorable quality assessment service can assist the use of citizen-generated content from social media. In particular, we want to study how users can articulate their personal quality criteria appropriately. A presentation of related work is followed by an empirical study on the use of social media in the field of emergency management, focusing on situation assessment practices by the emergency services. Based on this, we present the tailorable quality assessment service (QAS) for social media content, which has been implemented and integrated into an existing application for both volunteers and the emergency services.

Keywords: Social media · Information quality · Tailoring · End User Development · Emergencies

1   Introduction

In times of a widespread adoption of interactive web technologies and social media, the importance of citizen-generated content is increasing constantly. According to the definition of the Organization for Economic Co-operation and Development (OECD) [20], user-generated content is "content that has been made publicly available via the internet" and reflects a "certain amount of creative effort", and which is "created outside of professional routines and practices". In recent emergencies such as the 2012 hurricane Sandy or the 2013 European floods, both the people affected and volunteers alike used social media to communicate with each other and to coordinate private relief activities [11]. Since the involvement of citizens is mostly uncoordinated and the content is therefore not necessarily created in a structured way, a vast amount of resulting data has to be analyzed. Appropriate methods of valuation are essential for the analysis, whereby a consistent evaluation of the quality of information can be complex [6]. Especially in cases where a selection has to be made from a variety of information sources and formats, it is helpful if the evaluation can be made easier by applying diverse quality criteria.

© Springer International Publishing Switzerland 2015
P. Díaz et al. (Eds.): IS-EUD 2015, LNCS 9083, pp. 156–170, 2015.
DOI: 10.1007/978-3-319-18425-8_11

This design case study [41] aims to examine the challenges arising from the integration of citizen-generated content and especially the evaluation of information from social media. Based on a review of related work, we sommarize the results of our conducted empirical study on the use of citizen-generated content and social media by the emergency services. Based on the challenges focusing on individual and dynamic quality assessments of social media data, we have implemented a platform independent quality assessment service (QAS) for social media data. Further we have prototypically implemented and evaluated QAS into two reference applications [15, 27].

2   Related Work: Situation Assessment with Social Media

Information is essential for situation assessment during emergencies and has to be available at the right time, at the right place and in the right format [12]. Endsley [4] distinguishes between *situation awareness* as a "state of knowledge" and *situation assessment* as the "process of achieving, acquiring, or maintaining" that knowledge; and sees information gathering as a selection process leading to the construction of a mental model in accordance with individual goals. Since emergencies are not only time-critical but also unique, they generate a special demand for information that cannot be predicted. It is difficult to have all the essential information available [37]. The availability of as many sources as possible, which can be accessed without delay, would appear to be indispensable. At the same time, it is crucial to avoid a potential overload of information in such a way that the decision making is not influenced [10].

Information systems support both situation assessment [22] and decision making [40] in crisis management. It is, however, especially when dealing with such seldom used technologies within emergencies and while assessing social media that challenges still arise. Adaptations of these technologies and particularly of the information being considered are necessary and become especially important at 'use-time' [5, 21, 33]. Concepts of End-User Development (EUD) can support flexible adaptations by enabling end-users to adapt and reconfigure information systems independently [13]. EUD is understood as all "methods, techniques, and tools that allow users of software systems, who are acting as non-professional software developers, at some point to create, modify or extend a software artifact" [13]. One important concept of the discourse of EUD is tailoring, referring to the change of a "stable" aspect of an artifact [9]. However, what is 'tailoring' for the one person can be 'use' by another. Tailorability essentially has to be one important aspect of software with regard to its establishment in practice.

Mashups can enable EUD to combine services or information from various sources [1]. In addition to information that is provided automatically (meteorological data, water levels, etc.), there are two other kinds of information sources provided by people: emergency services in the field from whom information can be requested [16] and other individuals and organizations not actively participating in dealing with the emergency situation. In the case of a house coal, the number of residents can be requested from the registration office, but the estimation of the fire's size and the number of affected people can only be performed on-site. For example during a power blackout, electricity suppliers can provide the emergency services with better and faster information about which areas are affected than this information could be gathered on-site [12]. However, a lot of pictures of the emergency itself can be found on social media platforms. Such examples show that external information can speed up the process and sometimes cannot be gathered on-site. Thereby information provided by citizens is not always objective – opposed to data measured by sensors. However, sometimes citizen generated content is very accurate – illustrated at a comparison of Wikipedia and Britannica encyclopedia articles [8]. In some cases the subjectivity of citizen-provided reports can generate some sort of vigilantism [28]. Additionally, the misinterpretation of a situation – whether deliberate or not – can lead to potential misinformation; this can result from the reporter paying too little attention to some aspects of the situation or from an incorrect representation of the facts [36]. However some information cannot be obtained from other sources [42]. There are already approaches concerning the selection and use of citizen-generated content but which do not support a complete quality assessment:

- *Twitcident* [35] is used to select tweets by keywords, the type of message or the user and displaying them on a map. At the moment, quality assessment based on meta-information such as the time of creation is not possible. Further, it does not include any information from other social media platforms.
- *SensePlace2* [29] shows another possible solution for displaying georeferenced information on a situation map gained from tweets. The problem is, however, that it collects an extensive amount of data without quality assessment so that the information overload problem is not dealt with.
- *Tweet4act* [3] enables the tracing and classification of information published on Twitter. It is realized through matching every Tweet against an emergency-specific dictionary to classify them into emergency periods. Methods of machine learning based on dictionaries and language classification are used.
- With *TwitInfo* [18], information for a specific event can be collected, classified and visualized. Aside from a graphical visualization, additional information about the quality of the actual information is presented. A personal selection of the quality requirements of the user is not implemented.
- *Ushahidi* [19] enables citizens to exchange information. Additionally, this information can be made accessible for emergency services. The direct communication and the spread of unfiltered information can cause an information overload which forces the user to evaluate the information manually according to its quality.
- *Tweak the Tweet* [32] supports the evaluation and classification of information. Even though the syntax allows variations of the quality assessments, the evaluation of information in only one specific format disables the possibility to show them on a clearly arranged situation map.

In summary, it can be stated that there are already many studies and approaches which deal with citizen-generated content; but with regard to the subjectivity of quality assessment, the current approaches are missing a tailorable tool for assessing social media information. Our research question is therefore, how the concepts of EUD can be applied to support individuals in extracting relevant social media information.

3   Pre-study: Social Media Assessment by Emergency Services

To gain a deeper understanding of the impact citizen-generated content has on social media within emergencies, we analyzed the data from a previous empirical study on the current work practices of the emergency services (focus on fire departments and police) in two different regions of Germany. The results of this pre-study have already been published [15, 26] and we aggregate the main results within this paper.

3.1   Methodology

The bases for the data analysis were the results of multiple empirical studies from 2010 to 2012 [23]. The studies were embedded in a scenario framework describing a storm with many minor and connected incidents and energy breakdowns, which had been developed together with actors from the police and fire departments, county administration and an ENO. The purpose of the scenario was to be able to create a common understanding of an occurring emergency quickly and therefore it helped to increase validity and comparability in our interviews.

First we conducted observations in order to acquire knowledge regarding the practical work in inter-organizational crisis management. The observations took place in a control center on a normal working day (observation time: 9 hours); in the crisis management group and the operations management during a crisis communication practice course (4 hours); as well as at a major cultural event with about 400,000 visitors (6 hours). In addition to observations, we conducted 5 inter-organizational group discussions (W1-W5, each 4 hours with about 10 participants) to understand the communication methods of inter-organizational crisis management. Furthermore, we conducted 22 individual interviews with actors from the participating organizations (I01-I24). Each interview lasted between 1 and 2 hours and followed a guideline, which was separated into three parts. The first part focused on the participants' role, qualification, tasks and work activities under normal conditions. The second part covered the participants' tasks during emergencies in our developed scenario framework. The third part covered applied information and communication systems and perceived problems with these tools. To study mobile collaboration practices more closely, also in regards to the creation, exchange and use of information by the response teams and the control center, an additional 5, partially structured, interviews were conducted (IM1-5; each 1 hour).

Group discussions and interviews were audio recorded and later transcribed for subsequent data analysis. The analysis of the data material was based on the inductive approach found in *grounded theory* approach [34]. We chose this systematic methodology to discover insights about the work practices through the analysis of data. To be able to use this methodology, the transcripts were coded openly and the agents' statements were divided into text modules and later into categories. The knowledge previously acquired in the literature study was used to heighten *theoretical sensitivity* [34].

3.2   Results I: Use of Citizen-Generated Content for Situation Assessment

Generally it is not possible to base a situation assessment solely on the information gathered from one's own organization. External information can improve the information basis (W3). In addition to textual data, pictures provided by citizens are often used. These pictures enable better assessment of how the emergency was caused and what the actual situation looks like:

"If you look at information during demonstrations or other events, you can see that it is often provided faster via Twitter than we can manage on police radio or mobile phone [...]. When events are taking place, they can also often be found on the internet, accompanied by pictures and videos. We will have a lot more to do with that in the future; I am pretty sure about that." (I02).

One example is the debriefing of an event: *"Our investigators like to use fire pictures because obviously our criminal investigation department is not on-site when the fire starts. Of course, they depend [on them] [...] to see the fire behavior."* (I02).

But information is not always necessarily helpful: *"Information is only helpful when it affects my behavior. Any information that does not affect my behavior is a sensory overload"* (I06). An attempt is therefore made to gather only that information which is relevant: *"We try to obtain information from each and every caller"* (I15). Even in emergency situations, people on-site are becoming involved in supporting the emergency services: *"There are many special cases where you need basic skills or previous knowledge but there are also cases in which you can fall back on knowledge and skills provided by citizens"* (I11). Regardless of the large amount of information, the time factor exerts considerable pressure on the emergency services. Due to this, it is always important that each operation is executed promptly. There is *"no time to deal with strangers additionally"* (I02). The fact still remains that citizen-generated content may be defective and therefore requires information assessment.

3.3   Results II: Selection and Quality Assessment of Social Media Content

The question: *"Who is going to evaluate this now [...] and is it really going to help us to assess the situation?"* (I03) often appears in emergency situations. The sheer amount of citizen-generated content makes its use especially difficult: *"Above all, 290 [messages] of 300 are trash. You can only get something from ten reports"* (I02). The mass of information quickly raises the problem of how to handle it: *"You have to read them all. Of course it would be helpful if there was a preselection"* (I02).

For this reason, automatic selection is recommendable: *"It would be nice if there were a selection that separates the important from the unimportant"* (I03). Nevertheless, information has to appear in a certain quantity to render it trustworthy for the emergency services: *"It's a problem if I only have one source. It is certainly more reliable to have five sources than just one"* (I15). External sources are especially susceptible to providing misinformation (I14, I15) and have to be verified (I15) because of this: You *"have to be careful with the content because it does not always reflect reality"* (I14) – *"In such cases it becomes obvious that someone is trying to lead us up the garden path [...] and we have to evaluate the information for ourselves"* (I02). In these cases, misinformation is not always intended; potentially it can result from the subjective perception of the situation which can appear very different to a neutral observer. In conclusion, the use of citizen-generated content from social media fails because of the need for assessment by the emergency services: *"There is simply a bottleneck which we cannot overcome"* (I02).

Overall it is noticeable that *"the more precise information, the more relevant it is"* (I02). This kind of precision can be achieved by assessment. There has to be some form of guarantee that the selected information is useful for the emergency services (I02, I03). Global selection also proves to be difficult because *"it does not seem possible to me that we can select in advance what is important for the section leader. He might need the same information as the chief of operations – or not"* (IM01). This therefore necessitates the possibility of flexible assessment criteria (I19). Due to the time-critical aspect of emergency situations, it is imperative that the personal selection of information be supported since every member of the emergency team has to decide *"relatively quickly between the important and the unimportant"* (I19).

The first impression has to include some amount of significance and has to be helpful for the situation assessment: *"If someone he takes a photo of a window, I know that he was really there. But where is that window exactly?"* (I16). This shows that pictures need additional meta-information just as normal textual information does. Pictures can be especially helpful for assessing crowds of people at huge events: *"If someone had noticed that a relevant number of people were congregating in certain areas, you could have closed the entrance immediately with the help of the security"* (I06). Even though this entails gathering a lot of information, *"most people [...] do not [know] what counts and what kind of information we need"* (I02). There is therefore a risk that the information has no additional value and cannot be used in the emergency situation: *"I do not believe that who is not connected in some way to the police or the fire service is capable of providing useful information in these stress situations"* (I02). It is unusual for an untrained citizen to have knowledge of this sort. *"You have to be very careful with this kind of information"* (I14).

3.4   Results III: Responsibility and Decision Making

Ultimately, it is a member of the emergency team who has to take responsibility for actions taken and who also has to decide if the information is used or not (I15). Misinterpretation is possible both by humans as well as through computer support. It does not matter how good the assessment mechanism is: there *"remains a risk and the person in charge has to bear it, it is as simple as that"* (I15). That is the reason why the emergency services are so careful when using external information. In conclusion it can be stated that *"assessing information, assessing it correctly and dealing with it [...] is a challenging task"* (I15). Every single piece of information is an input to evaluate the whole situation: *"You add more and more flesh to the skeleton you start off with, so that in the end, you have a picture; not just a silhouette but a whole figure and any actions executed by the police are mostly based on that figure"* (I16).

Situation assessment influences the actions which in return influence the situation. However, it does not always make sense just to increase the amount of information. Because as the American political scientist Simon has early stated in 1971, the higher the amount of information, the higher the consumption of information, which in turn creates a "poverty of attention and a need to allocate that attention efficiently among the overabundance of information sources that might consume it" [30].

4   Concept: Tailorable Quality Assessment Service for Social Media Content

It is not only our literature review and the empirical study which have shown the quality assessment of mass information and extractions of relevant information to be a major challenge. It seems comprehensible that different circumstances require different assessment methods. The option to combine these methods could therefore contribute to the improvement of the quality assessment practice [15]. Several assessment methods have already been shown in section 2. In section 3 it has been shown that different assessment methods can support the subjective quality assessment in different situations. Our concept enables the assessment of (social media) content with 15 assessment methods (Table 1) which can be divided into four categories according to their technical execution:

1. The **rating of metadata** contains five assessment methods (author frequency, temporal proximity, local proximity, number of followers/likes, amount of metadata), in which either the deviation from the entered research criteria or the absolute appearance is determined by assessing the difference.

2. The **rating based on the content** provides two assessment methods (frequency of search keyword, stop words), that ascertain the appearance of certain words (or their synonyms) from a list.

3. The **rating based on the classification of the message** uses six assessment methods (sentiment analysis, fear factor, happiness factor, named entity recognition, emoticon, slang), which determine the appearance of words using word lists. In this way, information is graded in different categories.

4. The **rating based on scientific methods** applies two assessment methods (Shannon Information Theory (Entropy), term frequency, inverse document frequency).

   If the (non-specified) end-user of an application based on QAS has the possibility to choose several assessment methods, a subjective quality of information can be determined. Furthermore, this choice and the different categories allow further application of the quality assessment service within several scenarios.

Table 1. Implemented Quality Assessment Methods

#	Method / Criterion	Description
A	**Assessment of metadata**	
1	Author Frequency (Reputation)	Number of messages from the same author in the message set. The more messages an author writes, the more knowledge about the situation is assumed.
2	Temporal Proximity (Currency)	Temporal proximity of the messages to the center of the search period. The closer the message is to the search moment, the more certain it is that the information is relevant
3	Local Proximity	Distance between the place the message was created and the incident's place. The shorter the distance, the higher the probability that the message is about the current disaster.
4	Followers / Likes (Credibility)	An increasing degree of credibility is assumed in proportion to the growing number of likes / followers conferred on a particular message / author.
5	Metadata (Pictures/Links)	Using an image or other media material in addition to textual information can be useful. This assessment criterion measures the amount of metadata.
B	**Assessment based on content**	
6	Frequency of search keyword (Interpretability)	It is ensured that the keyword is not contained randomly in the message but actually addresses the issue. The message is also searched for synonyms.
7	Stop words	The number of stop words (e.g. "so") does not increase the validity of the message as these words do not provide information. Therefor the message utility increases as use of stop words decreases.
C	**Assessment based on classification of the message**	
8	Sentiment Analysis (Impartiality)	The message is evaluated regarding its emotional property. Emotional messages can distort the meaning, especially if they are motivated by fear.
9	Negative Sentiment (Fear Factor)	The Fear Factor measures the degree of expression of fear in the message by the frequency of words that are related to the subject of fear.
10	Positive Sentiment (Happiness Factor)	The Happiness Factor, measures the degree of expression of joy in the message by the frequency of words that are related to the subject joy.
11	Named Entity Recognition (NER)	Number of entities in the message. An entity indicates the connection of the information's content to another information source. Thus the information quality increases by the number of entities in a message.
12	Emoticon Conversion	Provides the ability to convert emoticons into language expressions supporting the readability for different audiences.
13	Slang Conversion	Provides the ability to convert slang words into standard language supporting the readability for different audiences.
D	**Assessment based on scientific methods**	
14	tf-Idf (term frequency – Inverse document frequency)	The appearance of individual search keywords (term frequency) with the frequency of appearance in all messages (inverse document frequency). Useful if more than one single keyword is used because the appearance of a fragment of the whole term which only occurs frequently in few documents is weighted higher than the appearance of a fragment which occurs in many documents but less frequently. $$tf(t, d) = \frac{f(t, d)}{\max\{f(w, d) : w \in d\}}$$
15	Shannon Information Theory (Entropy)	Shannon theory of information. The average amount of information contained in each message received. $$I(p_x) = \log_a\left(\frac{1}{p_x}\right) = -\log_a(p_x)$$

In general: At first, the individual messages are evaluated absolutely concerning the particular method. Afterwards, the relative score of each message is determined by searching for the highest and the lowest absolute score. The message with the highest absolute score is graded "1.0" (100%), the one with the lowest absolute score "0.0" (0%). Subsequently, single scores are weighted and an overall score is obtained. Additionally, in order to address both the requirements of querying multiple sources and enabling the subjectivity of quality assessment, the individual user must be given the opportunity to select the desired social media sources.

5   Implementation and Integration

5.1   Implementation of Social-QAS

The actual quality assessment service is realized as a service following the paradigm of a web-based, service-oriented architecture (SOA). Using such an architecture, it is possible to perform the rating centrally and thus enable its integration into different applications by providing assessment results along with the original data in JSON format (JavaScript Object Notation). The interface is called "via HTTP-GET" and query parameters are added at the end of the URL (separated by "&"). The server-sided information rating is expected to reduce the client's processing load. The APIs of the particular social network providers are used to extract data from the social networks [27]. Within the scope of this paper, Twitter and Facebook are considered especially as necessary APIs exist for them: these APIs provide a variety of opportunities to both export and import data regarding the related social network.

To gather semantic meanings of the content of the message, a Named Entity Recognizer (NER) (No. 11) is used. The Stanford NER[1] is available as Java library for free. The corpus "deWac generalized classifier" was deployed for the NER because it is especially suitable for German messages from social networks. The library Classifier4J[2] was used for the creation of a Bayes Classifier (No. 8), that allows the categorization of information into different classes because it can be skilled with lists of words. The list of synonyms (No. 6) was been generated using the Open Thesaurus web services[3]. A geographical reference is needed to visualize the information. As the majority of information does not contain any geographical metadata, it has to be geocoded. The Gisgraphy Geocoder[4] is usable by web services and geocodes location information for any map material. For reasons of speed, a list is applied for each location that has already been geolocated, whereof the coordinates can be determined without geolocation. GSON[5] provides an automatic generation of a JSON object by means of a java object model and is therefore used for conversion.

---

[1] http://nlp.stanford.edu/software/CRF-NER.shtml

[2] http://classifier4j.sourceforge.net/

[3] http://www.openthesaurus.de/

[4] http://www.gisgraphy.com/

[5] https://code.google.com/p/google-gson/

5.2   Available Data

While working with QAS based on the available type of social media different data attributes are accessible (Table 2). Furthermore some technical and business oriented limitations become apparent [27]. Therefore it is not possible to apply all quality assessment methods in the same way.

Table 2. Source-based data attributes

Attributes	Facebook	Google+	Instagram	Twitter	YouTube
Date, Time	Given	Given	Given	Given	Given
Sender	Given	Given	Given	Given	Given
Title	N/A	Given	Caption	N/A	Given
Tags, Keywords	N/A	N/A	Given	N/A	Given
Comments, Replies, Answers	Comments	Replies	Comments	N/A	Via Google+
Content	Given	Given	Caption	Given	Description
Number of views	N/A	N/A	N/A	N/A	Given
Number of likes	Likes	Plusoners	Likes	N/A	Likes
Number of dislikes	N/A	N/A	N/A	N/A	Dislikes
Number of retweets	N/A	N/A	N/A	Given	N/A
Number of shares	Given	Resharers	N/A	N/A	N/A
Person: Age	N/A	Age Range	N/A	N/A	Age Range
Person: Location	Given	Given	N/A	Given	Given
Person: Number of uploads	N/A	N/A	Given	N/A	N/A
Person: Number of watches	N/A	N/A	N/A	N/A	N/A
Person: Number of total posts	N/A	N/A	N/A	Given	N/A
Person: Real name	Given	Given	Given	Given	Given

5.3   Integration of QAS into a Web Application and a Facebook-App

To test the implemented service, we have integrated QAS into a web-based application specified for emergency services as well as a Facebook-app "XHELP" to support volunteer moderators during disasters. In the following we will outline prototypically the implementation into XHELP, which allows information to be both acquired and distributed cross-media and cross-channel [25].

Inside this application, it is possible to search for information using different quality parameters and to perform a quality assessment (Figure 1). For this, the user decides which assessment criteria to choose using a slider. Integrating the user in this way meets the requirements for a flexible and manageable quality assessment, as identified in the pre-study.

Fig. 1. Quality Assessment Service integrated into an application

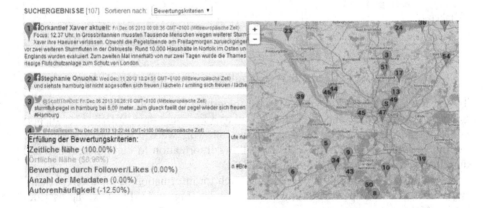

Fig. 2. Search results (left), degree of completion (lower left) and map presentation (right)

The results of a search are illustrated both as a table and visually, on a situation map. A wealth of meta information - such as the degree of completion of particular methods - is displayed as tool tips in the table. At the same time, the situation map enables the direct determination of the proximity of the information to the search location (Figure 2). This way, the user is able to choose from various procedures the mode in which s/he wishes to view the results, thus increasing the flexibility of the application. This user interface is only one of a range of ways in which QAS can be used.

5.4   Key Advantages

In summary, QAS unifies the following functionalities:

- The quality of information generated by citizens can be assessed on the basis of several methods.
- Assessment does not only take place on the basis of metadata, but additional on the basis of the content.
- The user decides how to weight each method. The subjective quality of a message emerges when all the assessments of every method have been combined.
- QAS is very flexible because it provides the opportunity to extend the sources and assessment methods very easily.
- The integration and usage in other applications is possible because the implementation is SOA-based.

6   Conclusion

This article illustrates how a tailorable quality assessment of citizen-generated information from social media can support the situation assessment practices of crisis management actors – both emergency services [15] as well as informal volunteers [25]. As a starting point, we analyzed the results of an already conducted empirical study involving emergency services regarding the use of citizen-generated content and social media within their current work practices [15]. Based on literature and empirical findings, we derived different quality criteria and applied them on information from social media. We implemented QAS, which not only incorporated all the quality criteria but also offered the user the chance to adjust them according to the requirements of the current situation. We contribute three results that extend the current state of the art:

1. An analysis of dealing with citizen-generated content in emergency situations through an empirical study which highlights the selection and quality assessment of citizen-generated content in emergencies.
2. A concept for a tailorable quality assessment service for social media as well as a running SOA-oriented and tailorable implementation that can be integrated into different applications (section 4 and 5.1)
3. A reference implementation of QAS inside an existing web-based application fpr emergency services [15] and an existing web-app for volunteers [25] (section 5.2).

In summary, the flexibility in form of tailoring options for source platform selection and quality assessment criteria is helpful due to the fact that situation assessment has been shown to be very subjective. Thus information needs depend on personal feelings, experience and the situation itself. Compared to the current state of the art, Social-QAS, developed within this work, has a number of advantages: in contrast to Vivacqua et al. [39], it is not just the emergency services who receive information; additionally, the work of unbound volunteers can be supported through flexible assessment and free accessibility. A very wide base of information is realized using several social networks as information sources [35]. Compared to Starbird et al. [31], who limit the amount of information by using a fixed syntax, in QAS all the information from various sources is considered. Verma et al. [38] place restrictions by only allowing the usage of a number of assessment criteria that can be combined with each other.

Our results could prove interesting for other application fields as well. Wherever information is gathered and analyzed and information systems are implemented to support the task, one question still poses a challenge: How can information systems be implemented in such a way as to allow the automatic selection of relevant data and, at the same time, afford end-users the possibility to adapt this automation, thus enabling tailorable quality assessment according to their needs [2]. This is especially of importance if situations and the context of work differ and if practices evolve over time. Concepts like Social-QAS will help to allow end-users to articulate their needs in a more appropriate way.

Our work still has some limitations. Not all the criteria that are relevant for quality assessment are included within QAS. Furthermore, according to the context, the amount of criteria might overburden the cognitive skills of end-users. It is, therefore, important to define standards and to allow end-users to adapt them, whereby different tailoring power might then require different skills, according to MacLean et al. [17]; thus local developers may be needed [7]. Another limitation is that Social-QAS needs a good data base to encompass all its rating mechanisms. But as table 2 has shown, currently not all social media services provide such a sophisticated data base. To get more details about what quality criteria method is appropriated within which scenario, we need to enhance our data base. In future work, we will therefore try to enhance the raw data base from social media to further improve quality assessment for social media content. Our endeavor will be to expand dynamic quality assessment not solely for cross-platform social media content [25] but also for other types of information sources, such as on-site volunteers [14].

Acknowledgements. The research project EmerGent' was funded by a grant of the European Union (**FP7 No. 608352**). This paper is an enhanced, refocused and improved version of a paper presented at the 2014 German Informatics Society Conference **[24]**.

References

1. Cappiello, C., Daniel, F., Matera, M., Picozzi, M., Weiss, M.: Enabling end user development through mashups: requirements, abstractions and innovation toolkits. In: Piccinno, A. (ed.) IS-EUD 2011. LNCS, vol. 6654, pp. 9–24. Springer, Heidelberg (2011)
2. Carr, N.: The Glass Cage: Automation and Us. Norton, New York (2014)
3. Chowdhury, S., et al.: Tweet4act: using incident-specific profiles for classifying crisis-related messages. In: Proc. ISCRAM, Baden-Baden, Germany, pp. 834–839 (2013)
4. Endsley, M.R.: Toward a theory of situation awareness in dynamic systems. Hum. Factors. 37(1), 32–64 (1995)
5. Fischer, G., Scharff, E.: Meta-design – design for designers. In: Boyarski, D., Kellogg, W. (eds.) In: Proceedings of the International Conference on Designing Interactive Systems, pp. 396–405. ACM, New York (2000)
6. Friberg, T., et al.: Analysis of information quality criteria in crisis situation as a characteristic of complex situations. In: Proc. IQ, Little Rock, USA (2010)
7. Gantt, M., Nardi, B.: Gardeners and gurus: patterns of cooperation among CAD users. In: Proc. CHI, pp. 107–117 (1992)
8. Giles, J.: Internet encyclopaedias go head to head. Nature 438, 900–901 (2005)
9. Henderson, A., Kyng, M.: There's no place like home: continuing design in use. In: Greenbaum, J., Kyng, M. (eds.) Design at Work Cooperative Design of Computer Systems, pp. 219–240. Lawrence Erlbaum Associates (1991)
10. Hiltz, S., Plotnick, L.: Dealing with information overload when using social media for emergency management: emerging solutions. In: Proc. ISCRAM, Baden-Baden, Germany, pp. 823–827 (2013)
11. Kaufhold, M.-A., Reuter, C.: Vernetzte Selbsthilfe in Sozialen Medien beim Hochwasser 2013 in Deutschland. i-com. 13(1), 20–28 (2014)
12. Ley, B., et al.: Supporting improvisation work in inter-organizational crisis management. In: Proc. CHI, pp. 1529–1538. ACM Press, Austin (2012)
13. Lieberman, H., et al.: End-User Development. Springer, Dordrecht (2006)
14. Ludwig, T., et al.: Crowdmonitor: mobile crowd sensing for assessing physical and digital activities of citizens during emergencies. In: Proceedings of the Conference on Human Factors in Computing Systems (CHI). ACM Press, Seoul, (2015)
15. Ludwig, T., Reuter, C., Pipek, V.: Social Haystack: Dynamic Quality Assessment of Citizen-Generated Content in Social Media during Emergencies. ToCHI (2015, in press)
16. Ludwig, T., et al.: What you see is what i need: mobile reporting practices in emergencies. In: Bertelsen, O.W., et al. (eds.) Proc. ECSCW, pp. 181–206. Springer, Paphos (2013)
17. MacLean, A., et al.: User-tailorable systems: pressing the issues with buttons. In: Proc. CHI. Seattle, USA (1990)
18. Marcus, A., et al.: Twitinfo: aggregating and visualizing microblogs for event exploration. In: Proc. CHI, Vancouver, Canada, pp. 227–236 (2011)
19. McClendon, S., Robinson, A.C.: Leveraging geospatially-oriented social media communications in disaster response. In: Proc. ISCRAM, Vancouver, Canada (2012)
20. Organisation for Economic Co-operation and Development (OECD): Participative Web: User-Created Content. http://www.oecd.org/internet/ieconomy/38393115.pdf
21. Pipek, V., Wulf, V.: Infrastructuring: Toward an Integrated Perspective on the Design and Use of Information Technology. J. Assoc. Inf. Syst. 10(5), 447–473 (2009)
22. Reuter, C., et al.: Ad Hoc Participation in Situation Assessment: Supporting Mobile Collaboration in Emergencies. ACM Trans. Comput. Interact. 21(5) (2014)

23. Reuter, C.: Emergent Collaboration Infrastructures: Technology Design for Inter-Organizational Crisis Management (Ph.D. Thesis). Springer Gabler, Siegen, Germany (2014)
24. Reuter, C., et al.: Entwicklung eines SOA-basierten und anpassbaren bewertungsdienstes für inhalte aus sozialen medien. In: Plödereder, E., et al. (eds.) Informatik 2014, Stuttgart, Germany. GI-LNI, pp. 977–988 (2014)
25. Reuter, C., et al.: XHELP: design of a cross-platform social-media application to support volunteer moderators in disasters. In: Proc. CHI. ACM Press, Seoul (2015)
26. Reuter, C., Ritzkatis, M.: Adaptierbare bewertung bürgergenerierter inhalte aus sozialen medien. In: Koch, M., et al. (eds.) Mensch & Computer 2014, pp. 115–124. Oldenbourg-Verlag, München (2014)
27. Reuter, C., Scholl, S.: Technical limitations for designing applications for social media. In: Koch, M., et al. (eds.) Mensch & Computer 2014: Workshopband, pp. 131–140. Oldenbourg-Verlag, München (2014)
28. Rizza, C., et al.: Do-it-yourself justice-considerations of social media use in a crisis situation: the case of the 2011 vancouver riots. In: Proc. ISCRAM, Baden-Baden, Germany, pp. 411–415 (2013)
29. Robinson, A., et al.: Understanding the utility of geospatial information in social media. In: Proc. ISCRAM, Baden-Baden, Germany, pp. 918–922 (2013)
30. Simon, H.A.: Designing organizations for an information-rich world. In: Greenberger, M. (ed.) Computers, Communication, and the Public Interest, pp. 40–41. The Johns Hopkins Press, Baltimore (1971)
31. Starbird, K., Palen, L.: Voluntweeters: self-organizing by digital volunteers in times of crisis. In: Proc. CHI, pp. 1071–1080. ACM-Press, Vancouver (2011)
32. Starbird, K., Stamberger, J.: Tweak the tweet: leveraging microblogging proliferation with a prescriptive syntax to support citizen reporting. In: French, S., et al. (eds.) Proc. ISCRAM. Seattle, USA (2010)
33. Stevens, G., Pipek, V., Wulf, V.: Appropriation infrastructure: supporting the design of usages. In: Pipek, V., Rosson, M.B., de Ruyter, B., Wulf, V. (eds.) IS-EUD 2009. LNCS, vol. 5435, pp. 50–69. Springer, Heidelberg (2009)
34. Strauss, A.L.: Qualitative Analysis for Social Scientists. Cambridge Press (1987)
35. Terpstra, T., et al.: Towards a realtime twitter analysis during crises for operational crisis management. In: Proc. ISCRAM, Vancouver, Canada, pp. 1–9 (2012)
36. Thomson, R., et al.: Trusting tweets: the fukushima disaster and information source credibility on twitter. In: Proc. ISCRAM, Vancouver, Canada, pp. 1–10 (2012)
37. Turoff, M., et al.: The design of a dynamic emergency response management information system (DERMIS). J. Inf. Technol. Theory Appl. 5(4), 1–35 (2004)
38. Verma, S., et al.: Natural language processing to the rescue? extracting "situational awareness" tweets during mass emergency. In: ICWSM, pp. 385–392 (2011)
39. Vivacqua, A.S., Borges, M.R.S.: Taking advantage of collective knowledge in emergency response systems. J. Netw. Comput. Appl. 35(1), 189–198 (2012)
40. Van de Walle, B., Turoff, M.: Decision support for emergency situations. Inf. Syst. E-bus. Manag. 6(3), 295–316 (2008)
41. Wulf, V., et al.: Engaging with practices: design case studies as a research framework in CSCW. In: Proceedings of the Conference on Computer Supported Cooperative Work (CSCW), pp. 505–512. ACM Press, Hangzhou (2011)
42. Zagel, B.: Soziale netzwerke als impulsgeber für das verkehrs-und sicherheitsmanagement bei großveranstaltungen. In: Koch, A., et al. (eds.) Geoinformationssysteme, pp. 223–232. VDE Verlag GMBH, Berlin (2012)

Short Papers

Instilling a Culture of Participation: Technology-Related Skills and Attitudes of Aspiring Information Professionals

Monica Maceli[✉]

Pratt Institute, School of Information and Library Science, 144 West 14th Street,
New York, NY 10011, USA
mmaceli@pratt.edu

Abstract. End users are increasingly frequent contributors to design and development activities. A fundamental necessity to these activities is the existence of a culture of participation, in which users are empowered to solve meaningful problems through technology. This combination of attitudes and skills provides the foundation for end-user-development activity. This preliminary study explores efforts to instill a culture of participation in students training to become information professionals. This demographic is uniquely suited for such research due to students' low incoming technology skillset, educational programs that often fail to heavily cover technology topics, and a high need for end-user-development activities in their future workplaces. This qualitative study explores the evolution of students' skills and attitudes throughout an introductory technology course, finding that common instructional techniques induced positive attitude and skills change in many, but negative or fearful attitudes towards technology were still present, suggesting future exploration is needed in this area.

Keywords: Culture of participation · End-user development · Meta-design · Technology education · Library and information science

1 Introduction

Until the relatively recent past, the design of technology was a process conducted by experts in a setting remote from the eventual setting of use. As time has passed and technology has evolved, this relationship has shifted, and much more design power is now shared with the end users of the system. End users are now frequent contributors to design and development activities. This may range from the simple (e.g. contributing a product review), to the complex (e.g. creating a functionally new mash-up), and our clear-cut roles of designer and user have subsequently blurred. Currently, some of the most interesting and relevant design problems center on how systems should be designed in a world increasingly full of end-user developer/designers.

Many of these challenges are highly technological, in creating the tools and interfaces to best facilitate these behaviors. However, in tandem with the technological aspects, there are many socio-cultural challenges inherent in instilling a *culture of*

© Springer International Publishing Switzerland 2015
P. Díaz et al. (Eds.): IS-EUD 2015, LNCS 9083, pp. 173–179, 2015.
DOI: 10.1007/978-3-319-18425-8_12

participation in potential end-user-developers. These ideas were highlighted in earlier influential works: notably Christopher Alexander's vision of an "unselfconscious culture of design" [1] where users had the skills and confidence to tailor their environment and Ivan Illich's concept of convivial technology tools [11] that would empower people to conduct creative and autonomous actions. These largely theoretical works described a fundamentally different culture of design, one which introduced complex questions around the goal of allowing and encouraging users to act as (and with) designers.

This culture of participation must be in place to shape users with the confidence and skills necessary to take on an active role in shaping their technological environments. One might even make the statement that without the underlying culture of participation, no end user design or development work may take place at all. These ideas are vital to the conceptual framework of meta-design; meta-design theory emphasizes that designers can never anticipate all future uses of their system. Users shape their environments in response to emerging needs and designers must therefore design with future flexibility in mind [e.g. 8, 9]. In 2011, Fischer and Hermann [10] identified key guidelines for the meta-design of socio-technical systems, including the need to *establish cultures of participation*.

This short paper explores an effort to establish cultures of participation in aspiring library and information scientists – a group of unique interest to the end-user-development (EUD) community as this field has become increasingly technology-heavy, with many LIS practitioners engaging in programming-related activities. Both incoming LIS students and current practitioners often lack formal training or background in information technology and some may have a generally fearful or resistant attitude towards technology. However, simply increasing end-user developer participation is not without its own risks; *participation overload* [e.g. 7] is a serious pitfall that may arise where an increasing number of individuals are called on to participate in end-user development activities, including those that may not be highly personally meaningful.

1.1   Technology in the Library and Information Science (LIS) Field

To understand the uniquely technological position that LIS professionals take today, and its interest and relevance towards the study of end-user-development, it is necessary to briefly explore the evolution of the use of technology in this field. Libraries have historically been a technological hub for the community, giving many patrons access to the Internet or printing services, during the 1980s and 90s. As library and information science work moved out of the traditional context of the physical library, e.g. into museum, archives, and digital libraries, the technological knowledge necessary for LIS professionals expanded immensely.

In the subsequent years, the explosion of online search and information retrieval tools necessitated a hard look at the function and purpose of the modern library. As technology use expanded outside (and within) the library, an increasing number of library functions and roles dealt directly with information technology, from working with integrated library systems, expanding to new search or discovery systems, website creation and even extending to mobile app development and the construction and operation of maker spaces [e.g. 2, 4]. Current LIS professionals are often involved in end-user-development activities: namely, creating mash-up web applications and generally crafting solutions from tools designed and provided by others (e.g. using APIs, creating maker-spaces, working with linked data and open source software, etc.) [2]. In particular, creating mash-ups has become a popular means of exposing library-related data to the public and amplifying it with others' data sets, with entire books dedicated to the topic in the context of LIS [e.g. 5].

In contrast to the current state of the field, many students enter LIS programs with little background in information technology and little intent to pursue such a direction, even though their future work may be necessarily technology-centric. Furthermore, LIS students may have completed their undergraduate work in the humanities or other non-technical specialties. This creates a student population with little formal background in information technology and programming, with a relatively short time (approximately 2 years as a full-time student) in a master's program in which to expand these skills. In the compressed time-frame of a master's program, technology-intensive courses must often complete with courses covering a more traditional LIS curriculum [4].

2   Research Study Design and Results

The research methods applied in this preliminary study were targeted towards 1) understanding the initial technological competencies and attitudes of incoming students and 2) assessing changes in attitudes and skills over the period of a 17-week semester. The participants were 31 LIS graduate students enrolled in two sections of the introductory technology course. At the beginning of the semester, students were asked to self-report their technology skills and interests. The findings indicated that few had significant technology experience (Table 1) and most of the experience reported was performed in the role of user.

Table 1. Self-reported technology experience at the beginning of the semester

Technology-related experience	# of Students
User role only (e.g. user of office productivity software, email applications, writing blogs)	17
Basic developer skills (e.g. simple HTML markup, customization on blogging platforms, web design)	13
Intermediate developer skills (e.g. e-commerce, programming, interface design skills)	1

The course included a dense 6-week module focused on building students' web design skills. During this heavily hands-on module, students were exposed to concepts such as client-server architecture, file formats, and character encoding, in addition to basic web design and development skills (e.g. hand-coding HTML/CSS/Javascript, working with text and WYSWIG editors, and graphics editors). For the majority of students, these concepts were challenging and the pace of the course was generally reported as fast, but accessible.

At two points during the semester, students were asked to anonymously answer several questions targeting their thoughts and feelings towards technology. At the culmination of the intensely hands-on portion of the semester, the survey results were transcribed and assessed through qualitative coding and thematic analysis (Table 2). Students' comments often expressed multiple themes of interest to the study (e.g. one student expressed an increasing understanding of the technological demands of the field as well as a lingering negative attitude towards technology – *"I'm beginning to feel much more comfortable with the idea of having to be well-versed with certain technology in order to meet career goals...Still mildly afraid of computers."*)

Table 2. Themes expressed in students' final responses

Theme	Code	Frequency
Positive	General positive attitude towards technology e.g. *"I'm excited about technology, it seems much more accessible than I ever imagined."*	12
	Increased confidence and comfort e.g. *"I definitely feel more confident in my tech skills"*	7
	Increased interest/desire to learn more e.g. *"I'm encouraged to take more tech classes next semester."*	7
Negative	General negative attitude towards technology e.g. *"not really a huge fan of technology"*	3
	Expressed confusion, feeling overwhelmed or fearful e.g. *"I'm feeling somewhat overwhelmed"*	7
Total codes observed (N=31 participants)		**36**

3   Discussion

As noted in previous literature [e.g. 12], the LIS demographic may need particular support in overcoming pre-existing negative attitudes or fears towards technology that impede the creation of a culture of participation. These attitudes were apparent at both the onset and completion of the studied introduction to technology course. Despite common perceptions that the younger populations are more tech-savvy, current LIS students (of all ages) do not necessarily have extensive technology experience. A 2013 study of "digital native" librarians revealed that the Millenial generation (born between 1982 and 2001) that is increasingly populating library schools tend to lack more advanced technology skills [4]. The findings suggested that such students "are accustomed to using technology, not creating it or understanding the back end infrastructure" [4]. This emphasis, on using rather than creating, was demonstrated in the incoming students' reported technology experience levels [Table 1 above].

These underlying skills and attitudes have direct implications on the field of EUD and the role of end-user developer. Existing research in this area often assumes that end users transition to developer roles when faced with personally motivating problems that can be tackled using novel technology. End-user-development activity can be considered a spectrum from simple manipulation or customization of fixed features, up to creating (or contributing to) functionality novel systems [Figure 1 below]. It has largely been assumed in the EUD literature that those who are strongly interested and highly personally motivated will make the transition from end user towards end-use-developer along the spectrum; therefore the end-user-developer population inherently consists of the most motivated and confident end users.

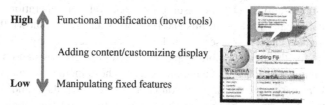

High Functional modification (novel tools)

Adding content/customizing display

Low Manipulating fixed features

Fig. 1. EUD activities represented as a spectrum of customization

In the LIS demographic, the work done by information professionals has become intensely and (largely) non-optionally technological. This creates a scenario in which end users that may not historically have been motivated to shift towards developers, find themselves in a situation where such behavior is required of them. For users that lack both the skills and the confidence (i.e. culture of participation) to begin the uphill battle towards developer of technology, in practice this process may currently be too difficult. The rapid adoption of technology contrasted with the relative lack of technology skills in current and aspiring LIS practitioners may make this community particularly vulnerable to the concept of *participation overload* introduced earlier in the paper.

A limitation of the study design was the relatively small group of participants and (due to the need to protect student anonymity) the resulting difficulty in tracking the progression in attitude on an individual level throughout the course. Further research addressing the questions posed below can correct for these potential limitations and further our understanding of end-user development in library and information science:

What technology teaching tools and approaches are most effective at instilling a culture of participation? This course employed a wide range of tools and instructional techniques commonly used to teach basic web design concepts (e.g. lectures and hands-on exercises, a diversity of design tools, text and WYSIWYG editors, etc.) Individual differences and motivations likely play a large role in overall success and attitude change during the course, but tools that provide a low barrier to entry and quickly give a sense of accomplishment may be ideal.

What aspects of the design of the information system affect the attitudes of end-user developers towards technology? Open source software products are very common within the LIS field and may generally lack the user-friendly interfaces to support novice users in gaining confidence and control over the system.

How can participation overload be effectively managed in this demographic? In a scenario where information professionals may be increasingly pushed towards becoming end-user developers, managing participation overload becomes a serious concern. Supporting LIS professionals with useful EUD tools and educational practices serves to facilitate the creation of a healthy culture of participation.

4   Conclusion

This research study begins to explore the process of fostering a *culture of participation* in students preparing to play diverse roles in increasingly technology-heavy information organizations. Despite assumptions that younger generations are inherently more technologically proficient, this and previous studies have shown these groups to have experience largely as users, not developers, of technology. This has serious implications for the field of library and information science which encompasses diverse and complex scenarios of technology use. These include frequent challenges in working with mash-ups, APIs, open source software, open data, and other technologies that have historically been of great interest to the EUD community. As the previous discussion section explores, there are several intriguing questions identified by this research in progress that have wide relevance to the study of EUD and the facilitating culture of participation. As emphasized earlier, an underlying culture of participation is a requirement for supporting end users in solving meaningful problems through information technology.

References

1. Alexander, C.: Notes on the synthesis of form. Harvard University Press, Cambridge (1964)
2. Breeding, M.: Library technology: The next generation. Computers in Libraries **33**(8), 16–18 (2013)
3. Carson, P.: Re-framing Librarians' Identities and Assumptions around IT. The Journal of Academic Librarianship **40**(3–4), 405–407 (2014)
4. Emanuel, J.: Digital native librarians, technology skills, and their relationship with technology. Information Technology & Libraries **32**(3), 20–33 (2013)
5. Engard, N. (ed.): More library mashups: exploring new ways to deliver library data. Information Today Inc., Medford (2014)
6. Farkas, M.G.: Training librarians for the future: Integrating technology into LIS education. In: Gordon, R. (ed.) Information Tomorrow: Reflections on Technology and the Future of Public and Academic Libraries, pp. 193–201. Information Today Inc., Medford (2007)
7. Fischer, G.: End-User development: from creating technologies to transforming cultures. In: Dittrich, Y., Burnett, M., Mørch, A., Redmiles, D. (eds.) IS-EUD 2013. LNCS, vol. 7897, pp. 217–222. Springer, Heidelberg (2013)
8. Fischer, G.: Meta-design: Expanding boundaries and redistributing control in design. In: Baranauskas, C., Abascal, J., Barbosa, S.D.J. (eds.) INTERACT 2007. LNCS, vol. 4662, pp. 193–206. Springer, Heidelberg (2007)

9. Fischer, G., Giaccardi, E.: Meta-Design: A framework for the future of end user development. In: Lieberman, H., Paternò, F., Wulf, V. (eds.) End User Development, pp. 427–457. Kluwer Academic Publishers, Dordrecht (2006)
10. Fischer, G., Hermann, T.: Socio-Technical Systems - A Meta-Design Perspective. International Journal for Sociotechnology and Knowledge Development 3(1), 1–33 (2011)
11. Illich, I.: Tools for Conviviality. Harper & Row Publishers, New York (1973)
12. West, J.: Technophobia, technostress, and technorealism. In: Gordon, R. (ed.) Information Tomorrow: Reflections on Technology and the Future of Public and Academic Libraries, pp. 203–215. Information Today Inc., Medford (2007)

Lessons Learned in the Design of Configurable Assistive Technology with Smart Devices

Bruno A. Chagas$^{(\boxtimes)}$, Hugo Fuks, and Clarisse S. de Souza

Departamento de Informática, Pontifícia Universidade Católica do Rio (PUC-Rio),
R. Marquês de São Vicente, 225, Gávea, Rio de Janeiro, RJ 22453-900, Brazil
{bchagas,hugo,clarisse}@inf.puc-rio.br

Abstract. Assistive Technology (AT) aims at compensating for motor, sensory or cognitive functional limitations of its users. We report on a study with a single tetraplegic participant using AT that we have been developing for interaction with multiple devices in smart connected environments. We wanted to investigate a user's reaction during his first encounter with this technology and to verify if needs and opportunities for AT configuration would emerge from study activities and interviews. Results show implicit and explicit configuration needs and opportunities suggesting that we must address both hardware and software configuration, some to be done by the end user, others by assistants. At this initial stage our contribution is to propose a structure for organizing the AT configuration problem space in order to support the design of similar technologies.

Keywords: Assistive Technology · Configuration · Wearable computers

1 Introduction

Assistive Technologies (AT) are resources that allow for compensating motor, sensory or cognitive functional limitations of their users [1]. One of the reasons AT are hard to design, produce and be used is the variability of kinds and degrees of disabilities and individual characteristics among users (physical, psychological, cultural, environmental, etc.). This variability can be addressed by means of configurations to improve production and adoption. However, before engaging in such endeavor we must answer questions like: what is configurable AT? What does AT mean to users (and to people around them)? There are, at least, two ways of defining AT: one is more technical, concerning the technology and its functions, as in the U.S. [2]; the other focuses on the disabled person, emphasizing the role of AT as equipment for social inclusion, which is the case in Brazil [1]. This work follows the second definition and explores issues beyond functionality and technology, but that can nevertheless influence the design of both. We conducted a case study with a single tetraplegic participant who controlled some devices using an AT platform operated simultaneously by gesture and voice interaction in a smart home environment. Based on our findings, we propose a set of dimensions for AT configuration. We believe our contribution is to propose a structure for organizing the AT configuration problem space to support the design of similar technologies.

© Springer International Publishing Switzerland 2015
P. Díaz et al. (Eds.): IS-EUD 2015, LNCS 9083, pp. 180–185, 2015.
DOI: 10.1007/978-3-319-18425-8_13

2 Related Work

Our work is currently investigating the intersection of three extensive research topics, depicted in Fig. 1. Of course, this section is not an exhaustive review of the research done in the three areas. We just want to point some work we think can show important approaches and advances, especially in the intersection between them. This might be useful to support the relevance of this research and to uncover its gaps. Our aim is to contribute to the design for user empowerment in the AT domain [3] towards an "ubiquitous accessibility" [4] to promote full social inclusion of disabled users.

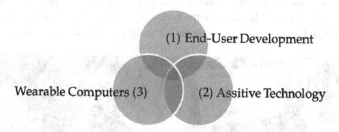

Fig. 1. A depiction of the research topics of our work

The intersection of (1) and (2) was investigated by Carmien & Fischer [5] applying the meta-design framework in systems for people with cognitive disabilities. Lewis [6] has pointed at configurability needs and some aspects of design, also in the domain of cognitive disabilities. Between (1) and (3), there are investigations of configurability in tangible computing [7], end-user programming of hardware platforms [8] and alternative (even "physical") means and languages for programming [9], but in different applications and domains. Between (2) and (3), the use of wearable computers as AT has been studied in [10] and advanced work has been done in the rehabilitation field using robotics [11]. Most of these focus on engineering aspects. Closer to us, Kane et al. [12] make recommendations for increasing configurability in the design of mobile accessible devices for users with motor impairments, but more is needed to clarify what it is and how it could be done. To the best of our knowledge, there is no significant volume of research focusing on the intersection of all three areas.

3 Case Study

We are working with a single tetraplegic participant who has come to our lab looking for new technology that could help him in his everyday life. We anticipated that configurability would be an issue, but had little idea of what should be configured and how. We so decided to investigate his reaction in first encounter with a concrete instance of the technology he was looking for. We wanted to see if needs and opportunities for configuration would emerge and how this would come about.

3.1   An Assistive Technology Platform Prototype for the Smart Home

After observations and interviews with the participant and some market research, we proposed a solution composed by three parts, which can be seen in Fig. 2:

1. An electronic cap – a wearable computer – that detects head movements and simulates a mouse. The cap can be plugged to up to four exchangeable switches that are used to do the clicks. It communicates wirelessly to mobile phones via Bluetooth;
2. A dock station for Android™ mobile phones, which controls a lamp, a TV set and a wireless dual connection headset (switching between phone and computer);
3. An Android™ mobile phone, which is "the brain" of the system and connects with the dock station via USB. The phone is equipped with an app designed to control each device individually, besides the native features provided by Android™.

Fig. 2. Our AT prototype platform: on the left, a user wearing the cap to control a lamp, a TV and a computer; on the right, the dock station connected to a mobile phone with our app.

3.2   Study Scenario

We designed a study split in two steps. First, we presented the platform to the participant, taught him the basic operation and allowed some time for him to play with it. Second, we proposed a task scenario specifically designed to include multitasking: he would be working on the computer doing some generic activity (e.g., reading e-mail, the news, etc.) when a friend (a role played by another researcher) would call him unexpectedly to discuss a spread sheet in his computer. Study session took place in the participant's home and lasted approximately three hours, including the interviews. Each step was video-recorded using the CAS (Capture & Access System) infrastructure, which allows for a complete capture and subsequent analysis of the scene observed from different angles [13]. The first author of this paper conducted and supported the participant during the session. At the beginning and at the end of each step we made oral open-question interviews about his expectations about what was coming next and about his impressions on what he has just experienced, respectively.

4 Results and Discussion

Our findings are based on two kinds of evidence: the participant's actions and behavior during study activity; and his utterances, during actions and when answering our questions. In the first step (technology introduction), we placed the cap on the participant's head, adjusted fit and position properly and tried out the different switches we could use. We quickly discarded two of them, because we noticed instability on the control and the participant's emerging fatigue, discomfort and frustration when testing them. The other two were placed and adjusted in such a way they could be activated comfortably, which we could notice and the participant verbally confirmed. We connected all the parts, taught the basics and then let him explore the equipment for some time on his own.

In the second step (task scenario), many things happened (mostly triggered by us as part of the scenario) to promote task switching and interleaving. They brought about interaction challenges that we saw and were also verbalized by the participant in the interview. Switching the voice from the computer to the mobile phone and answering the phone doing a "swipe" with his head was the greatest issue. It took our participant several attempts to accomplish that, because of failure in one or another intermediary stage and confusion about moving the mouse pointer up and down. We observed some tension and anxiety, which was later confirmed by him in the final interview. The participant, however, persisted in the task, not asking to abandon it (which he could easily do).

This study revealed many configuration needs and opportunities. First, there were **physical form and hardware options**, like the size of the cap, the switches to be used, their positioning and fit to allow for comfortable use. Then, there were **behavior configuration opportunities**. In the interview, the participant spontaneously suggested the creation of shortcut buttons (hardware switches) to allow for quick switching voice channeling from the computer to the phone. He also mentioned options for changing the behavior of the mouse pointer, like going up when he pitches down and vice-versa (the equipment worked opposite to his expectations). He even suggested the possibility to use the head gestures like keyboard arrow keys, he referred to it as being a "more primitive" kind of control that could be easier for him.

One may argue that a better design for our AT prototype might improve his experience, which is true. However, the desired actions for any given task are subject to change according to the situation (for example, if he receives a call while watching TV at high volume) and the contingent access conditions to control buttons (limited by range of physical movements the user can do). A configurable mechanism could provide means for defining shortcut actions using the available buttons (and combinations) that can be reconfigured according to context and task. Along this line, in the interview the participant referred to tetraplegic friends that he believes may act and think differently from him, for example, in the up-down head control preferences and in the ability to move the shoulders. A flexible system can effectively adapt to a broader population of users, especially when we consider that our participant represents a "best case", with high motivation levels, since he had anticipated the benefits of technology when he first contacted us on our lab.

As a result from our study, we propose three dimensions with which to organize the analysis of needs and opportunities of AT configuration:

— **The psycho-social dimension**, concerning the different form and behaviors factors that may be desired in different situations in a context-dependent way and determined by individual motivations and social environment. That includes: appearance and mobility, devices to be controlled, shortcuts for quick performing functions, and end-user definitions of contexts, tasks or situations of use. For example, the equipment to be used at home may be different from that to be used at school or work due to its appearance, portable abilities and devices to interact with. In the same way, the functions to be performed and how they will be achieved can be totally different in each context: there will probably be no TV at work, but the user may need to control a projector; using voice can be more convenient and practical alone at home, but not possible at a classroom or meetings;

— **The carrier dimension**, concerning the means by which a configuration can be done and the *substratum* where it will reside: whether it is a hardware, software or hybrid configuration and if is to be changed by the user himself or by somebody else helping him. That includes the fit of the cap, the switches to be used and their position, that will have to be put on him by somebody else helping him; at the same time, the outcome of a switch activation and the connections to other devices have the potential to be done by himself on the platform software;

— **The persistence dimension**, concerning the duration of a configuration, its timeliness and volatility: some configurations will be temporary, and some will last for a long time or be for ever. For example, a user's size and abilities to move his head and shoulders are unique, and will probably not change significantly over time, allowing for a persistent setup; however a task or context of use may begin and end making sense once the user changes activity, uses different devices, and so on.

Design features will often have to be considered from the perspective of more than one dimension. For example, the "look" (appearance) feature may vary between "discreet" and "impressive" in the psycho-social dimension (depending if the user is going to school or to a date with his girlfriend), whose effective configuration requires hardware changes, which in turn may entail changes in the carrier dimension. From the persistence dimension perspective, configurations might be kept only for a short time (say, the duration of a date outing or a class). The user might probably want to save it for use in similar situations. So, these dimensions play complementary roles that are all closely linked to each other and we cannot consider them separately during the design. All of them contribute for the achievement of specific goals. We find it useful to think about AT configuration in terms of these dimensions, as a way to clarify the options to be considered and the ways to set them.

5   Conclusion and Future Steps

In this work we proposed three dimensions to support the design of AT configuration options. This characterization of the problem space hasn't been proposed to date and we believe it can be a starting point for the incorporation of configuration features into most AT systems. We plan for a subsequent research cycle, where we will use these findings in a new design and then evaluate it with the same participant to investigate techniques, technologies and approaches that may suit each configuration need.

Acknowledgements. The authors thank the volunteers that participated in this study, as well as CNPq and FAPERJ for supporting them with research grants and scholarships.

References

1. Brazilian Presidency of the Republic: Act N° 3.298 on the National Policy for the Integration of Persons with Disabilities, December 20, 1999
2. United States (105th Congress): Assistive Technology Act of 1998, S. 2432, November 13, 1998
3. Ladner, R.E.: Access and Empowerment: Commentary on Computers and People with Disabilities. ACM Trans. Access. Comput. 1(2), Article 11, October 2008
4. Vanderheiden, G.C.: Ubiquitous Accessibility, Common Technology Core, and Micro Assistive Technology: Commentary on Computers and People with Disabilities. ACM Trans. Access. Comput. 1(2), Article 10, October 2008
5. Carmien, S.P., Fischer, G.: sssssesign, adoption, and assessment of a socio-technical environment supporting independence for persons with cognitive disabilities. In: Proceedings of CHI 2008, Florence, Italy (2008)
6. Lewis, C.: Simplicity in cognitive assistive technology: a framework and agenda for research. Universal Access in the Information Society 5(4), 351–361 (2007)
7. Dourish, P.: Where the Action Is - The Foundations of Embodied Interaction. Cambridge, M.I.T Press (2001)
8. Booth, T., Stumpf, S.: End-user experiences of visual and textual programming environments for arduino. In: Dittrich, Y., Burnett, M., Mørch, A., Redmiles, D. (eds.) IS-EUD 2013. LNCS, vol. 7897, pp. 25–39. Springer, Heidelberg (2013)
9. Eisenberg, M., Elumeze, N., MacFerrin, M., Buechley, L.: Children's programming, reconsidered: settings, stuff, and surfaces. In: Proceedings of the 8th International Conference on Interaction Design and Children (IDC 2009). ACM (2009).
10. Ross, D.A.: Implementing assistive technology on wearable computers. IEEE Intelligent Systems, 16(3), 47–53 (2001)
11. Dollar, A.M., Herr, H.: Lower extremity exoskeletons and active orthoses: challenges and state-of-the-art. Robotics, IEEE Transactions on 24(1), 144–158 (2008)
12. Kane, S.K., Jayant, C., Wobbrock, J.O., Ladner., R.E.: Freedom to roam: a study of mobile device adoption and accessibility for people with visual and motor disabilities. In: Proceedings of the 11th International ACM SIGACCESS Conference on Computers and Accessibility (Assets 2009), pp. 115–122. ACM, New York (2009)
13. Brandão, R., de Souza, C., Cerqueira, R.: A Capture & Access infrastructure to instrument qualitative HCI evaluation. In: Boscarioli, C., Bim, S.A., Leitão, C.F., Maciel, C. (eds.) Proceedings of 13th Brazilian Symposium on Human Factors in Computer Systems (IHC 2014), pp. 197–206. SBC (2014)

Analysing How Users Prefer to Model Contextual Event-Action Behaviours in Their Smartphones

Gabriella Lucci and Fabio Paternò[(✉)]

CNR-ISTI, HIIS Laboratory, Via Moruzzi 1, 56124, Pisa, Italy
{gabriella.lucci,fabio.paterno}@isti.cnr.it

Abstract. Developing context-dependent applications involves indicating the relevant contextual events and the corresponding actions. Based on an analysis of the usability and expressiveness of three Android apps for developing such applications, we have started a study that aims to identify a general solution able to better represent how users classify the relevant concepts in order to facilitate their manipulation during development. We report on a card sorting experiment carried out with 18 users for this purpose, and an analysis of its results, with suggestions for improving current designs and informing future solutions.

Keywords: End-user development · Context-dependent applications · Smartphones

1 Introduction

The main End-User Development (EUD) approaches have focused on the desktop platform and applications that are unable to adapt to the changing context of use [1]. For example, desktop spreadsheets have been the most used EUD tools so far. Some environments allow the development of applications for mobile devices, but still through the desktop platform. One example is App Inventor[1], which provides a graphical environment for creating Android applications.

Only recently have some contributions also started to consider the smartphone as a platform in which the development can be carried out. In this respect, one important point to clarify is that the adoption of mobile devices does not only imply that the development platform has a screen with limited size with which to interact through touch. It also means that the corresponding applications have the potential to dynamically detect relevant information on the context of use through several sensors, and thus adapt their behaviour accordingly. Such contexts can vary in aspects related to the users (tasks, preferences, emotional state, …), the technology (devices, modalities supported, connectivity, …), environment (light, noise, place, …), and social aspects, and only end users can know the most appropriate ways their applications should react to contextual events.

---

[1] http://appinventor.mit.edu/explore/

© Springer International Publishing Switzerland 2015
P. Díaz et al. (Eds.): IS-EUD 2015, LNCS 9083, pp. 186–191, 2015.
DOI: 10.1007/978-3-319-18425-8_14

One possible solution for developing context-dependent applications, still in desktop platforms, even if the obtained applications can then be executed in mobile devices, is IVO (Integrated Virtual Operator) [2]. In IVO the authors used the workflow metaphor in which the activities are triggered by events that are automatically generated at runtime by sensing the environment, either through the smartphone's own sensors, or using a sensor infrastructure external to the smartphone.

More recently, some contributions aiming to support end user development on smartphones have been put forward. For example, Puzzle [3] proposes the adoption of the puzzle metaphor to support development of Internet of Things applications on smartphones. The supporting environment has been designed to facilitate the composition of various pieces through a touch interface for a screen with limited size. Thus, the tool provides a usable solution but limited to the composition of functionalities for which a puzzle piece has been provided.

An attempt to apply the programming-by-example paradigm to a mobile development environment is "Keep Doing It" [4]. It provides the possibility of identifying context-dependent adaptation rules in the event / condition / action format according to the history of user interactions. The rules are represented through a natural language subset using "when", "if" and imperatives verbs. Another environment that aims to support the development of small reactive applications is IFTTT. It uses the textual syntax "IF This Than That" to specify the scheduling of execution of a certain action (That), and the occurrence of a specified event (This). Its distinguishing feature is that, besides being able to express "recipes" that concern and make changes in the hosting device, IFTTT communicates with widely used Web services, thus allowing the automatic execution of functions related to the internal state of apps. A recent study [5] found that trigger-action programming can express the most often desired behaviours in order to customize smart home devices. They conducted a 226-participant usability test of trigger-action programming, finding that inexperienced users can quickly learn to create programs containing multiple triggers or actions obtained by extending the IFTTT language, which has limited possibilities, since it only supports applications with only one trigger and one action. This shows that this approach seems suitable to support EUD of context-dependent applications, but needs to be improved in order to allow users to express the various desired combinations of events and corresponding actions.

Our aim is to reach a better understanding of the users' mental models when they want to specify how their interactive applications should behave according to the context of use, and to provide design suggestions for EUD tools that better match such models.

In this paper we discuss a recent study that carried out a comparative assessment of three Android apps in terms of expressiveness and usability [6]. We then report on a follow-up card sorting study that aimed to better identify how users logically organise the concepts supported by such apps. Lastly, we provide a discussion aiming to analyse the current designs and provide suggestions for new designs that better match the requirements identified.

2   An Analysis of Android Apps for Context-Dependent EUD

An input for our work has been a recent study [6] on how three Android Apps (Tasker[2], Locale[3], and Atooma[4]) aim to support non-professional developers in creating context-dependent applications by exploiting the smartphones' sensors and capabilities. The analysis of the three environments has been carried out from two viewpoints: expressiveness (to what extent they support the relevant concepts); and usability (for which a user study has been carried out).

They provide three different solutions according to the event / condition / action model. They tend to structure the relevant concepts in similar ways in terms of categories, elements, actions. However, they use slightly different vocabularies for the same concepts. In Atooma an application is called Atooma and is structured in an IF and a DO part. Locale supports the development of situations described in terms of Conditions and Settings. Tasker is used to create Profiles structured into Contexts and associated Tasks composed of Actions.

Tasker has the greatest expressiveness (more than double Locale's), with a number of actions that can be expressed (108) greater than the triggers (83). In Atooma the number of expressible conditions (70) is greater than the actions (48). In both triggers and actions, Locale has the same number of expressible elements (40) and is the one that has the lowest total expressiveness. Of a total of 80 features, 58 are obtained through plugins since few elements are directly integrated into the environment.

The three environments differ in terms of how they model what can be specified (events and actions). Right at the beginning Atooma asks users to select mainly from four main macrocategories. Locale provides a list of elements, which can be extended through plugins, while Tasker structures the selectable events and conditions in terms of six Contexts.

We have noted a lack of consistent terminology in such Apps: each environment provides different names for similar concepts, which does not help users to immediately understand them. The most expressive environment (Tasker) is also the one that was found most difficult to use (highest performance time, error numbers, and unsuccessful performance numbers).

In general, with the increasing number of categories for grouping the relevant concepts, there is also an increasing risk of misunderstandings unless familiar classifications, icons and metaphors are proposed to represent and manage such concepts. Since there are many possible elements to specify, they should be structured according to intuitive logical categories that match the mental representation of mobile users. The ordering in specifying events, conditions, and actions should be flexible without artificial constraints. It can also be useful to allow users to easily indicate flexible events, conditions and related actions in which the elements can be composed according to various logical and temporal operators, without any particular limitation on the number of events and actions to compose. In addition, the set of events and conditions to consider should be extensible.

---

[2] http://tasker.dinglisch.net

[3] http://www.twofortyfouram.com

[4] https://play.google.com/store/apps/details?id=com.atooma&hl=it

3   Card Sorting for Identifying User Conceptual Models

In order to identify a more intuitive classification of the concepts that characterize context-dependent applications, we have carried out a user study through card sorting and associated cluster analysis techniques.

The identification of the cards used in the study derived from the analysis of the three Android apps mentioned in the previous section. We used cards that were associated with all the event and action types supported by the three apps. Thus, we obtained 39 cards: 14 referring to only events, 6 to only actions, and 19 were used for both events and actions.

The card sorting was proposed to 18 users with ages between 18 and 35 (average 27), 72.2% were males. In terms of the most used mobile operating systems, 66.9% used Android, 16.6% iOS, 11.1 Windows, 5.7 Blackberry. 72.2% use the mobile to access interactive applications more than 5 times per day.

At the beginning we provided them with some basic concepts to introduce context-dependent applications, then the users had to group them logically and assign a name to each group identified. We did not provide any particular constraint regarding the number of groups to create or limit the possibility of creating sub-groups. They had to carry out the exercise twice: once to classify the 33 cards related to events and once for the 25 cards representing the possible actions. In order to avoid any possible bias, half started with the events and half with the actions. During the exercise the groups identified by the users were entered in the UXsort tool[5], which has been used to support the results analysis. By applying hierarchical clustering methods the tool is able to measure the linkage among elements groups and produces a dendrogram that represents the similarity among elements through a tree-like structure. The tool supports their analysis by using three clustering algorithms (single linkage, complete linkage, average linkage).

In order to select the most interesting results, we decided to focus on solutions that yielded a number of groups between 5 and 8. Such numbers were identified by the analysis of the numbers of groups supported by the current solutions: Atooma groups the elements in five macrocategories, while Tasker exploits six contexts (two of which contain 10 and 12 elements). In the user test mentioned in the previous section the greater number of elements managed by Tasker implied higher expressivity, but also required the subjects to take longer to find the desired elements, especially when they were located in unexpected places in the proposed logical hierarchy. In addition, we considered that less than five groups results in some groups containing many elements, which can become confusing when users look for a specific item, and with more than 8 groups the solutions tend to separate elements that people would expect to be together. In the analysis we used such criteria to identify the levels at which to cut the dendrograms (there were three dendrograms: for single, complete, and average linkage) and obtain clusters with the required cardinality.

In the case of the events, we thus obtained eight possible solutions, which required further analysis: some were then discarded since the resulting groups contained an unbalanced number of elements (as far as having a group with two and one with eighteen elements), while others were discarded since the contained elements were

---

[5] http://www.uxsort.com/

rather heterogeneous (for example, in one case elements such as SMS-Call-Signal were grouped with elements such as Gmail-Facebook-etc.). Thus, we ended up with three similar solutions in which the only differences were related to the location of the elements Silent and the pair Airplane mode and Silent mode, which could be located together with either the group SMS-Call-Supply-Display or the group Bluetooth-WIFI-Tag NFC – Roaming – Mobile Network.

By observing the element patterns in the groupings that occurred in both the events and actions classifications, we have identified the associations between elements and groups that users found most meaningful, and the corresponding group names that were assigned most frequently. We also discarded solutions with an unbalanced number of elements in the resulting groups or with a group whose name was not completely consistent with the actual elements (e.g Archive for a group containing the Media player element). A similar process was followed to analyse how users grouped the 25 action types. Also in this case we discarded solutions with nine groups since they contained a widely varying number of elements (even with groups with only one element). Thus, we obtained twelve possible solutions that all contain six groups of elements that are always together: 1. [Dock – SD Card], 2. [File –Image], 3. [Airplane Mode – Automatic Data Synchronization – Tag NFC – WIFI – Bluetooth – Mobile Network], 4. [SMS – Call – Audio – Display], 5. [Alarm-Notification], 6. [Gmail-Facebook-Twitter-Instagram-App-Dropbox]. In this set of solutions we discarded some that included groups that would be expected to be autonomous together with other elements. Thus, we obtained five solutions that differ by three elements (Media Player, Text-to-Speech, GPS).

The classification of the nineteen elements in common between events and actions has been consistent in the resulting solutions. The following fifteen elements have been grouped in the same way: 1. [Dock – SD Card], 2. [Call – SMS – Display], 3. [Tag NFC – WIFI – Bluetooth – Mobile Network], 4. [Gmail – Facebook– Twitter – Instagram – App – Dropbox]. Airplane Mode, Alarm, File and GPS were the common elements that have been classified differently. The reason for such differences was that each of these elements was strictly related to specific elements in either the events category or in the actions category, thus when users had to classify them when the connected element was not available, then they had to look for new ways to classify them. For example, the GPS event was always grouped with [Location – Movement], but such elements were not available in the action category.

Users also provided suggestions regarding the names to associate with the logical groups. For some groups, users assigned clear preferences regarding their names (as in the case of App, Phone, Hardware). Connections and Sensors received a good number of preferences as well and were more general than other choices for their groups (such as Net and Localization). In one case there was a similar number of preferences for both Archive and File; the latter seems more appropriate. In the end, we found a solution with two small variants that differ regarding the location of the GPS element, which could be included in the groups "Connections", "Sensors", or "Localization". In one case we obtained seven groups for both events and actions. The groups App, Phone, Hardware, File, Events, Connections (including GPS) in common for both, while for the events there was the Sensors group as well, and for actions there was the Multimedia group.

4   Design Implications

Of the elements considered in the card sorting exercise, 17 in the Atooma mobile category are classified differently from the results suggested by the users who preferred to distribute them across various groups. In contrast to Atooma, which supports the same classification for events and actions, in Tasker, while the events are grouped in six contexts (two of which with further subcategories), the actions are reachable through 20 categories, some of which still maintain the names of the event classification (Phone, Net, Display, App, ...). Thus, the Tasker classification of the actions is rather different from that resulting in the card sorting exercise. Since the number of groups is higher in Tasker   then some elements, which in the card sorting exercise are in the same clusters, are placed in different groups in Tasker. In general, Tasker supports a great number of operations, which provides for the use of a higher number of more specific categories. However, some similarities with the card sorting classification emerge as well. In the end, the new classification emerging from the card sorting exercise seems able to address some of the issues found in a previous user study [6], in which Tasker showed various usability problems. Such issues were mainly due to the high number of categories, for which it was difficult to find the elements of interest, and the use of Events and State macro-categories, which were difficult for the users to understand as well. Atooma revelaed usability issues as well because of the unbalanced distribution of the elements (most of them in the Mobile category), and the use of a graphical representation, which made it difficult to show all of them at the same time, thus making finding some of them problematic.

In terms of requirements for new solutions, this study highlights that they should facilitate the understanding of the event / condition / action paradigm, and the search and use of the elements of interest. Thus, a usable design should be able to graphically represent the cause / effect mechanism without imposing any temporal constraint regarding which to specify first. The elements of interest should be selectable from lists providing an appropriate number of elements, without having to deal with an excessive number because this makes it difficult to identify the desired elements.

References

1. Paternò, F.: End User Development: Survey of an Emerging Field for Empowering People. ISRN Software Engineering, 2013, Article ID 532659, 11 pages (2013)
2. Realinho, V., Romão, T., Dias, A.E.: An event-driven workflow framework to develop context-aware mobile applications. In: MUM 2012, vol. 22. ACM Press (2012)
3. Danado, J., Paternò, F.: Puzzle: Puzzle: A Mobile Application Development Environment using a Jigsaw Metaphor. Journal of Visual Languages and Computing 25(4), 297–315 (2014)
4. de A. Maues, R., Barbosa, S.D.J.: Keep doing what i just did: automating smartphones by demonstration. In: Mobile HCI 2013, pp. 295–303 (2013)
5. Ur, B., McManus, E., Ho, M.P.Y., Littman, M.L.: Practical trigger-action programming in the smart home. In: CHI 2014, pp. 803–812
6. Lucci, G., Paternò, F.: Understanding end-user development of context-dependent applications in smartphones. In: Sauer, S., Bogdan, C., Forbrig, P., Bernhaupt, R., Winckler, M. (eds.) HCSE 2014. LNCS, vol. 8742, pp. 182–198. Springer, Heidelberg (2014)

Interaction Anticipation: Communicating Impacts of Groupware Configuration Settings to Users

Raquel O. Prates[1,2(✉)], Mary Beth Rosson[2], and Clarisse S. de Souza[3]

[1] Department of Computer Science, Federal University of Minas Gerais,
Belo Horizonte, Brazil
rprates@dcc.ufmg.br
[2] College of Information Science and Technology, Pennsylvania State University,
State College, USA
mrosson@ist.psu.edu
[3] Department of Informatics, Pontifical Catholic University of Rio de Janeiro,
Rio de Janeiro, Brazil
clarisse@inf.puc-rio.br

Abstract. As collaborative systems have become more integrated into everyday life, designers have tried to bridge the social-technical gap by building more flexible systems that allow users to configure their interactions with other users (e.g. who sees their photos). Although researchers have studied configuration in groupware, we have not found any research on whether and how users can *anticipate* possible interactive paths that are defined as a consequence of their choices and how these paths might be impacted by *other users'* actions over time. In this brief paper we offer an initial framing of what we call the *interaction anticipation* problem and propose five challenges that designers must face in order to address it.

Keywords: Groupware configuration setting · Interactive paths · Anticipation

1 Introduction

In 2000, Ackerman identified a major challenge for the development of groupware systems, the social technical gap – the divide between the social behavior people expect from collaborative systems and what systems can support technically [1]. One of his examples was privacy and information disclosure: people follow nuanced social rules for sharing. The number of possible scenarios leading to exceptions could be unlimited, making it impossible to design a system that could support them all. A solution that has been broadly adopted is the creation of flexible systems that can be adapted by users to different contexts.

Research on groupware systems that can be adapted by users to specific contexts or needs is not novel. A variety of solutions have been proposed – from customization (activities that allow users to choose among behavior features already available in the application) to end user development or software engineering (when users engage in development activities to create, modify or extend a software artifact) [5, 4].

© Springer International Publishing Switzerland 2015
P. Díaz et al. (Eds.): IS-EUD 2015, LNCS 9083, pp. 192–197, 2015.
DOI: 10.1007/978-3-319-18425-8_15

Existing research covers a broad set of issues, such as how users collaborate to tailor a system (groupware or not) [8], toolkits and frameworks [11] that support the development of adaptive groupware systems, and how to support users in understanding the impact of their choices in groupware [3,9,10,7], among others. However, we have not found studies of how to support users in anticipating the effects of their configurations over time. This anticipation problem has become more relevant as Web 2.0 groupware systems present users with sets of configuration parameters that impact not only the status of the system, but also actions that can be taken by or are expected from other users; and these possibilities may evolve over time. In this brief paper we present an initial framing of the problem and propose five challenges that designers must face to address it.

2   Related Work

Our work is investigating how to support users in understanding the impacts – over time – of choices they make about configuration settings. In this direction, de Paula et al. [3] and Reeder et al. [9] have investigated support for users in understanding configuration settings and access rules related to shared files. In both works, the focus was on understanding the current state based on file control settings, and the possibility of changing this state through graphical interface manipulation.

Wulf and Golombek [10] also considered how to show users the status of current settings in a collaborative system, and also allowed them to experiment with effects of their actions on other users' interfaces. The goal was to create an exploration environment in which users could learn about tailoring by experimentation. They explore not only the state caused by a setting change, but also different possible interactions that may result from a combination of settings. However, they did not discuss how one might explore different states and possibilities over time.

More recently, Pereira Junior et al. [7] investigated the value of a simulation environment that may help users understand the effects of their privacy settings, including the impact on other users' actions. Their prototype allows users to ask "what-if" questions about the visibility of Facebook photos, by exploring how their settings affect what other users can see and do. In their discussion, the authors raise the issue we address in this paper, namely the need to support users in anticipating the interactive paths that may occur over time from a set of configuration changes.

3   Framing the Problem

Many Web 2.0 applications enable users to create and share content and to interact with a multitude of other users regarding this content. In order to support a large range of user profiles and contexts in such systems, designers often allow users to tailor the system, mainly through a set of configuration parameters. To define these parameters, designers must first understand what flexibility is needed by their users. For instance, social network system designers try to create flexible privacy schemes; course management system designers want to provide their users with flexible access and management of many types of educational resources.

Customization parameters are fixed at design time; users cannot revise customization *code*. It is up to the designers to envision all relevant states and transitions. Research has shown the relevance and challenges in conveying the system state that will result from a new combination of settings [3,9,10]; but in modern applications, users may need to anticipate not only the **next state** (i.e. the immediate impact of their specification decisions) but also the new **interactive paths** that will become available as a consequence of their choices (i.e. the possible states that may be generated in the future as a result of the possible interactions enabled by their decisions). To illustrate this more complex requirement for groupware systems we propose two scenarios.

Scenario 1 – Facebook privacy settings: *Jane went to Brazil recently and saw many beautiful places. She does not usually post pictures in Facebook, because she is a private person, but this time she posts a few pictures just to her friends. Lucy, a good friend, sees a beach in Maceió, in Northeastern Brazil, and thinks it is beautiful. She is now choosing a vacation spot with Amy and Becky, friends from work, so she shares Jane's pictures with them. Amy loves the picture of Jane at the beach. She tags Carlos, a Brazilian friend (even though he is not in the photo), so he can see the beach and she can ask him if it's a good vacation spot. Carlos recognizes the beach as Sonho Verde and adds the picture location.*

Jane is notified that Carlos (a person she does not know) wants to add a location to her photo. Jane already regrets having shared the picture: she has no idea of who Carlos is and why he can see the picture; she is uncomfortable that she no longer knows who can see her photos. She wishes she would have known before sharing them that people other than her friends would be able to gain access to her pictures.

The scenario shows how difficult it can be for users to understand the effects of their actions. Jane expected that by specifying that the photo should be shared with *friends*, only *her* friends would have access to it. However, in Facebook a shared picture can be tagged by other users, extending the sharing to the newly tagged people. So, the sharing state of Jane's photos depends on both what she does and on actions of other users. We do not intend to discuss which actions should or should not be available in such cases, but rather that these possible outcomes are not clear. Facebook does offer a solution in that direction – the "View as" function provides a preview of how a photo will be seen by other profiles (e.g. a friend or public). But the user has no insight into interactive paths that may be enabled in the future (e.g. a friend tags someone and that person now has access to the photo).

Scenario 2 – Digital legacy: *Jim is a professor who operates almost entirely in the digital realm. He is very organized with his email, redirecting accounts to Gmail, where he tags and separates files that are work related, that relate to bills or shopping or are personal. He also uses Google tools to save documents, pictures, videos and other types of data. When Paul, a good friend of Jim's passed away unexpectedly, Jim started thinking about what would happen to all his digital "stuff" if he were to die. He found that Google allows users to specify what to do when an account becomes inactive.*

He uses Inactive Account Manager to define who will have access to what, based on how his data is tagged. He wants all his bills, receipts and similar data tagged "Finances" to be accessible by his sister Ann. Regarding personal photos and videos he wants both Ann and his best friend John to have access. He dates many women, so he will delete data tagged as

"Relationship". Data tagged as "Research" should be accessible to Debbie, who co-leads their research group. Finally, data tagged as "Class" should be available to his Associate Dean of Education.

Jim has defined the destiny of his most important data. But he did not cover everything and wishes he could know what is left and what will happen to it. Also, he does not know what actions the people he's named as managers of his data will have available. He wishes he could better anticipate exactly what would happen to his data once his account is inactive, so he could make sure he had specified all the actions he had intended.

As in the first scenario, this one refers to many parameters and the final configuration depends not only on the current user's choices, but also on the actions that others might take. Anticipation of only the next state is clearly not enough to support a user's informed decision. Differently from the previous scenario, in this one the user would not be able to understand later on (like Jane did) that the impact of his decisions was not as intended. The additional legal implications underlying this scenario show how critical it is to be able to anticipate the impact of choices *over time*.

4   Challenges in Communicating Interactive Paths over Time

We point to five challenges in helping users to anticipate the unfolding consequences of parameter settings: Supporting anticipation; representation; anticipation cost-benefit; conflict mitigation and negotiation; and definition of default values.

Supporting Anticipation. Typically there will not be just one path but an indefinitely large set of interactive paths enabled by changes to a configuration state. Therefore, the challenge is to help a user understand many scenarios that may (or not) ensue from a set of parameters. If all the possible interactive paths were planned and anticipated at design time, they could be presented to users through help systems. However, this implies that users will visit the help system and read about all the possibilities involving parameter types and values. Wulf and Golombek [10] suggest instead that users should experiment with the interface, using mechanisms for simulating the impacts of their decisions in their own or other users' interface over time.

Configuration settings allow for a deterministic set of interactive paths; nonetheless this set could contain an unlimited number of new possibilities. Therefore, it might not be feasible to present users with all the possible scenarios that could result from a specific decision. In that case, it might be helpful to identify (or let users define at use time) which scenarios are of interest for exploration. Allowing users to choose the different options available would probably require the simulator to provide users with the possibility to ask what-if questions.

Representation. To provide users with a what-if simulator, designers must first decide how to represent the possible future scenarios to users. For example, should the system depict an abstract representation or one that simulates the actual interface? Wulf and Golombek [10] simulated the actual interface to support users in learning the impacts of display and filter configurations. In contrast, the prototype of Pereira Jr. et al. [7] presented users with an abstract model of a Facebook friendship network.

An abstract representation can offer an efficient overall view of interactive paths. However, users would need to learn the new representation and how it maps to the interface. Simulating the actual interface implies a smaller cognitive load to users. Nonetheless, it raises issues such as scale in representing the actual users, their information and their view of the system. For instance, representing in Facebook a user's friends of friends set could require the representation of thousands of people.

Anticipation Cost x Benefits. Supporting users in anticipating and understanding the possible impacts of a decision is important in making informed decisions. However, providing such information will have its own costs to users in terms of cognitive effort, especially if it requires learning new representations. When would the benefits of more informed decisions be worth the cost? If the cost of analyzing the impact is too high, users may decide to ignore the offer (i.e. decline to explore unfolding interactive paths).

Conflict Negotiation and Mitigation. When users' decisions may influence the actions or interactive paths not only of themselves but also of others, disagreements might arise in decisions to be taken (e.g., should Carlos be able to see Jane's photo?). It might be possible for users to negotiate such conflicts, even before an action is taken (e.g., notifying Lucy and Jane when Carlos is tagged). In that direction, Besmer et al. proposed a tool to allow users tagged in a picture in Facebook to negotiate with the poster who should be able to see or not the picture [2]. In a digital legacy scenario [6], it might make sense to have the trusted contact agree to act on behalf of the user before the specification is finalized.

To support conflict negotiation and mitigation, designers should first identify potential conflicts caused by users' actions, the users involved in the conflict and an infrastructure for negotiating it. In some contexts, a conflict may require a negotiation and an agreed upon solution, whereas in others it might be up to the user to decide if he/she wishes to negotiate or not a potential conflict.

Definition of Default Values. Offering configuration parameters to users requires designers to decide which default value would be most appropriate for each parameter. In user-centered design, the choice of default values often signals what designers expect to be most desirable to users in *present* and *typical* situations. Designers may also choose default values that communicate their hopes for how the system will be used (e.g., using "public" as a sharing default in an online social network system). In some contexts designers may also need to support anticipation of *atypical* or *undesirable* scenarios (e.g., digital legacy), in which case they may choose default values that communicate the use of the system in *possible worlds*. This might lead into a hierarchy (or a taxonomy) of default values that designers should *themselves* anticipate productively.

5   Final Remarks

The need to support groupware users in understanding the results of their configuration is not novel. As mentioned, other works have investigated how to support users in understanding the resulting state of their configurations [3,9,10]. This paper contributes to the existing body of work by showing that supporting users in understanding the resulting state of a system is not enough any longer. In some contexts, users should also become aware of a set of resulting *interactive paths* over time.

Framing a problem is the first step needed in order to investigate and propose solutions. In the paper we presented five challenges involved in proposing solutions to the interaction anticipation problem. This should help designers in reflecting and making decisions about the (re)design of configurable groupware systems. The challenges can also be used as guide in the analysis and evaluation of existing systems.

Our next steps in this research involve the description of other scenarios that can be used to illustrate the problem being investigated. For each scenario, we intend to perform a systematic analysis of an existing system in order to collect evidence of the problem, as well as to determine if and how system designers have dealt with the challenges presented in this paper (or others that we discover).

Acknowledgments. Raquel Prates thanks CNPq (grant #248441/2013-2) and the College of Information Sciences and Technology of Information Sciences at Penn State and Clarisse de Souza thanks CNPq (grant #307043/2013-4) and FAPERJ (grant #E-26/102.770/2012) for partially funding their research.

References

1. Ackerman, M.S.: The intellectual challenge of CSCW: the gap between social requirements and technical feasibility. Human–Computer Interaction, 179–203 (2000)
2. Besmer, A., Richter Lipford, H.: Moving beyond untagging: Photo privacy in a tagged world. In: Proceedings of CHI 2010, pp. 1563–1572. ACM, USA (2010)
3. de Paula, R., Ding, X., Dourish, P., Nies, K., Pillet, B., Redmiles, D.F., Ren, J., Rode, J.A., Silva Filho, R.: In the eye of the beholder: a visualization-based approach to information system security. International Journal of Human-Computer Studies **63**(1-2), 5–24 (2005)
4. Ko, A.K., Abraham, R., Beckwith, L., Blackwell, A., Burnett, M., Erwig, M., Scaffidi, C., Lawrance, J., Lieberman, H., Myers, B., Rosson, M.B., Rothermel, G., Shaw, M., Wiedenbeck, S.: The state of the art in end-user software engineering. ACM Comput. Surveys 43(3), Article 21, 44 pages (2011)
5. Lieberman, H., Paternò, F., Wulf, V.: End-user development. Springer, Netherlands (2006)
6. Maciel, C., Pereira, V.C.: Digital Legacy and Interaction. Springer, Heidelberg (2013)
7. Pereira Jr., M., Xavier, S.I.R., Prates, R.O.: Investigating the Use of a Simulator to Support Users in Anticipating Impact of Privacy Settings in Facebook. In: Proceedings of the Int. Conf. on Supporting Group Work (GROUP 2014), pp. 63–72. ACM, USA (2014)
8. Pipek, V., Kahler, H.: Supporting collaborative tailoring. In: End-User Development, pp. 315–345. Springer (2006)
9. Reeder, R.W., Kelley, P.G., McDonald, A.M., Cranor, L.F.: A user study of the expandable grid applied to P3P privacy policy visualization. In: Proceedings of the 7th ACM Workshop on Privacy in the Electronic Society (WPES 2008), pp. 45–54. ACM, USA (2008)
10. Wulf, V., Golombek, B.: Exploration environments: concept and empirical evaluation. In: Proceedings of Int. Conf. on Supporting Group Work (GROUP 2001), pp. 107–116. ACM, USA (2001)
11. Wulf, V., Pipek, V., Won, M.: Component-based tailorability: Enabling highly flexible software applications. International Journal of Human-Computer Studies **66**(1), 1–22 (2008)

Involving Children in Design Activities Using the ChiCo Exploratory Co-design Technique

Diego Alvarado[✉] and Paloma Díaz

Dept. of Computer Science, Universidad Carlos III de Madrid, Leganés, Spain
{dalvarad,pdp}@inf.uc3m.es

Abstract. This paper introduces ChiCo, a novel and exploratory technique for co-design with children based on Ecological Inquiry, aimed at obtaining user requirements for the design of a game. At the core of this technique, there's a technological platform conceived to empower children to partner with adults in a designers' team at the early stages of the creation of a game.

Keywords: Co-Design with children · Multi-touch interaction · Mobile interaction · Ecological inquiry

1 Introduction

When trying to design technology for children, children themselves have a huge potential as co-designers since they have their own conception of what is useful, fun and valuable, and adult designers are not always able to fully understand these aspects in order to fulfill children's requirements.

One of the biggest challenges of involving children in a co-design process is to make them work collaboratively with other children [3]. In order to engage them in scientific inquiry and collaborative explorations, some studies have leveraged the use of multi-touch interaction with tabletops, demonstrating its ability to elicit collaboration in children and support effective learning [5, 7].

In this study, we try to engage children in the co-design of a social game by which other children can learn by playing about emergency response in a natural environment, like home or school. The creation of a game of this nature entails exploration of the environment where the co-creation process is taking place, as well as embodiment of actions in order to print out ideas onto children's prototypes.

Based on findings obtained by Ecological Inquiry [9], we attempt to involve children in technology utilization, environment exploration and social practices, in order to support them in the production of ideas for the design of a game. This paper describes the foundations of a novel and exploratory co-design technique called ChiCo (Children Co-designing) and the implementation of its enabling technological platform.

© Springer International Publishing Switzerland 2015
P. Díaz et al. (Eds.): IS-EUD 2015, LNCS 9083, pp. 198–203, 2015.
DOI: 10.1007/978-3-319-18425-8_16

2   Related Work

In order to strengthen children's potential as design partner of an adults' team, low-tech prototyping tools have been used in a narrative-based methodology [2], and in participatory design sessions to involve children in the design of educational games [10]. A different method that arises cooperation in children is given by Vaajakallio et al. with Make Tools [11], a co-design technique in which tangible design materials (pieces of cardboard, markers, scissors, glue and so on) are provided so children generate new ideas by touching, cutting, pasting and reshaping, while adults moderate the sessions by encouraging teamwork among them. In order to avoid adult's intervention during the design process, the Embodied Sketching technique [4] makes use of activities like sketching, bodystorming and photo stories to motivate children and make them have fun. Embodied Narratives [3] is a performative co-design technique targeted to the early stages of the design process that fosters embodied interaction and social play in natural settings in order to facilitate the generation of ideas. All these techniques mentioned rely on tangible materials without making use of technology. One interesting use of technology to foster children's imagination in brainstorming sessions was made by leveraging and enhancing comicboarding [6]. This approach consisted in having a professional artist drawing what children narrate. What's interesting of it is that children couldn't see the artist but just a screen where drawings appeared "magically", meanwhile in another room the artist drew on a digital canvas connected to the screen that children were watching. This technique relies strongly on technology to make children come up with ideas during a brainstorming session. The POGO story world [8] also leverages technology in order to support children in story building through a narrative environment equipped with technological tools at children's disposal. Lastly, let us mention Ecological Inquiry [9], a methodological approach to design technology with children which analyzes the social aspects surrounding children's activities and their environment. The work introduced in this document is strongly based on EI due to the emphasis made on social practices and environment awareness when designing technology for children. The authors mention the need of a recipe of tools and techniques for the execution of their approach. This is the gap that is meant to be bridged through this study.

3   An Exploratory Co-design Technique

Motivated by the challenges of gathering children in a co-design process, we shaped a technique able to introduce technology without alienating the spatial and social aspects of the activity, but enforcing them in order to support children in the production of user requirements for a social game of which they would be the final users. Fig. 1 depicts a diagram of the ChiCo co-design process.

As suggested by the EI methodology [9], ChiCo iteratively combines inquiries in social practices, user environments and appropriation of technology. This technique is executed in three stages:

Brainstorming. It is in this stage when children start to come up with the first ideas. Children are instructed about the procedure of the activity and the use of the technological platform to their disposal. Then, they are left alone to discuss what they could do if they were to create a game to teach other children how to respond to an emergency. This stage lasts about 20 minutes.

The Process. In this stage technology, environment and social practices meet. The curved external arrows in Fig. 1 indicate that the process is iterative and that the three dimensions of EI are supposed to be explored repeatedly until the outcome is obtained. The fundamental piece at this stage is the ChiCo platform, a system that supports children in the production of a digital storyboard. More details about this platform will be given in the next section. This stage lasts about 45 minutes.

Debriefing. At the end of the session, children describe what they did to other children and researchers. Their storyboard is the input adult designers will use to gather user requirements for the creation of a social game. This stage lasts about 15 minutes.

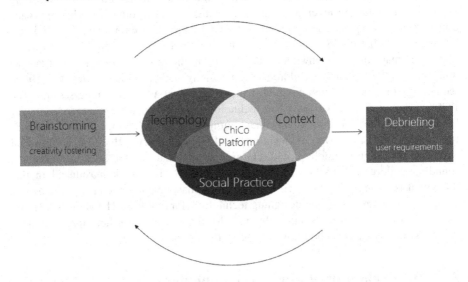

Fig. 1. Diagram of the ChiCo technique.

4   The ChiCo Platform

The core of the ChiCo technique is a technological platform able to facilitate the convergence of the three dimensions of an Ecological Inquiry: technology, context and social practices. The ChiCo platform was conceived as a whole system consisting of the integration of three main modules: a canvas main application running on a multitouch tabletop where the prototype is going to be crafted; a mobile application that will allow children to take photos while exploring the environment, and the middleware that will make possible the wireless communication between the mobile and the tabletop applications. This communication is needed since photos taken with mobile devices are transferred to the tabletop via Bluetooth. From the interaction point-of-view, this transfer was designed to occur when the user slides a photo out of the mobile screen with his finger towards the tabletop. Immediately after, the image appears onto the canvas where it can be manipulated with other application tools to create the storyboard of the game.

The multi-touch main application allows the following types of interaction:

— Multi-touch drawing on a digital canvas, so several children can draw at the same time.
— A set of tools to draw different geometric shapes, to draw by free-hand, to type-write using a virtual keyboard, to change colors, sizes and position of drawings and so on. However, only one tool can be used at a time, so as to favor agreement between team members and avoid independent or isolated working individuals.
— The drawings can be manipulated using commonly used multi-touch gestures like pinch-to-zoom, rotate, and move. This is especially useful for pictures sent to the canvas with the mobile application.
— A set of buttons to save the work as a static JPEG file or as an XML project to a specified location; and buttons to import images to the canvas in JPEG, GIF, PNG or TIFF format, and load an XML project from a specified location. This makes it possible to permanently digitalize children's work so it can be reused or modified in future sessions.

The platform was evaluated using Cognitive Walkthrough, with the help of 14 experts in the area of Human-Computer Interaction. The details of the evaluation can be found in [1]. Evaluators considered that the interface was usable, intuitive, and easy to get used to. They particularly enjoyed the mobile feature by which photos are transferred to the digital canvas by sliding the pictures out of the mobile screen. In any case, this was only a preliminary usability evaluation that doesn't empirically validate the utility of the platform. As a drawback, evaluators experienced some difficulties when trying to select some of the drop-down menus to pick an item; however, it wasn't due to the interface itself but to the hardware which occasionally incurs in touch misdetections. A workaround to overcome such an issue was to enlarge drop-down menus considerably so they could be easier to select.

5   Next Steps

The ChiCo technique was developed to embrace some favorable aspects for getting children to work in teams, collaborate, lose shyness and boost their creativity; all this in a playful manner. First, children's immersion in technology while exploring their environmental setting and incentivizing social practices, as inspired by Ecological Inquiry, is advantageous for empowering children as design partners in the early stages, instead of just involving them as informants or evaluators of technology.

Secondly, the slight level of restriction imposed in the platform, impelling children to work individually, contributes to enforce synergy among team members and make them actually work collaboratively.

The platform is now ready to be evaluated in a workshop with children. After that, the next directions for the technique will be discussed. One desirable update for the platform to be done after children use it for the first time is to provide them with pre-made templates, created according to the sort of stories and games that children create, in case they follow and identifiable pattern. If so, we could invite children to choose among different templates to start crafting their storyboard and help them save time with the initial steps and make emphasis on the creativity development.

6   Conclusions

This paper describes a new approach to co-design with children based on an Ecological Inquiry. In the near future, through a case study, we will be able to discuss how this technique is able to make children collaborate and work in teams to come up with a storyboard for adult designers to use as user requirements for the creation of a social game to help children learn how to respond to an emergency situation. This paper contributes to the theory of Ecological Inquiry by providing a technique for its application in a specific domain.

Acknowledgments. This work is supported by the project emerCien funded by the Spanish Ministry of Economy and Competitiveness TIN2012-09687.

References

1. Alvarado, D., Díaz, P.: Design and evaluation of a platform to support co-design with children. Proceedings of the 2014 International Working Conference on Advanced Visual Interfaces. ACM (2014)
2. Duh, H., Yew Yee, S., Gu, Y., Chen, V.: A narrative-driven design approach for casual games with children. In: Proceedings of SIGGRAPH Symposium on Video Games 2010, LA, USA, July 2010, pp. 19–24. ACM, NY (2010)
3. Giaccardi E., Díaz, P., Paredes, P., Alvarado, D.: Embodied narratives: a performative co-design technique. In: Proceedings of DIS 2012, Newcastle, UK, July 2012, pp. 1–10. ACM, NY (2012)
4. Hemmert, F., Hamann, S., Löwe, M., Zeipelt, J., Joost, G.: Co-designing with children: a comparison of embodied and disembodied sketching techniques in the design of child age communication devices. In: Proceedings of IDC 2010, Barcelona, Spain, ACM Press, 202–205 (2010)
5. McCrindle, C., Hornecker, E., Lingnau, A., Rick, J.: The Design of t-vote: a tangible table-top application supporting children's decision making. In: Proceedings of IDC 2011, Michigan, USA, June 2011, pp. 181–184. ACM, NY (2011)
6. Moraveji, N., Li, J., Ding, J., O'Kelley, P., Woolf, S.: Comicboarding: using comics as proxies for participatory design with children. In: Proceedings of CHI 2007, San Jose, USA, May 2007. ACM, NY (2007)

7. Olson I., Horn M.: Modeling on the table: agent-based modeling in elementary school with NetTango. In: Proceedings of IDC 2011, Michigan, USA, June 2011, pp. 181–184. ACM, NY (2011)
8. Rizzo, A., Marti, P., Decortis, F., Moderini, C., Rutgers, J.: The design of POGO story world. In: Hollnagel, E. (ed.) Handbook of Cognitive Task Design, pp. 577–602. Erlbaum, London (2002)
9. Smith, R., Iversen, O., Hjermitslev, T., Lynggaard, A.: Towards an ecological inquiry in child-computer interaction. In: Proc. of the IDC 2013. ACM (2013)
10. Triantafyllakos, G., Palaigeorgiou, G., Tsoukalas, I.: Designing educational software with students through collaborative design games: The We!Design&Play framework. Computers and Education 56(1), 227–242 (2011)
11. Vaajakallio, K., Mattelmäki, T., Lee, J.: "It became Elvis": Co-design lessons with children. Interactions 17(4), 26–29 (2010)

FaceMashup: Enabling End User Development on Social Networks Data

Daniele Massa and Lucio Davide Spano(✉)

Department of Mathematics and Computer Science, University of Cagliari,
Via Ospedale 72, 09124 Cagliari, Italy
danielemas87@gmail.com, davide.spano@unica.it

Abstract. Every day, each user produces and shares different contents on social networks. While developers can access such data through APIs, end users have less control on such information, since their access is mediated by the social application features. In order to fill this gap, we introduce FaceMashup, an EUD environment supporting the manipulation of the social network graph. Data types are represented through widgets containing the UI elements used in the social network application, which can be connected with each other through the drag and drop. We report on a user-test on the FaceMashup prototype, which shows a good acceptance of the environment by end-users.

Keywords: End user development · Social networks

1 Introduction

The availability of APIs for accessing social network (SN) data is a gold-mine for developers, since they are useful for creating a personalised application experience. Social Networks APIs such as the Facebook Graph API [3] apply strict privacy rules, and social network users must explicitly grant the access on their information. In contrast, even if users are the owners of this material, they cannot combine sources, filter results or perform specific actions if not explicitly provided by the interface. Even for third party developers it is difficult to provide support for unusual tasks, which have a smaller potential audience. Nevertheless such small groups consider the functionalities they need as useful. In this paper, we propose to fill this gap applying End User Development (EUD) techniques for enabling end-users to inspect and control their social network data, creating applications able to both retrieve and manipulate their contents. We describe the design and the implementation of FaceMashup, an environment allowing users to mix contents created friends and to perform actions on them.

2 Related Work

We have been inspired by different existing solutions for representing data and defining the application logic in other EUD applications in literature. We represent the social network through the UI elements used by the Facebook web

© Springer International Publishing Switzerland 2015
P. Díaz et al. (Eds.): IS-EUD 2015, LNCS 9083, pp. 204–210, 2015.
DOI: 10.1007/978-3-319-18425-8_17

application. In this way, the user recognizes the information by its appearance, associating intuitively the data semantics. Such technique has been applied successfully in [4], where the authors proposed a tool for creating mashups from existing web applications. Hartman et al. [5] follow a similar approach, requiring some programming knowledge for creating the data composition code. With respect to the application logic, FaceMashup requests the users to directly manipulate the data representation in order to infer the actions that the environment must perform on them (e.g. using a field as input for a search, or filtering some photos by date etc.). Such paradigm is derived from the *programming by example* [2] technique, which has been employed in different EUD tools. For instance, CoScripter [6] allows users to automatize searches and data extraction on web pages recording the user's actions. The tool automatically creates scripts, whose descriptions in natural language contain the procedure steps. Users can review, modify, load and save them through a dedicated panel in the web browser. Lin et al. [7] created a different interface for the same scripting engine, based on spreadsheets, which allows users to combine data coming from different websites.

3   End User Development Support

FaceMashup represents the Facebook Graph API data with the same elements used in the social network application interface (see figure 1), including them in dedicated widgets. Starting from these building blocks, the user can drag interface elements between different widgets for retrieving, combining and filtering data coming from the Facebook graph. In addition, she can perform actions on the selected entries, through a set of action widgets. We followed four design principles for creating the environment:

P1 No separation between the design and the runtime of a SNA. The user defines the SNA data and logic *while* executing the it. The goal is to require a lower abstraction effort for the end user, since she focus on a specific example [2].

P2 A data type is represented through the interface elements of the social network application UI, for exploiting the recognition mechanism and helping the user in understanding the semantics of a data type (e.g. a user profile is represented through the profile picture, the name etc.). The data *is* the UI element from the end user's point of view.

P3 The user exploits familiar interactions for defining the input of a routine element or for exploiting its output. She should consider them as UI objects that can be manipulated inside the environment like e.g. file icons.

P4 The environment should support the user guiding her actions while creating the application logic, in order to 1) avoid conceptual errors (e.g. data type mismatch) and 2) explore the possibilities offered by the environment for stimulating the learning process.

Fig. 1. A sample Social Network Application developed with FaceMashup

In FaceMashup, each widget represents a block for building the entire SNA. A widget retrieves data from the Facebook graph, or it modifies its state. In addition, a widget can be used for requesting simple direct inputs (e.g. a text or a number) to the user. Therefore, we group the FaceMashup widgets into three categories: *Content, Action* or *Input*. Content widgets are user-friendly representation of Facebook Graph data types. In FaceMashup, it is possible to insert the following content widgets: 1) *Login,* 2) *Photo* 3) *Post,* 4) *Video* 5) *Friend List,* 6) *Profile Information,* 7) *Like list*. According to P2, we maintained a UI similar to the Facebook one. Figure 1 shows different content widgets, with a blue background (login, photo, friend list and posts), and their similarity in appearance with respect to the correspondent information in Facebook.

The second type of widget we included in FaceMashup is the *Input*, which collects data inserted directly by the user of the SNA (e.g. text, date, number, URL, place etc.).

The last type of widget included in FaceMashup is the *Action*. Such widgets take as input a set of objects and modify their state or add new content on the Facebook graph. We included in the environment the following set of action widgets: 1) *Tagger*, which takes as input a set of contents (e.g. posts, photos videos etc.) and a set of user profiles, tagging all the profiles in all the specified contents 2) *Share* which allows to share a content on the Facebook wall, 3) *Like* which allows to like a set of contents, passed as input to the widget. Figure 1 shows an example of tagger widget in the bottom row.

Fig. 2. Example of user feedback while dragging a field from a widget into another

If we do not consider the input and the login, all widgets show contents or perform action according to some input data. The end-user defines which widget provides such input data while creating the SNA. In this way, she is able to create and control the flow of the routine she wants to automatize. According to P3 and P4, the data transport between two widgets is supported through a drag and drop metaphor: a UI element, which represents a data type or a data field, can be selected in a source widget and it can be dropped inside another one. Such interaction specifies that the data corresponding to the selected element is the input of the widget where it was dropped. When the user adds a new widget in the environment, it shows a help message for supporting the user in figuring out which kind of information it needs. In order to show which elements can be dragged from a widget, FaceMashup visualizes an immediate feedback to the end-user each time she clicks UI element. Such feedback contains information about the selected field, like its type and value, and also the number of dragged elements. Indeed, it is possible for the user to move more than one data object at a time, for instance dragging the entire content of a photo or friend list widget, by selecting the container box. Figure 2 shows an example of such dragging feedback in the left part, where the user is informed that she is dragging one data object, corresponding to the profile name. Finally, the tool guides the user for choosing one among all the available options for releasing the data she is currently dragging. It matches the selected data type with the input needed by all the widgets in the environment. For all widgets that may exploit the such data, FaceMashup shows an icon suggesting to drop the content, as shown in figure 2, right part. In this way, we prevent end-users errors, since we do not allow her to release the data elements into widgets that do not accept them. Once data is dropped inside a widget, it immediately updates its visualization for showing the retrieved content.

The connection defines implicitly a partial temporal ordering among the widgets, which can be automatically computed by the underling environment support. FaceMashup represents explicitly such ordering positioning the widgets inside the environment. It represents a sequential relationship between a widget A and B positioning B below A in the vertical axis. Instead, if the user may provide the information needed by both widgets at the same time (theoretically) or in any order (more practically), the widgets are represented in the same position in the vertical axis, aligned horizontally. This creates a grid of widgets, where rows represent sequential steps and columns parallel operations. For instance, the application in figure 1 allows the user to select a photo and tag all friends that published at least a photo or a post in the same place where the photo was shot. The SNA sequence requires her to login (first row), then to select the photo and retrieve the list of friends (second row), then it shows all photos and posts created by her friends in the same place (third row) and, finally, to tag them (fourth row) [1].

The end-user is able to recall which widget provides input to another one through hints in its presentation. If a widget receives data from a source, in the upper part there is a green icon with a small number indicating the cardinality of the input set. If the user clicks the icon, the environment highlights the corresponding source widget. In addition, the user can de-connect the two widgets simply dragging out the green icon.

Besides setting the widget input source, in FaceMashup end-users can control the contents retrieved by a widget applying some filters, in order to select the set of items according to an end-user defined criterion. In order to filter the contents, the user can follow two approaches. The first one is a manual selection of the contents from the set. The second option is to define a filter through the bottom part of a content or action widget. A filter defines a simple comparison between a data attribute against an end-user provided value with a comparison operator. The operator set changes according to the type of the comparison attribute. The value can be specified dragging data from another widget, as happens for a connection.

4 Evaluation

We carried out a usability test in order to evaluate the prototype and the techniques for controlling both the data and the control flow. Twelve people participated to the user test, aged between 36 and 20 years old ($\bar{x} = 25$, $s = 3.96$). None of them had programming skills, 8 used applications for organizing automatically personal data, and all users were familiar with Facebook.

After completing a demographic questionnaire and reading a one-page introduction to the tool, each user completed the following three tasks: **T1**) Create an application for retrieving all the photos of a user, **T2**) Create an application for retrieving all the photos created by all the friends of a user in a specific day,**T3**) Create an application allowing the user to select a photo and tag all friends that published at least a photo or a post in the same place where the photo was shot.

Finally, the users completed a post-test questionnaire in two parts: a standard SUS [1] and other five questions for evaluating the EUD specific features. Figure 3 summarizes the results of the first part of the questionnaire. All questions received high mean ratings and all users completed T1 and T2 successfully. Only one user was not able to complete T3. The mean SUS [1] score was good ($\bar{x} = 77.6$, $s = 16.1$). We registered a high variability for question 10 of the SUS questionnaire, which means that the next version of the prototype should focus more on the learning phase, providing support and help for users that

---

[1] A demo video is available at https://www.youtube.com/watch?v=4LhUislgFD8

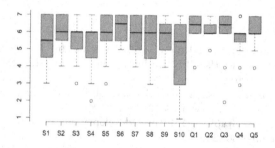

Fig. 3. Evaluation questionnaire results in a 1-7 scale. We inverted the rating for questions in [1] with a negative connotation.

are exploring the environment for learning. The additional five questions (Q1 - Q5 in figure 3) show a good rating of FaceMashup on the following aspects: Q1) satisfaction, Q2) usefulness, Q3) overall experience, Q4) aesthetics and Q5) completeness.

In summary, the users found the tool useful and they were able to complete the programming task, even the most difficult one. The interface was able to support them appropriately in creating applications with social network data. However, the evaluation highlighted also the need for a more effective help, in order to better convey the application concept to end-users. In addition, the environment should include more feedback and suggestions for the available actions, especially for the widget connections.

5   Conclusions and Future Work

In this paper, we described the design and the implementation of FaceMashup, a tool that empowers social network users, supporting them in creating their own procedures for inspecting and controlling their data. The tool represents the Facebook graph data through a set of widgets containing the interface elements exploited in the social network application. The preliminary user test highlighted both a good acceptance of the tool and a high completion rate even for complex tasks. More work is needed for providing a better user guidance during the widget connection, especially for identifying and selecting the UI parts that can be exploited for connecting widgets.

Acknowledgments. Lucio Davide Spano gratefully acknowledges Sardinia Regional Government for the Financial support (P.O.R. Sardegna F.S.E., European Social Fund 2007-2013 - Axis IV, Obj 1.3, LoA 1.3.1)

References

1. Brooke, J.: SUS: a "quick and dirty" usability scale. In: Jordan, P., Thomas, B., Weerdmeester, B. (eds.) Usability Evaluation in Industry, pp. 189–194. Taylor & Francis, London (1996)
2. Faaborg, A., Lieberman, H.: A goal-oriented web browser. In: Proceedings of CHI 2006, pp. 751–760. ACM, New York (2006)
3. Facebook: Facebook Graph API. https://developers.facebook.com/docs/graph-api (accessed: September 30, 2010)
4. Ghiani, G., Paternò, F., Spano, L.D.: Creating mashups by direct manipulation of existing web applications. In: Piccinno, A. (ed.) IS-EUD 2011. LNCS, vol. 6654, pp. 42–52. Springer, Heidelberg (2011)
5. Hartmann, B., Wu, L., Collins, K., Klemmer, S.R.: Programming by a sample: rapidly creating web applications with d.mix. In: Proceedings of UIST 2007, pp. 241–250. ACM, New York (2007)
6. Leshed, G., Haber, E.M., Matthews, T., Lau, T.: Coscripter: automating & sharing how-to knowledge in the enterprise. In: Proceedings of the SIGCHI Conference on Human Factors in Computing Systems CHI 2008, pp. 1719–1728. ACM, New York (2008)
7. Lin, J., Wong, J., Nichols, J., Cypher, A., Lau, T.A.: End-user programming of mashups with vegemite. In: Proceedings of IUI 2009, pp. 97–106. ACM, New York (2009)

SketchCode – An Extensible Code Editor for Crafting Software

Siemen Baader[✉] and Susanne Bødker

Department of Computer Science, Aarhus University,
Aabogade 34, 8200 Aarhus N, Denmark
{sb,bodker}@cs.au.dk

Abstract. We present SketchCode, a code editor that its users can augment with visual elements to represent domain and program concepts. We examine programming as sketching and identify the techniques of *postsyntactic augmentation, macro components,* and *interactive semantic enrichment.* Based on studies of programmers, we discuss these techniques as a promising way for code editing and tool appropriation.

Keywords: Programming · Crafting · Sketching

1 Introduction

Domain specific programming tools can be very effective at supporting development and workflows within their particular area. We note that programmers often act as end-user developers in the sense of Ko et al. [2], in that they create and appropriate tools to fit their domain and own ways of working. Similarily, designers make extensive use of sketching and model making as ways of expressing a design in the making. Lindell characterized both disciplines as 'crafting' [4], and we believe that programming and designing share similarities in their relieance on thinking through action and the creation of supporting structures as central activities. While the creative use of expressive materials is widely accepted within design professions, programmers do not have access to modifying their code writing tools in the same practical ways, and most end-user appropriation of programming tools is not very feasible beyond the configuration of standard editors and refactoring of source code. We report on early findings from a design-oriented effort to understand the end-user development aspects of programming. We ask *"What can we learn from design studies to support the expressive and appropriative aspects of programming practice, and how can we design programming tools to support this?"*

In this paper we report on two things: How end-user development in programming can be interpreted as design, in particular sketching, and which requirements this interpretation offers. Based on an empirical study of programmers we present SketchCode. We introduce the interface techniques of *postsyntactic augmentation*, which allows the inlining of rich visual editors in plain text code,

© Springer International Publishing Switzerland 2015
P. Díaz et al. (Eds.): IS-EUD 2015, LNCS 9083, pp. 211–216, 2015.
DOI: 10.1007/978-3-319-18425-8_18

macro components, which are rich interactive editors for domain and program concepts, and *interactive semantic enrichment*, which allows the insertion of non-parseable parts into source code. Figure 1 shows how source code is augmented and intermixed with components that represent higher level concepts.

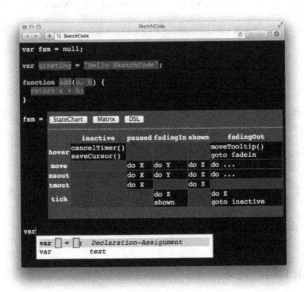

Fig. 1. The SketchCode extensible editor displays the concept of *postsyntactic augmentation*. It shows white plain text source code (top line), colored *macro components* of varying complexity, and *interactive semantic enrichment* via an autocompletion menu.

2   Programming seen from a Sketching Perspective

To identify theoretical requirements for a programming system informed by design studies, we rely in the concepts of crafting, reflective practice and sketching. Lindell [4] demonstrated that interaction designers and programmers share a crafting epistemology. Likewise informed by reflective practice, Buxton [1] and Lim et al. [3] studied the specifics of sketching techniques and prototypes in design. Applying these perspectives to programming results in the following perspectives on code and editors as a design material:

Backtalk. Reflective practice is a dialectic process and depends on backtalk from the code and editor in order to advance the solution (reflection in action) or to rephrase the approach (reflection on action). In programming, we have observed backtalk from four sources: running the code, reasoning about the code, feedback from static analysis, and representing the code differently (e.g. in a diagram). To support the cycle of reflective practice, a system can e.g. tolerate broken and pseudo code, simultanously allow different (e.g. visual) representations and perform automated reasoning.

Externalizing and Improvising. Lim et al. [3] introduced the notions of *filtering dimensions* and *manifestation dimensions* as ways to using protypes and sketches economically. In coding, filtering dimensions include properties like execution order, stateful situations like in user interfaces and visual properties like color codes. Effective manifestations include meaningful names and refactored code, but also graphical representations like charts, tables and formulae available in a modern browser.

Sketching and Modeling. Visualizations and automated reasoning approximate the agenda of modeling tools. Unlike offline sketches, models and representations in code can be reused and linked with the concepts they represent. However, modeling tools require the complete specification of models to work, and in order not to prevent other kinds of backtalk, a system informed by sketching should allow, but not require, complete modeling.

3   Programmer Studies

We conducted 6 participant observations of 30 minutes and semi-structured interviews with web-programmers in two startup companies. In addition we collected 103 scenarios of interest to the sketching perspective in the form of annotated screen shots from the first author's own programming practice.

Backtalk. The most direct mode of backtalk was making a change and executing the program to see the result. Programmers furthermore relied on mental execution to find bugs, e.g. reasoning about front-end code that was broken beyond execution. Static analysis was another source of backtalk, e.g. using the JSLint static analysis tool regularly without executing the code. A final source of backtalk comes from the representation, e.g. using state charts and transition matrices to reason about complex network interactions. We observed backtalk from a variety of sources, and rather than siding either with dynamic (backtalk from execution) or compiled languages (backtalk from static analysis), programming systems should provide backtalk suitable to the specific situation.

Representation. Several situations indicated that the programmers benefited from concise representations of the programing concepts at hand, e.g. preferring the concise JQuery library over the browser's verbose DOM API, or writing hexadecimal CSS color codes and repeatedly refreshing the browser in trial-and-error cycles to find a desired color.

Modeling. The situations of representing colors and the different state chart representations lend themselves not only to visual representation, but also to direct manipulation interfaces and concept-specific editing assistance. The issues of representation and receiving relevant backtalk go hand in hand with issues of modeling, i.e. elevating the source codes semantic level beyond the textual level.

Emergence and refining. The programmers saw static programming systems as heavyweight and dominated by boilerplate, which indicates that a system should be vary of imposing formal structures up front, and allow the coexistence of higher level concepts, visual representations and very crude code, and the gradual refinement of code into higher level components. One programmer e.g.

used Emacs because it allowed him to execute code in an anonymous buffer without having to name a file.

4   The SketchCode Extensible Code Editor

Figure 1 shows the SketchCode editor. It is implemented as a number of partly usable prototypes used to develop the conceptual design. The editor contains both source code in plain text (top line) and instances of *macro components* representing the declaration and assignment of a variable, a function, and one representing the configuration of a finite state machine using three panels (a state chart, a transition matrix and code). The programmer writes code and navigates the editor like a standard editor. However, macro components govern their own user interfaces and support and restrict editing according to their meaning. Since macro components can represent both very complex but also very simple concepts in code, the editor does not offer syntax coloring but instead provides macro components for basic concepts such as functions and variables.

The user inserts instances of macro components into the source code using an autocompletion menu, which we call *interactive semantic enrichment*. In Figure 1, the user is just about to insert another instance of a variable declaration and assignment component. Editors within macro components may recursively contain other macro components. At run time, the macro components are expanded to valid syntax within their surrounding region. E.g., a macro component representing a CSS color expands to the string #CC0000 within a CSS stylesheet, while it will expand to "#CC0000" to be a valid expression in a JavaScript context.

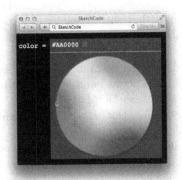
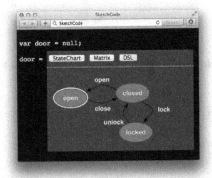

Fig. 2. Visual Macro Components: A CSS color wheel (left) and a state chart (right)

Macro components are built as small interactive web user interfaces, and integrate with the surrounding SketchCode environment in a standardized way. Figure 3 shows pseudo code for an interactive color picker to edit CSS color codes. Complex macro components such as the state machine contain executable code in their expanded representation, and to avoid name clashes, this should be implemented as hygienic macros.

The key aspects of this design consist of three parts. First, it allows the gradual refinement of plain text code into more semantic representations only as needed – the use of macro components is not enforced, and the editor can be used as a plain code editor until specialized macro components are needed. Second, the creation of macro components makes use of the skills that the programmers are proficient in. Third, the system integrates with the text-based ecosystems that programmers live in, like version control and interpreters.

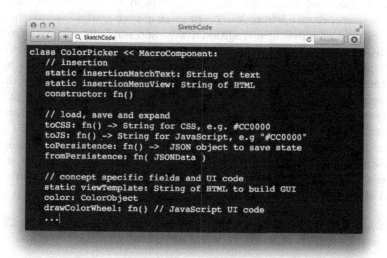

Fig. 3. The macro component programming interface shown in pseudo code

We conducted an early evaluation of the SketchCode concept by confronting the programmers with the prototype and discussing how they would use and extend it. Reactions ranged from excitement to skepticism with regard to the efficiency and uniform editing capabilities achieved in text-only environments. One sceptic noted that "everything can be expressed in text, and I believe it should". On the other end, one programmer noted that this was "a very interesting concept, I already build visualisations for my database." Two of them have since started implementing visual code editing in their own toolmaking.

We draw two main conclusions. First, lightweight tooling is important to the audience, and a running prototype must test if the system remains efficient and easy to use with an increasing number of macro components. Second, we have seen evidence of toolmaking and appropriation, but programmers are not fully aware of the effects of changing and evolving representations and should be educated in this way of thinking before the concept can be tested properly.

5   Discussion and Conclusion

We have introduced the perspectives of crafting and in particular sketching, identified central elements of it in programming practice and proposed the design of SketchCode and its key concepts of *postsyntactic augmentation, macro components* and *interactive semantic enrichment* to accomodate sketching better in code editors. With this, we argue for a more fine-grained view on the process of programming, its different kinds of backtalk, and how it can benefit from evolutionary creation of supporting semantic structures and visualizations.

Language workbenches address issues of backtalk from static analysis and representations well, but they require the programmer to work directly on the abstract syntax tree. This requires programmers to re-learn their editing tools and to define concepts up-front [6]. We propose a more gradual approach, where most code can be edited in a traditional way, and semantic editing introduced gradually as needed. Agentsheets [5] is another toolkit for creating and evolving (visual) programming languages, and differs mainly from SketchCode in that the latter uses plain text and web technology concepts from within the domain of the end users. Live programming systems such as Processing and Smalltalk cater more to getting backtalk from executing code than SketchCode, and less to backtalk from representation.

Overall, SketchCode presents a balance towards supporting backtalk from representation and domain specific editing support, while taking into account the needs for emergence, existing practices and known technologies within the domain of its user population.

Acknowledgments. We thank Joseph Kiniry for exceptional support, and Clemens Klokmose and our three reviewers for constructive feedback.

References

1. Buxton, B.: Sketching user experiences: getting the design right and the right design. Morgan Kaufmann (2010)
2. Ko, A.J., Abraham, R., Beckwith, L., Blackwell, A., Burnett, M., Erwig, M., Scaffidi, C., Lawrance, J., Lieberman, H., Myers, B., et al.: The state of the art in end-user software engineering. ACM Computing Surveys (CSUR) **43**(3), 21 (2011)
3. Lim, Y.K., Stolterman, E., Tenenberg, J.: The anatomy of prototypes: Prototypes as filters, prototypes as manifestations of design ideas. ACM Transactions on Computer-Human Interaction (TOCHI) **15**(2), 7 (2008)
4. Lindell, R.: Crafting interaction: The epistemology of modern programming. Personal and ubiquitous computing **18**(3), 613–624 (2014)
5. Repenning, A., Sumner, T.: Agentsheets: A medium for creating domain-oriented visual languages. Computer **28**(3), 17–25 (1995)
6. Voelter, M., Siegmund, J., Berger, T., Kolb, B.: Towards user-friendly projectional editors. In: Combemale, B., Pearce, D.J., Barais, O., Vinju, J.J. (eds.) SLE 2014. LNCS, vol. 8706, pp. 41–61. Springer, Heidelberg (2014)

Physical Prototyping of Social Products Through End-User Development

Daniela Fogli[1(✉)], Elisa Giaccardi[2], Alessandro Acerbis[1], and Fabio Filisetti[1]

[1] Dipartimento Di Ingegneria Dell'Informazione, Università Degli Studi Di Brescia, Brescia, Italy
fogli@ing.unibs.it, {alessandro.acerbis,filisetti}@gmail.com
[2] Department of Industrial Design, Delft University of Technology, Delft, The Netherlands
e.giaccardi@tudelft.it

Abstract. This paper presents a web-based toolkit that facilitates the physical prototyping of social products. Social products are a new generation of consumer products (e.g., clocks or umbrellas) that exhibit the ability to socially interact with their users via a variety of social media platforms such as Facebook, Twitter, Google+ and others. The toolkit has been built around three main activities that product designers perform in the physical prototyping of social products: (a) designing the appearance and behavior of the physical object; (b) implementing the code associated with the physical object; and, (c) testing if the physical object behaves as expected. Because the target users of the toolkit are not expert in software programming, an End-User Development (EUD) environment has been developed, which aims at facilitating the ideation process and providing simple mechanisms for automatic code generation and testing.

Keywords: Arduino · Internet of things · Physical prototyping · Social products

1 Introduction

A central issue in the education of industrial designers is becoming the development of toolkits and languages that can support *physical prototyping*, by making the design process of innovative interactive objects easier [1]. With growing interest in the Internet of Things [2], an additional issue for industrial design education has become how to support the design of *social products,* namely of physical objects able to interact with social media platforms.

Interaction between physical objects and social media platforms can be bi-directional: from objects to social media, and from social media to objects. In this paper, we focus on physical prototyping of social products able to interact with social networks in the first direction (from objects to social networks). To this end, we have iteratively developed a web-based toolkit to support the creation of Arduino-based products able to connect to a variety of social network APIs (Application Programming Interfaces). Indeed, in design schools, Arduino [3] is currently one of the most popular platforms to carry out activities of physical prototyping [4].

© Springer International Publishing Switzerland 2015
P. Díaz et al. (Eds.): IS-EUD 2015, LNCS 9083, pp. 217–222, 2015.
DOI: 10.1007/978-3-319-18425-8_19

The use of Arduino actually requires some programing skill; therefore, a variety of visual programming environments have been proposed over the years, such as ArduBlock, Modkit, and S4A (Scratch for Arduino), all using a building-block metaphor. However, these environments have limitations as well: they are sometimes perceived as confusing by non-expert programmers and more suitable to the modification and adaptation of existing programs rather than to program creation [5]. On the other hand, Intuino [6] is a much more intuitive authoring tool for physical prototyping with Arduino, but it is specifically oriented to the design of objects developed with organic materials and capable of moving in the real space.

Some toolkits have been then designed to provide mechanisms for Internet of Things scenarios [2], such as d.tools [7], iStuff [8] and Spacebrew [9]. However, either they adopt typical computer science-oriented notations (e.g., state-chart diagrams [7] or publisher-subscriber metaphor [9]) or show some limitations in terms of flexibility and scalability [8]. Temboo [10] provides hundreds of APIs for connecting Arduino Yún (a specific type of Arduino board with WiFi functionality) with a variety of social networks in a bi-directional way; however, it is still more oriented to expert programmers, who can integrate their code with the one made available by the Temboo site. reaDIYmate [11] is designed to support the creation of paper-made companions embedding Arduino boards, which are able to react to changes occurring in a social network or anywhere on the Internet (SoundCloud, RSS feeds, etc.).

All the approaches mentioned above pay attention to facilitating code generation by end users, and therefore support an end-user programming (EUP) activity. However, they often keep on adopting an implementation-oriented perspective rather than a design-oriented one: indeed, EUP is focused on 'functions' and 'operations' rather than on user experience and interaction design. The end-user development (EUD) research field [12], on the other hand, tries to bridge this conceptual gap between function creation and the ideation of software artifacts by end users. Several proposals in the EUD field advocate more attention on the development process of software artifacts carried out by domain experts and on the phenomena occurring around this process (e.g., [13,14]). Therefore, EUD offers a new perspective on the prototyping of social products, which requires that design ideas are made concrete and tested easily and quickly. In this paper, we describe *sense.me,* a EUD environment whose components support users to create the main features of an object (design), to automatically generate the corresponding Arduino code (implementation), and to verify if the object behavior corresponds to what is expected (test).

The rest of the paper presents the main characteristics of the system and its evaluation with users; discussion and plans for future work concludes the paper.

2   A EUD Environment for Physical Prototyping

An action-based research approach [15] was adopted to answer the research hypothesis of facilitating physical prototyping by students in industrial design. The activity started with a 'quick and dirty' ethnographic inquiry [16] of a semester-long master class in interactive prototyping at Delft University. One of the authors attended all lectures and project workshops, and participated in the course forum; furthermore, along the whole duration of the course, he has also provided the other students with technical support about software design and development, thus becoming perceived as an active member of the student community, rather than just as an external observer. He discovered that students, even though becoming able to create interactive physical prototypes in a relatively short time, find many difficulties during software development, due to their limited programming skills. Indeed, they tend to use available software libraries and operate in a trial-and-error way, by adjusting the code to their needs. The observation of students' behavior has led to the creation of a storyboard, and a set of scenarios and mock-ups, which have been presented to the students to discuss the characteristics of a toolkit that could facilitate the creation of social products. Then, an iterative design of the system has been carried out with a continuous interaction with potential users for defining the terminology, the functionality and the appearance of the system. This activity lasted 5 months and led to the first version of the system [17]; its evaluation provided feedback for iteratively developing, along a further 4-months period, the revised version of the toolkit described in the following.

2.1   The Toolkit: Key Concepts and Operation

The key concepts at the basis of the conceptualization of the toolkit are:

- *Virtual prototype:* it is the virtual counterpart of a physical prototype. It consists of a meaningful string used to identify a design project of social product.
- *Event:* it is the representation of either an *action* that the user can perform on the prototype or of a *state change* of the prototype. For example, the user could call "Shaking" the event associated with the shaking action performed on the object or "toDark" an event that represents the state change of the object when it is moved to a dark environment. The user may define many different events and associate them to each prototype. Every event is the trigger for a social behavior.
- *Social behavior:* it is the action on the social network (e.g. making check-in in Foursquare) that is carried out when the associated event occurs.
- *Sensor:* it is an object embedded in the physical prototype that allows capturing the actions performed on the prototype or changes of its state, and translating them into *sense.me* events.

The toolkit follows a EUD approach to social product prototyping that encompasses a design-implementation-test cycle, where each phase requires the user to carry out simple drag-and-drop gestures and parameter configuration.

In the *design phase*, the user must begin with the creation of a virtual prototype in *sense.me,* by defining a name for the prototype, choosing the type of Arduino board (Arduino without Internet connection, Arduino with Ethernet shield, Arduino with WiFi shield or Arduino Yún) and indicating the names of events. Then, for each defined event – e.g. "isMorning" and "isNight" in Figure 1 – one or more social behaviors can be selected from those available in the right part of the screen and dragged-and-dropped in the event container. Twenty social behaviors, related to eight social networks, are currently available in *sense.me.* (The integration of the underlying architecture with Temboo [10] allows adding further social networks and behaviors in the future). For example, Figure 1 shows that the user has associated the "Publish post (Facebook)" and "Get favorite tweets (Twitter)" behaviors to the "isMorning" event.

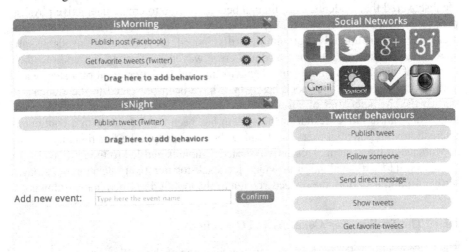

Fig. 1. Event creation and association with social behavior

In the *implementation phase*, the user must associate each defined event to a sensor or a combination of sensors he/she has embedded in the physical prototype. In this way, an event becomes the trigger for the associated social behaviors. The sensors available in *sense.me* can be classified as i) *analogue sensors*, including photo resistor, force sensor, temperature sensor, linear potentiometer, air pressure and infrared distance sensor; and ii) *digital switches*, including tilt sensor, button, and touch sensor. Furthermore, users with specific authentication credentials have also the possibility to easily add further sensors to the system by providing information about name, description and type (analogue or digital) of the sensor.

Users can also create AND/OR combinations of sensors: also in this case, the system provides a drag-and-drop interaction. Actually, the implemented solution is a compromise between simplicity and completeness: complex combinations are not allowed, but even designers with limited knowledge in Boolean logic can easily activate events using different sensors. Feedback from users obtained during development has confirmed that most of prototypes include few sensors in simple combinations.

After the event-sensor association and sensor configuration, the Arduino code can be automatically generated and uploaded on the selected Arduino board.

Finally, in the *test phase*, the user may test if the social product behaves as expected. In particular, the user can physically interact with the prototype, in order to trigger the events defined in *sense.me* and observe the corresponding social activities performed by the product in the *sense.me* web page devoted to testing. The same social activities can also be checked directly on the user's page of the social network.

2.2   Evaluation

A user study has been carried out to qualitatively evaluate *sense.me* both in terms of usability and of its integration within the design process.

Seven students (5 females and 2 males) in Industrial Design at the TU Delft volunteered to participate in the evaluation (age range from 22 to 34). Participants were provided with material for object construction (e.g., lego bricks, cardboards, etc.) and various types of Arduino boards and sensors. Sheets describing the available sensors and social behaviors were also given to the participants. The evaluation has been structured as an ideation workshop that required designing a product able to motivate people to use public transportation. One group of 3 students decided to work on a social device to be installed in a bus, and the other group of 4 students worked on the creation of a social advertising panel to be installed in a train station. Then, each participant used *sense.me* individually to generate the Arduino code for the ideated social product, without any previous training session. The experimenter observed the participants at work and annotated his own observations about usability problems and system bugs. A semi-structured interview was finally carried out with each participant with the aim of understanding users' opinion on *sense.me* and its integration within the creative process that brings designers from product imagination to prototyping.

Direct observation revealed some minor usability problems related to terminology and affordance of icons, but also one major problem emerged. It was concerned with a gap existing between the user's mental model and the system conceptual model: *sense.me* allows creating all desired events and associated social behaviors in the same page (see Fig. 1), whilst event configuration with sensors must be carried out in another page; however, the users expected to configure each event just after its creation and, in a subsequent time, associate it with social behaviors.

The semi-structured interview allowed gathering comments about the integration of *sense.me* within the design process. In particular, we were not evaluating creativity (e.g., whether participants came up with better ideas), but fluency in the design process itself. Almost all participants declared that the list of available sensors and behaviors represented a source of inspiration for new ideas of social products and this has facilitated their creative process. Some participants said that *sense.me* could be a limitation, because designers have to narrow their options depending on what is available in the tool; however, they also added that sometimes designers start with "crazy ideas", and knowing what one can do or cannot do allows converging towards feasible solutions. Having limited programming expertise, most of participants declared that they could not realize the same things without this system. A participant added that *sense.me* generates a useful code that an expert can tune at her/his own pace.

3   Conclusion

The *sense.me* toolkit aims to facilitate the physical prototyping of social products. To this end, it has been built around the social behaviors and physical sensors necessary to make design ideas about social products concrete, without the need of knowing any programming language and modifying the generated code. The continuous interaction with target users allowed us to focus on their needs, background and competencies, and create an environment that could sustain their design activity and foster their creativity. As future work, we are planning to extend *sense.me* by providing the support for creating physical objects that connects with social networks in a bi-directional way, namely that are also able to react with their actuators to data coming from social networks. Another possible extension could be the integration of *sense.me* with existing solutions supporting electronics design of Arduino-based objects.

References

1. Carulli, M., Cugini, U.: An integrated framework to support multidisciplinary design processes. In: Dagman, A., Söderberg, R. (eds.) NordDesign 2010, vol. 2, pp. 323–332. The Design Society, Bristol (2010)
2. Cvijikj, I.P., Michahelles, F.: The toolkit approach for end-user participation in the internet of things. In: Uckelmann, D., Harrison, M., Michahelles, F. (eds.) Architecting the Internet of Things, pp. 65–96. Springer, Heidelberg (2011)
3. Arduino. http://www.arduino.cc/
4. Kushner, D.: The Making of Arduino. IEEE Spectrum, October 2011
5. Booth, T., Stumpf, S.: End-User Experiences of Visual and Textual Programming Environments for Arduino. In: Dittrich, Y., Burnett, M., Mørch, A., Redmiles, D. (eds.) IS-EUD 2013. LNCS, vol. 7897, pp. 25–39. Springer, Heidelberg (2013)
6. Wakita, A., Anezaki, Y.: Intuino: an authoring tool for supporting the prototyping of organic interfaces. In: Bertelsen, O.W., Krogh, P., Halskov, K., Petersen, M.G. (eds.) DIS 2010, pp. 179–188. ACM, New York, USA (2010)
7. Hartmann, B., Klemmer, S.R., Bernstein, M., Abdulla, L., Burr, B., Robinson-Moscher, A., Gee, J.: Reflective physical prototyping through integrated design, test and analysis. In: Wellner, P., Hinckley, K. (eds.) UIST 2006, pp. 299–308. ACM, New York, USA (2006)
8. Ballagas, R., Ringel, M., Stone, M., Borchers, J.: iStuff: a physical user interface toolkit for ubiquitous computing environnments. In: Cockton, G., Korhonen, P. (eds.) CHI 2003, pp. 537–544. ACM, New York, USA (2003)
9. Spacebrew. http://docs.spacebrew.cc
10. Temboo. http://temboo.com/
11. reaDIYmate. http://www.readiymate.com/
12. Lieberman, H., Paternò, F., Wulf, V. (eds.): End-User Development. Springer, Dordrecht, The Netherlands (2006)
13. Costabile, M.F., Fogli, D., Mussio, P., Piccinno, A.: Visual Interactive Systems for End-User Development: a Model-based Design Methodology. IEEE Trans. on SMC - part A 37(6), 1029–1046 (2007)
14. Fischer, G., Giaccardi, E.: Meta-design: A framework for the future of end-user development. In: Lieberman, H., Paternò, F., Wulf, V. (eds.) end-user development, pp. 427–457. Springer, Dordrecht, The Netherlands (2006)
15. Hayes, G.: The Relationship of Action Research to Human-Computer Interaction. ACM Trans. on Computer-Human Interaction 18(3), 15:1–15:30 (2011)
16. Hughes, J., King, V., Rodden, T., Anderson, H.: The role of ethnography in interactive systems design. Interactions 2(2), 56–65 (1995)
17. Acerbis, A., Fogli, D., Giaccardi, E.: *sense.me*: a eud environment for social products. In: Paolini, P., Garzotto, F. (eds.) AVI 2014, pp. 329-330. ACM, New York, USA (2014)

Pervasive Displays in the Wild: Employing End User Programming in Adaption and Re-Purposing

Tommaso Turchi$^{(\boxtimes)}$ and Alessio Malizia

Department of Computer Science, Brunel University, London, UK
{tommaso.turchi,alessio.malizia}@brunel.ac.uk

Abstract. The declining hardware cost has enabled the wide spread of Pervasive Displays anywhere within urban spaces; these systems are composed of displays of various sizes and allow users to interact with the same public screens simultaneously, usually through new and engaging modalities, e.g. Tangible Interaction. Yet the frequent changes in users' needs dictate a continuous adaption and re-purposing of such systems with new and focused features, in order to prevent interest to wear off and overcome people's low expectations of their content value; currently this process has to be done by site managers, and this tedious and necessary task prevented long-term deployments. In this paper we propose to use End User Programming to empower users with the ability to adapt Pervasive Displays to their continuously evolving requirements. We conducted a preliminary study involving university students, gathering scenario's requirements and initial feedback on a prototype we developed.

Keywords: Pervasive displays · End user programming · Natural user interfaces · Tangible user interfaces

1 Introduction

In recent years digital displays have flooded urban areas, providing ubiquitous information hubs to everyone within their reach; lately, thanks to the cheaper hardware's availability and to the recent technology trends, public displays started engaging users through a richer interaction: these systems – called *Pervasive Displays* – are composed of various-sized displays (from hand-held devices to large displays) and support many-to-many interaction, allowing "many people to interact with the same public screens simultaneously" [1].

Because of their ubiquitousity, the interaction modality has to be easily graspable by everyone who comes across a Pervasive Display; this is the main reason why interactions are fostered through a new paradigm, namely Natural User Interfaces (NUIs): these interfaces are based on more innate human interaction paradigms, such as touch, vision and speech.

A fairly recent trend in Pervasive Displays' research studies is to deploy large and long term experiments outside their usual laboratory setting, without the close researchers' supervision, i.e. *in the wild*; this is mostly due to the recent

© Springer International Publishing Switzerland 2015
P. Díaz et al. (Eds.): IS-EUD 2015, LNCS 9083, pp. 223–229, 2015.
DOI: 10.1007/978-3-319-18425-8_20

definition of new methodologies within the Human Computer Interaction area [2], allowing researchers to evaluate technologies within people's daily usage contexts.

Yet, as pointed out by Hosio et al. [3], such new and long term deployments present two main drawbacks: (1) the expensive maintenance costs in terms of setup and mundane service activities and (2) the gradual loss of interest shown by users and site managers overtime.

The authors also suggested a viable solution: allowing a degree of appropriation when designing Pervasive Displays might enable site managers and users to understand how they could relate to the ordinary activities often taken for granted, leading to a more sustained use. Moreover, because of their public and moderated nature, these displays are usually equipped with just a small set of very specific features, e.g. displaying local points of interests on a map; yet users' interests and needs are heterogeneous and evolving overtime. Thus opening up such systems by empowering users to adapt and re-purpose them into entirely new usage contexts might promote a more serendipitous and prolong usage.

We argue that End User Programming (EUP) could be effective in enabling users to adapt and re-purpose Pervasive Displays without the intervention of site managers.

To test this statement, our main contribution is the design of a simple NUI-based application for Pervasive Display's ecosystems allowing users to collaborate with each other in a group work scenario; we then conducted a preliminary study with users in order to provide an initial validation of our prototype – which will inform the next stage of its design – and investigate practices and problems they face during their meetings, in order to get further insights on the tools they need.

2   Related Works

Employing EUP in Pervasive Displays' adaption dictates a paradigm shift; indeed, ours is not the first attempt of bridging EUP and NUI. The vast majority of studies focused on a subset of NUIs, namely Tangible User Interfaces (TUIs): the main idea is to give digital information a physical counterpart, acting as both its representation and control [4]. This predominance is mainly due to the effectiveness of matching digital constraints and properties with physical ones – and vice-versa; moreover, unlike Graphical User Interface-based EUP systems, with TUIs one can easily and more effectively foster collaboration between users.

The existing literature can be grouped in two main categories, according to the EUP paradigm employed, Programming by Instruction (PbI) or Programming by Demonstration (PbD); the first one – usually referred to as *Tangible Programming* in the TUIs domain – being the more traditional approach to programming, requires learning and using a syntactic construct (e.g. visual languages) in order to impart instructions to the system, while the latter enables users to teach the system new behavior by demonstrating actions on concrete examples [5].

Topobo [6] (proposed by Parkes et al.) falls under the second category, comprising a set of modular components that can be assembled and animated by pushing, pulling and twisting, then observing the system repeatedly play those motions back. Employing PbD to teach different movements to the system directly on the actuated physical object proved to be very effective and intuitive, therefore it forms the basis for Robot Programming by Demonstration [7].

Moving on to the PbI-based systems, Mugellini et al. [8] proposed the tangible shortcuts: they've used physical objects to improve information retrieval, enabling users to develop new shortcuts using a puzzle-based visual language.

To the best of our knowledge, ours is one the the first attempts at employing an EUP approach within the Pervasive Display domain. Due to their effectiveness and ease of use, we decided to build all the interactions with our application around a TUI, which will allow end users to easily customize and assemble – in a PbI fashion – the services provided through a puzzle-like metaphor.

3   Prototype Design

Our prototype is an application enabling users to develop simple workflows by assembling several functions together, thus falling under the PbI-based systems category; it runs on a horizontal display, offering a tangible interaction through the movements of the users' smartphones on the main display's surface.

Employing smartphones allows us to adapt the system to each different user, because they hold all users' personal information and can be used to display a wide range of widgets that can be presented to end users depending on the specific service (e.g. a virtual keyboard to input text).

To make the system easily graspable by every user, we based the interaction metaphor on a puzzle [9]: each available function is mapped to a piece, which will (possibly) require inputs and produce some outputs, as depicted in figure 1; constraints on inputs and outputs are afforded using different shapes. The smartphone itself is associated with the main puzzle piece (a circle representing the smartphone halo), which will move alongside the smartphone on the main display's surface; moving the main piece towards another one will add the latter's related function to the workflow – if the two shapes are matching, that is to say the latest output is compatible with the required input. If a single piece requires some additional inputs from the user, such as selecting an option between several ones or typing in some text, a dynamic widget will appear on the smartphone screen, allowing the user to do so.

We developed the first set of features keeping in mind the targeted scenario, thus the available puzzle pieces were: (1) fetch a file from Dropbox, (2) display a PDF or an image on the main screen, (3) search for a book in the library and get an image depicting its location, and (4) send a text document via email.

4   Preliminary Study

To get a better understanding of the scenarios where Pervasive Displays might be used, we carried out a study involving users in the university setting, where many public interactive displays are already being deployed and used. This particular study involved Computer Science undergrad students during their second year:

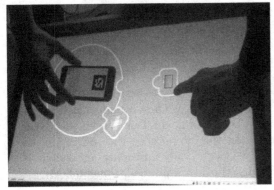
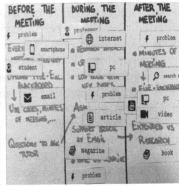

Fig. 1. An example of a workflow that can be assembled using our prototype; widgets are displayed on the smartphone once a new piece requiring some user input is assembled

Fig. 2. The rich picture generated by one of the groups participating in our study

as part of their degree, students have been clustered into groups of 4-6 people and assigned with an Android application to be developed during the course of the year, with the supervision of a teaching staff member, whom they usually meet all together once a week. Students have to work collaboratively and meet on a weekly basis, usually in a college's meeting room: our study took place in the same environment to simulate "in the wild" settings.

The study involved three different groups of students and was composed by two different activities, both carried out in the same session with the group as a whole: the first activity consisted of gathering the specific scenario's requirements from participants; we asked students to tell us about the tasks and tools they use during their meetings, trying to keep the discussion going with a semi-structured interview; we gave them a set of non-exhaustive sample icons representing some of the resources and tools they might be using, such as books, papers, search engines, smartphones, and so on. We asked them to place the icons on a sheet of paper, which had three different sections: before, during and after the meeting. As a result, we obtained an accurate picture of what is happening during a meeting, which tasks require some preparation and which ones trigger some other activities to be performed after the actual meeting (figure 2).

During the second activity we carried out a preliminary evaluation on the proposed interaction modality by explaining them how the system works and we let them play with it until they were satisfied, carrying out a semi-structured interview (mainly focused on the interaction modality).

Results of both the interviews are reported in the following.

4.1   Results

The first interview's results were structured with regard to the focused aspect, obtaining three ex-post generated categories.

Scheduling. Students use instant messaging tools to schedule meetings with each other and discuss urgent matters together; this happens before a meeting, thus they also can all agree on what should be discussed with their supervisor and build an agenda for the next meeting.

Reporting. Because the groups usually get together with their tutors once a week, one of the objective of their meeting is put together a report on what has been done so far; students describe how they've handled previously assigned tasks and report the problems they've encountered with the development.

Discussing. The discussion happens in all of the three phases: before the meeting, students discuss with each other (using instant messaging tools for pressing issues, emails for tasks requiring additional details) the tasks they were assigned and how they're addressing them, getting suggestions from the other members.

As for the results emerging from the second activity of the study, it seems that participants quite liked the idea we've pitched them through our prototype; feedback was mostly pointing towards the missing features and the interaction with the smartphone. Firstly, for the system to be really useful in the targeted scenario, it should have included a deeper integration with the online content manager used within the university and the ability to send several types of files via email. Secondly, it became clear how a TUI is an effective way of interacting with the system while composing the workflow, but it's not really effective when it comes to operating on their results: indeed, all of the groups attempted to drag the images displayed on the main screen with their fingers.

5   Discussion

Based on the results of our study, we noticed a clear distinction – in terms of the most suitable interaction modality – between the composition and the execution environment: while they are composing a workflow, users have to deal with abstract concepts – such as functions and type constraints – thus we argue that the puzzle metaphor coupled with a tangible interaction modality could help them building an effective mental model, allowing them to easily deal with such intangible concepts; when the system prompts users with the result of an application, the natural need of directly manipulating content takes over, thus users automatically shift interaction paradigm and try to operate directly on the resource, rather than keep on relying on an indirect control mechanism (i.e. the smartphone). This shift stems also from the literature on the difference between the PbD and PbI paradigms: there's a clear overlapping between the editing and the execution environment within the first paradigm – i.e. users operate on an artifact to impart instructions *and* to interact with the results, as in Robot Programming by Demonstration – while these two perspectives are definitely separated within PbI-based systems. We intend to study this problem more deeply in future, since PbI appears to be a more adequate paradigm to be employed in our scenario, being inherently less domain-specific.

One final remark follows directly from our research question: all the existing attempts of bridging EUP with TUIs (and more generally NUIs) deeply rely on Visual Languages. It's worth pointing out how employing such construct, which was developed back when Graphical User Interfaces were the widespread interaction modality, in a NUI environment might violate the latter's premises and act more as a barrier to an effective communication with the end user rather than easing it. It might be worth investigating new forms of communication with end users – highly coupled with NUIs principles – in order to exploit the real value of this modality, which already proved to be really effective in lowering technology's barriers and are heavily employed in public displays.

6   Conclusion

In this paper we outlined how EUP might be a suitable methodology in helping users adapt and re-purpose Pervasive Displays; adaption and re-purposing of Pervasive Displays, as proposed by Hosio et al. [3], might help overcome the progressive loss of users' interest in actively using such systems overtime.

We carried out a preliminary study with second year university students, whose aim was to gather scenario's requirements and feedback on our proposal. Finally, the study offered us new and interesting insights, as well as new and unforeseen issues, which will be highly relevant during the next design phases.

References

1. Terrenghi, L., Quigley, A., Dix, A.: A taxonomy for and analysis of multi-person-display ecosystems. Personal and Ubiquitous Computing 13(8), November 2009
2. Crabtree, A., Chamberlain, A., Grinter, R.E., Jones, M., Rodden, T., Rogers, Y.: Introduction to the Special Issue of "The Turn to The Wild". ACM Transactions on Computer-Human Interaction 20(3), 13:1–13:4 (2013).
3. Hosio, S., Goncalves, J., Kukka, H., Chamberlain, A., Malizia, A.: What's in it for me: exploring the real-world value proposition of pervasive displays. In: PerDis 2014: Proceedings of The International Symposium on Pervasive Displays, pp. 174–179. ACM Request Permissions, New York, USA, June 2014
4. Ishii, H.: Tangible bits: beyond pixels. ACM, New York (2008)
5. Lieberman, H.: Your Wish Is My Command: Programming by Example. a post-WIMP perspective on control room design. Morgan Kaufmann, New York, USA (2001)
6. Parkes, A.J., Raffle, H.S., Ishii, H.: Topobo in the wild: longitudinal evaluations of educators appropriating a tangible interface. In: CHI 2008: Proceedings of the SIGCHI Conference on Human Factors in Computing Systems, pp. 1129–1138. ACM Request Permissions, New York, USA, April 2008

7. Billard, A., Calinon, S., Dillmann, R., Schaal, S.: Robot programming by demonstration. In: Siciliano, B., Khatib, O. (eds.) Springer Handbook of Robotics, pp. 1371–1394. Springer, Heidelberg (2008)
8. Mugellini, E., Lalanne, D., Dumas, B., Evéquoz, F., Gerardi, S., Le Calvé, A., Boder, A., Ingold, R., Abou Khaled, O.: MEMODULES as tangible shortcuts to multimedia information. In: Lalanne, D., Kohlas, J. (eds.) Human Machine Interaction. LNCS, vol. 5440, pp. 103–132. Springer, Heidelberg (2009)
9. Danado, J., Paternò, F.: Puzzle: a visual-based environment for end user development in touch-based mobile phones. In: Winckler, M., Forbrig, P., Bernhaupt, R. (eds.) HCSE 2012. LNCS, vol. 7623, pp. 199–216. Springer, Heidelberg (2012)

Towards a Toolkit for the Rapid Creation of Smart Environments

Thomas Kubitza$^{(\boxtimes)}$ and Albrecht Schmidt

University of Stuttgart, Stuttgart, Germany
{thomas.kubitza,albrecht.schmidt}@vis.uni-stuttgart.de

Abstract. With the rise of rapid physical prototyping tools such as Arduino it has become very easy for designers, makers and developers to build smart devices, simple installations or other single device solutions. However, as soon as a room, floor or building-wide (prototype-) installation should be build consisting of various types of devices that need to communicate, the effort for building these environments still remains extremely high. A lot of this is due to three factors: programming for different platforms, bridging different communication technologies, and physically connecting devices to network and electricity. In this paper we present a concept that drastically reduces this efforts. Thus, designers and developers can focus more on the implementation of the behaviour of interactive environments. We have implemented this concept as a toolkit for on-site setups that allows to easily mash-up heterogeneous sets of devices using a common scripting language and a web-based IDE. We report from interactive installations in office and museum environments that have been realized based on this platform and we point towards new ways of programming environments.

Keywords: Smart environments · End user programming · Mashups

1 Introduction

Smart and interactive spaces are based on a common principle; different kinds of devices with sensors and actuators attached are statically installed in rooms, levels, whole buildings or are even worn by users. All these heterogeneous devices need to talk to each other or to an entity that constantly combines system state and generates system reactions. Multiple reasons make the setup of such environments a complex task. Firstly, similar functionality has to be implemented on various platforms ranging from microcontrollers to High-End computers. This requires expert knowledge in very specific programming languages and platforms as well as the management of various development environments (IDEs). Secondly, different communications technologies, protocols and formats have to be bridged so that devices can actually exchange data. Thirdly, devices have to be deployed in their target environment, supplied with electricity and wired or wireless communication infrastructure (e.g. WiFi access points). Especially the first two reasons put up high boundary for non-experts in electronics and programming. This limits its usage to small and mostly only professional user groups.

© Springer International Publishing Switzerland 2015
P. Díaz et al. (Eds.): IS-EUD 2015, LNCS 9083, pp. 230–235, 2015.
DOI: 10.1007/978-3-319-18425-8_21

We believe that the right tools can open up the creation of smart environments to a much larger audience in the same way as physical prototyping platforms such as Arduino made the access to microcontrollers much easier and in the same way as Apps made potentially everyone the programmer of his own cell phone (and the phones of millions of others). By empowering groups such as user experience designers, scientist, designers, artists, makers and hobbyists we envision the creation of a large set of truly useful applications evaluated in realistic environments and addressing a broad range of problems.

In this paper we present a toolkit that drastically reduces the technical complexity for creating and programming smart environments. Our approach consists of two main pillars: (1) A client software for each type of end device is provided which allows to remotely access and control all its abilities and to abstract from its specific platform. (2) A server software on a central computer node is provided to bridge between various communication-technologies and to provide unified access to all sensors and actuators of configured devices through a web-based JavaScript development environment.

This approach allows to quickly implement or change the behaviour of a system without the need to reprogram or physically access any of the associated or deployed devices. JavaScript, one of the most widespread and growing programming languages, is used to define the system behaviour in a single spot.

A simple scenario is used in following paragraph to illustrate the toolkit usage.

2   Simple Usage Scenario

Bob wants to set up a small WiFi enabled projector in the office floor that should inform about local events. He wants to use a distance sensor connected to a WiFi enabled Arduino that is mounted on the wall to turn on the screen only when somebody is close. He has installed the server part of our toolkit on a spare computer. With the help of the web-based user interface he installs the client firmware on the Arduino device and an App on the Android based WiFi projector. Both devices automatically pop up in the user interface and Bob continuous with adding a "display module" to the projector and a "IR distance sensor" to the Arduino from a list of available modules (see Figure 2a). Now, he switches to the "rules"-view and creates a new behaviour rule consisting of the following JavaScript code:

```
if (api.device.Arduino1.distanceSensor.value > 300)
    api.AndroidProjector1.WebDisplay.showUrl = "http://bob-site.org/news.html";
else
    api.device.AndroidProjector1.WebDisplay.showText = "";
```

Fig. 1. Bobs JavaScript code for controlling a projector using a distance sensor

During typing an auto-completion feature helps Bob to choose the right device-names, module-names and properties (Figure 2b). Bob saves his new rule and approaches the sensor deployed in the floor. When he is in a distance closer than 1.5 meters the news page of his website is displayed; as soon as he leaves the distance a black screen is shown. Bob decides to tweak the distance value in his rule so that the content is only shown when somebody is closer than roughly 1 meter.

Two major strengths of our approach are pointed out in this scenario: The central unified access to completely different devices and their easy mash-up. Access to devices is implemented via objects (`api.device.`). This allows using the full power of the JavaScript language and thus the implementation of short and simple rules as well as very complex ones (low threshold, high ceiling).

3   System Concept and Implementation

Conceptually our toolkit strictly follows a master-slave architecture; the client side software allows to treat each client device as a source of sensor events, a sink for actuation commands, or both. It allows abstracting from the underlying operation system and hardware as well as the communication technology and protocol. For each end device platform a specific client firmware has to be implemented. However, this implementation effort is done just once by experts for this specific platform; after that, users of our toolkit just need to install the firmware once and from that point on they can access and control all its abilities from the central server node.

The central server node provides a web-based user interface for the configuration of devices and the creation of behaviour rules. It includes a rule engine that triggers events and runs rules as soon as sensor data is received. Rules may then again trigger actuator commands which are instantly sent to the appropriate devices. In our example a change of the distance sensor value triggered the execution of Bob's rule, which resulted in the actuation of the Wifi projector output if the value was within a certain range.

The system components of the toolkit consist of one computer that runs the server software, an arbitrary number of client devices and an optional external network infrastructure (e.g. WiFi access points). A number of sensor and/or actuators can be attached to a client device (depends on a devices' abilities).

The server software is fully implemented in NodeJS - a framework specialized on the implementation of high-performance multi-protocol applications. This allows the server to be installed on any computer platform (e.g. Windows, Linux) and even on platforms with very limited resources (e.g. Raspberry Pi). The server node can be equipped with various (wireless) communication adapters such as Ethernet, Wifi, Bluetooth / BLE, XBee and RF Link which all work in parallel. The centralized approach allows to completely hide the network layer from the developer. Auto-discovery mechanisms allow a client to find a local server immediately after installing its client software. The web-based interface gives access to all functionalities from the device configuration to rule creation and monitoring. Its web-based nature especially allows to run the development environment on tablets; those can be taken into a smart environment and used to monitor and modify behavior on-site.

A good range of popular client devices is already supported at this stage. The list includes various Arduino devices, .NET Gadgeteer devices [1] and modules, Raspberry Pi, Beaglebone, Intel Edison, various Bluetooth Low Energy devices as well as Android and iPhone smartphones, tablets and projectors. The client software of these devices have the form of firmware, PC software or Apps and expose the full functionality of a device to the central server. Communication protocols and APIs between server and clients are well documented to allow an easy future integration of yet unsupported devices.

4   User Interface

Fig. 2. a) Device configuration view, b) Rules overview, c) Code auto-completion

The toolkit user interface runs in any browser and is structured in three sections: Devices, Events and Rules. New devices automatically appear in the device overview after the installation of their specific client software. In its initial state a device has no modules configured; this means no sensor or actuators are activated yet. In the device configuration view, modules can be selected from a list of supported sensors and actuator modules (Figure 2a). By double-clicking on a module, it is automatically assigned to a compatible and free port; this way users don't need to care about the right attachment of sensors beforehand, the device configuration steps already give visual hints about the right ports to connect to. After saving a configuration, it is instantly pushed to the device where the selected modules are activated.

In the rules-view an overview of available rules is given. These are structured in groups and consist of a name, a description and an execution priority. Groups allow to tie together rules which are logically associated or only apply to a certain space in the environment (e.g. "Office Floor 1"). Groups and rules can be enabled and disabled individually which allows easy instant switching of behaviour for single spaces or whole environments. Single rules can be edited any time and the changes are applied immediately. Syntax highlighting and auto-completion features help novice users to shimmy along available devices, modules and their individual properties without any previous knowledge; advanced users benefit from the coding speedup and correct referencing of objects. The following section briefly describes two exemplary applications in different environments that where realized using our toolkit.

5   Applications

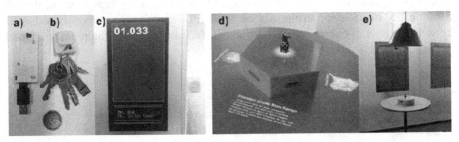

Fig. 3. a) Intel Edison BLE scanner, b) BLE key fob worn by users, c) Electric Imp doorscreen, d) Plinth with distance sensors, e) Projector lamp above plinth

The first setup is created in an **office environment**. It consists of 10 door screens and the same number of BLE scanner devices and BLE key fobs (Figure 3abc). Each key fob is associated to a person and the door-screen in front of this persons' office always indicates whether and where within the building the person is currently located; an "out of office" indication is given when the key fob of a person has not been seen for a while. This behaviour has been realized with a single rule consisting of 45 lines of code. The system is in daily use since multiple months.

The second example setup consists of an **installation for museums**. Three hexagonal plinths are placed within an exhibition room. Each is accompanied by a Pico projector hidden in a lamp above each plinth (Figure 3d-e). The plinth itself is equipped with a RFID reader and six IR distance sensors; this allows recognising exhibition objects on top of the plinth as well as movement (direction and distance) of people around the plinth. The projector permits projecting arbitrary content onto and around the plinth. One use case is the adaption of exhibit related content based on direction and movement of people around. Another use case lets museum visitors put replicas on the plinth in order to receive related digital information on the surrounding surface.

6   Related Work

We focus the discussion of related work on frameworks for rapid protoyping and software for the creation of mash-ups and web-based programming.

Two popular frameworks for the rapid physical prototyping of smart devices are Arduino and .NET Gadgeteer [1]. Latter, provides an ecosystem of modules that can be simply attached without any need for soldering. Both provide a desktop based IDE for programming and deploying firmware on single devices. In contrast to our toolkit these platforms focus on the creation of single standalone devices. However, our toolkit integrates both platforms and its module ecosystems. Other systems focus on the integration of massively widespread smartphones and their integrated sensors as sources for data [2]. Further, peripheral connectors for phones such as IOIO or WebClip [3] allow the attachment of external sensors and actuators.

The idea to use a centralised web hub for mashing up devices in local environments using simple rules has been introduced in [4] and [5]. The system was based on HTTP request, supported very simple sensor to actuator relations and didn't abstract from hardware or communication technology. In [6] a rather simple scripting language has been introduced for smart home setups; by using JavaScript in our toolkit we cover these very simple "If-this-then-that" use cases but also allow for the creation of highly complex rule sets. Another recent trend is the movement of full development environments into the web [7]. The strengths of this approch are for example demonstrated by the mBed IDE; a web-based toolchain for ARM microcontrollers.

7   Conclusion and Future Work

In this paper we have presented a toolkit for the creation and programming of smart and interactive environments that reduces much of the technical complexity and allows users to focus on programming the system behaviour. By choosing JavaScript as scripting language and providing a single web-based IDE we intend to empower a large user group, from novice to expert users, to create and experiment with their own smart environments.

This toolkit is part of an EU project and it is in ongoing development. Two major medium-term milestones are: the implementation of an easy sharing mechanism of smart setups for an online community using "recipes" as well as the experimentation with code that is automatically generated by physically demonstrating actions to smart environments. Further, assistive and visual programming aids (such as Blockly) that can lie on top of the JavaScript layer are currently evaluated. These approaches will be evaluated with cultural heritage professionals from three of our partner museums who will take the role of the smart environment developers.

Acknowledgements. This work is funded by the European Project meSch (http://mesch-project.eu, Grant Agreement No. 600851).

References

1. Hodges, S., Taylor, S., Villar, N., Scott, J.: Prototyping connected devices for the internet of things. IEEE Computer **46**(2), 26–34 (2013)
2. Shirazi, A., Winkler, C., Schmidt, A.: SENSE-SATION: an extensible platform for integration of phones into the Web. IoT (2010)
3. Kubitza, T., Pohl, N., Dingler, T., Schmidt, A.: WebClip: a connector for ubiquitous physical input and output for touch screen devices. Ubicomp, pp. 387–390 (2013)
4. Holloway, S., Stovall, D., Lara-Garduno, J., Julien, C.: Opening pervasive computing to the masses using the SEAP middleware. IEEE Pervasive, pp. 1–5, March 2009
5. Holloway, S., Julien, C.: The case for end-user programming of ubiquitous computing environments. FoSER 2010, p. 167 (2010)
6. García-Herranz, M., Haya, P., Alamán, X.: Towards a Ubiquitous End-User Programming System for Smart Spaces. J. UCS **16**(12), 1633–1649 (2010)
7. Kubitza, T., Pohl, N., Dingler, T., Schneegaß, S.: Innovations in Ubicomp Products Ingredients for a New Wave of Ubicomp Products. IEEE Pervasive Comp., pp. 5–8 (2013)

Making Mashups Actionable Through Elastic Design Principles

Carmelo Ardito[1(✉)], Maria Francesca Costabile[1], Giuseppe Desolda[1],
Markus Latzina[2], and Maristella Matera[3]

[1] Dipartimento di Informatica, Università degli Studi di Bari Aldo Moro,
Via Orabona, 4 70125, Bari, Italy
{carmelo.ardito,maria.costabile,giuseppe.desolda}@uniba.it
[2] Strategic Projects, Products and Innovation – Technology, SAP SE,
Dietmar-Hopp-Allee 16 69190, Walldorf, Germany
markus.latzina@sap.com
[3] Dipartimento di Elettronica, Informazione e Bioingegneria,
Politecnico di Milano, Piazza Leonardo da Vinci, 32 20134, Milano, Italy
maristella.matera@polimi.it

Abstract. This paper discusses motivations and requirements leading to *elastic environments* where relevant information and the functions that can be performed on it can be shaped by end users at runtime. As a solution for creating elastic environments, a framework is presented which exploits methods for the *mashup of heterogeneous resources* and elastic features that permit the easy transition of information between different task contexts according to the recently proposed notion of *transformative user experience.*

Keywords: End-user development · Transformative user experience · Data integration · Mashups · Composition platforms · Elasticity · Task semantics

1 Introduction and Motivation

Due to the new technological landscape (e.g., cloud computing, the software as a service (SaaS) paradigm, the new "API economy" and the resulting service eco-systems), an extraordinarily high number of data is available online. Today, almost any person uses sophisticated mobile devices supporting the pervasive access to data and applications; this determines an increasing demand by the end users (called "users" in the rest of this paper) to effectively access, integrate, and visualize the information offered by such resources. In this respect, platforms for service composition play an important role as they let users integrate heterogeneous information that otherwise would be totally unrelated [1]. Web mashups are indeed "composite" applications constructed by integrating ready-to-use functions and content exposed by public or private services and Web APIs [2]. As compared to consuming what is offered by each single resource in isolated ways, mashup platforms enable users to aggregate information coming from the various resources and create synchronized visualizations. In such ways, mashups generate new value.

© Springer International Publishing Switzerland 2015
P. Díaz et al. (Eds.): IS-EUD 2015, LNCS 9083, pp. 236–241, 2015.
DOI: 10.1007/978-3-319-18425-8_22

Several mashup tools proposed so far, the so-called mashup makers, provide graphical notations for combining services [3-6]. An example is Yahoo!Pipes [7] (for other examples see [2]). As compared to manual programming, such platforms alleviate the mashup composition tasks, but they require an understanding of the integration logic (e.g., data flow, parameter coupling, composition operator programming). Studies with users show that they are still difficult to use by non-technical users (e.g. [8]). According to the End-User Development (EUD) vision, enabling a larger class of users to create their own applications requires intuitive abstractions and notations. To reach this goal, we have developed a mashup platform, described in [1], which is based on the EUD vision and exploits a meta-design approach to support users in mashup creation. More details on how users create their own mashups with this platform are illustrated in [1, 9].

Our recent research on the EUD of mashups has led us to identify some strengths and weaknesses of the proposed approaches. In particular, on the basis of findings of user studies that we performed to validate our mashup platform [10], we believe there is still room for enhancing the mashup paradigm, to empower the users to play a more active role than just consuming the finally visualized information. Transitions across different usage situations, which imply different functionality to be applied on information, should become possible without requiring users to switch among multiple applications. This means that rigid schemas for information provisioning and fruition, generally adopted by isolated, pre-packaged applications, have to be overcome by instrumenting systems with an intrinsic flexibility. The application functionality must dynamically emerge at runtime, based on the users' actions that determined the current situation, i.e., the context and tasks performed.

This paper addresses such a need for *elasticity* and also presents, as a possible solution, a framework where mashup composition paradigms are revisited and potentiated through the notion of Transformative User Experience (TUX) [11]. TUX is a recently proposed approach that aims to natively support users in a variety of spontaneously self-defined task flows, not limiting them to work along highly specific use cases, as typical for applications which are driven by workflow engines or which adopt predefined patterns of guided procedures. The goal is to overcome common application boundaries enabling user interaction with information in terms of *task objects* (i.e., data elements, their visualization and specific functions used to perform a task) within dedicated, contextual task environments assembled through interrelated sets of *task containers*. The distinctive feature of such containers is that they provide functions to process the data they include that strictly relate to the current context as informed by the task actually performed by the users. Thus, the users' task flow is not predefined, but it is determined at runtime based on the users' actions, as the users select proper containers depending on the current situation and on the functionality (e.g., data manipulations) needed to further proceed with their task. In the architectural framework resulting from the integration of the mashup paradigm and TUX, elasticity is thus pursued by allowing users: *i)* to select and combine pertinent data sources through mashup composition; *ii)* to explore and manipulate the integrated data sets in ways that allow them to move across various task contexts while performing varying functions that become available depending on the current usage context. In this way, the information displayed by the mashup becomes actionable, thus really useful with respect to the users' concrete tasks and overall purpose.

In this regard, this paper proposes a systematic approach to establishing actionable mashups, outlining a framework in Section 2. The demo description provided in [9] reports a scenario motivating such framework.   Section 3 provides the conclusions.

2   A Framework for Actionable Mashups

This section describes how to extend the coverage of mashups by augmenting information exploration, generally operated on top of mashup data sets, towards more active *prosumption* (i.e., genuinely merging "production" and "consumption") and sense making. The important feature we focus on is to support the accomplishment of sophisticated sense making tasks on the visualized information thanks to additional manipulations driven by task semantics. In other words, we aim to enable a kind of *active* sense making, in which the presented information can not only be viewed differently and in meaningful ways towards the gaining of insights, but moreover transformed effectively towards the actual accomplishment of task goals. In this regard, the visualizations of data retrieved from data sources, that in a mashup environment can occur by means of *UI templates*, are enriched by augmenting the UI templates with the notion of TUX *task containers*, i.e., elements whose role is to supply task-related functions for manipulation and transformation of task objects along user-defined task flows [12]. As a consequence, through task containers and their particular task semantics, users are empowered to interact with the displayed information in a contextual manner, thus raising information in mashups to the level of task objects the user can act upon.

As represented in Fig. 1, *system objects* (i.e., data items), resulting from the mashup, and their visualizations within UI templates (*UI objects*) can be promoted to the role of *task objects* that in turn can be endowed with and treated according to the various *task functions* offered by the containers in which they are cast. Task objects - not simply data items or their representation in UI templates - become the very objects of user interaction, with the result that the users are not only allowed to consume the information displayed by the mashup, but they are also enabled to manipulate and transform it, i.e., to *prosume* it, in accordance with the tasks they intend to perform. In principle, mashups – without considering TUX principles – can be equipped with some functionality that has task-semantic character, exceeding the mere modification of data visualizations. Yet, in such cases the task semantics would reside in the application implicitly and in a rather hard-wired fashion. For example, a component for the visualization of products could be enriched with a functionality to send emails to vendors. However, this would be a hard-coded function, which the users could not adapt flexibly into their spontaneously defined task flow. According to TUX, it would be instead possible to apply the communication capability to other object types, for example to submit inquiries on the products to consumer forums.

Fig. 1 illustrates the organization of a framework supporting this new task-centric perspective on the organization of an EUD system based on the mashup paradigm. Modules supporting mashup composition and execution are integrated with modules for the manipulation of task objects according to TUX principles. Typical mashup modules are exploited to create the base of UI objects to be then manipulated as task objects. Within the *mashup engine*, the *data access module* extracts data from the services on which the system relies on (by means of the *mashup components* [2]). The *integration module* interprets user composition actions performed at the UI level and creates an execution model determining how system objects have to be integrated. The results, i.e., the integrated system objects, are rendered as UI objects within *UI templates*. Such UI objects provide the actionable information on which task functions can be applied. In this sense, UI objects are promoted to the level of task objects by virtue of the functionality provided by the *task-semantic layer*. In Fig. 1, the dotted-dashed line connecting a UI template (used for rendering various views of UI objects) and a task container (hosting task objects) makes this promotion explicit.

The task-semantic layer then provides for the identification of the current task contexts, based on the interpretation of user actions as they manipulate *task objects* by applying container-specific task functions; it also supports the *casting* of task objects within and across various *task containers*. At the UI level, a task container "wraps" mashup UI templates, so that the user can act on the displayed UI objects by means of the task-related manipulations. This results in treating UI objects as task objects by virtue of their interpretation through the context, which is defined and provided by each task container. Different UI templates within a task container can be used for providing different views of the same task objects without changing however the semantics of the objects as implied by the task container. Changes of views would in fact still be in line or even supportive of the particular task semantics.

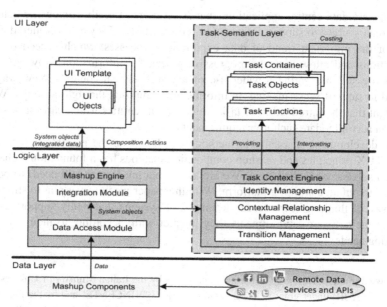

Fig. 1. Overall organization of the framework supporting the interaction with mashups enhanced according to TUX principles

It is worth noticing that, in order to associate different task semantics to data extracted from heterogeneous resources, it is important to maintain continually the relation of the elements representing the task objects to their original context. According to the framework shown in Fig. 1, establishing and maintaining the identity of task objects (as data returned by a given resource) is supported by the *task context engine*, in particular by its *identity management* component.

Another challenge is to deal with the need of users to endow objects with meanings that depend on the task they choose to accomplish. From the system perspective, a *contextual relationship management* module (see Fig. 1) allows task objects to be augmented by users with subjective meanings and functions that relate to the task semantics of the selected containers where the interaction with the objects takes place. More specifically, this is handled by the generic function of *casting,* which implies that task objects are exposed to the aforementioned container-specific task semantics.

In any concrete scenario, users may interact with task objects in a sequence which spans multiple containers, along spontaneously defined trajectories that however have to keep track of the sequence of the various task semantics a given set of task objects was subjected to. The overall process can thus be considered a kind of "sequential casting" that in the framework of Fig. 1 is managed by the *transition management* module.

3   Concluding Discussion

Mashups are data-centric applications that assist users in easily composing heterogeneous data sources to support information retrieval tasks. They are considered a solution for the important trend of data exploration processes, which exceed one-time interactions and allow users to progressively seek for information. However, some factors are still preventing a wider use of mashups in real contexts. New ways are needed to support sense making on information composed through mashups. We are confident that the introduction of task containers, as entities which carry task semantics, can accommodate such user requirements.

The development of a suitable methodology based on the possible synergies between TUX principles and mashup composition methods has a foundational character that can solve several challenges. We are aware that much work still needs to be done in order to obtain a working platform. With this paper we however aim to stimulate a new way of thinking towards the definition of systems that really support users in shaping the software environments they interact with, according to their actual and emerging needs.

Acknowledgments. This work is partially supported by the Italian Ministry of University and Research (MIUR) under grant PON 02_00563_3470993 "VINCENTE" and by the Italian Ministry of Economic Development (MISE) under grant PON Industria 2015 MI01_00294 "LOGIN".

References

1. Ardito, C., Costabile, M.F., Desolda, G., Lanzilotti, R., Matera, M., Piccinno, A., Picozzi, M.: User-Driven Visual Composition of Service-Based Interactive Spaces. Journal of Visual Languages & Computing **25**(4), 278–296 (2014)
2. Daniel, F., Matera, M.: Mashups – Concepts, Models and Architectures. Springer, Heidelberg (2014)
3. Ennals, R., Brewer, E., Garofalakis, M., Shadle, M., Gandhi, P.: Intel Mash Maker: join the web. SIGMOD Rec. **36**(4), 27–33 (2007)
4. Copeland, T.: Presenting archaeology to the public. In: Merriman, T. (ed.) Public Archaeology, pp. 132–144. Routledge, London, UK (2004)
5. Wong, J., Hong, J.I.: Making mashups with marmite: towards end-user programming for the web. In: SIGCHI Conference on Human Factors in Computing Systems (CHI 2007), San Jose, California, USA, pp. 1435-1444. ACM, New York, NY, USA (2007)
6. Daniel, F., Casati, F., Benatallah, B., Shan, M.-C.: Hosted universal composition: models, languages and infrastructure in mashArt. In: Laender, A.H.F., Castano, S., Dayal, U., Casati, F., de Oliveira, J.P.M. (eds.) ER 2009. LNCS, vol. 5829, pp. 428–443. Springer, Heidelberg (2009)
7. http://pipes.yahoo.com/pipes/ (Accessed 4 March 2015)
8. Namoun, A., Nestler, T., De Angeli, A.: Conceptual and usability issues in the composable web of software services. In: Daniel, F., Facca, F.M. (eds.) ICWE 2010. LNCS, vol. 6385, pp. 396–407. Springer, Heidelberg (2010)
9. Ardito, C., Costabile, M.F., Desolda, G., Latzina, M., Matera, M.: Hands-on actionable mashups. In this volume
10. Ardito, C., Bottoni, P., Costabile, M.F., Desolda, G., Matera, M., Picozzi, M.: Creation and Use of Service-based Distributed Interactive Workspaces. Journal of Visual Languages & Computing **25**(6), 717–726 (2014)
11. Latzina, M., Beringer, J.: Transformative user experience: beyond packaged design. Interactions **19**(2), 30–33 (2012)
12. Beringer, J., Latzina, M.: Elastic workplace design. In: Wulf, V., Randall, D., Schmidt, K. (eds.) Designing Socially Embedded Technologies in the Real-World. Springer, London (2015)

Assisted Composition of Services on Mobile Devices

Nikolay Mehandjiev[(✉)], Lu Ning, and Abdallah Namoun

University of Manchester, Manchester, UK
n.mehandjiev@mbs.ac.uk

Abstract. Composing software services on mobile devices is especially challenging when attempted by non-programmers. In this paper we compare two alternative supporting strategies: using generic task templates and scripting together condition-response fragments. The first is exemplified by a prototype called ACOM (Assisted Composition on Mobiles), the second by a commercially available alternative called IFTTT (IF This Then That). The paper uses a comparative observational study to highlight the benefits and drawbacks of both approaches, and to derive lessons for their improvement.

Keywords: Assisted service composition · Mobile mash-ups · Mobile EUD

1 Introduction

The increased sophistication of mobile devices leads to extended scope of users' interactions with them. Users even create "mashups" by connecting web services to provide combined functionality or information. Providing effective support for such activities on mobile devices is still a developing research topic, with only a handful of user-centric systems reported in the literature (notably Puzzle [6] and MobiMash [7]).

Desktops tools claiming to support "mashups" exist, yet these tools are difficult to learn by non-programmers, requiring the understanding of advanced programming concepts such as loops [1]. An exception is Yahoo Pipes![1], which employs "pipe and filter" metaphor for connecting components through information pipes, yet its models are not scalable, the type of information to be processed is limited and users experience difficulties in localising faults [2]. Converting these tools to mobile platforms is far from trivial, facing a number of platform-specific challenges. Success depends on choosing an appropriate strategy and ensuring effective representations.

This paper presents our initial steps in this direction, exploring the effectiveness of two alternative support strategies for mobile service composition by end users: using generic task templates and scripting condition-response fragments. The second strategy is implemented in the commercial tool IFTTT (IF This Then That) [5], which enjoys a growing user community. We have a tool supporting the first strategy, called Assisted User Composition (AUC) [3], yet this is designed for desktop platforms.

In this paper we report on the conceptual adaptation of our AUC approach to mobile platforms, called *ACOM: Assisted Composition on Mobiles;* and on the results of an observational study comparing our adapted approach with IFTTT.

---

[1] http://pipes.yahoo.com/pipes/

© Springer International Publishing Switzerland 2015
P. Díaz et al. (Eds.): IS-EUD 2015, LNCS 9083, pp. 242–248, 2015.
DOI: 10.1007/978-3-319-18425-8_23

2   Assisted Composition on Mobiles (ACOM)

Our Assisted User Composition tool [3] uses a set of templates organised in a taxonomy. Each template corresponds to a key generic activity of our users [4] and comprises a number of tasks. Once a user selects a template, the tool uses the information encoded in the template to select a set of services for each task in the template. These are listed underneath the task name in a tabular format, and the user is expected to select a service for each task. Using the semantic information encoded in the templates and in the actual services, the tool indicates all services which are incompatible with the ones selected so far. Further details are available elsewhere [3].

Adapting the interface ideas of this tool to the features of a mobile platform was the first step in our investigation. We decided to deconstruct the tabular layout into a set of tabbed panes, one tabbed pane for each column of the table, and to hide the taxonomy of templates once the initial selection has been made. The adapted approach was prototyped using the JustInMind prototype tool[2], with the result shown on the left in Figure 1. Once the service selection is complete, the prototype lists all selected services on a single screen as shown to the right in the figure.

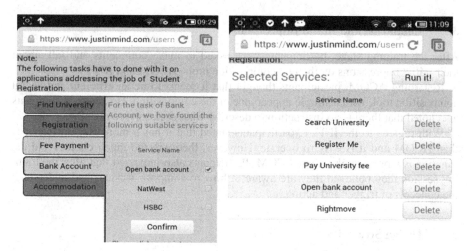

Fig. 1. Service Selection in ACOM (left) and list of selected services (right)

3   Experiments and Results

The aim of this study was to evaluate two alternative approaches to supporting end users when they try to compose services on a mobile device: using generic templates, exemplified by ACOM, and scripting together condition-response patterns, exemplified by IFTTT [5]. To that end we designed a within-subjects comparative observation study, where our participants were asked to complete two composition tasks of different complexity per tool. The task pairs across the tools were based on scenarios

---

[2] http://www.justinmind.com/

with similar complexity. Eight participants with average age of 23.4 years were selected for this experiment (four males and four females). All had low experience of similar tools, and only three of them had IT background. The participants were divided into two groups of four participants. Group 1 used ACOM first and then IFTTT, whilst Group 2, used IFTTT first and then ACOM. Participants alternated from different groups to reduce skewing due to learning by the moderator.

The experiment involved three stages as follows:

(1)   Training stage, where participants completed user information forms, attended a tutorial and then completed a pre-observation questionnaire.
(2)   Composition stage, where participants performed first a simple and then a complex composition task whilst verbalizing their thoughts. Voice and interactions were captured on the device using a screen recording tool.
(3)   Rating stage, where the participants rated the adaptability and usability of the composition tool, as well as end user development experience.

The second and third stages were repeated for each of the two tools.

After the experiments, data were analyzed using thematic analysis for the qualitative observations and statistical analysis for the quantitative data.

3.1   Comments and Initial Impressions

After the training stage, participants were asked to make comments and talk about their initial impressions on the two composition tools, ACOM and IFTTT.

Regarding ACOM, participants thought that it seems to be an efficient and useful composition tool, with a simple appearance of the composition. However, participants also noted that there is no instruction to describe what each service is doing.

With regards to the IFTTT, participants stated that it has a more elegant interface than ACOM and it is easy to operate. However, there are too much choices and the function is more complex than ACOM. Participants also indicated that after the training session they believed they are aware of how to compose services and understand the concepts of trigger and action.

3.2   Design Strategies

Participants were able to understand the two ACOM scenarios, and to follow the instructions for both to completion. During the composition session for the simple scenario, participants were able to understand the instructions and information flow, and quickly completed the task without particular problems. However, when users composed services according to the complex scenario, they were confused between the name of the overall scenario and the name of one the tasks within. The lack of detailed information about each service was reiterated, users pointing out that they could not know what each service is used for. They were also able to delete a specific service quickly and accurately after composing services and then run the composition tool. The services that a participant composed are shown in Figure 1. Notably, participants with IT background spend less time on using ACOM than those without.

Similarly for IFTTT, all participants completed the simple task successfully and in a short time. The information flow for the complex scenario was easy to understand and users could find appropriate services according to the hints or keywords of required services. However, half of the participants pointed out that it was a little difficult for them to find the right services for tasks because of the large amount of services in IFTTT. Therefore, users spend too much time on looking for services. Furthermore, participants were confused by similar services, such as Android SMS and SMS, some selecting inappropriate services. When deleting services, they were also not able to find the "delete" button in a short time.

3.3   Pre-observation and Post-observation Questionnaires

The comments and observations from the previous sections are reflected in the pre-observation and post-observation questionnaires completed by the 8 participants.

Table 1. Common questions and their codes, version for ACOM

Q1	It is difficult to understand the notations used in ACOM.
Q2	It is difficult to understand the instructions for ACOM.
Q3	The interface of ACOM is concise and simple.
Q4	The function of ACOM is practical and useful.
Q5	It is easy to use ACOM.
Q6	It is easy to navigate ACOM.
Q7	It is easy to find the right services using ACOM.
Q8	It is easy to delete services using ACOM.
Q9	I feel confident using ACOM.
Q10	I feel confused using ACOM.
Q11	The interface of ACOM fits the screen of mobile.
Q12	It is a difficult task to compose/aggregate services for me.
Q13	It is time consuming to develop assisted composition applications on mobiles.
Q14	I know which services and modules to combine in order to develop my composite application.

The questions listed in Table 1are answered through a 7-point Likert scale, where 7 is "strongly agree" and 1 is "strongly disagree". The scores for questions formulated in a negative manner, have been inverted to allow comparison with the positive questions. Figure 2 shows average response values for questions similar across both tools.

ACOM scored better than IFTTT on the majority of the questions. The ones which are statistically significant using a two-tailed t-test at 90% are Q5 (ease of using the tool) and Q6 (ease of navigation). Overall, the participants preferred the concise and simple interface, the ease of understanding instructions and the navigation of ACOM. Also, participants did not find the development of applications using ACOM to be time consuming nor difficult. Finally, participants demonstrated that they knew more about service composition after this experiment and they showed strong interest in service composition and in learning more about EUD in the future.

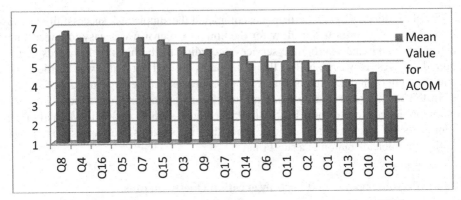

Fig. 2. Mean values of answers (7 is best) in decreasing order for ACOM

In addition to common questions, there were a few questions specific for one of the tools. The mean of the score for Q18ACOM (The application produced by ACOM is helpful to accomplish a student registration) and the mean of the score for Q22ACOM (ease of understanding the final list of services) for ACOM are nearly 7. It means that participants thought ACOM was helpful for the job of student registration and the final selected service list was also easy to understand. The mean value of Q18IFTTT (limitation of functions in IFTTT) is 4, which means participants' opinion for this question is neutral. They thought the functions in IFTTT are sufficient for general use.

3.4   Post-observation Comments and Suggestions

After observation, participants completed a post-observation questionnaire, where they commented on features they like most and least, and provide suggestions for improvement in Table 2.

Table 2. Suggestions for Improvements

ACOM	IFTTT
Adapt UI for mobile devices, for example enlarge the buttons and checkboxes	Simplify the way applications appear to end users to avoid confusion
Improve the security of the system to protect the privacy of the users	Add history recording, especially for searches and results
Add more descriptions for each service on the screen	
Improve the aesthetic design of user interface	

Table 3 shows the results from the thematic analysis of participants' comments on ACOM and IFTTT. In summary the comments relate to:

User Interface: Both interfaces were considered simple and elegant.

Notations: Participants expressed weak preference for the ACOM notation, finding both notations easy to understand but lacking details about the services

Navigations: Participants thought the two composition tools were easy to use and navigate without programming skills. Most participants thought that the navigation of IFTTT is better and easier than ACOM.

Functions: The functions of both tools were perceived as useful, yet ACOM had limited services and scope of use, whilst IFTTT had too many services, making the choice of service too slow. Besides, both tools were found lacking a good searching function. The number of comments suggests the functions in ACOM were better regarded than those in IFTTT.

Table 3. Times of mentioning aspects of the tools

Themes	ACOM	IFTTT
User Interface	7 (5 positive and 2 negative)	4 (4 positive)
Notations	2 (1 positive and 1 negative)	2 (2 negative)
Navigations	5 (3 positive and 2 negative)	6 (6 positive)
Functions	9 (7 positive and 2 negative)	12 (7 positive and 5 negative)

4   Summary and conclusions

The constraints of this study meant only eight participants were used, focusing analysis on qualitative comments. This initial feedback will be used to develop an operational ACOM prototype to be evaluated in a future study with more participants.

Despite its limitations, the current study achieved its objectives in comparing two alternative approaches to service composition on mobiles and highlighting requirements for further improvement. For example, clear information about each service would help users deal with a large amount of unfamiliar services. The findings are generally in line with our earlier work on mental models [3], e.g. confirming end user difficulties in following data dependencies and other dependencies between services. Other interesting requirements were the need for search history, the preference for larger icons and simpler service composition interfaces. The participants were able to perform the simple composition tasks without the help of the moderator, and provided an overall positive opinion about the ease of use of ACOM, and about the usefulness of such tool in the task which is supported by it.

References

1. Zang, N., Rosson, M.B., Nasser, V.: Mashups: who? what? why?. In: Proceedings of CHI, Florence, Italy (2008)
2. Jones, M., Churchill, E.: Conversations in developer communities: a preliminary analysis of the yahoo! pipes community. In: Proceedings of the 4th International Conference on Communities and Technologies, PA, USA (2009)
3. Mehandjiev, N., Lecue, F., Wajid, U., Namoun, A.: Assisted service composition for end users. In: Proceedings of ECOWS 2010, pp. 131-138. IEEE CS, Washington, DC (2010). doi=10.1109/ECOWS.2010.30

4. Sutcliffe, A.: Domain Theory: Patterns for Knowledge and Software Reuse. L. Erlbaum Assoc. Inc., Hillsdale (2002)
5. IFTTT 'Put the internet to work for you. - IFTTT' (2015). http://ifttt.com (accessed: March 13, 2015)
6. Danado, J., Paternò, F.: Puzzle: a visual-based environment for end user development in touch-based mobile phones. In: Winckler, M., Forbrig, P., Bernhaupt, R. (eds.) HCSE 2012. LNCS, vol. 7623, pp. 199–216. Springer, Heidelberg (2012)
7. Cappiello, C., Matera, M., Picozzi, M., Caio, A., Guevara, M.T.: Mobimash: end user development for mobile mashups. In: Proceedings of the WWW 2012 Companion, pp. 473–474. ACM, NY. doi=10.1145/2187980.2188083

Everyday Tools Used for Avionics User Modifiable Software Automatic Generation

Miguel Sánchez-Puebla[1,2(✉)], Roberto Sobrino[1], and José Martín[1]

[1] Airbus Defence and Space, Getafe, Spain
{Miguel.A.Sanchez,Roberto.Sobrino,Jose.A.Martin}@airbus.com
[2] Computer Science Department, Universidad Carlos III, Madrid, Spain
masrodri@inf.uc3m.es

Abstract. User Modifiable Software is designed to allow for limited modification by aircraft operators without certification efforts. User Modifiable Software is not new in concept. Nevertheless, development of technology, combined with a strong demand for cost reduction and the worldwide use of desktop applications like office automation favor the use of common tools like spreadsheet applications for automatic generation of User Modifiable Software embedded in avionics equipment in modern aircrafts.

Keywords: User Modifiable Software · Automatic software generation · Spurious failures · Common tools

1 Introduction

In many industries, increasing tension exits between the desire of manufacturers producing standard product which allow cost reduction and the desire of the end-users to have standard product with a reduced acquisition cost but also a very customized product to minimize overall operational costs. Typically, users cannot afford full customization even if there are not any certification needs. Even more users cannot afford unique maintenance efforts and custom development, including specific tools and dedicated training.

Aircraft operators emphasize on overall cost reduction and demand for commercial and very familiar tools as environment for User Modifiable Software (UMS) modification.

On aircrafts, one of the earliest successful attempts was the use of jumper wires as a standard way for limited 'programming' the performance of the embedded computers. Jumper wires [6] were used to change mathematical behaviors of the systems, or reconfiguring the components of a system composed with different components without modifying the internal design. For instance, by using a sequence of jumper wires, an aircraft altimeter could be "programmed" by the user to set the altitude of the center of gravity of the aircraft. UMS is a more sophisticated solution to provide customized systems while still allowing the equipment manufacturer to maintain lower costs through standardization.

© Springer International Publishing Switzerland 2015
P. Díaz et al. (Eds.): IS-EUD 2015, LNCS 9083, pp. 249–252, 2015.
DOI: 10.1007/978-3-319-18425-8_24

Airborne software standard [4] provides a detailed discussion of early thinking on the subject. Modern software standards [2] and its last version [3] formally recognize User Modifiable Software and provide guidelines for system safety and certification.

The system containing UMS must be designed such that the safe operation of the non-modifiable software component is not affected by the operation or any change to the modifiable component.

The extent of modifiability can range from simply setting a bit to select an option to providing code, which implements a major function.

Safety is the overriding consideration in determining what areas can be modified and the implementation techniques used. This places practical constraints on what is reasonable to allow users to modify.

Once technology and broad industry changes has made UMS practical and usual, the challenge is now the use of low cost desktop, laptops, tablets, … and low cost office automation for making modifications at a reasonable cost and without specialized trainings.

This paper proposes the use of everyday tools as a valuable and very affordable mean for automatic UMS generation used on modern aircrafts.

2   User Modifiable Software Applications

Perhaps in the avionics arena, the best-known and widest use of UMS for many years has been the wide spread adaptation by airlines of Aircraft Condition Monitoring Systems (ACMS). These systems monitor thousands of signals during in flight and process the data into succinct reports and also extensive files about aircraft and crew performance that can be down linked via radio links, printed, or placed on recorders. Examples include the monitoring of engine parameters, oil pressures, and fuel consumptions and flows.

Several manufacturers have provided ACMS designed to be modified by the airline user. An airline can upload a modification to the system's software to provide nearly any type of report desired. The modifications are programmed on a PC or a workstation using a combination of commercially available software packages and specialized software tools.

Another well-known use of UMS in the last years is the filter used on the Central Maintenance System (CMS). CMS is fully intended for maintenance purpose, not for flight crew operation. CMS provides means to correctly identify and isolate failed avionics equipment and wirings by generating maintenance messages [1]. CMS shall not be confused with flight crew confidence tests, and failure annunciation/warning functions.

As a main component the line maintenance, CMS' function consists of the identification or confirmation of a fault condition, the isolation of the fault to a single equipment or interface, aids the replacement of the faulty equipment, adjustments required to return the system to an operational configuration, and verification that proper system operation has been restored [1].

CMS is basic to assist maintenance personal to provide timely responses that should be fast, accurate, and unambiguous when identifying equipment replacement and corrective actions. The increasing complexity of modern aircraft implies that CMS could report a significant number of spurious failures inducing unjustified removals of systems components, which are traditionally a major cost factor.

3   Implemented Solution

In-Service Experience addresses real behavior of the certified design in real conditions. Airlines' in-service experience shows more than half of maintenance failure messages reported by onboard electronic diagnostic functions are spurious, i.e. not real failures. Spurious messages lead to unnecessary expensive maintenance actions. Preventing already identified spurious from being declared by their CMS saves undoubtedly huge resources.

An imaginative way to reduce the number of spurious failures no requiring an extra cost of recertifying some pieces of onboard software is the inclusion of a software filter embedded on the CMS. This filter is a type of UMS that allows the containment of unscheduled maintenance actions already confirmed as spurious. An error on the filter has no safety effects but only maintenance cost implications.

However, the growing number of aircrafts with many allowed configurations fosters a rapidly increase of filter versions diversity, producing the subsequent escalation on the cost for the aircraft manufacturer. On the other hand, the complexity and multiplicity of aircraft configurations make the set of known spurious failures almost unique for every aircraft configuration. Therefore, adapting the spurious filter is an interesting asset for Operators.

One plausible solution is set the end-user in the loop for the software filter generation by using dedicated tools provided by CMS manufacturers. End-users of the filter in charge of aircraft maintenance are the best connoisseurs of their aircraft configuration and the best ones positioned in the generation of the desired software filter. They only need that the tools required for the software filter generation would not have the same level of complexity as the tools used for software developers or the tools used by CMS specialists. Even more, this software filter is been described as a character-separated value file (CSV), widely supported by everyday tools, thus allowing a successful substitution of specialized and frequently expensive software packages. Besides, the authors have developed a human interface based on office automation, allowing easy modifications, both on the software filter and the interface itself. In this way, end-users are enabled to interact with the software filter with their everyday tools requiring neither additional efforts nor training in a self-sufficient scope.

```
# Filter file for MSN777 filter development: v1.0
#FALSE TYPE BITE ID SIDE Fault Code Starting (Event 1)
  Finishing (Event2) FIN Part Number Class FDCE Type FWS
FDCE Starting (Event 3) Priority FMC Multy-Occurence
#PFR Report Relevance Comments to CMS team Reason for
usage in FilterLock Delete
```

```
FALSE FM  8 2 2473F8TT  * EVENT [w] * * 6 * * * high  2001
#   Action Status: Resolved with correction\s
Root:Limitation
FALSE FM  8 1 2473F59B  * EVENT [w] * * 6 * * * high  2001
#   Action Status: Resolved with correction\s
Root:Limitation
FALSE FM  8 3 2473FCC9  * EVENT [w] * * 6 * * * high  2001
#   Action Status: Resolved with correction\s
```

[Example of a filter file in CSV format]

The use of everyday tools [5] is deemed as a very suitable option. This approach allows end-users afford full customization of the filters without requiring expensive and specialized tools only used for this purpose, also avoiding the need of skillful personnel only devoted to this tasks and the matching periodic training. Then, end-users can maintain, up to some extent, complex systems like modern aircraft without requiring additional certification efforts, always expensive and painful in terms of time.

4   Future works

Even if the software filter files are described in plain-text, modifications are error prone and require special attention.

A further step in the UMS arena is the use of interfaces based on everyday tools daily used, and developed by the users themselves. Macro features and predefined widgets already existing in these everyday tools are of a big help in defining and implementing those interfaces.

Users can benefit from these interfaces optimizing the modification process and producing filter free of errors.

References

1. Airlines Electronic Engineering Committee, ARINC 652, Software Management Guidelines (1993)
2. Radio Technical Commission for Aeronautics: RTCA DO-178B, Software Considerations in Airborne Systems and Equipment Certification (1992)
3. Radio Technical Commission for Aeronautics: RTCA DO-178C, Software Considerations in Airborne Systems and Equipment Certification (2011)
4. Airlines Electronic Engineering Committee: ARINC CHARACTERISTIC 624-1, Design Guidance For Onboard Maintenance System (1993)
5. Fund Action: Pros: Use 'Everyday Tools' To Communicate. ISSN: 1054-5956, November 15, 2010
6. Williams, R.: Real-Time Systems Development. Butterworth-Heinemann (2005)

Doctoral Consortium

Investigating the Barriers Experienced by Adult End-User Developers When Physical Prototyping

Tracey Booth[✉]

Centre for Human-Computer Interaction Design, School of Mathematics,
Computer Science and Engineering, City University London, London, UK
tracey.booth.1@city.ac.uk

Abstract. Previous research has not explored to great extent the barriers end-user developers face when developing physical prototypes with popular platforms such as Arduino. In this paper I motivate and describe an upcoming exploratory study investigating end-user developers' mental models of some of the fundamental concepts involved in physical prototyping, and the learning barriers encountered in both electronic circuit construction and programming. I will present the preliminary results of this study at the Doctoral Consortium.

1 Introduction

The Maker Movement and technologies it has spawned, such as the popular Arduino platform, continue to entice end-users - artists, designers, researchers, hobbyists - into constructing and programming microcontroller-based prototypes. Referred to as *physical prototyping*, this type of activity requires applying programming and electronics concepts, and understanding how the two relate. However, new end-user developers (EUDs) may lack experience in one or both areas. While the platforms now available make it easier to connect sensors and actuators to a microcontroller and program their behaviour, it is still unclear to what degree the learning and application barriers have been lowered for adult EUDs.

The overarching aim of my PhD is to identify how physical prototyping systems can be designed to best support EUDs and integrate both the physical and virtual aspects of physical prototyping effectively [5]. Knowing how EUDs *naturally* think, reason and behave in the act of physical prototyping will be key to understanding how physical prototyping systems can be designed for optimal usability [4] for EUDs.

Findings from an earlier study I conducted identified potential *learning barriers* for end users new to programming Arduino [1]. In an upcoming exploratory study, described below, I will investigate EUDs' *mental models* of some of the fundamental concepts involved in physical prototyping and look deeper into learning barriers encountered in both circuit construction and programming.

© Springer International Publishing Switzerland 2015
P. Díaz et al. (Eds.): IS-EUD 2015, LNCS 9083, pp. 255–258, 2015.
DOI: 10.1007/978-3-319-18425-8_25

2   EUDs' Learning Barriers and Mental Models

The main goal of EUD is *'empowering end-users to develop and adapt systems them-selves'* [3]. In the context of physical prototyping, I expand development to include the physical prototypes themselves, not just the software programs that control their behaviour. Decades of research has taught us much about end-user programmers (EUPs) and EUDs, in domains such as web development and spreadsheets, but rela-tively little is known about the barriers faced by EUDs when physical prototyping.

Ko et al. [2] identified six learning barriers frequently encountered by novice EUPs, that can stall progress: *design barriers, selection barriers, coordination barri-ers, use barriers, understanding barriers* and *information barriers*. The main barriers found in my previous study of novice EUPs using Arduino involved the selection and use of programming constructs and understanding unexpected program output, in-cluding compiler errors [1].

As mental models play a key role in problem solving and the assimilation of new information, barriers can result from inadequate or faulty ones. Experts have struc-tural ('how it works') mental models that provide abstract, generalised schema to draw upon, whereas novices have functional ('how-to-use-it') mental models that are frequently incomplete and potentially inaccurate. Misconceptions in mental models of electricity and circuit theory make learning advanced concepts more difficult and can lead to confusion when interpreting or designing circuits. Poor or erroneous mental models have also been shown to be a significant source of novice programmers' diffi-culties. Incomplete or incorrect mental models of programming and electronics may limit EUDs in their prototype development ambitions, lead to frustrating bouts of troubleshooting, or even prevent them from completing their projects. More research is needed to determine how best to support EUDs developing physical prototypes so that they can overcome the barriers they face.

3   Study Outline

The study aims to answer the following main research questions:

RQ1. What learning barriers do EUDs encounter when constructing and program-ming physical prototypes?

RQ2. What mental models of physical prototyping concepts do EUDs hold?

RQ3. Are there common incorrect mental models that impact EUDs' physical pro-totyping progress and success?

Participants.
Participants will be 20 adults who actively use the Arduino platform to develop physical prototypes for personal use, rather than as their primary job function. The target profile is deliberately broad, to attract people of varying background and ability in both programming and physical prototyping. I will recruit participants via hacker-spaces and other maker community groups.

Procedure.

Participants will be sent an online questionnaire, gathering data about their background and experience in programming, electronics and physical prototyping. Once this has been completed, each will attend an hour-long session in a usability lab, structured into four phases: First, they will complete a self-efficacy questionnaire to measure their confidence in developing physical prototypes. Second, they will answer a number of questions to elicit their *existing* mental models of physical prototyping concepts. Third, they will perform a physical prototyping task. Fourth, the participant will be asked, in the form of a semi-structured interview, to explain the workings of the prototype they have developed, and I will probe them on any specific issues observed, including misconceptions or areas of difficulty. The session sequence takes into account the potential for each activity to affect data gathered in subsequent phases.

For the physical prototyping task participants will be asked to construct and program a physical prototype that displays the values of an analogue sensor using the Arduino platform (microcontroller board and IDE) and a starter kit of labelled electronics components. Participants will have access to the Arduino IDE's built-in help and online resources, as they would during real-world prototyping activities. A verbal protocol (think aloud) will be used, and both on and off-screen actions will be video recorded. The prototypes will be photographed and the programs saved.

Data analysis.

Analysis will involve mixed methods. RQ1 will be addressed by coding the recording transcripts for learning barriers - I will look for types and frequencies of barriers encountered and compare the findings to those of my previous study. To answer RQ2 I will perform a thematic analysis of the mental models elicitation data to determine the mental models held by EUDs of physical prototyping concepts. To answer RQ3 I will identify common mental model types, misconceptions and knowledge gaps in this thematic and investigate whether these are correlated with physical prototyping performance and efficacy. In addition, I will look for correlations between participants' backgrounds, their self-efficacy scores, their mental models and the learning barriers they experience. The task recordings will also allow me to analyse participants' strategies for prototype development, such as whether and how they seek out and use existing examples or instructions, and their behaviour and efficacy in the use of help content.

4   Future Work

My next steps will be influenced by the findings from the study. One avenue is to investigate how to provide in situ supports to help EUDs overcome barriers encountered during physical prototyping tasks. Another is to focus on solution exploration, or 'tinkering', and how it relates to the development of mental models and overcoming learning barriers.

References

1. Booth, T., Stumpf, S.: End-user experiences of visual and textual programming environments for Arduino. In: Dittrich, Y., Burnett, M., Mørch, A., Redmiles, D. (eds.) IS-EUD 2013. LNCS, vol. 7897, pp. 25–39. Springer, Heidelberg (2013)
2. Ko, A.J., et al.: Six learning barriers in end-user programming systems. In: Proceedings of the 2004 IEEE Symposium on Visual Languages and Human Centric Computing, pp. 199–206. IEEE Computer Society, Washington, DC, USA (2004)
3. Lieberman, H., et al.: End-user development: an emerging paradigm. In: Lieberman, H., et al. (eds.) End User Development, pp. 1–8. Springer Netherlands (2006)
4. Myers, B.A., Pane, J.F., Ko, A.: Natural programming languages and environments. Communications of the ACM 47(9), 47–52 (2004)
5. Tetteroo, D., Soute, I., Markopoulos, P.: Five key challenges in end-user development for tangible and embodied interaction, In: Proceedings of the 15th ACM International Conference on Multimodal Interaction, pp. 247–254. ACM, New York, NY, USA (2013)

EMA IDEs: A Challenge for End User Development

Nikolaos Batalas[(⊠)]

Eindhoven University of Technology, Den Dolech 2, 5600MB Eindhoven,
The Netherlands
`n.batalas@tue.nl`

Abstract. With the proliferation of smartphones and wearables, Ecological Momentary Assessment (EMA) methods[1] are evolving into an indispensable component of practices that seek to collect data from a population of participants, through the use of their devices. In fields ranging from clinical psychology, to product design, to marketing and mHealth, the mobile devices owned by a population of participants can be made use of, and gather insights into how their daily lives unfold, by collecting data as reported from the participants themselves, or sensed by the devices. End-user programmable systems can aid these professionals and researchers manage the challenges that may arise in employing EMA methods with such devices.

1 Introduction

With the proliferation of smartphones and wearables, Ecological Momentary Assessment (EMA) methods[1] are evolving into an indispensable component of practices that seek to collect data from a population of participants, through the use of their devices. In fields ranging from clinical psychology, to product design, to marketing and mHealth, the mobile devices owned by a population of participants can be made use of, and gather insights into how their daily lives unfold, by collecting data as reported from the participants themselves, or sensed by the devices. End-user programmable systems can aid these professionals and researchers manage the challenges that may arise in employing EMA methods with such devices.

In this paper, we reflect on our experience with EMA studies so far, and discuss how researchers who perform the data collection, from conception to configuration, to execution and to conclusion, tend to follow a linear progression that can be likened to a waterfall model. We attribute the reason for this to the familiarity that researchers traditionally have, both from literature and practice, in using paper as the principle means of disseminating questionnaires.

We argue that the conception of the EMA study with digital means in direct analogy to former paper-based processes can be problematic, even with end-user configurable or programmable systems. We propose a re-conception of EMA - and by extension mHealth- platforms as Integrated Development Environments

© Springer International Publishing Switzerland 2015
P. Díaz et al. (Eds.): IS-EUD 2015, LNCS 9083, pp. 259–263, 2015.
DOI: 10.1007/978-3-319-18425-8_26

for a platform abstracted to a level higher than the client-server architecture, and discuss potential merits of the approach.

2 Tempest

We built Tempest, initially a software tool in support of the Experience Sampling Method[2] on smartphones. Most tools for ESM allow the composition of questionnaires with standard form elements (textfields, multiple choice items, etc) as offered by the frameworks they had been built with.

Our intent was to allow richer, more complex interfaces to also be employed in the service of eliciting data from participants, and we built a modular system that can be easily configured and also extended with custom widgets of any functionality[3]. In this way, Tempest[4] allows traditional questionnaires to be served, but also custom interfaces like a sketchpad widget, or mini applications such as cognitive tests (Stroop, PVT, Trail Making). It consists of a server where the process is programmed by the researchers, and participant clients that perform the data collection.

Tempest has been used in a number of cases. To give an indication, some of these have been:

- to examine user behavior in video content exploration
- to study the social interactions of women with premenstrual syndrome (PMS)
- with a similar protocol, to study bullying behaviours in social interactions
- in the setting of a steel galvanization factory, to capture moments during workers' shift and construct a model of the tasks they undertake daily[5]
- to study how sleep quality affects people's performance during the day on a barrage of cognitive tests
- to perform an experience sampling study of participants with schizophrenia, asking questions about their mental imagery several times during the day

Tempest has been used in several other contexts as well and in different capacities as a subsystem for larger applications[6], for data collection related to advertising, evaluating ambient technologies, or mobile applications.

In most cases, researchers seeking to employ the system for their studies have received some initial instruction and support from us. It often happened though that they have had extensive teams of collaborators and assistants, whom they allocate different parts of the process to, and all of which also become users of the system, with tasks such as building variants of questionnaires, managing a subset of the participant population, or extracting data.

Most of our researchers have had previous experience in conducting EMA studies, involving either paper forms, or a dedicated personal device. Traditionally, these studies are conducted in a linear fashion[7]. The checklist indicates how researchers understand the process:

- Determine resources
- Set study parameters(type of protocol, sampling period)

- Choose equipment (choose software, perform purchases)
- Implement security measures
- Implement the study (configure and pilot devices, create documentation, anticipate participant issues, maintain equipment)
- Data Issues (data backups, data cleaning)

In practice, implementing a study requires considerable effort. The fact that resources and knowledge are often distributed amongst team members can make it hard to any single team member to maintain awareness of the state the study is at any given point in its implementation, and it is also hard for a study to scale to large participant populations without significant effort from the researchers. Also importantly, this linear process cannot easily support cases where the assessments of participants need to be fed back into strategies for interventions[8].

Also, as different participants with their own devices are brought into studies, several types of errors can occur. In our cases, these have involved stumbling onto bugs in the software code, but oftentimes could also be attributed to how understanding of the software's functions, the study's goals, and the way participants go about their daily routines is shared amongst researchers, assistants and participants. The longer such issues remain undiagnosed, the more likely it is for the data collection to perform suboptimaly. In the next section we propose a way in which software systems can move forward to better support EMA methods

3   Progressing the software platform

As materials for implementing an EMA study are translated from physical form into software artefacts, the transformation affects how their design, implementation, and potential malfunctions can be understood[9]. Additionally, the professionals that conduct data gathering, by way of using end-user programmable systems, become themselves software authors and vendors, who release the software instruments for their participants to use.

Yet, an interesting tension exists: For the software developer of the EMA platform, the product functions correctly when any software instrument can function (or be made to function by the researcher) for any participant, at any point in time. On the other hand, correct function from a researcher's point of view has been achieved when the particular instance of the software instrument, released to the particular participant population, succeeds in gathering an adequate amount of data from an adequate portion of the population, for a sufficient amount of time, in fulfillment of the initial experimental design.

We theorise that, from the point of view of a researcher conducting the data collection, it is the combination of the particular instance of the data collection software, and the participant population that constitutes the platform which can be meaningfully put to use for the researcher's purposes. Both the participant and the device process and generate information. It can be useful to treat this combined, socio-technical system as a computational platform and describe its processes in terms of source code. Philosophical and methodological support for such an approach can be sought in the field of computer science, where the metaphor of the computational lens[10] provides new insights and ways of thinking about the relation between computation and the natural science. Furthermore, the ternary computing approach[11] investigates from a computer-scientific viewpoint, the opportunities that can be found coupling and interaction of the human society, the cyberspace, and the physical world.

In this case, what follows is to conceptualize the tools that enable the authoring and execution of EMA and mHealth processes in general, as Integrated Development Environments, where source code for the cyber-physical platform can be developed, its execution monitored, and its dysfunctions debugged. Futher potential benefits from this conceptualization would be the unambiguous, formal description of the EMA process in code, source code sharing and reuse between studies, proliferation and encapsulation of successful design patterns for EMA.

Tempest is a simplified programmable runtime environment on its own, with a memory storage for saving and loading values for named variables, and the sequential execution of abstracted procedures such as rendering a particular page on the screen of the device, reading sensors, or branching the execution path according to a logic statement evaluating to true of false. In this way, the level of abstraction is raised above its client-server architecture. With its GUI, researchers can declare variables and compose structured programs that can vary in outcomes according to data provided by participants. Participants are also stateful objects accessible by the EMA process.

4   Conclusion

Conducting Ecological Momentary Assessments is an integral basic component of an mHealth ecosystems. In the pragmatics of conducting EMA studies with software, researchers are called to undertake various roles, in order to setup and manage processes that are bound to be increasing in complexity. There is opportunity to support them, with end-user development environments, that operate on appropriate abstractions. We propose that the challenge is not only to implement the end-user development tools, but also define and deliniate the programmable platforms that these tools are used for, and which would expose concepts that align well with the end-user's domain.

References

1. Stone, A.A., Shiffman, S.S., DeVries, M.W.: Ecological momentary assessment (1999)
2. Larson, R., Csikszentmihalyi, M.: The experience sampling method. In: Flow and the Foundations of Positive Psychology, pp. 21–34. Springer (2014)
3. Batalas, N., Markopoulos, P.: Considerations for computerized in situ data collection platforms. In: EICS 2012, pp. 231–236 (2012)
4. Batalas, N., Markopoulos, P.: Introducing tempest, a modular platform for in situ data collection. In: NordiCHI 2012, pp. 781–782 (2012)
5. Kieffer, S., Batalas, N., Markopolous, P., et al.: Towards task analysis tool support. In: 26th Australian Computer-Human Interaction Conference (2014)

6. Capatu, M., Regal, G., Schrammel, J., Mattheiss, E., Kramer, M., Batalas, N., Tscheligi, M.: Capturing mobile experiences: Context-and time-triggered in-situ questionnaires on a smartphone
7. Christensen, T.C., Barrett, L.F., Bliss-Moreau, E., Lebo, K., Kaschub, C.: A practical guide to experience-sampling procedures. Journal of Happiness Studies **4**(1), 53–78 (2003)
8. Heron, K.E., Smyth, J.M.: Ecological momentary interventions: incorporating mobile technology into psychosocial and health behaviour treatments. British Journal of Health Psychology **15**(1), 1–39 (2010)
9. Floridi, L., Fresco, N., Primiero, G.: On malfunctioning software. Synthese, 1–22 (2014)
10. Karp, R.M.: Understanding science through the computational lens. Journal of Computer Science and Technology **26**(4), 569–577 (2011)
11. Xu, Z., Li, G.: Computing for the masses. Communications of the ACM **54**(10), 129–137 (2011)

End User Development System
for Adaptive Augmented Environments

Álvaro Montero[✉]

University Carlos III, Madrid, Spain
ammontes@inf.uc3m.es

Abstract. The objective of this work is to empower artists, designers or teachers with non-technical profiles with the ability to design and produce Adaptive Augmented Reality (AAR) experiences. Thus, their specific domains might benefit from augmented reality (AR) technology. As a first step towards this goal we present a conceptual model of a system which takes into account information about current context, user profile, devices and objectives to produce an experience tailored to the specific requirements of the final user.

Keywords: EUD · End-User Development · AR · Augmented reality · Adaptive systems · AAR · Adaptive Augmented Reality

1 Introduction

This work is focused on End-User Development (EUD), Augmented Reality (AR) and Adaptive Systems (AS). The term EUD makes reference to the methods and techniques that aim to help non-professionals programmers to develop, modify or extend applications [1]. Nowadays, there are many commercial EUD tools that help users to perform plenty of tasks without requiring the assistance of computer professionals [2,3]. In the specific case of AR applications there also exist some tools that aim to simplify the process of development [4,5,6]. However, most of them still require the user to exhibit programming skills, and they are mostly focused on the design and development of AR applications for a specific domain, device or AR technique. There is still a unfortunate lack of AR solutions for some areas in which AR has been demonstrated to be particularly useful [7,8].

The objective of this work is to empower users with non-technical profiles to design and develop AR applications enhanced with adaptation capacities, so applications can automatically adjust themselves to the user's preferences, devices or context of use. As a first step towards that goal we present a conceptual model of AR platform that organizes the different features and components of an application of this kind. The rest of the paper is structured as follows. Section 2 presents some related work in the area. Section 3 introduces the proposed model. At the end of the document, conclusions and future lines of work are presented.

© Springer International Publishing Switzerland 2015
P. Díaz et al. (Eds.): IS-EUD 2015, LNCS 9083, pp. 264–267, 2015.
DOI: 10.1007/978-3-319-18425-8_27

2   Related Work

During the last decade we have witnessed an increasing interest in exploring the possibilities of using AR technology in different areas, such as education [7] or computer games [8]. This trend seems set to continue with the advent of cheaper, more powerful and more ergonomic devices such as smartphones or AR glasses [9]. However, the full potential of AR technology has not yet been fully realized. The development of AR applications entails high costs and complexity, as it requires combining skills and knowledge from different domains related to computer vision, mobile and wearable technology, and the area in which the AR system is intended to be used.

At present there are different platforms and tools that facilitate the development of AR applications. One of the first AR libraries available was ARToolkit [4], which allows recognizing fiducial markers and visualizing 3D model over them. This library is intended to be used by programmers. Among the solutions specifically devised for end users stands out the Dart toolkit [5], which provides a graphical interface to allow developing AR applications in a similar way as the process followed in video composition. The user organizes animations, models or videos along a time line, and programs the actions and events making use of high-level scripts. The toolkit specially addresses the needs of designers, game developers and artists. In addition to these libraries and toolkits, there are also some proposals of conceptual frameworks that organize the components of an AR system. This is the case of UMAR (Ubiquitous Mobile Augmented Reality) [6], a context-aware system [10] that takes into account the user preferences to retrieve and deliver information through a mobile phone. Finally, examples of systems that exploit the use of AS techniques in AR are scarce. One of them is ARtSENSE [11], an application that allows visitors to experience personalized cultural encounter in museums.

One area in which there already exists a wealth of research into the use of adaptive systems is in the area of hypermedia. Instead of providing a "one size to all" experience, Adaptive Hypermedia Systems (AHS) are able to adjust themselves to the specific preferences and objectives of the user. To perform this task, most adaptive systems make use of at least three different models [12]: (1) user model, which contains the relevant information about the user; (2) domain model, which defines the elements that can be modified and changed and (3) interaction model, which stablishes interrelation between the elements of the other two models. Making use of these models AHSs are able to carry out different types of adaptations such as adaptive presentations, which modify the way the content is presented to the user, or adaptive navigation support, which modify the way the content is linked and accessed. AHSs have been used in different domains such as information retrieval, e-commerce, education, training [13].

3   An Adaptive Augmented Reality System Model

As a first step towards the goal of allowing end users without technical knowledge to design and develop AAR applications, we present a conceptual model for an AAR system (Figure 1). The architecture of the system is divided in three layers: (1) High-level EUD Layer, (2) Low-level Development Layer and (3) Adaptation Layer. End users interact with the system through the topmost layer, defining links and relationships between entities of the real world, such as a person, and entities of the virtual world, such as a person profile. The second layer provides links between the entities of the first layer and different representations and identification techniques provided by the system. This way, the entity "person" of the first layer could be linked with a identification method which make use of a photography of the person, or just a fiducial marker. In the same way the virtual world entity that depicts the person profile can be defined as a 3D graphical model, a text or an audio file. The system would adapt the user experience by automatically selecting the best way to identify the real entity in a given moment, and to represent the corresponding virtual one. To support this task the system makes use of a third layer, which provides information about four types of adaptation factors: (1) context, which includes information related to the environment of use, such as lighting, GPS coverage or level of noise, (2) user profile, which could include age, preferences and skills, (3) devices, which detail the characteristics of the devices available to display the AR information, and (4) goals, which describes the intended purpose of the augmentation experience. These factors might impose restrictions in the way the real world entities are identified and the virtual world entities represented. For example, under some lighting conditions the system could identify the person using facial recognition, whereas in a crowded room it might rely on RFID. In the same way, the person's profile could be delivered by displaying textual or graphical representations on the glasses screen, or through headphones as an audio file.

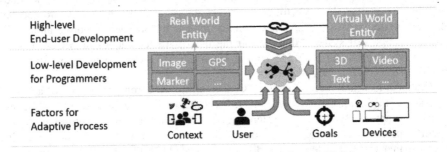

Fig. 1. Adaptive Augmented Reality Application Model

The model will be validated through different use cases consisting in the design and development of different types of AAR applications. Currently, we are working in a new version of the ALF system (Augmented Learning Feedback system) presented in [14], which aims to supports communication between teacher and student during a lecture. The teacher is equipped with a pair of AR glasses that allow him or her to visualize visual cues that depict the current knowledge status of the students during the presentations, and that these select using their mobile phones. The new version of the system is being designed according to the model premises. Hence, the real entities have been made correspond with the students, whereas the status information is matched with the virtual entities. Based on the current context and the device used the system will modify the way the status are represented. For example when the system is used in crowded classrooms, or when using glasses with a limited augmented field of vision, as the Google Glass [15], the system will present the students status information summarized in a pie chart. In other cases the information will be displayed as individual graphical visual cues depicted on top of each student's head.

4   Conclusions and Future Work

In this paper we introduced a conceptual model for AAR applications. This model seeks to hide the complexity of developing AAR applications for end users such as artists, designers and teachers. This could empower them to design and develop AAR experiences tailored to the specific requirements or wishes of their pupils, clients, audience etc. .

We plan to explore two main lines of future work. On the one hand we will develop an authoring tool   based on the proposed model. On the other hand we are extending the model to cover the possibility of interaction design with real objects. Thus, the future model will support the definition of a wider range of AR applications.

References

1. Lieberman, H., Paternò, F., Klann, M., Wulf, V.: End-user development: an emerging paradigm. In: Lieberman, H., Paternò, F., Wulf, V. (eds.) End User Development, pp. 1–8. Springer, Netherlands (2006)
2. Spreadsheet Software Programs | Excel Free Trial. https://products.office.com/en-US/excel
3. WordPress; Blog Tool, Publishing Platform, and CMS. https://wordpress.org/
4. ARToolKit Home Page. http://www.hitl.washington.edu/artoolkit/
5. Macintyre, B., Gandy, M., Dow, S., Bolter, J.D.: DART: a toolkit for rapid design exploration of augmented reality experiences. In: ACM Symp. on User Interface Software and Technology (UIST 2004), pp. 197–206 (2004)
6. Henrysson, A., Ollila, M.: UMAR: ubiquitous mobile augmented reality. In: Proceedings of the 3rd International Conference on Mobile and Ubiquitous Multimedia, pp. 41–45. ACM, New York (2004)
7. Kaufmann, H., Schmalstieg, D.: Mathematics and geometry education with collaborative augmented reality. Comput. Graph. **27**, 339–345 (2003)
8. Piekarski, W., Thomas, B.: ARQuake: The Outdoor Augmented Reality Gaming System. Commun. ACM. **45**, 36–38 (2002)
9. Epson Moverio BT-200 Next Generation Smart Glasses - Epson America, Inc. http://www.epson.com/cgi-bin/Store/jsp/Landing/moverio-bt-200-smart-glasses.do
10. Dey, A.K.: Understanding and Using Context. Pers. Ubiquitous Comput. **5**, 4–7 (2001)
11. Damala, A., Stojanovic, N.: Tailoring the adaptive augmented reality (A2R) museum visit: identifying cultural heritage professionals' motivations and needs. In: 2012 IEEE International Symposium on Mixed and Augmented Reality (ISMAR-AMH), pp. 71–80 (2012)
12. Benyon, D., Murray, D.: Applying user modeling to human-computer interaction design. Artif. Intell. Rev. **7**, 199–225 (1993)
13. Brusilovsky, P.: Adaptive Hypermedia. User Model. User-Adapt. Interact. **11**, 87–110 (2001)
14. Zarraonandia, T., Aedo, I., Díaz, P., Montero, A.: An augmented lecture feedback system to support learner and teacher communication. Br. J. Educ. Technol. **44**, 616–628 (2013)
15. Google Glass. https://developers.google.com/glass/design/index

Workshops

Cultures of Participation in the Digital Age: Coping with Information, Participation, and Collaboration Overload

Barbara Rita Barricelli[1], Gerhard Fischer[2], Anders Mørch[3],
Antonio Piccinno[4], and Stefano Valtolina[1(✉)]

[1] Università degli Studi di Milano, Via Comelico 39/41 20135, Milano, Italy
{barricelli,valtolin}@di.unimi.it
[2] University of Colorado at Boulder, Campus Box 430, Boulder, CO 80309-0430, USA
gerhard@colorado.edu
[3] University of Oslo, Postboks 1092 Blindern 0317, Oslo, Norway
anders.morch@iped.uio.no
[4] Università degli Studi di Bari, Via Orabona 4 70125, Bari, Italy
antonio.piccinno@uniba.it

Abstract. The spread of social computing, cloud computing, Internet of Things, and co-creation tools pushes the use of technology toward a more social dimension and toward the creation of enormous quantity of data. Cultures of participation aims at providing end users that are not experts in computer science nor have the skills specific to the domain at hand, with tools to actively participate and solve problems that are personally meaningfully to them, without necessarily the intervention of skilled professionals. The CoPDA Workshop is in its third edition, after the first one that was held in 2013 during the International Symposium on End-User Development (IS-EUD) in Copenhagen (Denmark)[1] and the second one held in 2014 during the International Working Conference on Advanced Visual Interfaces (AVI) [2]. This edition focuses on problems, tools, techniques and strategies for coping with information, participation, and collaboration overload.

Keywords: Cultures of participation · Information overload · Participation overload · Collaboration overload · Internet of Things · End-User Development · Meta-design · Collaborative design · Collective intelligence · Co-creation · Makers culture

1 Introduction

Nowadays, advances in technology provide end users with access to a more virtual social dimension for interacting with others and enable their active participation in social computing, cloud computing, Internet of Things. This led to the creation of a great mole of data that on a day to day basis may lead the users to feel overwhelmed and, in the long run, may lead to disaffection toward the use of technologies – because it becomes too time consuming and not easy to visualize, analyze, and exploit. But

© Springer International Publishing Switzerland 2015
P. Díaz et al. (Eds.): IS-EUD 2015, LNCS 9083, pp. 271–275, 2015.
DOI: 10.1007/978-3-319-18425-8_28

information overload is not the only problem: participation and collaboration overload follows behind and may cause severe problems in communication. A high level of complexity in participation and collaboration may also cause consumption and engagement difficulties. Therefore, information, participation, and collaboration overload may emerge as unanticipated side effects when we design Web, mobile, wearable, and pervasive applications that enable collaborative user experiences through End-User Development (EUD) and co-creation approaches.

EUD (and specifically the required active engagement in cultures of participation) open up new and unique opportunities for mass collaboration and social production, but they are not without drawbacks. One such drawback is that humans may be forced to cope with the burden of being active contributors in personally irrelevant activities, leading to participation overload. "Do-it-yourself" societies empower humans with powerful tools, but those tools also force them to perform many tasks that were done previously by skilled domain workers, serving as agents and intermediaries. An example is in [3]. Although this shift of agency provides power, freedom, and control to customers, it also has urged people to act as contributors in contexts for which they lack the experience of skilled professionals. This is the case, for example, of public EUD, in which the outcome of end user participation, i.e., the EUD activity, is aimed to be shared with other end users [4]. More experience and assessment is required to determine the design trade-offs for specific contexts and application domains in which the advantages of cultures of participation (such as extensive coverage of information, creation of large numbers of artifacts, creative chaos by making all voices heard, reduced authority of expert opinions, and shared experience of social creativity) will outweigh the disadvantages (accumulation of irrelevant information, wasting human resources in large information spaces, and lack of coherent voices).

Co-creation is grounded on new forms of constructive interaction among all relevant stakeholders in a democratic society: academia, government at all levels, business, public science, the third sector, and citizenship. All these actors collaborate in creative processes of delivering innovation based on principles of participation, empowerment and mutual responsibility. Through engaging citizens to redesign and remake their environment and communities can lead to improved outcomes such as job creation, social cohesion and inclusion, quality of life, more efficient and effective public administrations, improved market functioning, open government, innovation capacity and cross-fertilization of all sectors.

The Copd@ 2015 workshop built on the two previous events [1], [2] which one of the main outcomes has been a special issue of the IxD&A Journal on "Culture of Participation in the Digital Age Empowering - End Users to Improve their Quality of Life" edited by the organizers [5]. This year's event will provide a forum to discuss the following research questions:

- Information overload is a widely recognized problem — which techniques (providing promises and pitfalls) are available and should be developed to cope with it?
- If information overload is a problem, are participation and collaboration overload (as consequences that people are engaged EUD activities) even more serious problems as they require more time and engagement?

- If more and more people can contribute, how do we assess the quality and reliability of the resulting artifacts? How can curator networks effectively increase the quality and reliability?
- What is the role of trust, empathy, altruism, and reciprocity in such an environment and how will these factors affect cultures of participation?

2   Organization and Organizers' Background

The workshop aimed to extend the research agenda initiated during its first two editions. The topics are likely to be of interest to several researches and studies in human-computer interaction, social computing, interaction design, and software engineering. The purpose of this interdisciplinary workshop was to bring together researchers and practitioners. Authors were invited to submit 4-5 pages position papers. The submissions were peer-reviewed for their quality, topic relevance, innovation, and potentials to foster discussion.

Organizers' background are in the following.

Barbara Rita Barricelli is Research Fellow at the Department of Computer Science of Università degli Studi di Milano (Italy) where she obtained her M.Sc. and PhD in Computer Science. Her research interests are Human-Computer Interaction, Computer Semiotics and Semiotic Engineering, Sociotechnical Design, End-User Development, and UX. She has been involved in several International and Italian projects in collaboration with universities, research institutes, and private companies.

Gerhard Fischer is Professor of Computer Science, Fellow of the Institute of Cognitive Science, and Director of the Center for Lifelong Learning and Design (L3D) at the University of Colorado at Boulder. He is a member of the Computer Human Interaction Academy (CHI) and a Fellow of the Association for Computing Machinery (ACM). His research is focused on: (1) learning, working, and collaborating with new media; (2) human-computer interaction; (3) cognitive science; (4) assistive technologies; and (5) transdisciplinary collaboration and education.

Anders Mørch is Professor of Informatics at Department of Education (IPED), University of Oslo, Norway. He received his PhD in informatics from the University of Oslo and an M.S. in computer science from the University of Colorado, Boulder. He developed educational software at NYNEX Science and Technology Center, New York. His research interests are in technology-enhanced learning, learning analytics, collaboration and learning in social worlds and serious games, co-creation tools, end-user tailoring and evolutionary application development, and design-based models of human learning and development.

Antonio Piccinno is assistant Professor at the Computer Science Department of University of Bari "Aldo Moro". He is member of the Interaction, Visualization, Usability & UX (IVU) Lab. Since July 2001, after he got his laurea degree in Computer Science, he has been working at the Department of Computer Science of University of Bari, with different positions: research collaborator, fixed term researcher, lecturer, and finally as assistant professor. He received the PhD in Computer Science at the University of Bari. His research interests are in Human-Computer Interaction,

End-User Development, Visual Interactive Systems, Theory of Visual Languages, Adaptive Interfaces, Component-Based Software Development, Multimodal and Multimedia Interaction.

Stefano Valtolina is assistant Professor at the Computer Science (DI) Department of Università degli Studi di Milano. He obtained his PhD in Informatics from Università degli Studi di Milano and an MSc in Computer Science from the same university. His research interests include: Human-Computer Interaction (HCI), Creative Design, as well as studies in semantic, social and cultural aspects of information technologies with an emphasis on the application of this knowledge to interaction design. His research activity is directed toward the study of aspects of Human Computer Interaction and Database Management investigating methods, interactive systems, and tools for Knowledge Management and Fruition.

3   Program Committee

- Jose Abdelnour-Nocera (University of West London, UK)
- Paloma Diaz (Universidad Carlos III de Madrid, Spain)
- David Díez Cebollero (Universidad Carlos III de Madrid, Spain)
- Francesco Colace (Università degli Studi di Salerno, Italy)
- Daniela Fogli (Università degli Studi di Brescia, Italy)
- Angela Guercio (Kent State University, USA)
- Rosa Lanzilotti (Università degli Studi di Bari, Italy)
- Angela Locoro (Università degli Studi di Milano-Bicocca, Italy)
- Monica Maceli (Pratt Institute, New York, USA)
- Maristella Matera (Politecnico di Milano, Italy)
- Dao Minh-Son (The National Institute of Information and Communication Technology (NICT), Japan)
- Marisa Ponti (Chalmers University - University of Gothenburg, Sweden)
- Daniel Tetteroo (Eindhoven University of Technology, The Netherlands)

Acknowledgment. We would like to thank the organizers of IS-EUD 2015 for giving us the opportunity to organize this workshop. We are also grateful to our international program committee of experts in the field for their reviews and collaboration.

References

1. Díez, D., Mørch, A., Piccinno, A., Valtolina, S.: Cultures of participation in the digital age: empowering end users to improve their quality of life. In: Dittrich, Y., Burnett, M., Mørch, A., Redmiles, D. (eds.) IS-EUD 2013. LNCS, vol. 7897, pp. 304–309. Springer, Heidelberg (2013)
2. Barricelli, B.R., Gheitasy, A., Mørch, A., Piccinno, A., Valtolina, S.: Culture of participation in the digital age: social computing for learning, working, and living. In: International Working Conference on Advanced Visual Interfaces, pp. 387–390. ACM, New York (2014)

3. Cabitza, F., Fogli, D., Piccinno, A.: Fostering participation and co-evolution in sentient multimedia systems. Journal of Visual Languages and Computing **25**(6), 684–694 (2014)
4. Cabitza, F., Fogli, D., Piccinno, A.: "Each to his own": distinguishing activities, roles and artifacts in EUD practices. In: Caporarello, L., Di Martino, B., Martinez, M. (eds.) Smart Organizations and Smart Artifacts. LNISO, vol. 7, pp. 193–205. Springer International Publishing, Switzerland (2014)
5. Díez, D., Mørch, A., Piccinno, A., Valtolina, S.: Special issue on Culture of Participation in the Digital Age Empowering - End Users to Improve their Quality of Life. Interaction Design and Architecture (s) Journal (IxD&A) **18**(Autumn) (2013)

EUD-Playground

Searching in a Playful Manner

Markus Latzina[✉]

Products & Innovation, Technology – Strategic Projects, SAP SE,
Dietmar-Hopp-Allee 16 69190, Walldorf, Germany
markus.latzina@sap.com

Abstract. Search having become the dominant metaphor for information-oriented web usage and being commonly projected on other domains of human-computer interaction (HCI), still seems to be a largely undervalued topic in the field of user experience in general and human-computer-interaction design towards joy-of-use in particular. Therefore, the proposed search UI 'DISCO' aims not only at demonstrating how search can be embedded in an integrated and app-like environment, in which information objects can be leveraged considerably across various functional areas. The purpose of DISCO is to showcase how this kind of interoperability on the level of UI can occur in a playful manner. Therefore, given the prominent role of search functionality as part of computer-mediated artifacts, DISCO bears the promise to serve as an ideal for how design efforts within EUD can be inspired, resulting in end user applications which not only provide rich functionality for retrieving and manipulating information but which are also fun to use and embody aesthetic qualities.

Keywords: Search · Visual language · Design · Human-computer interaction · Incremental query specification · Joy-of-use · End user development

1 Introduction and Motivation

This playground contribution features an experimental prototype implementation of a search UI, code-named *DISCO*. On one hand, it can be deployed as a stand-alone search UI for the typical tasks of information retrieval, on the other hand, it can be regarded as an integral part of a larger environment, 'Discovery UI', which is designed according to the principles of *Transformative User Experience* (TUX) [1]. As such, during use time, *DISCO* can be stepwise extended towards a more comprehensive functionality which ranges from simple information retrieval, to tasks which are oriented towards discovery and exploration or even towards rather active sense making, including the manipulation and transformation of retrieved information according to end users' particular purposes.

As far as the orientation of *End User Development* (EUD) is concerned, the proposed approach aims at reducing the gap which commonly exists through the separation between design time and runtime, or, for our purpose, *use time*. In the case of search UIs which have become the predominant entry point to many applications or services – if not even a complete UX genre of its own kind - this applies specifically to the design of the query definition (alias "search input"). Commonly, from a consumer perspective, the

© Springer International Publishing Switzerland 2015
P. Díaz et al. (Eds.): IS-EUD 2015, LNCS 9083, pp. 279–282, 2015.
DOI: 10.1007/978-3-319-18425-8_29

query definition is narrowed down to a search input field. When users insert a few search keywords this results in a huge number of "hits", raising the effort of inspecting them to identify the desired information. For professional users advanced search UIs are an option. However, they mostly follow the database format and require knowledge of some, even if very basic, principles of database-centric query formulation (e.g., inserting input according to predefined attributes, or, using logical operators).

2   Design Approach

The search UI DISCO is largely informed by the design principles of TUX which can be characterized as a particular evolution of direct manipulation interfaces in the framework of activity theory-based Human-Computer Interaction (HCI). Following the orientation of direct manipulation, the UI in endowed with visuo-spatial qualities in several ways: it supports user interaction by means of visual containers and blocks [2, 3], it encourages to manipulate these visual entities, and, it uses spatial metaphors. E.g., assuming a left-to-right reading culture, a query definition (short, a query) which is arranged by the user in the leftmost position in relation to other queries, is interpreted as the most important query. One of the particularities which is introduced by the TUX approach is the context-dependent treatment of objects. In the case of DISCO, moving a result item (as embodied in a visual block) from the *Results* to the *Query-Building* container, implies, that this item should be used as a new query for triggering the instant retrieval of similar results. As to the *Query-Building* container, users can create visual blocks with a query from a predefined template or reuse previous queries and modify them. Also, users can rearrange various query blocks and immediately observe the effects in the container *Results*. This is expected to result in a rather intuitive interaction, since users can experience an increased level of efficacy or control by this direct feedback.

The rationale behind using the spatial order of query blocks for defining the complete query is that users can intuitively comprehend that each query block receives a weight which is analogous with its rank in the order of query blocks. Simultaneously, users are relieved from the burden to assign a nominal value to any of the queries [4]. Finally, the underlying metaphor of weights alleviates the users from understanding logical functions (in particular, OR and AND) and how they should be combined effectively to express a particular search intent.

The analogy between spatial arrangement and relevance is further pursued with respect to categories which are dynamically retrieved on the basis of actual content. When users fill the search field of a predefined query template with some free text, the database is instantly queried and fields ("categories") in which the query term appears are retrieved. In this case, users can disambiguate the query by rearranging these category terms according to their preference. Such a rearrangement of category terms is instantly echoed in the *Results* container.

3   Description of the Planned Hands-on Activity and Assumptions on the Experience of Qualities

The environment DISCO including the search UI will be presented through a common browser which requires a PC, monitor, pointing device (computer mouse or trackball), and a high-speed internet connection. The UI is meant to be self-explanatory, using common help functions, mainly optional tooltips. Settings can be accessed in a typical fashion, allowing users to select various predefined layouts or data sources.

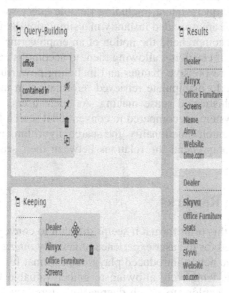

Fig. 1. Screenshot with the containers *Query-Building*, *Results*, and *Keeping*, each including various visual blocks. Blocks can carry some buttons for triggering functions. E.g., a new query block can be created by cloning an existing query block and changing some of its values.

The overall rationale of the design is to invite users to explore the UI on their own and learn by doing. Therefore, a demo is considered as optional.

As an example, the database may contain works of authors and artists. Users then can decide to search for particular works, e.g., literature on Mozart's opera *Magic Flute*. In one search task, users could be encouraged to find a particular work on the *Magic Flute* in their favorite language, e.g., taking into consideration whether this would contain a translation of the original libretto, or merely a reference to the opera.

Given the overall orientation to support tasks with explorative character the question needs to be posed how well the aspirations of this UI design can be assessed with traditional methods which are geared towards established performance indicators of effectiveness and efficiency. In this regard, the author believes that the very claim about the playfulness of the interaction can be appraised best in rather subjective, individual ways, in terms of truly experiential qualities. Specifically, as elasticity is introduced as a novel interactive quality this may require some use time until it becomes tangible for users and they can – tentatively – learn to appreciate it. Therefore, on one side, the expected experience of elasticity and playfulness is expected to initially remain largely seamless and intuitive, on the other side, possibly only through discourse between users and researchers such experiences can potentially become apparent and subsequently accessible to a more articulated and explicit reflection.

4   Objectives and Learning Goals for the Activity

By using the incremental and visual search functionality of DISCO, users should learn to appreciate the flexibility of visual query construction and the options for incremental expression of their query intent, including flexible query specification and observation of results which are provided instantly in a simulation-like fashion.

Also, users should comprehend the notion of an empowering UI framework which embodies the quality of elasticity, allowing them to accomplish their tasks in a highly flexible, situationally responsive manner and including powerful tools with rich task functionality, suitable to manipulate retrieved information in meaningful ways, e.g., towards a rather sophisticated sense making. As such, users can gather a sense of transparency of the system, as compared to conventional search UIs which commonly hide the core of the search functionality, the search algorithm, as a kind of black box (thus, impeding to comprehend the relations between their search input and search results).

5   Concluding Remarks

By the limitations of this print format it seems difficult to convey the interactive qualities which are claimed for the user experience of actually *interacting* with the DISCO UI. In this respect, the newly introduced playground format for the symposium could prove highly suitable, tentatively allowing to gather valuable feedback from actual end users, to directly explore to which degree the aspired qualities of elasticity and playfulness get noticed or even appreciated. As such, this undertaking promises to become a research practice which is in tune with notions of meta design and design which is informed by reflective practice.

References

1. Latzina, M., Beringer, J.: Transformative User Experience: beyond packaged design. Interactions 19(2), 30–33 (2012)
2. Krebs, D., Conrad, A., Wang, J.: Combining visual block programming and graph manipulation for clinical alert rule building. In: CHI 2012 Extended Abstracts on Human Factors in Computing Systems (CHI EA 2012). ACM, New York, pp. 2453–2458 (2012)
3. Fujima, J., Lunzer, A., Hornbæk, K., Tanaka, Y.: Clip, connect, clone: combining application elements to build custom interfaces for information access. In: Proceedings of the 17th Annual ACM Symposium on User Interface Software and Technology (UIST 2004). ACM, New York, 175–184 (2004)
4. Fagin, R., Maarek, Y.S.: Allowing users to weight search terms in information retrieval. IBM Research Report RJ 10108 (March 1998)

IS-EUD 2015 Studio: Exploring
End User Programming of Interactive Spaces

Thomas Kubitza[✉]

University of Stuttgart, Stuttgart, Germany
thomas.kubitza@vis.uni-stuttgart.de

Abstract. We live in a world with a rapidly growing number of devices in our environments and on our bodies. Even though these devices often have network connectivity they rarely work together to achieve a higher level goal. This is mainly due to their different platforms, communication technologies and the missing "glue" that ties everything together and defines the behaviour of such a distributed set of heterogeneous devices. In this studio we introduce a novel toolkit that simplifies the integration of arbitrary devices and the creation of smart and interactive spaces to writing some lines of JavaScript code in a single web-based user interface - changes come to effect immediately without the need for individual reprogramming of devices. Participants will have the opportunity to prototype fully functional interactive setups consisting of arbitrary stationary and wearable devices. This practical experince should lead to a focused discussion on the applicability of various flavours of end user programming for the creation of smart and interactive environments.

Keywords: Smart environments · Interactive spaces · End user programming · Mashups

1 Introduction

Smart and interactive spaces are based on a common principle; different kinds of devices with sensors and actuators attached are statically installed in rooms, levels, whole buildings or are even worn by users. All these heterogeneous devices need to talk to each other or to an entity that constantly combines system state and generates system reactions. Multiple reasons make the setup of such environments a complex task. Firstly, similar functionality has to be implemented on various platforms ranging from microcontrollers to High-End computers [1]. This requires expert knowledge in very specific programming languages and platforms as well as the management of various development environments (IDEs) and compilation tool chains. Secondly, different communications technologies, protocols and formats have to be bridged so that devices can actually exchange data. Thirdly, devices have to be deployed in their target environment, supplied with electricity and wired or wireless communication infrastructure (e.g. WiFi access points). Especially the first two reasons put up high

© Springer International Publishing Switzerland 2015
P. Díaz et al. (Eds.): IS-EUD 2015, LNCS 9083, pp. 283–286, 2015.
DOI: 10.1007/978-3-319-18425-8_30

boundary for non-experts in electronics and programming. This limits its usage to small and mostly only professional user groups.

Based on former experience in using and creating rapid prototyping tools for smart standalone devices [1][2] we believe that the right tools can open up the creation of smart environments to a much larger audience in the same way as physical prototyping platforms such as Arduino made the access to microcontrollers much easier and in the same way as Apps made potentially everyone the programmer of his own cell phone (and the phones of millions of others). By empowering groups such as user experience designers, scientist, designers, artists, makers; hobbyists and end users we envision the creation of a large set of truly useful applications evaluated in realistic environments and addressing a broad range of problems.

Within the IS-EUD studio we want to give participants the chance to gain hands-on experince with a novel toolkit that drastically reduces the technical complexity for creating and programming smart environments. Our approach consists of two main pillars: (1) A client software for each type of end device is provided which allows to remotely access and control all its abilities and to abstract from its specific platform. (2) A server software on a central computer node is provided to bridge between various communication-technologies and to provide unified access to all sensors and actuators of configured devices through a comfortable web-based JavaScript development environment.

This approach allows to quickly implement or change the behaviour of a system without the need to reprogram or physically access any of the associated or deployed devices. JavaScript, one of the most widespread and growing programming languages, is used to define the system behaviour in a single spot. In the following section we briefly describe the envisioned agenda of our studio.

2   Studio Proposal

The proposed studio will start with a quick introduction of the toolkit and a general overview of its functionality and purpose. Multiple examples of interactive and smart spaces that have been created based on our toolkit will be shown to illustrate its potential. This theoretical part will be quickly followed by the first "Hello World" hands on experience: Participants can use the browser of their own computer to mashup the first two devices with just four lines of JavaScript code. Based on that simple example more advanced building blocks will be introduced and the integration and configuration of additional devices (potentially also devices that users have brought with them) will be shown.

The second part of the studio will consist of tasks that have to be solved in groups. Therefore participants will split up in up to four groups and choose one of multiple prepared tasks. Each task will sketch a specific interactive behavior of a smart space that can be implemented using the platform and the available devices, sensors and actuators brought by the organizer. Group members can split up work and independently implement parts of the overall functionality through the web based interface. One organizer will be available for helping out anytime. After a fixed time, each group will quickly present and demonstrate their interactive setup and solution – the group tasks will be prepared by the organizers such that each group solution (optimally) could be combined with the other groups solutions so that a new, more complex interactive setup could be potentially created (e.g. group #1 builds a distributed display, group #2 builds a person tracker – both combined may easily result in a smart presence system).

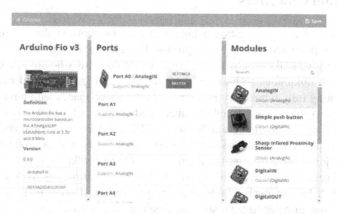

Fig. 1. Device configuration view for a Arduino device – modules can be added to free ports with a double-click. The device is automatically reconfigured and hints are given how to physically connect chosen sensors and actuators.

The presentations will end up in a group discussion where participants reflect their experiences and report strengths and weaknesses of the used toolkit as well as the overall approach. A short overview of future functionality that is planned for the toolkit will be introduced by the organizer and discussed together with the participants. Some of this additional functionality such as configuration (instead of programming) of behaviour, visual programming and simulation of sensor events may already be implemented by the time of the studio and can be demonstrated as part of the overall toolkit.

```
1   if (api.device.Arduino1.distanceSensor.value > 300)
2       api.AndroidProjector1.WebDisplay.showUrl = "http://bob-site.org/news.html";
3   else
4       api.device.AndroidProjector1.WebDisplay.showText = "";
            GadgeteerSpider.            device
            RPI10.                      device
            PicoPix01.                  device
            RPI8.                       device
            Blidget.                    device
            Blidget0.                   device
            ArduinoFio.                 device
            AndroidTablet.              device
```

Fig. 2. JavaScript code of simple rule that mashes up a distance sensor and a projector. An auto-completion feature helps in identifying the right devices, modules and properties

No specific prior technical skills or experience in programming or electronics are required – all important building blocks will be introduced step-by-step. People with different backgrounds (e.g. not related to computer science or engineering) are explicitly encouraged to participate.

3   Studio Objectives

Creation of and experimentation with smart environments is due to its technical complexity still limited to small user groups. By running a studio at the IS-EUD we want to both give EUD experts from very different domains who are interested in the application of ubiquitous technology the opportunity to gain personal experience in rapidly creating fully functional prototypes of interactive spaces with a novel toolkit - and we want to collect the valuable feedback and opinions of experts in the domain of EUD. Based on experience from former workshops we have organized [3][4] we believe that the individual hands-on experience will lay a good foundation for a subsequent joint discussion on the applicability of our toolkit in various domains as well as the general validity of our approach. We hope that the discussion and mutual exchange will lead to further high level insights for the domain of EUD applied to ubiquitous computing environments which may result in future publications.

4   Supporting Web Documents

We will provide further information on the studio on our website at http://iseud15. hcilab.org.

Acknowledgements. This work is funded by the European Project meSch (http://mesch-project.eu, Grant Agreement No. 600851).

References

1. Kubitza, T., Pohl, N., Dingler, T., Schneegaß, S.: Innovations in Ubicomp Products Ingredients for a New Wave of Ubicomp Products. IEEE Pervasive Computing, 5–8 (2013)
2. Kubitza, T., Pohl, N., Dingler, T., Schmidt, A.: WebClip: a connector for ubiquitous physical input and output for touch screen devices. In: Proceedings of Ubicomp, pp. 387–390 (2013)
3. Kubitza, T., Schmidt, A., Pohl, N.: Tools and methods for creating interactive artifacts. In: Proceedings of TEI, pp. 385–388 (2014)
4. Kubitza, T., Dingler, T.: Rapid Physical Prototyping Workshops for HCI-labs. http://blog.hcilab.org/gadgeteer/workshops

Creating Interactive Content in Android Devices: The Mokap Hackaton

Ángel Serrano-Laguna[1], Dan-Cristian Rotaru[1], Antonio Calvo-Morata[1],
Javier Torrente[2(✉)], and Baltasar Fernández-Manjón[1]

[1] Department of Software Engineering and Artificial Intelligence,
Complutense University of Madrid, Madrid, Spain
{angel.serrano,balta}@fdi.ucm.es, {drotaru,antcal01}@ucm.es
[2] Department of Computer Science, University College London, London, UK
j.torrente@ucl.ac.uk

Abstract. We propose the organization of a Mokap hackathon. In this activity participants will have the opportunity to develop interactive content using the Mokap Android app, either individually or in groups. Mokap is a new authoring tool for creating interactive content, developed by the e-UCM research group. It allows composing scenes by combining text, hand drawings, pictures and elements imported from an online repository. Mokap also supports basic animation and interaction. Users can take advantage of this functionality to create presentations, training materials, simulations, postcards and even simple games. We will start the activity with an introduction to Mokap, followed by a quick demo. Then we will help participants design their own mokaps and implement them. At the end of the activity participants will be given the possibility to share their mokaps with the rest of the audience. Participants will vote online to choose the best mokap developed during the session, which will be awarded a symbolic prize.

Keywords: Mokap · Serious games · Authoring · Educational games · Mobile learning · Interactive content

1 Description of the Activity

1.1 Topics Covered and Relevance to the EUD Community

This activity will cover how users from all backgrounds can create simple games and other interactive and playful pieces of content with Mokap. Digital games are a very popular type of content, especially in mobile devices which are a platform on the rise for casual gaming. However, their creation is usually limited to highly motivated authors with a certain background in programming. Some tools allow users with little technical background create their own digital games, but they are still complex to use for the great public. Besides, most game creation tools are oriented to the PC, a declining platform for personal computing. Game creation environments should start considering smartphones and tablets, as these are becoming predominant for all types of users. In fact, mobile devices are still rather unexplored in terms of supporting interactive content authoring, an activity only available in desktop platforms.

© Springer International Publishing Switzerland 2015
P. Díaz et al. (Eds.): IS-EUD 2015, LNCS 9083, pp. 287–290, 2015.
DOI: 10.1007/978-3-319-18425-8_31

We believe this hackathon is of great relevance for the End-User Development community, as the creation of games and interactive content is an extraordinary rewarding and creative activity that, unfortunately, has been out of reach for most end-users.

1.2   Goals and Detailed Description of the Planned Hands-on Activity

In this activity, we will cover the next goals: (1) Introduce the Mokap authoring tool; (2) Introduce basic game design concepts and game authoring; (3) Game authoring as a creative and social experience. During the activity, organizers will collect usage data and participants' feedback on the Mokap authoring tool to improve its usability and functionality.

This is the detailed outline for the activity:

- Welcome and introduction to the activity, leaded by the organizers [10 min].
- Basic introduction to game design and authoring (organizers) [30 min].
- Introduction to the Mokap authoring tool (organizers) [15 min].
- Brainstorming about projects that could be developed with Mokap. Examples: "directions to reach the coffee break room", "happy birthday card", "shoot'em up game with organizers' faces" (participants and organizers). [10 min].
- Initial feedback and discussion (audience and organizers) [10 min].
- Supervised project development [2 hours].
- Towards the end of the event, participants will be invited to share their finished (or work-in-progress) mokaps with the rest of participants [5 min].
- Participants will be given the opportunity to campaign for their mokaps before both participants and organizers vote for the best mokap of the session [20 min].
- Online voting is set up (audience, organizers) and voting starts [5 min].
- Voting poll is closed, winners are announced (organizers) [5 min].
- Final remarks and farewell (organizers) [10 min].

1.3   Logistics and Organizational Aspects

Cost of Material and Hardware. Organizers cannot supply smartphones and tablets to all participants, and thus they are expected to bring their own Android devices. However, organizers will make available for borrowing a small number of Android devices (5-6) with Mokap pre-installed for participants that may lack access to an Android device. Mokap is available for free and it runs on any modern Android tablet or smartphone (requirements: Android 2.3.3 and above, although 4.0.0 and above is preferable). Large screens (5" and above) are recommended for a better user experience.

Logistics Requirements. The room should be powered with a projector. WiFi connection is also necessary, as Mokap integrates a repository of graphical assets that requires Internet access and may consume considerable bandwidth. Power sockets should be available in the room so participants can recharge their devices if needed. USB chargers will be supplied by organizers.

Selection Criteria and Expected Number of Participants. Up to 20 participants from all backgrounds are welcome to participate in this session. No previous technical knowledge is required. However, participants are encouraged to bring their own Android devices (see above).

Expected Length. This activity is expected to last no more than 4 hours.

2   Project Description and Website

Mokap is a novel authoring tool for creating animated and interactive content like presentations, postcards, simulations and simple games. A first version of Mokap was just released in March 2015. Among its current features, it supports scene composition, text edition (Figure 1), hand drawing, image edition (through the Pixlr external app), integration of photos and elements from an online repository, basic animation and scene transitioning. With its current functionality, it cannot be expected to be used for the creation of very complex pieces of content, like full-featured games. Nonetheless, the project has set an ambitious long-term roadmap in the aim of making Mokap a real alternative for creating high-quality interactive content in general, and games in particular, that is affordable to the general public.

Fig. 1. Two snapshot fragments from the Mokap tool. Left fragment shows scene transition configuration, right fragment shows element animation.

We are also very interested in exploring how Mokap can be used to support serious game development (that is, games applied for a purpose beyond recreation, like education or health). Serious games usually require gathering to work together both technical experts (usually people with a strong background in game programming) and domain experts (people with valuable knowledge of the field the game has to capture and/or transmit) like teachers, doctors, etc. Technical and domain experts usually have diverse backgrounds and approach serious game development from different perspectives, which hinders communication. As a result, knowledge elicitation and requisite capturing are hard to accomplish in serious game development. We believe that a tool like Mokap can facilitate collaboration between technical and domain experts and speed up serious game development, especially in early design stages where flexibility, creativity, agile prototyping and ability to rapidly adapt to design changes is more important than having full functionality. Since Mokap is designed for mobile devices, it can be used in co-design meetings to make sketches, mockups and prototypes. Second, as Mokap values agility and simplicity over full functionality, those prototypes can be created on the spot, so they can be rapidly verified and discussed among technical and domain experts. Once a basic consensus on the game design is agreed, game experts can take it from there and further integrate and develop the prototypes created using Mokap Builder, a programming framework compatible with the Mokap authoring tool.

Mokap is an open source project, licensed under the LGPLv3 license. Developers interested in the project can join our small but vibrant community at GitHub: https://github.com/e-ucm/ead/. More information can also be found on the official website: http:/www.mokap.es. The app can be downloaded for free from Google Play following the next link: https://play.google.com/store/apps/details?id=es.eucm.mokap.

3   Organizers' Biographical Statement

Ángel Serrano Laguna works for the e-UCM e-learning group at the Complutense University. His research focuses in the design and implementation of Serious Games and tools to ease their introduction in the classroom, as well as the application of Learning Analytics techniques for assessment in Serious Games.

Dan Cristian Rotaru and Antonio Calvo Morata work as contract researchers for the e-UCM group at the Complutense University of Madrid, where they got their BSc in Computer Science in 2014.

Javier Torrente got his PhD in Computer Science from Complutense University of Madrid in 2014. Currently he works as a post-doc researcher at University College London. Formerly he worked as a contract researcher for e-UCM. He is coauthor of more than 70 academic papers published in international conferences and journals in the field of Serious Games.

Baltasar Fernández-Manjón, PhD, IEEE Senior Member, got his PhD in Physics from the Complutense University. He is currently Full Professor at the ISIA Dpt., UCM. He is director of the e-UCM research group and his main research interests include e-learning technologies, e-learning standards and serious games on which he has published more than 120 research papers.

Acknowledgements. The e-UCM research group has been partially funded by Regional Government of Madrid (eMadrid S2013/ICE-2715), by the Ministry of Education (TIN2013-46149-C2-1-R) and by the European Commission (RAGE H2020-ICT-2014-1-644187).

Spatial Awareness in Mobile Devices to Compose Data Source: A Utilization Study

Giuseppe Desolda[1(✉)] and Hans-Christian Jetter[2]

[1] Dipartimento di Informatica, Università degli Studi di Bari Aldo Moro,
Via Orabona, 4 70125, Bari, Italy
giuseppe.desolda@uniba.it
[2] University of Applied Sciences Upper Austria,
Campus Hagenberg Softwarepark 11 4232, Linz, Austria
hans-christian.jetter@fh-hagenberg.at

Abstract. The growing amount of low cost mobile devices over the last years allowed almost each person to be equipped with their personal device. This situation is leading researchers to investigate new possibilities to exploit the physical presence of several mobile devices for purposes like co-located collaborative activities. For example, today it is a common situation that a group of users tries to satisfy situational needs by using their mobile devices without the possibility to 'integrate' or join them to make more use of their full potential. In this paper, we propose a study to evaluate a new paradigm designed to compose data sources available on each mobile device through their spatial arrangement on a desk. HuddleLamp is a device that allows each mobile device to be spatially-aware of all other mobile devices on the desk. The main goal of this study is to understand if spatial awareness features can support co-located collaborative tasks to satisfy situational informational needs.

Keywords: Multi-device environments · Spatially-aware interfaces · User study

1 Introduction

In the last 30 years, the technological progress has encouraged the proliferation of different types of mobile devices. Their use has substantially changed over the time. Initially designed to call or send text messages to other people, they are now used primarily to visit web pages, chat, share content, pay an item, take a picture or record a video, listen music, etc. Despite the enormous advances in terms of functionalities offered by these mobile devices, until now little attention has been dedicated to the possibility of providing new opportunities by physically combining devices located in the same environment. In fact, we can now safely assume that all people in a co-located group carry a personal device, but this is rarely supported in the ways we can use multiple devices together. For example, while users are discussing a certain topic, they might want to find some information on the Web using their devices; in this case, they typically use their devices individually or, at best, by communicating by means of apps that are usually not designed to support information sharing in a

© Springer International Publishing Switzerland 2015
P. Díaz et al. (Eds.): IS-EUD 2015, LNCS 9083, pp. 291–294, 2015.
DOI: 10.1007/978-3-319-18425-8_32

group of co-located people. To better understand this problem, let us consider the following scenario.

Alice, Rudin and Bob are three friends that have decided to move to London for studying. They meet at Alice's home to discuss renting a shared apartment. First, Alice opens on her smartphone the site Zoopla (one of the most important property rental sites in the UK) and sets some parameters like price range, number of bedrooms, property type. Then she writes 'London' in the search box and the site shows a list of about 500 results ordered by price. Rudin says that he prefers a property near a bus or metro station, thus he opens on his smartphone a UK site to retrieve information about public transportation in London. A list of transport stations is shown on his device. Furthermore, Bob opens on his smartphone a site with information about air pollution in UK to retrieve a list of air pollution stations in London. The discussion continues on the basis of property parameters, air quality and availability of public transportation. Every time they decide to consider a different location (e.g. by refining the query with a specific area of London), they have to manually refine the query on each device. At a certain point, Alice takes her tablet and opens Google Maps because she prefers to visualize the results of the smartphones on a map. From now on, each time they want to know the location of a point of interest (house, transport station, pollution air station) on the map, Alice has to query Google Maps by typing in the specific address.

In this scenario, the users are not adequately supported by ad-hoc mobile device mechanisms to perform their tasks because the devices act in isolation, thus information and queries must be manually synchronized across device boundaries by their users. Today these types of informational needs that involve different data sources are typically supported by mashup platforms that allow end users to compose their own web application on a desktop PC also providing remote collaboration mechanisms [1]. Nonetheless, these existing solutions are not intended for supporting a collaborative co-located scenario with mobile devices.

We have designed a novel paradigm that allows people to physically combine their devices and their data based on a recent technology called HuddleLamp. It is a desk lamp with an integrated depth and RGB camera that allows users to compose their mobile devices in an ad hoc fashion, just by putting them under this desk lamp and without instrumenting them with custom-built sensing hardware or markers [2]. By using HuddleLamp, each device under the lamp is tracked in space and also becomes aware of the locations of all other mobile devices on the desk. This enables our newly designed composition paradigm that allows groups of users to combine the data sources from each device (e.g., different web sites) by means of their spatial position on the HuddleLamp desk. Users are enabled to formulate their query and reconfigure the flow of data between devices by simply rearranging them in the space, ideally achieving a new kind of EUD that feels "natural": rather than feeling like "development", this paradigm resembles natural arranging of devices in space, similar to how we constantly arrange non-digital objects like sheets or piles of paper, books, or folders on our desks or conference tables. According to [3], being manipulations part of a physical and spatial "mother tongue" that we all share, such a paradigm should facilitate the composition activities performed by the users independently by their culture and context.

We have elicited the spatial interactions for this paradigm in 2 pilot studies from 8 end users. Then we conducted 5 focus groups with 26 end users. Details about these studies are out of the scope of this paper and will be subject of future publications. However, in brief, three types of device compositions were elicited in these studies: 1) how to query multiple devices with same keyword(s) by performing the query only on one of them? 2) Given two devices A and B, how to query B with portions of text displayed on A? 3) Given the device A that shows data with a certain visualization (e.g. list of items), how we can move these data into the device B that shows input data with another type of visualization (e.g. map)? The results of the elicitation study in terms of the composition paradigm are summarized in Fig. 1.

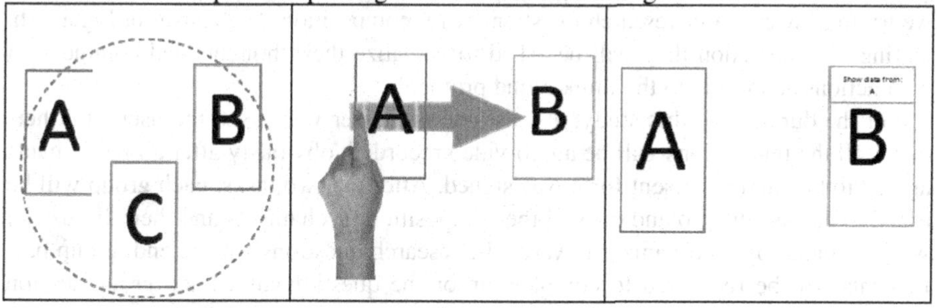

Fig. 1. a) A group of devices physically close are queried with same keyword(s) executed on one of them; b) a swipe gesture from a portion of text in the device A towards the device B causes a query on B with the swiped text; c) a menu on the device B allows to choose the device(s) A on the desk in order to visualize the results of A on B in different way.

The main goal of the hands-on activity is to understand if the spatial awareness functionality provided by HuddleLamp supports the co-located collaborative tasks performed by the end users participating in the activity. In particular, we address the following research questions: RQ1: *Are the users able to perform real co-located collaborative tasks by exploiting spatial awareness mechanisms?* RQ2: *Do the users like to have spatial awareness mechanisms to perform co-located collaborative tasks?* RQ3: *Do the users prefer to exploit spatial awareness mechanisms in other ways?*

In order to answer to these questions, we designed a utilization study described in the following section.

2   Hands-on Activity: a Utilization Study

During the days before the playground session, to motivate and recruit passers-by in participating, we will install HuddeLamp to allow anyone to interact with some demo application. We will recruit 16 people that will be divided in groups of four people. Each group will be scheduled in one-hour slots during the playground session. For each group, we will start with a quick introduction about the HuddleLamp technology. Some demo applications will be shown to explain the spatially–aware interaction. Afterwards, we will briefly introduce the three composition techniques by showing them on the

HuddleLamp desk. Then participants will be asked to perform two tasks with a balanced complexity, so that they can be accomplished with or without spatial awareness mechanisms. Concretely, in the first task they will be asked to find a cheap property in a specific zone of London. The property has to be very close to a metro station and in a non-polluted zone (i.e., pollution value below a threshold). With this task, we try to answer our research questions w.r.t. the composition mechanisms in Fig. 1a and Fig. 1c. With the second task, each group has to choose an upcoming musical concert at their favourite location. They will be asked to use a specific web site and, if the information provided by that site are not enough to choose the concert, they should use other sites to gather further information (e.g. YouTube, Wikipedia, and Google Maps). With this task, we try to answer to our research questions w.r.t. composition mechanism in Figure 1b. During the interaction they will be asked to verbalize their thoughts and comment on their actions according to the think-aloud protocol.

For the duration of this study, at least one organizer will assist the users. Furthermore, all the interactions will be audio-video recorded, obviously after all participants agreed to this and a consent form was signed. After the two tasks, each group will be asked to discuss the pro and cons of the composition mechanisms and their discussion will be guided by an organizer towards the research questions. At the end, group participants will be requested to complete an online questionnaire. Each group session will be 1 hour long.

The planned study aims at investigating the proposed spatially-aware composition paradigm by involving real end users and EUD experts. On the one hand, interaction of real end users with our system could give us important feedback about understating and acceptance of the proposed paradigm. On the other hand, EUD experts will provide important opinions and comments from a more theoretical perspective. We are confident that both viewpoints will contribute to assess and improve our composition paradigm and our insights about spatially-aware cross-device interactions in general.

Acknowledgments. This work is partially supported by the Italian Ministry of University and Research (MIUR) under grant PON 02_00563_3470993 "VINCENTE" and by the Italian Ministry of Economic Development (MISE) under grant PON Industria 2015 MI01_00294 "LOGIN".

References

1. Ardito, C., Bottoni, P., Costabile, M.F., Desolda, G., Matera, M., Picozzi, M.: Creation and use of service-based Distributed Interactive Workspaces. Journal of Visual Languages & Computing **25**(6), 717–726 (2014)
2. Rädle, R., Jetter, H.-C., Marquardt, N., Reiterer, H., Rogers, Y.: HuddleLamp: Spatially-aware mobile displays for ad-hoc around-the-table collaboration. In: Proceedings of the Ninth ACM International Conference on Interactive Tabletops and Surfaces (ITS 2014), Dresden, Germany (2014)
3. Ardito, C., Costabile, M.F., Jetter, H.-C.: Gestures that people can understand and use. Journal of Visual Languages & Computing **25**(5), 572–576 (2014)

Hands-on Actionable Mashups

Carmelo Ardito[1(✉)], Maria Francesca Costabile[1], Giuseppe Desolda[1],
Markus Latzina[2], and Maristella Matera[3]

[1] Dipartimento di Informatica, Università degli Studi di Bari Aldo Moro,
Via Orabona, 4 70125, Bari, Italy
{carmelo.ardito,maria.costabile,giuseppe.desolda}@uniba.it
[2] Strategic Projects, Products & Innovation – Technology, SAP SE,
Dietmar-Hopp-Allee 16, Walldorf 69190, Germany
markus.latzina@sap.com
[3] Dipartimento di Elettronica, Informazione e Bioingegneria,
Politecnico di Milano, Piazza Leonardo da Vinci, 32 20134, Milano, Italy
maristella.matera@polimi.it

Abstract. This paper describes how to involve end users without expertise in programming in a session where they will be asked to accomplish some tasks according to a new paradigm for actionable mashups. The goal will be to understand what the advantages of this new paradigm are with respect to traditional methods for mashup composition and information exploration.

Keywords: End-user development · Transformative user experience · Data integration · Mashups · Composition platforms

1 Introduction

In several application domains there is an increasing demand by end users (simply called "users" in the rest of this paper) to effectively access, integrate, and visualize multiple resources available online. In this respect, platforms for service integration, and especially End-User Development (EUD) paradigms for mashup composition, play an important role as they let users integrate heterogeneous information that otherwise would be totally unrelated [1]. Web mashups are "composite" applications constructed by integrating ready-to-use heterogeneous resources exposed by public or private Web services and APIs [2]. They offer in particular the possibility to integrate such resources at the presentation layer, an aspect that enables the creation of full-fledged applications whose user interface (UI) is easily achieved by synchronizing the UIs of the different components. Several works in the last year have been proposing platforms for mashup composition. Some of them offer novel paradigms to allow users to construct interactive and pervasive information spaces [2]. One such tool is proposed in [1]. Let us briefly describe how a user creates mashups with this tool.

Maria, a teenager keen on rock music, interacts with a web application on a PC to retrieve and explore various information about musical events by means of mashups. Maria can browse information provided by different online services and classified by

© Springer International Publishing Switzerland 2015
P. Díaz et al. (Eds.): IS-EUD 2015, LNCS 9083, pp. 295–298, 2015.
DOI: 10.1007/978-3-319-18425-8_33

various categories (e.g., video, photo, music, social). Maria decides to access the information through SongKick, a service registered into the platform that provides information about music events. From a number of UI templates provided by the system, Maria chooses the map (in particular, using the Google Maps service) for displaying the retrieved music events in the form of pins on the map. She also decides to visualize some further details on each single event, this time using a table view. By selecting a pin on the map, the details of the corresponding event get visualized accordingly. Fig. 1 depicts an example of the created mashup, rendered within a web browser. By typing "Afterhours" in the search box, Maria retrieves the forthcoming events of this rock band, which are visualized as red pins on the map. Maria clicks on one pin and a table appears showing the details of that event.

Fig. 1. Example of mashup created with the platform in [1] for monitoring rock concerts

The example illustrated above shows that, with the platform described in [1], the user performs the mashup without writing any code, but only using visual interaction mechanisms. However, Maria could not accomplish much more than visualizing a list of data, modifying the way data are visualized, or inspecting data details. Additional features would be needed in order to make the mashup information *actionable*, which means that Maria can act on the information resulting from the mashup, manipulate and even transform it according to her specific task. The proposal to achieve actionable mashups is to adopt TUX (Transformative User Experience) principles [3]. As discussed in [4], TUX indeed provides a framework for designing such task-oriented features. Therefore, besides adopting exclusively UI templates as containers supporting the access and the visualization of the information provided by services (as described in [1]), according to the TUX framework the mashup platform can exploit the notion of *task containers*, i.e., extensions to UI templates in charge of providing *task semantics.* In other words, when moved in a task container, information items are considered *task objects* to which *task functions*, specific to this container, can be applied [5]. As described in the next section, the participants to the hands-on activity will interact with a mashup platform integrated with TUX principles; the goal of this activity will be understanding whether by means of the TUX extensions users perceive a greater utility of the mashup data with respect to the possibility to fulfil some goals which go beyond the mere retrieval of information.

2   Hands-on Activity

People participating to the hands-on activity will be end users without specific expertise in programming. The interaction with the platform is individual. Each participant is briefly introduced to the scenario: he or she acts as Maria, who wants to attend a musical event with her friends. She uses the platform to search for forthcoming music events. She also gathers information that can inform the discussion with her friends about which event to attend. In the following paragraph, we describe in more details the tasks executed by Maria, i.e., by each participant.

By means of a PC, Maria logs into the web platform that offers a workspace where she can retrieve information by mashing up services and act on the information through specific functions provided by task containers. The workspace has been previously customized to provide the tools required to carry out the hands-on activity. The platform is equipped with services providing data on music events, plus some other services of generic utility, e.g., map services. In order to enlarge the set of available data to be integrated in the mashup, a polymorphic data source, exploiting the information structured in the Linked Open Data cloud, is provided [6]. The workspace also offers a collection of task containers. Each container is represented as a box widget with a labelled icon that indicates its intended purpose by highlighting a primary task function, e.g., a World globe for browsing, two side-by-side paper sheets for comparing, a call-out for communicating. When needed, a container representation can be moved by the user from this collection into the main area of the workspace, in order to activate its full functional scope.

(Step 1): Maria selects the task container "Events" and chooses "music" as event type. A map is displayed: every music event is represented as a pin at specific coordinates. The details of each event can be inspected by clicking on the corresponding pin. *(Step 2)*: Maria now adds the "Selecting" container and she makes a pre-selection by dragging from the "Events" container those events she is more interested in. She further refines her selection by means of a "Comparing" container, which offers features supporting the comparative inspection of items. After this analysis, Maria chooses the three most promising events and removes the others from the "Selecting" container. *(Step 3)*: Maria drags the "Housing" container in the main area of the workspace and she synchronizes it with the "Selecting" container by partially overlapping them. Three lists of hotels, one for each different event place, are visualized. For each hotel, a thumbnail photo, name, price and guests' rating are displayed. Maria performs those actions usually allowed by hotel booking web sites, i.e., changing dates,

ordering, filtering, inspecting details. She selects a couple of hotels for each location. On the basis of the housing information, she reduces the candidate events to only two and eliminates the third from the "Selecting" container. *(Step 4)*: Maria wants to send an email with a summary of the information related to the two chosen events. Thanks to the "Communicating" container, she is not forced to use an email client external to the workspace. She drops the items from the "Selecting" to the "Communicating" container, where she selects the recipients and the communication channel, e.g., a post on a social network or an email. She decides to send an email. The email addresses of her friends are displayed and the email body is prefilled automatically with the information about the events and the hotels. The message can be edited by Maria before sending. It is noteworthy to remark that Maria is not constrained to a predefined flow: for example, she could directly move events from "Selecting" to "Communicating", thus deliberately skipping the "Comparing" or the "Housing" container.

3   Objectives and Learning Goals for the Activity

The proposed activity allows users to interact with a system that enables them to express and respond to their task needs rather directly and dynamically. By observing the end users while using this system we aim to assess the validity of our ideas on the integration of mashups and TUX principles, and to verify whether making mashups actionable actually provides an added value with respect to the users' needs and expectations. We also aim to propose new EUD paradigms that can empower users to shape up software environments that can really support their situational needs.

Acknowledgments. This work is partially supported by the Italian Ministry of University and Research (MIUR) under grant PON 02_00563_3470993 "VINCENTE" and by the Italian Ministry of Economic Development (MISE) under grant PON Industria 2015 MI01_00294 "LOGIN".

References

1. Ardito, C., Costabile, M.F., Desolda, G., Lanzilotti, R., Matera, M., Piccinno, A., Picozzi, M.: User-Driven Visual Composition of Service-Based Interactive Spaces. Journal of Visual Languages & Computing **25**(4), 278–296 (2014)
2. Daniel, F., Matera, M.: Mashups - Concepts, Models and Architectures. Springer (2014)
3. Latzina, M., Beringer, J.: Transformative user experience: beyond packaged design. Interactions **19**(2), 30–33 (2012)
4. Ardito, C., Costabile, M.F., Desolda, G., Latzina, M., Matera, M.: Making mashups actionable through elastic design principles. In: Díaz, P., et al. (eds.) IS-EUD 2015. LNCS, vol. 9083, pp. 236–241 (2015)
5. Beringer, J., Latzina, M.: Elastic workplace design. In: Wulf, V., et al. (eds.) Designing Socially Embedded Technologies in the Real-World. Springer, London (2015)
6. Desolda, G.: Enhancing workspace composition by exploiting linked open data as a polymorphic data source. In: IIMSS 2015, June 17-19, Sorrento, Italy (2015)

A Platform for Creating Digital Educational Games as Combinations of Archetypical Games

Telmo Zarraonandia[✉], Paloma Díaz, Ignacio Aedo, and Alvaro Montero

University Carlos III, Madrid, Spain
{tzarraon,pdp,ammontes}@inf.uc3m.es, aedo@ia.uc3m.es

Abstract. In this work we present a platform that allows educators to design and develop 3D Digital Educational Games (DEG) rapidly and easily. The games are described as combinations of four simple game archetypes, which can be played sequentially or simultaneously along different missions and episodes. This seeks to provide educators, with no prior knowledge on game design, with a comprehensive approach for describing educational game experiences.

Keywords: Digital educational games · End-user development · Serious games · Game design · Authoring tool

1 Introduction

In this work we present GREP (Game Rules scEnario Platform), a system to aid educators in the process of creating DEGs. The platform is able to interpret descriptions of EGs expressed in XML files and to generate 3D games based on them. The descriptions of the games should follow the schema of the GREM model (Game Rules scEnario Model) [1], which provides a set of components and design entities for defining EGs. GREP provides different types of implementations for these game components, activating for each game the ones that suit better their descriptions in the XML files. The system has been implemented using the Unity game engine [2]. In order to aid the educator in the process of describing DEGs the platform includes two authoring tools: the *Game Scene Editor* and the *Game Rules Editor*.

The *Game Scene Editor* allows the educator to describe the virtual 3D environments in which the game action takes place. The tool includes a *Game Entities Repository,* which contains a collection of pre-defined game entities definitions. Each entity definition specifies an entity name, a list of entity attributes and states, and a set of graphical models and animations that will be used to represent those states. As shown in Figure 1, the editor provides a view of the scene and an interface to add (or remove) instances of the entities by dragging and dropping their names from the list of game entities to the desired position in the scene. The graphical model of the entity will be added, and a pop up window will be displayed to allow modifying the default values for its attributes. Once the scene has been arranged, the final design is exported into an XML file.

© Springer International Publishing Switzerland 2015
P. Díaz et al. (Eds.): IS-EUD 2015, LNCS 9083, pp. 299–301, 2015.
DOI: 10.1007/978-3-319-18425-8_34

Fig. 1. Screenshots of the Game Scene Editor (left), and the GREP Player (right)

Once the game scenes have been defined the educator should describe the rules that will govern the game action using the *Game Rules Editor* (Fig. 2), which implements the combinative approach for describing DEGs presented in [3]. This technique aims to decrease the difficulty of the game design task by describing the DEGs as combinations of more simple games that can be played simultaneously or in sequence at each different game stage. This saves the designer from having to fill in large forms detailing all the possible events, triggers and activations that the description of the rules of a game could require. Currently, the tool supports combining four archetypical games: *treasure hunts*, in which the player should collect certain items, *avoid dangers*, in which the player should avoid contact with some objects, *races*, in which the player should reach a position of the scene marked as goal before a time limit expires, and *adventures*, in which the player should activate tools from and inventory to fix specific problems and obtain new items. The DEG is defined as a sequence of game missions, in which up to four of these archetypical games can be active simultaneously. The educator describes the game missions and the rules that establish the order in which they should be presented to the learner, and exports the design as an XML file. These files can be uploaded to the platform player, which interprets the game designs contained within them and generates the gameplays for the learner (Fig. 1).

Fig. 2. Screenshot of the Game Rules Editor

To clarify the use of the platform we illustrate it with an example of a game for helping young students to learn about animals. Firstly, the educator would use the *game scene editor* to design of the scenes of the game. These scenes could depict a farm or a forest, for example, and the designer would populate them with animals models retrieved from the *game entities repository*. Once the scenes are defined the educator would upload their description files to the *game rules editor* and start generating games for them. For example, in one game the player could be asked to identify animals of a certain characteristic, for example ruminants. This game could be described using the *treasure hunt game* archetype, simply by defining ruminant animals as the pieces of treasure that the player should search and collect. To penalize the player when he or she tries to collect a non-ruminant animal, the educator can also activate the *avoid danger game*, linking the non-ruminants animals with the dangers. As another example, the player´s knowledge about animals could be tested by requiring him or her to feed them. This game could be described as a combination of a *treasure hunt game*, in which the player has to search for suitable food for the animals, and an *adventure game*, where the food collected should only be selected and used with the corresponding animal that can digest it.

2   Objectives and Activity Description

In this activity the users will participate in a hands-on exercise in which they will design and develop a DEG. Working in groups they will specify the scenes and the rules for a game experience to support learning on a specific subject of their choice. They will learn to use the different tools the GRE platform provides for supporting the game design task, exploring the possibilities of the combinative technique for describing DEGs.

The activity will be organized as follows:

- Introduction to the GRE platform
- Tutorial: GRE platform tools
- Brainstorming: DEG concept
- Design and development of the DEG
- Presentation of the DEGs

Not prior knowledge on programming or game design is required to participate in the activity. Limit: up to 20 participants.

The participants will be provided with laptops with working installations of the GRE Platform.

References

1. Zarraonandia, T., Diaz, P., Ruiz Vargas, M.R., Aedo, I.: Designing educational games by combining other game designs. In: Proceedings of the 12th IEEE International Conference on Advanced Learning Technologies (ICALT), Rome, Italy (2011)
2. Unity (2014). http://unity3d.com (accessed February 1, 2014)
3. Zarraonandia, T., Diaz, P., Aedo, I., Ruiz Vargas, M.R.: Designing educational games through a conceptual model based on rules and scenarios. Multimedia Tools and Applications, 1–25 (2014). http://dx.doi.org/10.1007/s11042-013-1821-1

Author Index

Printed in the United States
by Bookmasters

Printed in the United States
By Bookmasters